AN INQUIRY INTO

THE COLONIAL POLICY

OF THE EUROPEAN POWERS

VOLUME II

AN

INQUIRY

INTO THE

COLONIAL POLICY

OF THE

EUROPEAN POWERS

BY

LORD BROUGHAM

VOLUME II

[1803]

REPRINTS OF ECONOMIC CLASSICS

AUGUSTUS M. KELLEY · PUBLISHERS
NEW YORK 1970

(Edinburgh: *Printed by* D. Willison, *Craig's Close,*
for Balfour, Manners & Miller, and Archibald
Constable, *Edinburgh;* T. N. Longman &
O. Rees, *London,* 1803)

Reprinted 1970 by

AUGUSTUS M. KELLEY · PUBLISHERS

REPRINTS OF ECONOMIC CLASSICS

New York   New York   10001

.   .   .   .

I S B N   0 678 00658 X

L C N   75 118017

.   .   .   .

PRINTED IN THE UNITED STATES OF AMERICA
by SENTRY PRESS, NEW YORK, N. Y. 10019

AN INQUIRY

INTO THE

COLONIAL POLICY

OF THE

EUROPEAN POWERS.

IN TWO VOLUMES.

By HENRY BROUGHAM Jun. Esq. F. R. S.

VOL. II.

Edinburgh:

PRINTED BY D. WILLISON, CRAIG'S CLOSE,
FOR E. BALFOUR, MANNERS & MILLER,
AND ARCHIBALD CONSTABLE, EDINBURGH;
AND T. N. LONGMAN & O. REES,
LONDON.

1803.

CONTENTS of VOL. II.

BOOK II.

Of the Foreign Relations of Colonies.

BOOK III.

Of the Foreign Relations of States, as influenced by their Colonial Relations.

BOOK IV.

Of the Domeſtic Policy of the European
Powers in their Colonial Eſtabliſhments.

SECT. I.

SECT. II.

AN INQUIRY

INTO

THE COLONIAL POLICY OF THE
EUROPEAN POWERS.

BOOK II.

OF THE FOREIGN RELATIONS OF COLONIES.

INTRODUCTION.

THE external relations of any independent state, that is to say, its influence upon its neighbours, and its interest in their affairs, must always be regulated by its relative importance, and its relative position. When a state is not independent, but inseparably connected with another country, or attached to it as a subordinate branch of its empire; in a word, when the state in question is a colony, or a distant province, its relations to other colonies or independent states in the neighbourhood, must be influenced chiefly by the external relations of the

metro-

metropolis. * There are, however, certain circumſtances in the ſituation of different con‑ tiguous colonies, which may be conſidered a‑ part from the foreign relations of the mother countries, and which influence the mutual re‑ lations of thoſe colonies. Thus, independent of any foreign conſideration, a ſudden in‑ creaſe of power in the colonial dominions of any one nation, or an alliance between the co‑ lonial forces of two powers, would materially affect the ſecurity of the neighbouring colo‑ nies. In a word, colonies may be conſidered as ranged together in ſeparate communities or claſſes, mutually related to each other, and to the neighbouring ſtates, in the ſame manner as if they were independent powers. Thus, we may talk of the great Colonial Republic, in the ſame manner as we talk of the great Eu‑ ropean Republic. Within certain limits, too, we may ſpeak of the Colonial balance, as we ſpeak of the European balance of power, al‑ though the various relations of the parent ſtates muſt conſtantly enter into every calcu‑ lation which we make concerning the equili‑ brium of the colonial ſyſtem. In this point of view, we may conſider the different claſſes of European colonies, as forming ſo many dif‑ ferent

* Book I. Sect. I.

ferent fyftems of federal power, analogous to
the great political machine of Europe. Thus,
there is one fuch fyftem in the Afiatic, and
another in the American fettlements of the
European powers. The trifling eftablifhments
in Africa, are at prefent altogether fubordinate and fubfervient to the two great colonial
communities of the Eaft and Weft.

The foreign relations of any one member of
thofe fyftems, are, either its relation to the other
colonial eftablifhments in the fame part of the
world, or its relation to the independent ftates
which exift there, including what are commonly called the native powers. In the Afiatic eftablifhments, the weight of the native
powers is very great. In the New World,
the independent ftates form a very fmall and
infignificant portion of the political fyftem.
The events of late years, however, may furnifh juft grounds for apprehending that a very
formidable addition to their number will, at
no diftant period, be the confequence of the
blind policy of thofe nations which have poured into the Antilles the favage tribes of Africa.

I purpofe to confine myfelf, in the following
Book, chiefly to the mutual relations of the A-
merican colonies, and that principally for two
reafons. In the firft place, becaufe, for many
years, all colonial balance appears to have been
utterly

utterly deſtroyed in the Eaſt Indies, by the decided preponderance of the Britiſh power, and the almoſt total annihilation of its natural enemy. And, in the ſecond place, becauſe the difcuſſion is thus reduced to the relations between the Britiſh colonies and the native powers; a fubject of infinite difficulty, and almoſt boundlefs extent, where the materials are very fcanty, and where our conclufions muſt be regulated, not ſo much by general principles, as by the caprice of individuals, from the fluctuating and defpotic nature of the Eaſtern governments. It will, however, be found, that our general conclufions apply to all colonies, although our particular details are confined to thofe of the New World. In this Book, therefore, I ſhall confider the mutual relations chiefly of the American colonies; and thofe relations depend, in a great meafure, upon fome circumſtances which have already been explained in detail. So that the prefent Inquiry would be limited to an application of the conclufions formerly eſtabliſhed with refpect to the relative importance of the different fettlements, if fome peculiarities in colonial affairs did not occur to diverfify this fubject, and to introduce new difcuſſions, altogether unconnected with any of thofe in the Firſt Book.

The

The circumftances to which I allude, are chiefly of two kinds—the tendency of colonies, in certain circumftances, to feparate from their mother countries ; and the diftinguifhing fingularity in the fituation of the American colonies, arifing from the introduction of a race of men, differing equally from the original natives of thofe countries, and from the Europeans, who partly extirpated, partly enflaved them. The former of thofe circumftances is of a general nature, applicable to all colonial fyftems ; but, from various peculiarities, which we have already defcribed, and which are particularly applicable to the American eftablifhments, we fhall find that it is one of the moft powerful deranging caufes which can operate upon the modern colonial fyftem. The other circumftance is almoft entirely peculiar to the colonies of America. Its effects are ftill more powerful and univerfal ; the frequent recurrence of its dangerous influence is much more to be apprehended ; and at no period was it ever fo juftly the caufe of alarm as at the prefent. But although, for this reafon, we may look upon the times in which we live as a great colonial crifis, yet it is evident that the intermixture of races is a fundamental part of the colonial fyftem, and fo effentially interwoven with the whole fabric, as to prefent us with general confiderations and

con-

conclufions, not of a temporary nature, but applicable at all times to colonial affairs, fo long
as the bulk of the American population fhall
confift of perfons in a fervile condition, and of
a different race from their mafters. Thus, any
principles which we may deduce from our experience of paft years, will be applicable, not
only to the prefent pofture of affairs, but to all
future times, while Europeans fhall poffefs territories in the New World, and fhall remain
feparated from the inferior claffes of the people,
by phyfical differences and political privileges.
The inferences, too, which we fhall draw from
the ftate of things in the Weft Indian fettlements, (the moft interefting object of attention,
at the prefent moment), will be applicable to
thofe continental territories, alfo, where flavery
is permitted, and the difference of race exifts,
fince thofe communities are all haftening towards the fame crifis to which fuperior wealth
and induftry have already brought the iflands.
Nay, many of our conclufions, although ftated
for the particular cafe of the African negroes,
will be applicable to the ftate of all communities compofed in a great meafure of oppreffed and uncivilized men, unconnected, by
natural ties or fimilarity of circumftances, with
their oppreffors. The fubject, then, to which
we are now to proceed is, in fact, neither of a
local,

local, nor temporary nature; although our fpeculations, from a conftant reference to practice, may often affume the appearance of minute detail.

The two great circumftances of difmemberment, by a rebellion of the colonies, or the
eftablifhment of civilized and independent ftates
in the colonial territories—and the feparation
of the colonies by a rebellion of the inferior
races, or the eftablifhment of uncivilized and
independent communities in the colonial fyftem, are now to be confidered, not with refpect to their effects upon the interefts of the
mother country, or upon the internal ftate of
the fyftem (compofed of colonies and mother
country) in which the circumftances operate;
but with refpect to their effects upon the interefts of the neighbouring colonies, or upon
the internal arrangements and ftructure of the
colonial fyftem, that is, the mutual relations of
the different colonies viewed independently of
their parent ftates. Thus, we are to confider
the effects of fuccefsful revolt, or fuccefsful
negro rebellion, in the French fettlements, not
upon the interefts of France, but upon thofe
of her neighbours in America; and we are to
inquire, what the probable confequence of fuch
changes would be to the colonial interefts of
thofe neighbours.

Befides

Befides the two leading circumftances which I have ftated, there are fome others, unconnect-ed with them, and of more eafy confidera-tion, which will properly come under our ob-fervation in the next Book. The prefent In-quiry, therefore, divides itfelf into three parts, which I fhall confider in their order.

In the *firft* place, I fhall endeavour to ex-plain the effects of colonial independence be-ing eftablifhed in any part of the colonial fyf-tem.

In the *fecond* place, I fhall confider, more particularly, the probable effects of independ-ence being eftablifhed in the Weft Indian co-lonies, and the probable confequences of tran-quillity being reftored in the revolted iflands, either by the re-eftablifhment of the ancient order of things, or by the fubmiffion of the negroes to the authority of the laws under a fyftem of freedom.

And, in the *third* place, I fhall examine the natural confequences of the French iflands re-maining in a ftate of revolt, and of negro in-dependence.

SEC-

SECTION I.

OF THE MUTUAL RELATIONS OF COLONIES WITH RE-
SPECT TO THEIR DEPENDENCE ON THE MOTHER
COUNTRIES.

I⟶ may be obferved, in general, that a colony is much weaker, and lefs fitted for vigorous meafures, either of defenfive or offenfive
warfare, than an independent ftate, of the fame
natural refources.

The diftant poffeffions of a defpotic fovereign are never ruled with that energy which
is characteriftic of abfolute government in the
parts near the centre of the fyftem. An unlimited monarch is always afraid of arming his
deputies with the fame power which he himfelf enjoys, left they fhould turn it againft his
fupremacy ; and never entrufts them with the
delegated authority for a length of time fufficient to render it folid and effective. The
fame regulations which would fecure the vigorous adminiftration of the colony or remote
province, would endanger its dependence upon
the parent ftate. Thefe muft, of neceffity, confift in fuch arrangements as tend to render each
fubordinate agent dependent wholly on his immediate fuperior, in order to preferve complete
difcipline,

difcipline, regularity and promptitude in every part of the fyftem ; and to prevent the inevitable dangers that refult from delay, from the
jealoufy of office-bearers, and from the opportunity of an appeal or complaint to the government at home. A vigorous government can only be infured, by entrufting fome one with dif-
cretionary powers, and keeping as much as poffible out of view, the fountain from which this
delegated authority is derived. But thefe are
the very circumftances moft dangerous to the
maintenance of dependence, and moft repugnant to the views of all rulers. In every government there muft exift abfolute authority
fomewhere. In colonial or provincial governments, this power refides at a diftance. In
every vigorous fyftem of adminiftration, the
executive power muft be concentrated within
the feweft hands poffible. In whatever manner it is vefted in the mother country, the executive power in the colonial government muft
be divided between two claffes of rulers, one in
the colonies, the other at home. In fact, the
former are fubordinate and dependent ; the
latter effentially poffefs the fupreme power.

In all the defpotifms of the Eaft, it has
been obferved, that the farther any part of the
empire is removed from the capital, the more
do its inhabitants enjoy fome fort of rights and
privileges ;

privileges ; the more inefficacious is the power of the monarch, and the more feeble and eafily deranged is the organization of the government. Montefquieu has fancifully compared the condition of the people, under fuch a fyftem, to the ftratification of the earth according to the geological theories of the ancients. Whilft the centre is devoured by perpetual fire, and the middle regions are the fcene of barrennefs, the furface is bleft with falubrity,. and clothed with verdure.

The authority of the Viceroy in Spanifh America, though far more unbounded than that of any governor of the New World, is, neverthelefs, limited, according to the maxim *divide et impera*, by the right of appeal, and the independent judicial powers vefted in the Audiences by the legiflative and inquifitorial fupremacy of the great council of the Indies ; but chiefly by the fhortnefs of the period during which any one is allowed to hold fo magnificent a ftation. In this refpeét, the Spanifh government has imitated the jealous policy of fome republics and ariftocratic commonwealths towards thofe domeftic office-bearers whom, contrary to their general fyftem of fufpicion, they thought proper to entruft with confiderable privileges and powers. The extent of the authority was always in an inverfe

BOOK
II.

verfe proportion to its duration. The Doge of Venice, whofe office lafted for life, had fcarcely the fhadow of power. ' *Rex in pur-* ' *pura* ' (fays the Venetian proverb, fo admirably defcriptive of this office); ' *fenator in cu-* ' *ria ; in urbe captivus ; extra urbem priva-* *tus.* ' In Genoa, the Doge had more influence, from his right of exercifing a *veto*, befcre as well as after difcuffion; but he only remained two years in office. The fmaller republics in Italy were ftill more jealous of the executive power; partly becaufe the members of fmall communities are naturally more careful of their liberties; partly becaufe, in thofe ftates, abufes of power are more felt. They deprived their chief magiftrate of all real power, and limited, at the fame time, the duration of his office. The Capitani of St Marino were chofen for fix months only. The Gonfaloniere of Lucca was changed every two months. The Rector of Ragufa held his place for a fingle month; and the Governor of the Citadel was changed every day. It is from a jealoufy, much more natural, of their colonial adminiftration, but no lefs fatal to all energy and vigour of government, that the Spanifh Monarchs have endeavoured to counterbalance the effects of that extenfive delegated power which the diftance and magnitude

tude of their colonial dominions render abfolutely neceffary, partly by fowing the feeds of
diffenfion among the different conftituted authorities, partly by limiting the duration of the
moft fplendid appointment which any fubject
in the world enjoys. They have endeavoured
to unite energy of government with a fyftem
of checks and counterpoifes; to reconcile a
vigorous adminiftration with the very circumftances which weaken and paralyze all the
movements of delegated authority.

The powers of the governor in the French
colonies, under the ancient fyftem, were much
more limited, and his means of acquiring influence far more confined. His office was feldom allowed to continue for more than three
years. His conduct was carefully watched at
home by the Council of Commerce, who had
branches in every feaport town, to examine all
perfons returning from the colonies, and to
encourage, fyftematically, all manner of com-
plaints againft his adminiftration. His prerogative in the colonies was limited by the rights
of the fuperior councils, and the influence of
the colonial affemblies. His moft important
functions were fhared by the intendant, who,
on the other hand, was fupreme in his own department of finance. From this fyftem of divided power refulted an adminiftration equally
vexatious

vexatious to the inhabitants, and deſtructive of
all efficacy and vigour, and, in the end, ruinous alſo to the intereſts of the Crown.

In all thoſe ſyſtems of colonial government,
the undivided energy and quickneſs of execution which characteriſes the primary operations
of abſolute power, has been ſacrificed to that
jealous timidity ſo conſpicuous in its conduct
towards ſubordinate agents, and ſo deſtructive
of its beſt intereſts in all ſchemes of delegated
authority. The problem which Velaſquez ſo
often attempted to ſolve, will always preſent
the ſame difficulties to thoſe who, by deputy,
would perform great actions, or govern extenſive and diſtant territories. After a Cortez
has been found, the moſt difficult part of the
enterprize remains to be achieved : the neceſſary contradiction muſt be reconciled, of retaining in ſubjection him who is fit to conquer
or to rule ; and of calling forth, at the ſame
time, all thoſe powers which lead to victory,
or command obedience.

Monteſquieu * has obſerved, that a republic
governs its conquered provinces with more abſolute and intolerable ſway than a monarchy: that
its remote poſſeſſions ſuffer all the evils, without
enjoying any of the advantages of monarchical
government :

---

* Eſprit de Loix, Liv. X. chap. 7, 8, & 9.

government : and that the diftant provinces of an ariftocratic commonwealth are, in this re-fpect, in the fame fituation with thofe of a republic. Here, as in many other fpeculations, the love of conceit and paradox appears to have mifled this witty and ingenious author. That the government which a commonwealth eftablifhes in its colonies and provinces muft of neceffity be extremely different from its domeftic adminiftration, and that the fubjects of the diftant territories will always enjoy very different portions of liberty from thofe in the capital and the neighbouring provinces, cannot be difputed. It is, indeed, a propofition fo extremely evident, as fcarcely to acquire corroboration from the uniform example of all the republics which have ever plundered and infefted the world. But it is rather fingular, that Montefquieu fhould difcover any thing in the nature of this form of government more friendly to the prerogatives of deputies and governors of provinces, than in the monarchical conftitution ; more efpecially as, in the very chapter before, he had explained the dangerous tendency of intrufting extenfive powers to fubordinate agents in a commonwealth, and accounted, upon this principle, for the apparent unwillingnefs of the Carthaginians that Hannibal fhould fucceed in his enterprife againft Rome.

Rome. The Roman proconfuls, indeed, (whom, in another part of his work, * he de-fcribes with great animation as the bafhaws of the republic) exercifed over the provinces a power unknown in Latium during the free days of the ftate. But their office only lafted for a year ; they were fubjected to various checks and controuls ; and they owed the maintenance of their authority, during that fhort period, not to any influence which they had an opportunity of acquiring over the peo-ple, but to the terror of the Roman name, of which they were the reprefentatives, and to the legions of which they received the com-mand when they fet out for their government. It may be worth while to attend a little more minutely to the ftructure of the Roman pro-vincial governments, as this fubject, fo full of political inftruction, has been very much mif-underftood.

While Rome continued under a republi-can form of government, the conquered coun-tries were in general converted into provinces, and committed to the care of the confuls or prætors, but more commonly to proconfuls and proprætors—magiftrates whofe fole occu-pation was the provincial adminiftration. They were chofen by the Senate ; clothed with extenfive

---

* Liv. XI. chap. 12.

tenfive powers of civil government and jurifdiction ; and invefted by the people, in the
comitia curiata, with the chief military command. But this high authority was limited
in two ways :—they received their appointment
only for a year ; and they were accompanied
by a quæftor, likewife chofen by the Senate,
whofe department was that of the finances,
and who was always an officer of high authority and fplendid rank. Under the republic,
the governor was fometimes accompanied alfo
by an officer called *Legatus*, the lieutenant, or
fecond in command. We are told, indeed, that
the clofeft connexion fubfifted between the governor and his quæftor : ' *Ea neceffitudo*, ' to
ufe the words of Cicero, ' *ut illi proconful pa-*
' *rentis loco effet.* ' But as the quæftor's appointment was altogether independent of the
governor, as his feparate functions were of
great importance, and as his own private ftation
was always one of great dignity in the republic, it is fcarcely to be imagined that the power
of the governor fhould receive no modification
from the privileges of this affociate. That a
great familiarity fhould fubfift between them,
and a mutual complaifance fhould be cultivated
by both, was certainly neceffary for the management of the public bufinefs ; and would, in general, be conducive to their own intereft and eafe.

But

But if the prefence of the quæftor was not intended
as a controul upon the proconful or proprætor, it.
is not eafy to fee the ufe of his appointment. The
whole bufinefs might have been entrufted to
the governor himfelf. He was commiffioned
to adminifter civil and criminal juftice, as well
as to command the forces; and his powers
might have eafily been extended to the management of the revenue, and the arrangement
of the accounts of provincial expenditure, for
the infpection of the Senate. We may therefore conclude, that, befides the limitation of
the governor's power by the fhort duration of
his office, he was farther checked by the quæftor, whofe office feems, in many points, to have
refembled that of the Intendant in the government of the French colonies.

Auguftus introduced a new arrangement
into the provincial adminiftration. He took
upon himfelf the management of a great part of
the provinces, and left the reft to the care of
the Senate. The former were called *provinciæ Cæfaris;* the latter *provinciæ populares.* The
imperial provinces were committed to magiftrates called *præfides,* and fometimes *rectores,*
invefted with as full powers as had ever been
enjoyed by the proconfuls or proprætors, but
accompanied by *rationales,* or *procuratores
principis,* who refembled the quæftor in the
                                         nature

nature of their offices, and exercifed, it is probable, a fimilar controul over the governors.
The popular provinces continued under the
government of proconfuls and proprætors :
but Auguftus no longer allowed thofe magiftrates, chofen by the Senate, to command the
forces of the republic. * One province, Egypt,
feems to have been referved by the Emperor
exclufively, and with peculiar concern. It
was governed by a *Præfectus Auguftalis*, whofe
powers were apparently of a ftill more extenfive nature than thofe of any provincial governor during the republic ; for no fenator
was allowed to enter the province without fpecial permiffion ; and Tacitus, talking of Egypt
under the new form of government, fays—
' *Ægyptum copiafque quibus exercetur, jam inde*
' *a Divo Augufto equites Romani obtinent loco*
' *Regum.* ' † But though not accompanied either by a quæftor or procurator, his powers
were controuled by a magiftrate of high judicial authority, called, *Juridicus civitatis Alex-
andrini*—' *qui præfecti actiones fpeculatus vide-*
' *tur, ne res novas moliretur.* '

All thefe officers, then, *quæftores, procuratores principis, rationales Cæfaris,* and *juri-
dici,*

***

* Heineccii Antiq. Rom. lib. I. Append.—Tit. ff. de
off. Proconf.—Ibidem, de off. Præfidis.

† Hiftor. lib. I. cap. 11.

dici, appear to have ferved the purpofe of the French intendant ; the two firft by the management of the finances, and by their perfonal dignity ; the laft by the exclufive adminiftration of juftice.

Under fome of the emperors, however, there is reafon to believe, that the prerogatives of the *præfes* or *rector* were extended, and thofe of the affociated offices curtailed. Indeed, the neceffity of that fuperior energy which belonged to the imperial adminiftration, for the government of countries not completely fubdued, was the pretext upon which Auguftus obtained the new arrangement of the provinces, and their divifion into fenatorial or popular, and imperial. In both, the affociated officer remained in his place during the Emperor's pleafure. *

From a paffage in Tacitus, † we learn, that Claudius (A. U. C. 806.) refolved to make the decifions of his *procuratores* of as much effect as his own, and obtained a decree of the Senate, invefting them with powers, ' *plenius et uberius* ' *quam antea.* ' It is true, that Heineccius, in his Commentary on the Pandects, ‡ makes the term *procurator,* in this paffage, apply to the *rationalis ;* and conceives that Claudius intended, by his

* Dion. Caff. lib. LIII. cap. 13.
† Annal. lib. XII. cap. 60.
‡ Tom. I. p. 19.

his new law, to beſtow the jurifdiction of fiſcal caufes upon that officer. But this is quite in-conſiſtent with the context. ‘ *Nam* ’ (conti-nues Tacitus) ‘ *divus Auguſtus apud equeſtres* ‘ *qui Ægypto præſiderent lege agi, decretaque eo-* ‘ *rum proinde haberi juſſerat, ac ſi magiſtratus* ‘ *Romani conſtituiſſent : mox alias per provin-* ‘ *cias, et in urbe pleraque conceſſa ſunt, quæ* ‘ *olim à prætoribus noſcebantur. Claudius omne* ‘ *jus tradidit, de quo toties ſeditione aut armis* ‘ *certatum, cùm Semproniis rogationibus equeſter* ‘ *ordo in poſſeſſione judiciorum locaretur, aut rur-* ‘ *ſum Serviliæ leges ſenatui judicia redderent.* ’

This is a diſtinct aſſertion, that Claudius ex-tended to the governors of provinces, though of equeſtrian rank, thoſe powers of jurifdiction which the Servilian law had reſtored to the Se-nate. Neither the ſeditions of the Gracchi, nor the laws of Servilius, had any particular re-ference to fiſcal cauſes. The term, *procurator,* is often uſed to ſignify the Emperor’s delegate or preſident in the provinces. Many of the leſſer provinces were governed altogether by magiſtrates bearing this title ; as Judea, * Cor-ſica, † and Thrace. ‡ The powers of the pro-vincial governors were ſtill farther extended by the Emperor Alexander in the year 225, and
　　　　　　　　　　　　Conſtantine

---

* Tacit. Annal. lib. XV. cap. 44.

† Id. Hiſt. lib. II. cap. 16.

‡ Id. Hiſt. lib. I. cap. 11.

authority, than the monarchs of the Eaſt were
in their commiſſions to commanders and ſatraps.
It is probable that both received the ſame ſhare
of delegated power, becauſe they received their
appointments from Sovereigns equally jealous
of agents placed beyond the immediate ſphere
of their controul, and had to exerciſe their functions upon theatres where the ſame exertions of
authority were required.

In modern times, we find, that ariſtocratical
and republican commonwealths, and limited
monarchies, have inveſted their deputies with
powers ſimilarly reſtricted.

The governors of the Venetian podeſtas
were not indeed fettered by the various re-
ſtraints which reduced the authority of the
Doge to a mere name ; becauſe the provinces
were governed without the complicated ſyſtem
of ariſtocratic tyranny which prevailed in the
city. Yet the ſubjects of the republic in the
terra firma were ruled by ſo gentle a ſway, as
made the inhabitants of thoſe provinces which
were conquered in the war that followed the
league of Cambray, lament their ſeparation
from the dominion of Venice, whilſt this relaxa-
tion of the provincial government certainly contributed not a little to the unfortunate iſſue of
that conqueſt. *

It

* The collection of Venetian laws, entitled, ' *Parti è*
' *bandi Veneti,* ' contains various edicts limiting the powers
of the governors of provinces.

It was not to be expected that the States-
General, whofe extreme jealoufy of all fubordinate authority cramped the operations of their
generals with the prepofterous invention of field
deputies in the campaigns on the Rhine, fhould
entruft their commanders in South America
with that unlimited power, without which the
poffeffion of diftant fettlements can fcarcely be
acquired, and can never be long retained. Accordingly, the rapid conquefts in Brazil, which
the Republic owed entirely to the enterprizing
genius of Prince Maurice, and the patriotic zeal
of the whole nation againft Spain, were facrificed to that cautious and timid policy which
fubjected his meafures to the controul of a mercantile board appointed to watch his operations,
and to prevent him from counteracting the vigour fuddenly acquired by the Portuguefe government, under the newly eftablifhed dynafty of
the houfe of Braganza.

The conftitutions of the Britifh colonial governments in North America were formed upon
the model of that admirable fyftem of domeftic
policy, which has fecured the happinefs of the mother country, raifed her to an unexampled height
of profperity, and, notwithftanding its theoretical
defects, left her in a fituation of envied tranquillity, and folid practical freedom, amidft all the
political experiments and convulfions that have
fhaken

BOOK
II.

shaken the other nations of Europe. The governments of the British West Indies are still
constructed upon the same excellent plan. But it
is impossible to deny, that this form of government, of which we are so justly proud at home,
has communicated to our fellow subjects in the
New World, few of those advantages that we
ourselves enjoy under it. The author of the
' *Wealth of Nations* ' seems not to have consi-
dered this matter with his usual accuracy *,
when he says, that the English colonists had their
rights secured to them, in the same degree, and
by the same means, with their fellow citizens in
Britain ; and that the colonial forms of government approached still more nearly to the perfection of liberty, than the model upon which they
were originally constructed. In theory, indeed,
this is the case. They had, almost all of them,
two Houses of Legislature, and a governor entrusted with the executive power. The consent
of these three branches of the constitution was required in every public act of legislation. But it
appears very clear, that the relation of depend-
ency which a colonial establishment supposes,
could never be ensured by a delegation of that authority to the governor, or an extension of those
rights to the people, which give energy to the executive power, and secure complete liberty to the
                                            subjects

---

* Book IV, chap. 7.

fubjects on this fide of the Atlantic. To take one example, only, of the radical difference between the two fyftems. The influence of the Commons, from their power of withholding fupplies, which almoft always prevents the negative of the Crown from being exerted in Great Britain, and is indeed the great corner ftone of the Britifh conftitution, has, evidently, almoft no exiftence in the Colonial fyftem. Accordingly, every meafure propofed by the Colonial Legiflatures, that did not meet with the entire concurrence of the Britifh Cabinet, was fure to be rejected, in the laft inftance, by the Crown. So that, whilft the directing influence of the people of Great Britain prevents the Crown from exerting its conftitutional prerogative, and in a great degree regulates all the operations of the Royal authority; in the colonies, the direct power of the Crown, backed by all the refources of the mother country, prevents any meafure obnoxious to the Crown from being carried into effect, even by the unanimous efforts of the Colonial Legiflature; and indirectly obtains from it all the meafures that are defired.

If examples were required, we might refer to the hiftory of the abolition of the flave trade in Virginia. A duty on the importation of negroes had been impofed, amounting to a prohibition. One Affembly, induced by a temporary peculiarity of circumftances, repealed this law by a bill which
received

BOOK received the immediate fanction of the Crown.
II. But never afterwards could the Royal affent be
obtained to a renewal of the duty, although, as
we are told by Mr Jefferfon, * all manner of
expedients were conftantly tried for this purpofe, by almoft every fubfequent Affembly that
met under the Colonial government. The very
firft Affembly that met under the new conftitution, finally prohibited the traffic.

Nor is this political arrangement, which altogether reverfes the balance of the powers in
the government of the colonies, the confequence
of any arbitrary or accidental part of the fyftem.
It is effential to the dependence of the colonies,
and a neceffary part of the fubordinate conftitution. It is the legal mode of enforcing fubjection, confiftently with the forms of the Britifh
government. It can only be counteracted by
fuch a growth of refources, as may prepare the
independence of the colonies, and muft, in the
end, produce a complete feparation. This event
will of courfe be more fpeedily brought about in
the colonies of free ftates ; but, even in them,
we have had fatal experience of the obftinate
ftruggle with which fuch a confummation is always likely to be attended.

We may conclude, then, that the provincial
or colonial government eftablifhed in the diftant dominions of commonwealths and mixed

---

* Notes on Virginia, Qu. 8.

ed monarchies, although more free than that with which an abfolute fovereign rules his diftant territories, is neverthelefs extremely different, in its principles, from the conftitution of the parent ftates ; and that, as the delegates of the abfolute monarch, though armed with power fufficient to annihilate all freedom, yet rule with far lefs fway and energy than their mafters at home : fo, the fubordinate fyftems of free governments fecure, in a very inferior degree, the rights and privileges of the colonial or provincial fubjects, without falling into the oppofite extreme of defpotic government. Hence, one confequence muft inevitably follow ;—neither of the two fyftems of delegated power will poffefs the advantages, either of a defpotic or of a free conftitution, in thofe fituations which call for the exertions of national force. While the one is deftitute of that undivided energy, and appropriate promptitude in all military operations, with which a defpotic government is always armed, the other, poffeffed in a ftill lefs degree of this advantage, muft likewife want all that force which a popular form of government exclufively derives from the united exertions of a free people. In the conduct of military operations, therefore, whether defenfive or offenfive, all colonial governments muft be extremely imperfect ; and the colonial governments of

free

free ſtates more imperfect than thoſe of deſpotic
or abſolute monarchies.

But it is not merely from the neceſſary ſtructure of their governments, that colonial eſtabliſhments are ill adapted to the meaſures of vigorous warfare. The very circumſtance of their
dependence on another ſtate at a vaſt diſtance,
muſt be productive of conſequences the moſt fatal to promptitude of counſel, and activity of
exertion. Suppoſing that an abſolute Monarch
may ſafely delegate undivided power to his re-
preſentative, and that a free ſtate may organize
the government of its colonies, ſo as to com-
municate to the inhabitants the moſt ample privileges ; ſtill, ſuch diſtant poſſeſſions, of whatever kind, are in a very different ſituation from
primary ſtates. In them, it is not to be imagined that the influence of the government upon the internal adminiſtration, can operate ſo
ſtrongly as in the mother country. The principle of fear, or loyalty, or religion, or whatever it is that renders the people thoughtleſsly
ſubmiſſive to abſolute power, exiſts in a much
leſs degree, where the Monarch appears in the
perſon of his deputy, than where he ſhines himſelf in the magnificent fulneſs of deſpotic glory.
The feelings of patriotiſm, or virtue, or political expediency, or whatever it is that inclines a
free people to obey its rulers, can have very little

tle force in a fmall part of a ftate, cut off from
the reft by phyfical boundaries, connected with
the whole by no common intereft, and regulated
by a government which is itfelf dependent on a
diftant power.

Indeed, if we confider the kind of men by
whom colonies are always peopled, we fhall be
convinced that they are neither fit for fubmitting
to the difcipline of abfolute monarchy, nor for
being animated by the fpirit of a free conftitution. They are either fettled, for a time, with
the view of increafing their fortunes, and then
returning to their native country; in which cafe,
it muft be a matter of indifference to them in
whofe hands the poffeffion of the province is
placed, provided they are not themfelves mo-
lefted : or they have taken up their refidence
in the province, and made it their abode for
life ; in which cafe, they are much more likely
to feel the defire of feparating from the parent
ftate, than of efpoufing its quarrels.

Whenever, then, a free ftate would carry on
war from its diftant provinces, it has not only to
attack the enemy, but to retain its own fubjects
in tranquillity and fubordination. To look for
vigorous affiftance from thofe fubjects, is abfurd.
They cannot be expected to fight and to toil,
that others may wear the laurels, or divide the
fpoil. To them, it is much the fame thing what
nation

nation receives the taxes and contributions which they muſt pay; and if their exertions are to turn the fate of campaigns in the planning of which they had no ſhare, it ſeems but reaſonable that they ſhould continue thoſe exertions a little longer, in order to render themſelves independent, ſo that they may reap the fruits of their own dangers and toils.

But, beſides the nature of colonial governments, and the ſituation of the inhabitants over whom they are eſtabliſhed, other circumſtances eſſential to diſtant and dependent ſettlements, muſt always weaken and diſtract the operations of provincial warfare. It is ſeldom that a cabinet ought, in prudence, to entruſt a general with full command, unfettered by any reſtrictions ; and more rarely ſtill, that a cabinet can be found willing to grant ſuch diſcretionary powers, when circumſtances render it neceſſary or prudent. When plans are to be formed by a council or prince on one ſide of the globe, and executed by their delegates on the other, all the bad conſequences may be expected to oppoſe the ſucceſs of each meaſure, which can ariſe from local ignorance, and from conſtant delay. If a general has been found worthy of bearing the moſt unlimited commiſſion, and a cabinet wiſe and liberal enough to grant it, ſtill the fate of the conteſt is periled on a ſingle

gle ftake—his perfonal fafety and good conduct : for it is fcarcely to be expected, that
one army will contain two fuch men : and, before time has been given to form them, or to
felect them from the bulk of the forces, their
fervices are indifpenfably required. As to the
middle expedient of councils of war, they feldom or never produce any good effect. If
they are appointed as a check, they muft hamper the general, and do nothing but mifchief.
If they are confined to the office of giving advice, they may ftill have the effect of controul-
ing him ; and, at all events, they muft fhare
that refponfibility, which can never fall with
too undivided a force upon the fingle head of
the leader.

On the other hand, when the government
is near its military agents, they may fafely be
entrufted with ample authority, and can be directed by continual inftructions. Their conduct is clofely watched—their deficiencies eafily fupplied—their places foon filled up. No
great plan of operations can, in fuch a cafe, be
fruftrated by a random fhot. The ftate which
has the beft troops, and moft ample refources,
will, in general, find a fucceffion of able men
to command the one, and direct the other.
Had Cortes been cut off in any of thofe enter-
prizes which fo rapidly fucceeded each other
during

during the whole of his vaft and hazardous career, the Mexican empire was faved, at leaft for
a feafon. But when Montezuma was flain, a
Quetlavaca was eafily found to meet the increafed difficulties of the emergency ; and, on
his accidental death, in the courfe of a few
weeks, there was no difficulty in finding a
Guatimozin, who difplayed talents that would
have faved his country againft any ordinary
combination of dangers.

But, further ; troops may always be expected to fight better in prefence of their countrymen, in fcenes with which they are acquainted,
and under climates to which they have been
habituated from their birth. With how many
additional difadvantages have thofe forces to
ftruggle, which are fent into diftant regions ;—
where the people with whofe defence they are
entrufted, and the enemies whom they have to
combat, are almoft equally ftrange and foreign to them ;—where they may languifh in
an unwholefome air, after fpilling their blood
in the field ; and muft fubmit to all the rifks
and delays of a tedious return, before they can
receive the meed of their country's applaufe,
for the victories which their fcars and their
toils have won ? Nor are the leaders themfelves on equal terms. They have not the
fame eyes watching their conduct ; they do
not

not take the field with the fame local knowledge; they are called upon to act in a ftrange
country, at a vaft diftance from their fupplies ;
and having in their rear, fhould they be forced
to retreat, if not an enemy's territory, at leaft
one which belongs to a lukewarm friend. In
fhort, the nation that carries on war in its colonies, either for their defence or extenfion,
acts under the principal difadvantages to which
every power is fubject, when it engages in offenfive warfare, and which, other circumftances
being equal, muft always turn the fortune of
war in favour of an enemy who fights on his
own ground.

The hiftory of the Greek and Roman colonies will probably occur to my readers, as
furnifhing exceptions to the propofition which
I have been endeavouring to eftablifh. The
fubjection of the moft flourifhing of the former,
although independent of the mother country,
and the great affiftance which the Romans derived from their colonial fettlements, in extending and fecuring their conquefts, may at firft
fight appear to preclude the application of the
foregoing remarks, at leaft to the policy of ancient ftates. But, a little attention to the real
nature of thofe eftablifhments will fhow us, that
their hiftory prefents, in fact, nothing anomalous to our view.

The

The Greek and Roman colonies, as we have already fhown, * were effentially different in their conftitution and origin. The former arofe from emigrations caufed by an overgrown population, and feldom retained any dependence on the parent ftates. The latter owed their eftablifhment principally to the ambition of Rome; and they remained in ftrict fubordination to her power. But another difference between the two forts of colonies has not been fo much regarded. The colonial fettlements of the Greeks were planted in diftant countries, and amongft barbarous tribes. They were eftablifhed, not in Greece, or in the ftates immediately in the neighbourhood which had already been well peopled, but in Gaul, Sicily, and the fouth of Italy; in Cyrene, and Egypt; in Illyria, and Afia Minor. The Roman colonies, on the other hand, were planted in the immediate vicinity of Rome. During the fecond Punic war, the city was furrounded by no fewer than thirty eftablifhments of this kind, † which ferved as fo many garrifons or advanced pofts, for her defence. Ancient authors mention no lefs than one hundred and fixty-four colonies fettled in Italy, from the foundation of Rome to the death of Auguftus. ‡

It

---

* Book I. Sect. I.   † Livy, lib. XXVII.
‡ Onuphrius Panvinius; Imper. Rom. cap. VI.—Note B b.

It was not until after a neighbouring ſtate had been completely conquered, that the Romans thought of colonizing its territories. In laying the plan of a new acquiſition, their firſt ſtep was, to ſecure the alliance of ſome ſtate in the vicinity of the power marked out for plunder or deſtruction, and, if poſſible, to excite diſſenſions in the interior of the country itſelf. Having ſucceeded in this enterprize, they faithleſsly involved their allies in the ſame ſubjection. An advantageous treaty of peace, ſecuring the payment of tribute, and preſcribing a change in the form of the government or the perſons of the rulers, generally terminated the firſt war. This treaty was then treacherouſly broken, and hoſtilities recommenced, for the complete ſubjugation of the country, with circumſtances of barbarity and oppreſſion, which at once deſtroyed the ſpirit and the force of the vanquiſhed.

It was now that theſe ſavage plunderers of the world poured into the conquered territory a band of hungry adventurers, leagued by a conſtitution ſimilar to that of the parent city. Syſtematically regardleſs of the rights of property, they uniformly introduced thoſe ſettlements by an Agrarian law, which transferred part of the ſubjugated territory to the allied

powers

powers who were not yet fwallowed up, and
divided another portion among the Roman foldiers. The vanquifhed people eafily incorporated with their new mafters, whom they nearly
refembled in manners and in warlike habits;
and the colonies, by which Rome was furrounded, became, in fact, neither more nor lefs than
an integral part of her own territory, lying contiguous to the centre of the ftate, governed by
fimilar laws, and peopled by the fame fort of
mixed and warlike breed. The Social war was
thus, as we formerly remarked, a civil war, in
the ftricteft fenfe of the word. It was a conteft
between the inhabitants of the country, and thofe
of the city, for the poffeffion of certain political privileges, formerly difregarded, becaufe they
conferred no advantageous diftinction; but now
more highly prized, becaufe they ferved to mark
the fuperiority of the Romans over the inhabitants of the provinces or remote territories. It
muft, however, be obferved, that the tranfma-
rine and tranfalpine poffeffions of the republic
were in a very different predicament from its
Italian dominions. They were indeed fubdued
by force of arms and intrigue, by bafenefs and
political profligacy of every fort, juft as the body of the ftate had been more flowly added to
the city; but they were not retained and fecured
                                              by

by the fyftem of colonizing and incorporating.
They continued to form diftinct ftates, though
governed by Roman magiftrates and laws ; and
they were kept in fubjection by Roman armies.
They did not contribute to the farther conquefts
of the republic, unlefs by the tribute which they
paid, and the paffage which they afforded to the
republican forces. After the fecond Punic war,
in which the enemy was reduced to the loweft
ftate of humiliation compatible with the prefervation of nominal independence, no lands
were feized, no colonies planted, no provincial
government eftablifhed, in Carthage. But the
jealoufy of Mafiniffa was excited againft that
neighbour, whom common danger fhould have
taught him to confider as his beft ally : and full
fcope being given to that fyftem of policy which
conquers by dividing, and by fomenting wars,
the arms of Mafiniffa were employed to fmooth
the way for the total deftruction of the Carthaginian name, and, ultimately, for the accomplifhment of his own ruin alfo ; while the forces of
both, fo long as they retained any power, were
directed againft the independence of Macedonia
and Greece.

When the Romans would avail themfelves
of one conqueft, in order to make another,
they adopted a middle line of policy. They did
not at once complete any part of their work,
however

however eafy. Inftead of reducing a fubjugated ftate to the form of a Roman province, they allowed it to remain under its own laws ; and, by means of its conquered rulers, who were permitted to retain their places, they fwayed its fceptre, and appropriated its refources : a method of proceeding, not peculiar to thofe crafty warriors, but adopted by military communities, in all ages, and in every part of the world ; by the Tartar hordes, by the conquerors of the Mogul empire, by the Princes of Abyffinia, and, ftill more recently, by the French chiefs, who have furrounded their dominions with directories, and vice-prefidents, and landamtmans, and petty monarchs ; as the conquerors of the Eaft did with cawns, and nawaubs, and fultauns.

It appears then, firft, that the Roman colonies were, in moft material refpects, totally different from thofe of every other country : and, fecondly, that the Romans never extended the policy of conquering, or ruling, by means of colonies, to their diftant fettlements. But the hiftory of the Roman policy, rich in every fpecies of inftruction, furnifhes us alfo with pofitive proofs of the weaknefs of colonial eftablifhments, when attacked by the confolidated power, and energetic adminiftration peculiar to independent ftates.

The

The firft conqueft that the Roman arms made beyond the bounds of Italy, was the ifland of Sicily, and, foon after, thofe of Corfica and Sardinia. The greater part of the firft, and the whole of the two laft, were fubject to the provincial government of Carthage : they were all ceded to Rome by the treaty which terminated the firft Punic war. Spain, the firft country on the continent of Europe in which the Romans obtained a footing, had, immediately before the invafion of Scipio, been conquered by the troops of Carthage.

The rapid progrefs of the Punic arms under Hannibal, and the wonders which that fingular man performed, chiefly with a force collected from the conquered countries, may rather appear an inftance againft our general principle. But before drawing fuch a conclufion, we fhall do well to confider the chance which any nation has of producing fo great a captain as Hannibal. The events of the fecond Punic war, and the victories of Epaminondas, form, perhaps, the only inftances in the hiftory of the world, wherein great changes of affairs have, for a time, been brought about entirely by the accidental appearance of extraordinary men upon the theatre of human affairs. It is, in fact, the aftonifhing part of Hannibal's ftory, that, even according to the accounts of his enemies, he fucceeded, to a certain degree, in o-
vercoming

vercoming thofe phyfical and moral obftacles
which all other men have found infurmount-
able. ' *Ac nefcio, an mirabilior adverfis, quàm*
' *fecundis rebus, fuerit. quippe qui, quum et in ho-*
' *ftium terra per annos tredecim, tam procul ab*
' *domo, variâ fortunâ bellum gereret, exercitu non*
' *fuo civili, fed mixto ex colluvione omnium gentium,*
' *quibus non lex, non mos, non lingua communis ;*
' *alius habitus, alia veftis, alia arma, alii ritus,*
' *alia facra, alii propè Dei effent : ita quodam uno*
' *vinculo copulaverit eos, ut nulla nec inter ipfos,*
' *nec adverfus ducem feditio exftiterit ; quum et*
' *pecunia fæpe in ftipendium, et commeatus in ho-*
' *ftium agro deeffent.* ' *   Such were the circumftances natural to a war carried on againft an
independent ftate, from the remote provinces
of the invading power.   They were circumftances which may be expe&ed with certainty
to recur in fimilar fituations, and inevitably
to baffle fimilar attempts, unlefs carried on under the aufpices of fuch a leader as Hannibal.
In modern times, indeed, the more complicated
fyftem of warfare, and the more combined operations of foreign policy, which regulate the
intercourfe of ftates, render it ftill more unlikely, than formerly, that the appearance of a
fingular genius, or any other fortuitous occurrence, fhould again produce confequences of
importance

---

* Livy, lib. XXVIII. cap. 12.

importance fufficient to make them be confidered as exceptions to the general pofition I
have maintained.

And, after all, it fhould be remembered,
that even in the cafe before us, Hannibal was
not completely fuccefsful. The Roman colonies and provinces in Italy, as yet but partially
confolidated, readily joined the invaders. * The
jealoufy, and weaknefs of the motives which
ruled the Carthaginian councils, as well as
the great diftance of the fcene of action, and
the length of the war, prevented proper fupplies from being fent to Hannibal. The Romans, fighting on their own ground, refufed,
after their ufual manner, to hear of any terms,
until the enemy fhould, as a preliminary, eva-
cuate Italy. Every defeat rendered them more
obftinate ; concentrated their forces ; and inflamed them with the valour of defpair. The
talents of Hannibal himfelf, could not infpire
his troops with thofe fentiments ; becaufe they
were a mixed and difunited race, debauched
by fuccefs, fighting chiefly for plunder, at a
vaft diftance from their homes. All thefe circumftances were neceffary to the relative fituation of the parties, and might fairly be taken
into the calculation, as fure to influence the
ultimate fate of the conteft. They are among
the

---

* Livy, lib. XXI. cap. 38. & lib. XXII. cap. 61.

the neceſſary obſtacles to a warfare, carried on
from colonies or provinces againſt primary and
independent ſtates ; and in the end, they over-
powered even the wonder-working genius of
the Punic commander.

Nor is the hiſtory of the Greek colonies in
Aſia Minor, any exception to the propoſition
which I have been attempting to illuſtrate.
They were indeed conquered, as many other
ſtates have been, by powerful neighbours. The
Aſiatic Greeks occupied a narrow ſtripe of territory, furrounded on all ſides, excepting the
weſt, by the great empire of Lydia. Like
many other communities of men as well as of
nations, in ſimilar circumſtances, although oppoſed by a common enemy, they did not lay
aſide their hereditary antipathy, derived from
diverſity of origin, and the ancient rivalry of
their European anceſtors. The federal conſtitution of each ſtate was ill adapted to promote
the union dictated by their obvious intereſts ;
and, ſo far from the two nations agreeing in
any military combination, it was ſeldom that
the different cities of either, could be brought
to act in one way. While the ariſtocratic
government prevailed in Sweden and Poland,
it was not wonderful that Ruſſia ſhould acquire
an abſolute preponderance in. their affairs, and
ſeize upon part of the latter. The mutual
                                    animoſity

animofity of the Northern Powers has, for the laſt century, rapidly augmented the influence of their natural enemy over them both ; and the diviſions of the Germanic Empire have enabled France to dictate at Vienna, Berlin, and Ratiſbon. Divided councils are fatal; becauſe they are weak and irreſolute, and never effective but in ſome tranſient fit of a ſtill more dangerous raſhneſs and precipitancy. Diſtant councils have the ſame imperfections in a degree little inferior ; and the difference is more than compenſated by the diviſion of ſupplies, and the various delays eſſential even to the moſt active and energetic ſecondary government. If the ſcheme entertained by the cabinet of Verſailles upon the Poliſh crown, previous to the Auſtrian alliance in 1756, had ſucceeded, and a French prince had been eſtabliſhed in ſubordinate authority at Warſaw, the events of 1794 and 1795, would in all likelihood have taken place in 1774, after a ſhort and ineffectual ſtruggle. If Philip II. had ſucceeded in reſtoring the Spaniſh dominion over the Dutch Netherlands, the armies of Lewis XIV. would not have been forced to retreat from the gates of Amſterdam, and we ſhould never have heard of the family compact.

The hiſtory of America preſents us with a variety of examples, all ſtrongly confirming the

ſame

fame pofitions. It was from colonies, indeed,
and from colonies recently eftablifhed in the
iflands, that the firft conquefts of the Spaniards
on the continent were made with a rapidity
which aftonifhed all mankind. But although
the Crown of Caftile reaped the whole benefits
of thofe brilliant exploits, they were almoft entirely the achievement of private adventurers,
and refembled, in their energy and fuccefs, rather the fpeculations of mercantile adventure,
than the operations of a diftant cabinet. The
fettlements in Cuba, Jamaica, and St Domingo, ferved only as fo many convenient points
of attack—fo many ports where the adventurers were collected, and from which the voyages were fitted out. The enemy, though numerous, was greatly inferior in all the arts of
policy, as well as in military fcience; and,
though his force was concentrated, he was
not in a fituation to make reprifals, or attempt a diverfion. Yet, with all thofe advantages, it is manifeft that the Spaniards muft
have failed, had they not followed the maxims
of the Roman conquerors, and paved the way
to each fuccefs, by forming alliances, and fomenting divifions. The Peruvian empire was
fubdued entirely by perfidy and intrigue. The
invafion of Chili was fruftrated, partly by dif-
fenfions among the plunderers, partly by the
better policy of the native tribes; and it is
worthy

worthy of remark, that the fubjection of Mexico was effected by conquering, in detail, the
remoteft provinces in the kingdom, and acquiring at the fame time the firm alliance of
the Tlafcalans, a powerful and diftant appendage of the empire, without whofe affiftance
Cortes could never have reached the capital,
and whofe antipathy to their former mafters
faved him from utter deftruction in his retreat.

We have already taken notice of the effects
which the Dutch policy produced upon the operations of Prince Maurice, and the power of the
States-General in South America. The comparative trial of force, indeed, between an independent nation, and a province or colony in
the new world, has never yet been fairly made.
The European power in that quarter of the
globe, has never, till very lately, received any
check, either from the growth of the white population, or the increafed number of the African labourers; and the wife policy of the United
States has kept them at peace with all their
neighbours, fince they became independent of the
mother country. But, in the very firft year of
the unhappy conqueft which brought about that
event, a ftriking proof was exhibited, of the dangers to which the beft regulated colonial eftablifhment is expofed, by the neighbourhood of

an

an independent community, even during its early infancy, and its ftruggles for exiftence. My
readers will immediately perceive, that I allude
to the celebrated expeditions of Allen, Montgo-
mery, and Arnold. While the moft fanguine
friends of American independence fcarcely ven-
tured to hope that the colonifts would be able
to maintain their ground againft the forces of
the mother country, they aftonifhed the world,
by commencing offenfive operations. The very firft campaign of that unhappy war, was fig-
nalized by a fuccefsful expedition of the revolt-
ers againft the ftations of the Britifh forces on
the frontiers of Canada ; and the gates of that
province were thus thrown open to a moft formidable invafion, which threatened the total
conqueft of the country before the end of the
fame year. The gallant leaders to whom thofe
operations were entrufted, actually reduced the
whole of Upper Canada, and were only foiled
in their attempts on Quebec, by the ill choice
of the feafon, owing chiefly to the divifions of
opinion that conftantly attend the offenfive meafures of governments newly formed upon a popular model ; the union of the befieged in defence of their large property, which they were
taught to believe would be expofed to the plunder of the rebels ; and the extenfive powers
wifely confided by the Britifh government to
General

General Carleton—powers formerly unknown in any of the colonies, and utterly inconfiftent with a government bearing the fainteft refemblance to a popular form. Thus had the infant re- public of America, immediately at the com- mencement of feparate operations, and above half a year previous to the formal declaration of independence, almoft fucceeded in the conqueft of a Britifh colony, ftrong by its natural pofition, by the vigour of its internal adminiftration, by the experience of the veteran troops who defend- ed it, and by the fkill of the gallant officer who commanded thofe forces ; while the only advan- tages of the affailants confifted in the romantic valour of their leaders, the enthufiafm of men fighting in their own caufe, and the vigorous councils of an independent community.

Let us now fuppofe, that in any other part of the American colonies, a free ftate was efta- blifhed, either with the confent of the mother country, or by forcibly difclaiming her authori- ty. Let us conceive, that this new community is placed in the neighbourhood of colonies not connected with the new ftate by the ties of blood, or habits of fubjection to the fame go- vernment, but inhabited by a people whofe proxi- mity of fituation, diverfity of origin, and fimila- rity of purfuits, as is uniformly the cafe, render- ed them a rival or hoftile nation ; and that, of
                    confequence,

confequence, in any conteſt that may take place
between the two communities, neither of them
can labour under the diſadvantage of a diſputed
title to independence, as was the caſe in the A-
merican war.   Let us, for inſtance, ſuppoſe that
the cabinet of Liſbon, weary of the dependent
ſituation in which it is placed by every political difference among the European powers, ſhall
abandon ſo trifling a portion of its territory as
Portugal, and transfer the ſeat of government to
the great body of its dominions, the Brazils.
In its preſent ſtate, Portugal can neither preſerve
her independence in Europe, againſt the united
force of that power which, ſince the acceſſion of
John IV. in 1640, has been her natural enemy, and of France, the natural ally of Spain ;
nor can ſhe, by a diverſion in South America,
ſecure the ſafety of her European poſſeſſions ;
nor can ſhe again look for ſuch a ſeries of good
fortune, as that which, in the war of 1762, enabled England to ſave her from the power of the
Bourbons, by the brilliant campaigns in North
America and the Weſt Indies.   But if the Court
of Liſbon, with the military and naval force of
the kingdom, and the nonreſident proprietors
of American eſtates, remove to St Salvador, and
adopt ſuch reforms in the adminiſtration, as a
complete change of any kind may be ſuppoſed to render leſs terrific than innovation generally

nerally is to abfolute governments; then the colonies of France and Spain in South America,
will have to contend with a people poffeffed of
a fertile, extenfive, and compact territory, more
populous in Europeans and Creole whites, than
any other portion of that vaft continent ; and,
above all, forming an independent ftate, governed by a cabinet in the centre of its dominions.
Difputes have even already arifen between the
Spaniards and other nations, about the limits of
poffeffions which, under the Spanifh government,
feem fated to remain a wide defert ; and the
Portuguefe fettlers have repeatedly endeavoured
to injure their neighbours in America, and to
increafe a territory already too extenfive. But,
in the cafe which we have fuppofed, it is not neceffary to affume, that views of ambition in the
new world fhall actuate the tranfplanted cabinet. The fafety of the territories which it will
retain in Europe, forms a more legitimate and
more probable object of anxiety. While the
court of Madrid, then, continues to prefer the
rich colonies of Peru and Grenada, to the undivided poffeffion of the Spanifh peninfula ;
while France is unwilling to increafe the dominions of Spain in Europe, at the expence of
thofe territories in Guiana which have coft her
fo many millions ; at the expence, too, of a great
diminution of the Spanifh empire in America ;
and

and while Portugal retains a wifh to figure as a European power, to poffefs ports in the neighbourhood of her beft markets, and to retain the territories to which fhe owes her name and origin : fo long we may expect to fee, in confequence of the propofed change, the prefent arrangement of dominion maintained in America, as well as in Europe ; but with this difference, that Portugal will have become independent of all foreign affiftance, and will have greatly increafed the value and ftrength of her South American poffeffions ; fhe will owe the fafety and aggrandizement of every branch of her empire to the vaft fuperiority which all primary ftates poffefs over colonies in fimilar circumftances. This fuperiority, although the fituation of her European poffeffions may prevent it from actually increafing her American territories, will, neverthelefs, raife her to a far more exalted rank than fhe at prefent holds, and will, in every fenfe of the word, augment her refources, and extend her power. *

The fame confequences will follow, if any of the European fettlements in the Weft Indian Archipelago fhall, by whatever means, become independent of the mother country. The power of France to attack the neighbouring iflands of Jamaica, Cuba, and Porto-Rico, from St Domingo,

* Note C c.

mingo, is much more limited than the power
of St Domingo would be, were an independent
government, and a primary nation, either of
whites, mulattoes, or negroes, or of a mixture
of the three races, eftablifhed there, by whatever means; always fuppofing that the population and natural ftrength of the ifland is fufficient to enable it to ftand without the fupport of the mother country. Now, as any revolution of this nature muft, in all probability,
take place directly againft the will of the mother country, it is manifeft, that the colonies
will never be emancipated before they can exift
independent of her aid.

In general, then, it appears that the emancipation of any colony, or its eftablifhment as a
primary ftate independent of the mother country, is dangerous to the neighbouring colonies
which retain their dependence, although we
fhould not confider the very powerful effects of
example, and the contagious nature of revolt, in
all communities fimilarly circumftanced. Such
an event will be dreaded by all the powers
having colonies in that quarter, as directly fub-
verfive of the colonial balance, and the firft ftep
towards the ruin of their own colonial fyftem.

We have feen, during the eventful hiftory
of the laft twelve years, how fatal to the balance
of Europe the fudden changes in the internal
affairs

BOOK
II.
affairs of one great nation have been. Although various opinions have been entertained
with refpect to the merits of that revolution,
confidered in itfelf; although many have doubted the juftice and expediency of interfering
with its progrefs; although fome have even
maintained that its confequences, in the end, will
be favourable to the interefts of other ftates:
no one has ever denied, that the great fyftem
of European power has, in the mean time, been
deranged, and that the caufe of the derangement muft be looked for in the new energies
which the French revolution has developed, and
in the views of policy which have regulated the
actors in the great drama. Befides all thofe
difturbing caufes which a colonial emancipation
would immediately introduce into the fyftem,
others which we have pointed out, of no lefs importance, are peculiar to the colonies; and the
nature of fubordinate governments would deprive thofe fettlements which ftill remain dependent, of the energy and vigour fo neceffary
for meeting the new crifis of affairs.

It may be remarked, in general, that where
a number of nations are placed in fimilar circumftances, no change of importance can ever
happen in one, without inducing a fimilar change
in the reft alfo. This arifes chiefly from three
caufes;—from the force of example upon nations

tions united by conftant intercourfe, and placed in fimilar degrees of refinement ; from the direct neceffity which every increafe of power in one member of the national community impofes on all the other members, of providing for their fecurity by fimilar means, or from the power which any diminution of refources in one member affords to the others, of diminifhing their preparations for felf-defence ; and, laftly, from the circumftance, that every great change in one part of the fyftem which is not wholly accidental, muft be prepared and brought about by a certain combination of events common to the other parts, and may confequently be expected to take place nearly about the fame time, and in a fimilar manner, in thofe other parts alfo.

The whole hiftory of that collection of fmall ftates which occupied the territory of ancient Greece, as well as of the petty ftates into which the North of Europe was formerly divided, furnifhes us with conftant illuftrations of this general fact, that changes, but more particularly flowly progreffive changes, are always equable and regular over the whole members of fuch national fyftems as we are at prefent contemplating. But the hiftory of modern Europe affords ftill more ftriking and recent examples of the fame truth. Confolidated

dated into one fyftem of provincial government under the empire of Rome, the different
ftates, of which Europe is now compofed, were
feparated from their unnatural union, by the
fame caufes, and nearly at the fame time. Reduced by a people whofe character and manners were never effaced by the moft rapid
conquefts, or moft remote emigrations ; they
were formed into divifions, under conftitutions of the fame nature, peculiarly calculated to preferve that uniformity of cuftoms
which originally marked the whole. The
progrefs of political government has been
fimilar in all, from the dominion of the nobles
to the tyranny of the prince, and, in thefe later times, to the freedom of the people. That
fpirit of commercial intercourfe, which produces a perpetual connexion, little known in
the ancient world, has confpired with fimilarity of fituation, and the refemblance of manners, to render Europe a united whole within
itfelf, almoft feparated from the reft of the
world ; a great federacy, acknowledging indeed no common chief, but united by certain
common principles, and obeying one fyftem of
international law ; a vaft fyftem, compofed of
parts fimilarly conftituted, liable to be affected
in the fame manner, and nearly in the fame
degree, by every external event, mutually influencing each other, and keeping pace with
each

each other's improvements, in fcience, in liberty, and in national refources. Thus, to
take a more particular inftance, as foon as the
grand improvement of ftanding armies was introduced into one part of Europe, by the rife
of the more peaceful arts, and the diminution
of the power of the barons, the fame important change was effected about the fame time,
and by fimilar fteps, in all the nations of Europe. The progrefs of this improvement, and
its remote effects, were likewife fimilar in all.
It was extended, by the ambition of princes, to
the keeping of a large force, for the purpofe
of enflaving their fubjects, and enlarging their
dominions. This improvement was firft introduced into France; and the example was followed by the neighbouring ftates, both as a
ufeful invention of policy for fecuring the
prince's power, and as a meafure neceffary for
the fafety of nations expofed to the new refources with which this important change had
armed the French king.

A circumftance, not fo obvious, appears to
have regulated the formation of moft of the
European ftates, and prefents an illuftration,
equally ftriking, of the principle which I have
explained. There can be no doubt, that the
confolidation of the fmaller dynafties into
which the different European empires were
once

once divided, took place, in all, about the
fame period. The united empire of the Franks
under Charlemagne, was too formidable a
neighbour to the heterogeneous maffes of divided power, which were then prefented, on all
fides, by Britain, Spain, Italy, and the Northern kingdoms. Accordingly, we find that, in
the fpace of little more than half a century,
all the great unions took place, of which the
prefent nations of Europe are compofed. The
empire of Charlemagne was completed in the
beginning of the eighth century; the Saxon
Heptarchy was united under Egbert the firft
King of England, in 827; the Piɕts and Scots
by Kenneth II. King of Scotland, in 838; the
Norwegian petty lordſhips into one kingdom
by Harold Hafager, in 875. The more contiguous of thofe ftates were confolidated at the
very fame time; the reſt within a few years
afterwards.

A number of colonies, fituated in the fame
quarter of the globe, planted about the fame
time, by the fame people, and placed in almoft
every material refpeɕt in fimilar circumftances,
will always form a national fyftem, the members
of which are mutually affeɕted by each other's
fortunes. Any great change of circumftances
in one important colony, will be followed by a
correfponding revolution in the reſt. The
                                                    fudden

fudden emancipation, for inftance, of the flaves, or abolition of the flave traffic in one fettlement, will foon be followed by a general ceffation of the flave fyftem in all the Weft Indian colonies. In like manner, a fudden feparation of one important colony from the mother country, will, ere long, be followed by a general deftruction of the colonial fyftem.

Hitherto, we have only viewed the mutual relations of the American fettlements from a point whence their appearance is uniform in itfelf, and the fame with that of all colonies. The deductions to which we have been led, are accordingly of a very general nature, and apply to every colonial or provincial fyftem dependent on diftant governments. But the fame conclufions will derive additional force, as applied to the following Inquiry, if we attend to thofe peculiarities in the fituation of the Weft Indian iflands, which diftinguifh them from all other provincial and colonial fettlements. This forms, in part, the fubject of the next Section.

SEC-

SECTION II.

OF THE INTERESTS OF THE EUROPEAN COLO-
NIES, AS CONNECTED WITH THE RE-ESTA-
BLISHMENT OF THE FRENCH POWER IN
THE WEST INDIES.

BOOK
II.

I have explained, in the laſt Section, the
reaſons why a colonial eſtabliſhment is always,
other things being equal, a more harmleſs neighbour than a primary ſtate ; and why the ſeparation of any one important member of the colonial ſyſtem, from its relations of dependence
upon the mother country, would be moſt probably followed by a univerſal ſeparation of the
colonies. I now proceed to examine, *first*, The
peculiar circumſtances which render the application of this concluſion to the ſtate of the Weſt
Indian ſettlements particularly ſtriking ; and *next*,
the peculiar circumſtances in the ſituation of
the French ſettlements, which render the concluſion moſt particularly applicable to them.

The reſult of this inquiry will enable us to
determine the probable conſequences of a total
re-eſtabliſhment of the French colonial ſyſtem,
and to compare the effects of this event, with
thoſe of a total ſeparation of the French colonies,

nies, to the other powers who have dominions
in thofe parts of the world.

I. The Weft Indian colonies differ from colonial eftablifhments in general, chiefly in the
following particulars—

1. They are not peopled by feparate nations, like the countries of Europe, or the
larger colonies upon the two continents of A-
merica.

The fate of war has frequently transferred
the dominion of almoft all the iflands from one
power to another. Sometimes the permanent
fovereignty of the conquered iflands has been
transferred by treaty; fometimes a ceffion of
territory has taken place by purchafe or exchange. In the Seven-years war, Britain was
in poffeffion of all the French Windward
iflands. In the American war, fhe loft, to
France, almoft all her own: and during a great
part of the late war, fhe poffeffed feveral of
the Dutch and French fettlements. In the
treaties which concluded each of thofe wars,
indemnities and equivalents were fought for, by
the belligerent powers, among the Weft Indian
iflands. The Dutch owe their whole continental colonies to an exchange with England:
and the Swedes, having long ago loft their

continental

continental territories, are indebted to a bargain with France for their only fettlement in
the new world. The confequence of all thofe
changes of poffeffion, whether temporary or
permanent, is, an intermixture of the different
races of Europeans, who inhabit the Weft Indian Archipelago.

But the fpirit of commercial intercourfe
has produced the fame effect, perhaps, in as
great a degree, even in thofe fettlements which
have conftantly remained under the fame mafters. The temptation of cheap and fertile land,
large profits of ftock, and high wages of labour, have been found fufficiently powerful to
overcome the attractions of home; and adventurers, after leaving their native country, have often found it eafy to make a fecond change, from
the fame inducements, and to remove to foreign iflands. The policy of almoft all the
ftates of Europe towards foreigners, in their
colonies, has been fuch as to render their privileges and fecurity equal to thofe of the natives : And, as a refidence in any of the Weft
Indian iflands, is commonly a temporary exile,
fubmitted to for the acquifition of wealth *, the
comparative advantages of the different colonial governments, are objects only of fecond-
                                        ary

---

* Book I. Sect. I.

ary confideration, as each conftitution fufficiently confers fecurity of perfon and property.

Thus, the mixture of inhabitants in the different iflands, co-operates with the identity of the
climate and other phyfical circumftances, the fimilarity of purfuits and of complexion (an important confideration in countries where colour
is the grand mark of diftinction) to coalefce the
white inhabitants of the different iflands into one
people, united by a common origin and common
interefts. Although nominally diftributed into
different political focieties, and participating in
the views of their refpective mother countries,
only in fo far as their immediate intereft feems
to be concerned, colonies and provinces never can feel, in any ftrength, thofe national antipathies which divide primary ftates, and draw
their fuel from independence, whilft they excite or blow up the flames of war. But leaft
of all can we expect to fee principles of this
fort arife in focieties formed after the manner
which we have juft defcribed, fo long as they
remain in the ftate of colonial or provincial de-
pendance. If, however, a feparation from the
parent ftate takes place, the newly formed community is placed in the fituation of all nations
at their firft eftablifhment. With the new political inftitutions, a diftinction of manners, characters and habits, begins to appear in its members,

BOOK
II.
bers, and to divide them from the neighbouring colonies, unlefs they, too, have followed
the fame courfe, and joined themfelves in one
community with the reft.

2. In another point of view, the circumftances of the Weft Indian colonies are peculiar.
The attachment of the white inhabitants to the
foil, is perhaps weaker there than in any other
part of the world. I have already traced the
great outlines of the Weft Indian character,
and contrafted it with that of the North American colonifts. * I have enumerated the
circumftances which tend to form that character; and have particularly remarked, as a
leading feature in their fituation, the temporary nature of their connexion with the iflands,
and the want of wives and families. The prevalence of the negro flavery, too, and its effects on the manners of the whites, have alfo
been noticed. † It is eafy to perceive how little a fociety, thus conftituted, partakes of that
compact and folid form in which national
ftrength confifts, and how deftitute it muft
be of the great bulwark of nations—that animated zeal and warm intereft which men take
in the fafety and honour of a particular country,

* Book I. Sect. I.   † Ibid.

try, becaufe it contains their property, the place of their birth, the habitation of their fathers, the fcenes of their childhood, the perfons of their friends, their wives and their children.

Thefe views can fcarcely acquire additional ftrength, from the recollection of that extreme unwillingnefs which Weft Indians have ever fhown to take a part in military fervice, unlefs for the immediate purpofe of repreffing infurrection. The hiftory of St Domingo during the adminiftration of the Prince de Rohan, is well known to every one who is converfant with colonial affairs ; and the opinions of fome of the moft enlightened planters upon this point demonftrate, that their repugnance is defended by them on principle, as well as manifefted in practice. *

Now, it is not difficult to perceive the magnitude of the change which will immediately be operated upon the ftructure of fociety in the Weft Indian colonies, by any political revolution which fhall deftroy their connexion with the European powers. The peculiarities in the ftate of the population, muft indeed render the abolition of colonial fubordination a difficult tafk. But if the Weft Indian dominions of

one

* Laborie, Coffee-planter of St Domingo, Appendix.—
Malouet, Mem. fur les Colonies.

one of the European powers fhould become independent, by any of thofe revolutions in the
affairs of nations, which all the events of the
laft thirty years forbid us to confider as chimerical, or be abandoned in confequence of
fome change of views, not impoffible, on
the part of the European ftates, then we
may fafely conclude, that the face of things
will undergo a rapid alteration in the new
community, and that a ftate of fociety will be
introduced widely different from that which we
have been contemplating as one of the diftinguifhing features of the Weft Indian colonies.
The iflands which remain in their prefent circumftances will then be expofed, in all the im-
becility of their unnatural fituation, to the
ftrength of a neighbour, animated with the
ardour of fpirit, and armed with the new-
born energies of an infant ftate poffeffing the
ordinary refources of an independent community, inhabited by a race of men connected with
the place of their refidence, as the conquerors
of Xerxes and Darius were with Greece, and
the warriors of Stockach and the Nile were with
Auftria and England.

3. But the grand feature, which, more than
all the reft, diftinguifhes the Weft Indian iflands
from other colonial eftablifhments, and chiefly
merits our attention in this inquiry, is the proportion

portion of flaves to free men—of flaves, too,
whofe race is totally different from that of their mafters, who are diftinguifhed from them as much by their habits and their character, and by the extent of their progrefs in civilization, as by the formation of their bodies, and the co-lour of their fkin.

If even colonies of free men, connected with their mother country by a common origin and fimilar habits, mingled in the fame body, fo as to form homogeneous communities, and unit-ed to each other by a fimilarity of intereft and character ; if fuch eftablifhments are inferior to independent ftates in folidity and political ftrength : how vaftly is the difference aug-mented, by the exiftence of a foreign nation in the heart of the colony, held, by force and intrigue, in fubjection to the handful of white inhabitants, who, by violence or fraud, have tranfported them from their native country ? Military operations muft increafe beyond all calculation the danger and infecurity of this unnatural ftate of fociety. It is not the free fubjects only whom a diftant government has to keep in fubordination, and animate to acti-vity and vigour. The flaves, in number and force far more formidable than any European enemy, muft be held in obedience, whilft their mafters are engaged in the field, or divided by the

the factious difputes fo natural to a colonial
government.   Under whatever fyftem of policy the iflands are adminiftered, it is evident
that their capacity for the operations of warfare is extremely weakened by the mixture of
their inhabitants.

Thofe who are delighted to contemplate the
grandeur of ancient commonwealths, or the
romantic exploits of conquerors in the dark
ages, may perhaps be inclined to doubt, whether the external fecurity and glory of a community is fo incompatible with domeftic flavery as we have maintained.

With refpect to the bondmen or villeins of
the Gothic nations, they were evidently of the
fame race with their liege lords ; and they appear to have been moft peaceable fubjects, degraded indeed by their fituation, but contented
with their lot ; entirely ignorant of any higher
condition, and in a great meafure deftitute of
the capacity for enjoying it.   It is a fact, known
to fuch as have vifited thofe parts of Europe,
where the inftitution of villenage ftill fubfifts,
that the peafantry have no defire for emancipation.   After the Auftrian law had been introduced into that part of Poland which fell to
the Emperor's fhare by the partition of 1773,
it was found neceffary to furround many parts
of the new frontier with imperial troops, to

prevent

prevent the efcape of peafants into thofe parts
of Poland where they might ftill be received into the poffeffion of a mafter. *

But in the Greek and Roman republics, it will be faid, the influence of domeftic flavery, in its fevereft form, neither deftroyed the fecurity of the ftate, nor embarraffed the operations of war. I will not infift on the radical difference between the character and compofition of the free population in thofe countries and in the Weft Indian colonies, nor expatiate on the ftructure of their laws, and the tenor of their cuftoms, by which every citizen was made a foldier, while the flaves were devoted to the meaneft and moft enervating occupations. It will be fufficient to remark, that in two particulars, a difference ftill more effential to the comparifon, exifted between the flave fyftem of ancient, and that of modern times—the diftinction of race, and the relative proportion of the numbers. The captives taken in war, and ftill more their defcendants; the homeborn flaves, although of foreign extraction, and therefore denominated ' *Barbari;* ' were men of the fame complexion, and in the fame ftate of fociety with their mafters. When liberated, they immediately amalgamated with the mafs

of

---

* Voyage de deux Francois, tom. V. p. 106.—Note D d.

of the free population; and whilſt in a ſtate of
ſlavery, they differed as much from each other
as from their maſters. It was once propoſed
at Rome to diſtinguiſh the ſlaves by a particular
habit; but this idea was ſoon abandoned, for
fear of the conſequences which might reſult—
' ſi ' (as Seneca ſays) ' nos ſervi noſtri nume-
' rare poſſent. ' In Attica, they were obliged to
diſtinguiſh themſelves from the citizens; but
in practice, partly, we may preſume, from the
vanity of the ſlave, and partly from the policy
of the maſter, theſe diſtinctions were ſo much
neglected, that ſevere penalties were inflicted
upon him who ſtruck another man's ſlave,
' leſt, ' (ſays Xenophon) ' he ſhould, by miſ-
' take, injure the ſacred perſon of a citizen. ' *
In the colonies where negroes are employed,
the marks of ſlavery are plain and indelible.
' Nos ſervi noſtri numerare poſſunt. '

The number of ſlaves in the capital of the
Roman empire, at the period of its greateſt
luxury, is reckoned by Mr Gibbon to have been
equal to that of the free citizens. † We are told,
that the citizens of Attica, including ten thouſand freed men and foreigners of free condition,
amounted to ninety thouſand; and, the ſlaves

to

* Rep. Athen. p. 693.
† Decline and Fall, chap. ii. (vol. I. p. 68. 8vo. edit.)

to four hundred thoufand ; which is about the
proportion of one to four and one half. It is probable, that this number of flaves is exaggerated,
otherwife the Athenians would fcarcely have
enacted the laws above mentioned, to diftinguifh the two claffes of inhabitants. * However, that refined people treated their flaves
with the greateft indulgence ; and to this we
may afcribe their uniformly peaceable behaviour. The flaves in Laconia are faid to have
been fomewhat more numerous ; but the poverty of the Lacedemonians induces one to fufpect an error in the calculation. The helotes,
for inftance, may have been confounded with
the flaves. The helotes were an intermediate
clafs between the δουλοι and the ελευθεροι ; but
they had always the chance of obtaining the
right of citizenfhip by their fervices and good
behaviour. They were engaged in agriculture,
and allowed to farm the lands at a very low
rent. However, the cruel treatment and injuftice of the Spartans frequently excited revolts, both among them and the flaves, particularly after the conqueft of Meffenia had increafed their numbers. Nor could any thing
have kept thofe inferior claffes in fubjection, but
the perpetual ftate of difcipline, and the martial
habits

* Note E e.

habits which peculiarly diftinguifhed the free
barbarians who inhabited Laconia. In Thef-
faly, the great flave market of Greece, there
was a clafs of ferfs, refembling the helotes, occupied like them in agriculture, and renting the
land from the free citizens, on very moderate
terms. In that country, rebellion among the
flaves was very frequent, which muft have a-
rifen from the large proportion of imported and
unfeafoned hands, as it is not probable that a
great ftock of flaves would be kept up for fale.

The proportion of flaves to free men in the
colonies and provinces of Rome, muft have been
much fmaller than in the city, from the inferior wealth and luxury of the inhabitants, and
their greater diftance from the great flave market. In Sicily, where the fertility of the foil,
and the near neighbourhood of Rome, may be
fuppofed to have encouraged agricultural fpeculations, and diffufed greater riches among the
inhabitants, the flaves appear to have been very
numerous. Accordingly, that ifland was the
fcene of the moft formidable fervile infurrection
recorded in ancient hiftory. In the cruelty of
the flaves ; the influence of fanaticifm and for-
cery over their conduct ; the extent of the in-
fection, which feems to have fpread over the
whole ifland, and to have broken out repeatedly
after being quelled :—in the fucceffes of the rebels

bels againſt the Roman commanders, who, after many defeats, only ſubdued them at laſt by
famine,—this ſervile war ſeems to have borne a
cloſe reſemblance to the rebellions of later
times.

When the Roman empire was tottering by
its own weight, or verging to decay amidſt the
various dangers that beſet it ; among the cauſes
of its internal debility, we certainly cannot
reckon the mixture of ſlaves.   Long before
this period, the ceſſation of conqueſts had prevented the poſſibility of importing new ſlaves,
and had turned the attention of maſters to breeding, and conſequently to gentle treatment, as
the only means of keeping up their ſtocks. The
public law, and the policy of the emperors, concurred with, or aroſe out of the intereſts of the
citizens, and reſtrained the maſter's powers
within narrow limits.   The reſtrictions on e-
mancipation were removed, and the privileges
of ſlaves were increaſed, while their treatment
became milder.   By degrees, they came to
form a ſubordinate claſs of men, in the ſame
community with their maſters, and attached to
the ſame country ; neither formidable by their
numbers, nor ſeparated by their character and
conſtitution, nor alienated by the hardneſs of
their lot.

The

The proportion of negroes to whites in the
Weſt Indies, is extremely different from that
of the ſlaves to their maſters in the worſt times,
and in the moſt wealthy parts of the ancient
ſtates. The average in the Britiſh colonies
was, in 1790, about ten to one, excluſive of
Barbadoes, the Bermudas, and the Bahamas.
In the French colonies, the proportion was
nearly that of fourteen to one; and in the
Dutch colonies, it was that of twenty-three to
one. The average of the whole Weſt Indies,
was about ten to one. This average varies
from the proportion of twenty-three to one,
to the proportion of four to one. Inſtead of
abounding in the towns where the free men
are moſt numerous, and the government moſt
vigorous, as was the caſe in the ancient ſtates,
the negroes are chiefly diſtributed over the
country. The capital of Jamaica contains between one fourth and one fifth of the whole
white population of the iſland, and not above
one fifteenth of the negroes. In Italy or
Greece, theſe proportions would have been
juſt reverſed.

The proportions of ſlaves to free men, in the
Spaniſh and Portugueſe colonies, on the continent, and in the ſouthern ſtates of North America, more nearly reſemble thoſe of the ancient
nations. In the Portugueſe colonies, too, and
in

in moft of the Spanifh fettlements, the employment and diftribution of the negroes, are
fomewhat fimilar to thofe of the flaves in ancient times.

To the wide diftinction of race, and the difference in the relative proportions of the numbers, we have to add the various advantages of
the Weft Indian flaves over the citizens, in bodily ftrength, activity, and fitnefs for the climate, none of which diftinguifhed the ancient
flaves from their mafters ; and we fhall be convinced, that in this, as well as many other
points, the fituation of ancient ftates differed
widely indeed from that of nations in the prefent times, and that the greateft caution is neceffary in applying the examples of their policy and hiftory to the affairs of modern communities.

We may reft affured, then, that the ftructure of fociety in the Weft Indian colonies, is
in an eminent degree unfavourable to internal
fecurity at all times, and ftill more fo to fecurity or ftrength in a ftate of warfare.

But, on the other hand, there can be as little doubt, that the fatal difproportion of the two
claffes, the great proportion of imported negroes, and the cruel treatment of the flaves in
general, would be all materially altered by any
revolution that fhould feparate the colonies from
the parent ftates, whilft the more vigorous ad-
                                    miniftration

miniftration of an independent community would leffen the danger arifing from fuch a mixture of negroes, or fuch abufes of the flave fyftem as might ftill remain.

We have frequently had occafion to obferve, that the cultivation of the Weft Indies, or, what is the fame thing, the importation of African labourers, is carried on in a great meafure by credit obtained in the mother country, and by the funds of mercantile houfes, which embark in Weft Indian fpeculations, but are chiefly engaged in the European trade, or at leaft in the trade of importing or carrying Weft Indian commodities. Now, the greateft part, if not the whole, of the capital thus employed in loans to planters, will be withdrawn as foon as the government of any ifland ceafes to be dependent. Men are never fond of rifking their money in the hands of foreign merchants, out of their fight, fubject to the rapacity of a different government, and only recoverable by the laws of another ftate. How little of the monied capital of individuals in Great Britian has ever been drawn to Hindoftan, by the temptation of enormous intereft, although recoverable by action in an Englifh court of law! How much lefs has been lent to traders in Batavia! Nay, how feldom does any Britifh capital find its way acrofs the channel to countries fuch as France and Holland, the mercantile

tranfactions

tranfactions of which are as well known on
the 'Change of London, as in Paris or Amſterdam! If any traders continue to riſk their
ſtock in plantation loans, the intereſt muſt be
raiſed as a temptation; and this will have the
immediate effect of retarding improvement, and
diminiſhing the importation of negroes. As the
planters of one iſland, or confederacy of iſlands,
will not have it in their power to lay the increaſed rate of intereſt upon their commodities, and
as the produce of their grounds will not be augmented, the net produce will be diminiſhed by
the riſe in the demands of creditors. The planters who employ a ſmall borrowed capital, and
they who add a borrowed capital to their own
ſtock, in order to make up a ſufficient ſtock for
carrying on the buſineſs, will be unable to continue in the planting trade; and a number of
ſmall capitals, both real and borrowed, will thus
be thrown out of the plantation employment.
But the demands of European creditors, who
reſolve to withdraw their capitals; the riſe of intereſt required by others, as the price of the increaſed riſk and inconvenience; and the impoſſibility of ſmall traders now continuing in the
buſineſs; muſt immediately cauſe a number of
planters to diſpoſe of their whole ſtock, and
many others to ſell a part of theirs. The conſequence of their neceſſities will be, that their
lands,

lands, buildings and negroes, will be fold much
under their real value. This cheapnefs will tempt
the rich planters to lay out their furplus capital in
fuch purchafes, inftead of engaging in the lefs profitable and more hazardous fpeculation of clearing new land, by importing, or purchafing imported negroes. Or if, inftead of purchafing
lands, they affift the debtors with money to fatisfy the European claims, the rate of intereft
will be increafed, by the amount of the bonus :
fo that the lenders will be fatisfied, without em-
barking their money in new fpeculations of
clearing and importing. This cheapnefs will
at the fame time attract fettlers from other
countries ; and the old planters, reduced in
their circumftances by the change, will probably, from their knowledge of the bufinefs,
be employed on the eftates, and in the ware-
houfes of the new owners.

Thofe capitalifts, then, who, under the colonial fyftem, would have employed their ftock
in importing negroes, will now employ it in
fupplying the place of the capital withdrawn
by the merchants in the mother country, while
the old fyftem of credit, being almoft wholly
at an end, every proprietor will refide upon his
lands, inftead of employing a factor or attorney. Great care will be taken of the ftock of
negroes in hand. The proportion of creole to
imported

imported negroes will be much increafed; and
humane treatment of the flaves will produce its natural and conftant effect—fidelity and attachment on their part. The condition of the whole body of negroes being greatly ameliorated, they will gradually improve in habits of fobriety and voluntary induftry; they will become more civilized and fafer inmates of the community. In the mean time, the diminifhed demand for negroes will not occafion much capital to be withdrawn from the Guinea trade, at leaft for fome years; but its profits will be lowered; and nearly the fame quantity of flaves being imported to the Weft Indies as before, the planters of the iflands remaining under colonial government, will buy them cheaper than formerly; they will be tempted to engage in more extenfive fpeculations, and to manage their ftock with much greater careleffnefs. While the dangers of the independent iflands are diminifhed, and their internal weaknefs is corrected, the fettlements that remain in the ftate of colonies will be placed in circumftances of increafing danger and weaknefs.

But, in the new communities, a rapid change will alfo take place upon the numbers and characters of the whites. We have formerly had occafion to remark the difference between the conduct of thofe whofe refidence in a country is only temporary—whofe object is to accumu-

late

late wealth in order to return home, and thofe
who live at home and fpend their money where
they make it. * The ftock of whites in the new
ftate will not be kept up by emigration, but
increafed by marriage. The connexions with
mulattoes and negreffes will be abandoned, or,
if they are continued, their fruits will be confidered as lawful children, and the people of colour will thus be blended with the whites. In
a fhort time, the difproportion of females will
ceafe, and the augmentation of population will
be carried on by natural means. Additional
good treatment of the negroes may be expected
to refult from the improvement of manners, and
the greater ftake which mafters will have in the
country that contains their wives and families,
even if the admixture of women in the compofition of the fociety fhould fail to humanize
the manners of the people, and ameliorate directly the condition of the fubordinate race.

It is thus, that the change which we are
fuppofing to take place in the political condition of any one of the iflands, muft abfolutely,
as well as relatively, increafe its refources and
internal fecurity, and counteract the evil effects
which the negro flavery produces upon the military ftrength of the ftate.

4.

---

* Book I. Sect. I.

4. But, in another point of view, the Weft Indian colonies, and the other provincial fettlements of the European ftates, are placed in peculiar circumftances; namely, by the fyftem of foreign policy which has arifen out of the relative fituation of the European powers in modern times.

When a ftate, whofe territories are of moderate extent, and whofe dominion is not eftablifhed over diftant provinces, engages in warfare, its refources may all be called forth in one effort; its attention is not diftracted by remote and oppofing interefts. A fingle victory may permanently increafe its dominions, or a fhort reverfe of fortune reduce its power. A ftate, on the other hand, whofe poffeffions are widely diffufed over different parts of the globe, expofes, in every contention, a variety of points to the attacks of the enemy. In refolving upon hoftilities, all thofe dangers muft be taken into account. The weaknefs of a particular fettlement belonging to a rival power, is not more to be confidered than your own defencelefs fituation at fome diftant point. While the inducements to maintain a peaceable demeanour are increafed, the chances of various fuccefs in war are multiplied. As complete good fortune in all quarters can fcarcely be expected: fo, neither need total difcomfiture

ture in every part be apprehended. The chances of fuccefs and failure during a war between nations placed in fuch circumftances, are always much more likely to balance each other, than in any fingle and narrow conteft between ftates poffeffing fmall and compact dominions. If an unlucky campaign forces one of them from part of its poffeffions in the eaft, a contrary event may turn the fcale in the weft. The obvious convenience of retaining each its ancient territories, founds the treaty of peace, in general, upon a mutual reftitution of conquefts, and commonly leaves the territorial extent of the two powers nearly the fame as before the war.

But the policy of modern times has ftill farther diminifhed the probability of fudden changes in the diftribution of national dominion. The fimilarity in the fituation of the European powers ; the refemblance of their languages, manners, and laws ; the extenfion of their intercourfe by travelling and foreign refidence ; their union by the relations of fcientific and commercial purfuits—have given birth to an intimate connexion in times of peace, and a common feeling of intereft in maintaining the exiftence of the prefent ftate of affairs. Each power, then, views with folicitude the dangers which befet the reft, and feels itfelf attacked
when

when any of the weaker ftates are expofed to
the infults or oppreffions of their more formidable neighbours—in the fame manner that each nation watches over the fecurity of its diftant poffeffions, and prepares to put all its forces in motion, when any aggreffion in thofe remote quarters calls for revenge. As the power which would feize on a defencelefs province or diftant colony of another ftate, muft be prepared to meet the whole force of the mother country, and defend all its own remote fettlements : fo, the power that would encroach upon the territories of any one feeble neighbour, muft lay its account with preferving the ufurpation, by expofing its whole dominions and colonies to the combined attacks of the other ftates, who will immediately unite to reftore the former balance of power. Such, at leaft, is the theory of political equilibrium ; and we have only to lament, that an impolitic ambition, or thoughtlefs fecurity, fhould have fo frequently prevented its full application to the affairs of modern Europe. Yet we may eafily perceive how great the influence of the fyftem has been in maintaining the independence of the different ftates, if we only confider the very trifling extent of the changes which have taken place in the relative fituations of the European powers, and in the diftribution of the Continent, under

BOOK
II.
der feparate governments, during the long and fplendid period of modern hiftory.

In like manner, we may remark, how few alterations have taken place upon the pofition of the European ftates in the Weft Indies, and the diftribution of thofe valuable iflands, unequally as the ftrength of the different ftates in that quarter is proportioned. During the five long and eventful contefts of the eighteenth century, the only change which took place owing to the fate of war (if we except the expulfion of the French inhabitants of St Kitts), was the ceffion of Tobago by Britain, of Grenada by France, and of Trinidad by Spain. The firft of thofe iflands had only been annexed' to the Britifh Crown for twenty years, and the laft had juft begun to be planted by the Spaniards. The furrender of St Bartholomew to Sweden, and' of the eaftern divifion of St Domingo to France, can in no degree be imputed to the fortune of colonial war. The former of thofe changes was the refult of a tranfaction between two powers, who had remained during the whole century in conftant alliance ; and the latter was an acquifition made by France, through her preponderance in Europe, at a time when fhe had more territory in the Weft Indies than fhe could govern. So few have been the permanent transferences of colonial poffeffions in that

that part of the world where war has reigned the moſt conſtantly ; where every campaign has been attended with ſome important conqueſt ; and where every iſland, except Jamaica, Barbadoes, and Porto-Rico, has experienced a temporary change of maſters.

But if any of thoſe European ſettlements were to become independent of the mother country, and to remain unconnected with the other parts of the globe, it is evident, that the fate of Weſt Indian warfare would be inſulated on the part of the new ſtate, and would be productive of conſtant changes, which oppoſite events in different quarters could not modify or correct. If, for example, the French Weſt Indies had, during the American war, been unconnected with Europe immediately, and mediately with Aſia and North America, the peace of Verſailles could never have reſtored the conquered iſlands to the Britiſh crown. Britain muſt have loſt them for ever, and with them, moſt probably, her larger ſettlements alſo, unleſs ſhe could recover each conqueſt directly by force of arms. The ſame may be ſaid of the Britiſh conqueſts during the Seven-years war, and during the late war, reſtored on account of the North American colonies in the one caſe, and of the Aſiatic ſettlements in the other. In the Spaniſh war of 1740, the reſtoration of Cape Bre-

ton

ton affords a ftriking illuftration of the pofition for which we are contending. That important fettlement was taken almoft entirely by the exertions of the North American colonifts; and it was reftored by the peace of Aix-la-Chapelle, in order to procure the reftoration of our principal Eaft Indian fettlement taken by France. If Pondicherry and Cape Breton had not belonged to the fame European power, it is evident, that the events of that war would have transferred the poffeffion both of Calcutta and Cape Breton.

In all fuch circumftances as we are now fuppofing to be combined, the fortune of Weft Indian warfare alone would decide the poffeffion of Weft Indian territory. We fhould no longer hear of America being conquered in Germany; nor of balances or fets-off; nor of treaties on the footing of the *ftatus quo ante bellum*. The chance of war, in a few campaigns, confined to the Charaibean Sea, would determine the permanent fovereignty of the iflands. The right of property would be vefted by the mere act of occupancy, without the neceffity of confirmation by convention, or acknowledgment by the other nations; and the *uti poffidetis* would of courfe be the bafis of each pacification.

Now,

Now, it may be faid, that the independent ftate which we are fuppofing to arife in the Weft Indies, will be deprived of the fecurity arifing from a power of making reprifals upon an enemy in diftant quarters ; that, of confequence, though more unembarraffed in its offenfive operations, it will be expofed to hoftile neighbours, likewife lefs hampered ; and that its defeats will be as irretrievable as its victories will be fecure.

To a certain degree, indeed, this muft be the cafe. The new community cannot unite all the advantages of compactnefs and infulation with the benefits arifing from extended and remote dominions. But we muft remember, in the *firft* place, that while it is placed at a diftance from the great commonwealth of Europe, it cannot be an object of fo much jealoufy and apprehenfion to the ftates compofing that body, as any of the European powers poffeffing colonies in the Weft Indies muft always be. Suppofe St Domingo to be the independent fettlement, and that it is conquered by the Spanifh government in the neighbouring ifland of Cuba : Great Britain, we may be affured, would view with greater alarm this aggrandizement of Spain by the conqueft of St Domingo, than the aggrandizement of St Domingo by the conqueft of Cuba. We have indeed

proved,

proved, that an independent community in
thofe parts, would be a more dangerous neighbour, than a colonial fettlement to thofe colonies which fhould remain dependent.   But
this danger would only affect the colonial interefts of Great Britain; the acceffion of
wealth and power to any of her European
neighbours, brings the danger nearer home ;
and Spain, the natural ally of France, would
not be allowed to retain her conqueft without
a war in Europe or Afia.   I do not affert that
this policy would be the moft enlightened ;
but I maintain that it would be the moft confiftent with that fpirit of national rivalry which
divides the European powers, which is the
great corner-ftone of the balancing fyftem, and
which, notwithftanding its many evil confequences, has certainly done more to preferve
the independent exiftence of nations, than all
the refinements of abftract politicians, their
treaties of guarantee, and their codes of public law.

In the *fecond* place, whatever might be the
wifh of European powers, their opportunity of
checking the growth of the independent ftate,
and of preventing it from being conquered by
a neighbour, is extremely different.   In order
to check its growth, they can only interfere by
direct attack on the fpot ; in attempting to
prevent it from being conquered, they have all
the

the opportunities of attack which extended and fevered poffeffions prefent. To revert to the fuppofition which we have juft now made— The permanent conqueft of Cuba by St Domingo could only be prevented by a recapture of the one, or an invafion of the other. But the permanent conqueft of St Domingo by Spain, could be oppofed in Florida, in Cuba, in Mexico and South America, in the Mediterranean, and in the Philippine iflands. All the powers of Europe muft be averfe to any change, either at home, or in the neighbourhood of their diftant fettlements. If their interference can prevent or correct one kind of revolution or change of power ; and if this interference cannot be effectual in oppofing another : we may be affured, that without completely weighing the comparative evils of thefe events, or inquiring how far the prevention of the one may tend to bring about the other, they will intermeddle, as foon as the occafion prefents itfelf in which their interference is likely to be attended with effect.

Laftly, we may remark, that the powers of Europe poffeffing territories in the Weft Indies, are, from their relative pofition at home, always ranged on oppofite fides of the great European balance. Such a change of international policy, as fhould unite France, Spain and
Holland,

Holland, with Britain and Portugal, is not to
be fuppofed in any practical queftion.

However clearly, then, the colonial interefts
of thofe powers may point out to them the policy of a combination againft any one of the
colonies which fhall have thrown off its dependence on the mother country, fuch a coalition can fcarcely be expected to be vigorous
and fincere. Notwithftanding the guidance of
the moft enlightened ftatefmen, the councils of
nations are often impelled by paffion and prejudice, as well as thofe of lefs abftract beings.
A more immediate and more urgent danger than
the neighbourhood of the new ftate, whofe exiftence we have been figuring, would probably
be neceffary to induce Great Britain to rifk a
direct increafe of the French power, by uniting with the councils of the Thuilleries, or the
court of Verfailles, in an offenfive Weft Indian
league ; and if the rulers of the nation were
guided by thofe wife and temperate views, they
would have to encounter the ftrongeft prejudices of the people, whom the fpirit of our
free conftitution arms with a power fufficient
to fway even the foreign policy of our national
councils. We have not forgotten the part
that France, Holland and Spain, took in our
own colonial difputes againft their moft obvious tranfatlantic interefts, which they facrificed, perhaps with fufficient wifdom, to the
                                          defire

defire of curbing our more formidable maritime fuperiority in Europe. Upon fome occafions, the right and prudent line of public conduct may be adopted. We fhall afterwards
endeavour to prove, that a policy is recommended by the prefent colonial crifis, fimilar
to that which we at prefent maintain is the
one always leaft likely to be adopted. But
furely it is very fair to argue upon any meafure, from the probability that, in many cafes,
perhaps in a great plurality of inftances, the
unwife and popular views of foreign policy
will predominate in the councils of feveral
ftates.

The new Weft Indian power, then, will
probably find allies even among the ftates
whofe American fettlements lye expofed to its
attacks. But, admitting that a community of
interefts in thofe parts may unite all the rival
ftates againft the new nation; it will find warm
and powerful allies among the other commercial countries of Europe, which have no nearer
intereft in American affairs, than that of obtaining a market for their goods, and attract-
ing to their dominions a fhare of the rich produce of the Weft Indian territories. Ruffia,
Auftria and Pruffia, not to mention the Italian
States, are perfectly unconcerned in the diftribution of the colonies, unlefs indeed that
they would profit by any change which might
overthrow

overthrow the whole fyftem of colonial fovereignty. It is not eafy to conceive a ftronger
inducement to either of thofe ambitious powers, than the profpect of obtaining a footing in
the Weft Indies, or the advantages of a favourable commercial treaty, which the new power
would readily grant them in any crifis of its
affairs. *   Things are widely changed fince the
time when the proud fpirit of Katharine refufed
to acknowledge the independence of the United
States.   That thirft of dominion and territory
which has guided the Houfe of Brandenburgh
fince the days of the Great Elector, and which
neither the neighbourhood of Ruffia, or of
France, have been able to fubdue, is only e-
qualled by the defire of the Pruffian monarchs
to extend their mercantile refources ; and the
nineteenth century has opened with the foundation of maritime policy in the extended Imperial dominions.   It is manifeft, that the u-
nion of the Germanic powers with the ftates
immediately concerned in the affairs of America, could only be occafioned by a rapid extenfion of Ruffia over the Northern and Eaftern parts of Europe ; an event which would,
on the other hand, render the alliance of the
great Baltic ftate no very difficult achievement
of policy to the new power, whofe independent
exiftence in the Weft Indies we have figured.
                                                        We

* Note F f.

We may conclude, then, that befides the refources of internal ftrength, this ftate will not be
deficient in thofe of a federal nature, and that,
while it expofes no diftant territories to the
arms of its natural enemies or its rivals, it may
avail itfelf of divifions arifing from their relative
pofition in all parts of the globe, and of alliances
with their natural enemies and rivals in Europe.

It is furely no fpeculative inference, from all
the facts and principles which have been ftated,
that fo long as the European powers fhall per-
fevere in the fyftem of colonial policy, the eftablifhment of any independent dynafty in the
Weft Indies muft be immediately and directly
hoftile to their interefts.

II. Hitherto we have compared the relative
ftrength of a colony and an independent ftate
in general, and of a colony and an independent
ftate in the Weft Indies, without entering into
the circumftances of the particular fettlements
in that quarter. It remains to be confidered,
whether the different colonies are not diftinguifhed by diverfity of circumftances, and whether the French dominions in the Weft Indies
are not placed in a ftate of fingular weaknefs
by the peculiarities of their fituation, by the e-
vents which have lately happened, and by thofe
which muft accompany the reftoration of tranquillity.

The

The ftate to which the whole Archipelago,
as well as the furrounding continent, once belonged, ftill poffeffes the beft eftablifhed, though
far from the moft valuable empire in the new
world. Vaft extent of territory, towns and fettlements thinly fcattered chiefly over thofe parts
which are fartheft from the other colonies, a policy fingularly adapted to preferve internal tranquillity, and a free population to which the negroes bear but a fmall proportion; thefe import-
tant circumftances concur to render the continental poffeffions of Spain as fecure as provinces
fo remote can well be. The infalubrious nature of
the climate on the eaft fide of South America and
Mexico, while it has kept the fettlements on that
coaft in the ftate of a defert, except at particular
feafons of commercial refort, effectually prevents
any fuccefsful invafion from the Weft Indies, and
takes away the inducement to invade, by deftroying all the immediate objects of attack. In no part
of the South American colonies are fo few negroes
employed as in the Spanifh fettlements; and their
treatment is better there, than in any other of the
European colonies. Both in the Spanifh and
Portugueze dominions on the Continent, the
white population is much more flourifhing than
in the Weft Indies. Vaft bodies of emigrants
have been conftantly fettling there fince the conqueft, as in the North American ftates. The
Creoles form a large part of the community;
and

and their numbers increafe with confiderable rapidity, though not fo quickly as they would under a better form of government, a lefs corrupted religion, and a lefs indolent ftate of manners. The whites in the Spanifh colonies a-mounted in 1550 to fixty thoufand; at prefent they are not under a million. Yet the ftructure of the fociety does not endanger the dependence of thefe colonies. So much of the national importance, both of Spain and Portugal, has always been thought to depend upon their American poffeffions; and fuch large fupplies have been received from thence, in the form by which governments are moft apt to be tempted, that a very large fhare of attention has uniformly been paid to colonial affairs in both thefe countries. Particular councils and minifters have been appointed to fuperintend them. A regular fyftem of colonial government has been formed, and every thing hurtful to the fupremacy of the mother country has been carefully prevented from finding admittance. In the Spanifh colonies, particularly, the Papal jurifdiction, fo abfolute over the mother country, has never been allowed to acquire a footing; and the tithes, the difcipline, and the patronage of the Church (the inheritance of the Triple Crown all over the Pontifical dominions) have been monopolized by the temporal monarchs of Caftile.

There

BOOK
II.

There has refulted, from this attention conftantly paid to American affairs by both the powers
of the Spanifh peninfula, a fyftem of divifion
highly favourable to the fecurity of permanent
rights. A fpirit of difunion is carefully fomented between the Spaniards and Creoles ; and a
fuperiority is given to the former, which greatly
diminifhes the dangers of a feparation, encou-
rages the habit of temporary refidence, and thus
corrects the tendency of the increafing Creole
population to promote the independence of the
fettlements. A fimilar fuperiority is beftowed
upon the negroes over the Indians ; and a divifion is cherifhed between thofe two claffes, which
gives the whites an opportunity of uniting with
either againft the other, and generally attaches
to their interefts the leaft numerous though
moft warlike of the two races. A policy of the
fame nature has connected the Europeans with
the Indians in the French and Dutch fettlements of Guiana, where the negroes are by far
the moft formidable both in numbers and in
ftrength. In thofe continental colonies of Spain
and Portugal, then, as well from their pofition
and extent, as from the ftate of their popula-
lation and their fyftems of policy, there is lefs
danger of a feparation, and lefs rifk from foreign
attempts, than in the fettlements of Guiana ;
and lefs danger and rifk in all thofe continental
fettlements, than in the Weft Indian iflands.

We

We have before remarked, that the indolence S E C T. and want of adventurous fpirit, fo confpicuous in II. the Spanifh character, as well as the reftrictive fpirit of the colonial laws of Spain, has prevent- ed the iflands of Cuba and Porto-Rico from be- ing cultivated, like the other colonies, by the rapid importation of African labourers ; but, of late years, this difference has been fenfibly diminifh- ing. The mercantile company under the Af- fiento which lafted from 1769 to 1779, carried to the Havanna, yearly, from two thoufand five hundred to three thoufand negroes, for the ufe of Cuba and Trinidad, and only carried half that number to Carthagena and Portobello, for the ufe of the northern and weftern parts of the continent. * The field negroes of Cuba were found, by actual enumeration in 1787, to be fifty thoufand in number. Since that time, the ordinance of 1789 permitting the free importa- tion of flaves, granting a bounty on field negroes, and impofing a yearly poll-tax on houfe negroes, muft have greatly increafed the numbers of the former. But, ftill, the mild treatment of the flaves, provided for by new laws which keep pace with the increafed importation, the great proportion of whites, and the numbers of free blacks (eftimated at twenty thoufand in the Havanna

---

* Report of Committee 1789, part VI.

vanna alone), who are always attached to the
Europeans, and ferve with diftinguifhed zeal in
their regiments, muft render the poffeffions of
Spain in the Weft Indies more fecure, in thofe
particulars which we have been confidering,
than the colonies of the other European powers.

The Dutch iflands are in a fituation very
different from their colonies on the continent,
as we have formerly fhown, * and equally different from the other Weft Indian iflands. But,
whatever may be their internal fituation, their
trifling extent muft always render them an eafy
prey to any neighbouring Weft Indian power,
which may be tempted to attack them by the
hopes of mercantile plunder. The Danifh and
Swedifh iflands are in the fame fituation with
the French and Britifh iflands ; fo that our attention is now confined to a furvey of the predicament in which the latter would be placed
fhould the tranquillity of the former be reftored.

It is impoffible to deny, that the dominions
of France in the Weft Indies, are more extenfive
and more fertile in natural refources, than thofe
of any other power except Spain ; neither can it
be diffembled, that the reftoration of tranquillity
will put her in poffeffion of a much more extenfive and fcatterred territory than any independent
power in thofe parts can be expected to confoli-
date

* Book I. Sect. III. Part I.

date under its dominion for fome time after its

emancipation. But the example of Spain, both in the Old and New World, and of France her-felf, in Europe, may convince us, that political importance and national ftrength, are not fo much proportioned to the natural refources and capability of a country, as to the ftate of its fo-ciety and the nature of its inftitutions. The re-lative influence of France and of Great Britain, in Europe, is not lefs proportioned to their na-tural refources, than their relative power in the Weft Indies is to their colonial refources. What-ever may be the fertility and extent of any co-lony peopled by a mixture of whites and ne-groes, the inhabitants cannot avail themfelves of their advantages according to the flave fyf-tem, without diminifhing, at the fame time, their fecurity and military ftrength; and this ex-actly in proportion to the rapidity with which they increafe their wealth. Every hundred hogfheads of fugar or rum, whereby their annual produce is augmented, muft be purchafed at the expence of that fecurity which is deftroyed by a propor-tional addition to the ftock of negroes, and an augmentation in the proportion of the imported to the Creole flaves. A colony which continues to raife the fame quantity of produce, will fend home fewer overgrown fortunes, and augment, in a fmaller degree, the mercantile opulence of the mother country; but it will enjoy greater

fecurity,

fecurity, and have lefs to fear from its powerful
neighbours, than if it had been conftantly increafing in point of wealth.

It muft indeed be admitted, as we formerly
ftated, that the fame number of negroes in the
French iflands, from the fuperior fertility of the
foil, yield a greater quantity of produce. * But
the tendency of this fuperiority, is by no means
to fave either the labour or the importation of
flaves : It operates, on the contrary, as an encouragement to extravagant fpeculations, and
carelefs management of the ftock. The treatment of the flaves in the French iflands has
been alleged by fome † to be gentler than that
of the Britifh flaves ; and Dr Smith, in particular, feems to take this for granted, as a matter of common notoriety. ‡ Others have afferted,
that this clafs of men are nearly upon a level,
in point of comforts, in the colonies of both
nations ‖. But, from the inquiries of the committee of 1789, it appears clearly, that the
mortality among the negroes in the French
iflands, is much greater than in the Britifh. It
was computed, that of thofe imported, one third
died in three years, and of the Creoles, one
fifth

* Book I. Sect. III. Part IV.
† Laborie's Coffee Planter, Appendix.
‡ Wealth of Nations, book IV. chap. VII.—Note G g.
‖ Edwards' Hiftory of St Domingo, chap. i.

fifth yearly more than the number born ; *
while the annual diminution in Jamaica was
only one fortieth *per cent.*; and, in feveral of
the iflands, the ftock was kept up, and even increafed, without any importation. I have frequently had occafion to notice the vaft importation of flaves annually made into the French
iflands, and the confequently rapid increafe of
the numbers during the ten years immediately
previous to the revolution. It is manifeft, however, that the total increafe was far from being
in proportion to the number imported, either
before or during that period, admitting that
the births had been nearly fufficient to fill
up the blanks occafioned by the deaths, and
allowing for the difproportion of females in the
numbers imported. †

It would appear, therefore, that the natural
advantages of St Domingo will never be turned
to account without a very dangerous increafe in
the negro population. But, in another point of
view, this ifland, and indeed all the French colonies, are in a fituation much lefs favourable
to folid power than the Britifh poffeffions, and
more apt to render their independence a caufe
of comparative ftrength.

I have already had occafion to notice the
extenfive fyftem of commercial credit, interwoven

terwoven with the cultivation of all the West
Indian islands, and to point out the probable
effects of their independence upon this system.
But there are several other circumstances connected with it which well deserve our attention.
The credit upon which planters speculate, and
in many cases exist, is not of a solid and permanent description, like the credit interposed by
commercial confidence in the transactions of European merchants and manufacturers. The risk
is much greater, the profits of consequence
higher, and the spirit of gambling more intimately connected with it. A rapacity of gain,
and, in many instances, an eagerness of specu-
lation approaching to the desperation of the
gaming-house, influences both the creditor and
the planter. The fair idea of reciprocal advantage does not always preside over such transactions ; and a capitalist frequently risks his money
to a planter in circumstances nearly desperate,
in order to have a claim upon his estate, and to
obtain it at a price prescribed by the necessities
of the debtor. The complicated difficulties under which a great proportion of the planters labour from these causes, has been admitted by
writers on both sides of the great question that
has divided political inquirers into colonial affairs. The facts which the advocates of each o-
pinion have brought forward, with the most opposite

pofite views, are extremely important. The immediate confequence of the difficulties which thus opprefs the planters, is an eagernefs for quick returns upon their ftock of negroes, and a conftant demand of new fupplies from the Guinea trader. The flaves are worked out ; breeding is of courfe neglected ; and the numbers are kept up or increafed by importation. Accordingly, the demands of creditors, and the neceffities of debtors, have been uniformly pleaded by the fupporters of the African trade, as arguments demonftrating the neceffity of its continuance ; while the advocates of the abolition have urged the very fame facts to fhow the evil effects of the trade, as well upon the happinefs of the mafter, as upon the condition of the flave. * The new actions, we are told, which are raifed in the different courts of Jamaica, amount annually to three thoufand, of which the greater part are actions upon bond ; and of thefe, nine tenths are brought by flave factors as creditors. † In three years, half a million Sterling paffed through the hands of one Sheriff, in confequence of judicial fales on executions chiefly arifing from fuch bonds ; and the principal

part

---

* Edwards' Weft Indies, b. IV. c. 4. ; and Parliamentary Debates 1791 & 1792.

† Clarkfon's Impolicy of the Slave Trade, part 2, cap. 1. fect. 3.

part of the debtors in jail during that period were confined in confequence of thofe obligations. * A fimilar account is given by authors who wrote long before the queftion of abolition had begun to divide the public opinion, particularly by Mr Long, in his valuable Hiftory of Jamaica. †

But the planters in the French iflands have always been involved ftill more deeply in this ruinous and cruel fyftem, partly from the fuperior temptations of more fertile and extenfive lands, partly from the deficiency of capital, both among the creditors and colonifts, but chiefly from the grofs defects of the French laws refpecting the recovery of debts. In the Firft Book of this Inquiry, I have explained the fingular effects of thefe circumftances upon the ftate of property in the French iflands. Cultivators placed in the fituation which I there defcribed, have no immediate intereft in what is called their property. The care of their ftock is the laft method of increafing it that ever enters into their minds. Immediate returns, by whatever means, are the only method of improvement that occurs to them ; and as for any danger to be apprehended from increafing the number of the negroes, that belongs to the
whole

---

* Clarkfon's Impolicy of the Slave Trade, part 2. cap. 1. fect. 3.

† Vol. 1. p. 437.

whole community at once, and therefore affects none of its members until it is realized. ' Things will laft my time,' fays the Weft Indian farmer, as men have faid before him in all ages, and in every part of the world—financiers on the brink of national bankruptcy, and princes, or their favourites, on the eve of a revolution.

If this was the ftate of the French iflands in the year 1789, it is eafy to conceive how the fyftem muft have been affected by the events which have happened fince that time. The reftoration of tranquillity in the revolted colonies, cannot at once render them a defireable refidence. Thofe only will repair to the fpot, or remain there, whofe money has already been vefted in Weft Indian property, from the temptations held out to purchafers during the period of the greateft confufion, or whofe eftates have remained on their hands for want of purchafers. The men poffeffed of fuch extenfive capital as is required in Weft Indian fpeculations, will be ftill lefs inclined now, than before, to fuperintend a plantation in St Domingo. The cultivators will, as formerly, confift, in a great degree, of perfons inclined to rifk their health, and facrifice the comforts of home, for the chance of acquiring a competency—perfons of fmall capital, or mere adventurers. The devaftations of the revolutionary times, with the accumulated

BOOK
II.
accumulated intereſt of old debts, will render credit at once more neceſſary, and more expenſive than ever. Indeed, to ſuch a ſtate have the proprietors been reduced, that the beſt informed perſons ſeem to deſpair altogether of the colonial affairs of the republic. The interference of government will probably be neceſſary; and the nature of the expedients propoſed by ſome of the moſt intelligent planters, affords, as I before remarked, * abundant proof of their deſperate ſituation. Any aſſiſtance which the government can afford, will, at the very utmoſt, only enable the planters to go on. They are ſtill in a ſituation infinitely more deſperate than before the revolution—borrowing money at higher intereſt—forced to extract more labour from their ſlaves, in order to extend their culture, or reſtore their deſolated plantations. Some correction of the evils ariſing from the ſtate of the colonial laws, may indeed be expected—more particularly, the recovery of debts may be facilitated. But, beſides that this muſt, in the firſt inſtance, increaſe the neceſſities of the planters before it can lower the demands of their creditors for intereſt, we may obſerve, that the imperfections of the colonial laws ariſe, in a great meaſure,

_____

* Book I. Sect. III. Part IV.

fure, naturally from the circumftances of the
iflands, and cannot be wholly removed fo long
as the dangers of a tropical climate render im-
prifonment a punifhment of the higheft feverity, and fo long as creditors are willing rather to obtain the chance of repayment, or
profit, by enabling their debtors to work, than,
by completing their ruin, to lofe all chance of
getting either, without repairing to the fpot.

The low ftate of credit, and the complicated
difficulties of the planters, will always produce
confiderable derangement in the adminiftration
of the colonies. The firft affiftance which government may find it neceffary to give, will be
the abatement of fome colonial impofts, fuch
as the poll-tax on flaves ; and the encouragement of abolifhing the duties formerly known
by the name of ' *droits du domaine d'occident.* '
The adminiftration of the iflands, and their defence, will thus fall a burthen on the exhaufted
finances of the mother country. As foon as
the cultivation has begun to revive, we may be
well affured, that the government will attend
more to the direct expences, than to the indirect advantages of fuch eftablifhments. Like
all governments, it will view thefe iflands in
the fifcal fpirit, and will alienate the oppreffed
planters, by impofing on them the charge of
ruling and defending themfelves. We have
already

already feen what their opinions are upon the
fubject of colonial militia, even in the moft
eafy and peaceable times. It is not probable
that they will now grudge their labour lefs
when their occafions are much more prefling.
To the troops or fervices required for fup-
prefling infurrection, they may poffibly make
no objections. But the furtherance of any
views of conqueft, or even the meafures neceffary for their internal fecurity, will be viewed
as encroachments upon their exhaufted refources, and will either be oppofed or received with decided averfion. As to conqueft, it
muft be clearly againft their intereft to be at
variance with the neighbouring colonies ; and
the dominion of England would probably be preferred to that of France, as was the cafe about
the beginning of the revolution, if fhe burden-
ed them with the expence or interruption of
providing againft an invafion. So long, indeed, as the plantations depend upon credit
from the mother country, their proprietors can
have no objection to be connected with that
nation whofe trading capital is the moft extenfive, and whofe government is the mildeft
and moft equitable of any in the world.

Thefe confequences which, I apprehend,
may be fairly expected to refult from the late
calamities, and the prefent ftate of the Weft
Indian

Indian colonies, are by no means to be confidered as accidental, or peculiar to the circumftances in which they have been placed. It is
the lot of every diftant province of an empire
to experience many difadvantages which the
contiguous diftricts never feel ; and when fuch
provinces are involved in any unufual calamity, much lefs care is beftowed upon their
re-eftablifhment, than if the like misfortune
had happened to a nearer part. I have explained the reafon of this in various parts of the
Firft Book. A colony or remote appendage is,
by the policy even of thofe ftates which have moft
favoured the colonial fyftem, confidered merely
as a mine from which wealth is to be drawn in
the form of direct revenue, or, at the utmoft,
as a fpot to which the overflowing population
of the metropolis may refort in order to acquire opulence. Any unforefeen expence which
this poffeffion may coft, is always grudged, as
fo much actual and uncompenfated lofs. In
feafons of calamity, it is left in a great degree
to ftruggle with the burden of its own adverfity.
After the ftorm is over, it is left to recover as
it beft can. The contiguous provinces, on the
other hand, are viewed as neceffary and integral parts of the empire, whofe misfortunes
muft be fhared by all the reft, while they muft
be nurfed with fedulous care, for their own
fakes,

fakes, in every unforefeen difafter, and cherifhed without a murmur, not from the profpect of future revenue, but becaufe they form
an infeparable portion of the community. Calamities, then, from which the contiguous provinces foon recover without fuftaining any ferious or permanent injury, are long and feverely felt by the colonies or remote provinces.
Coldnefs or difguft arifes between them and
the mother country ; and the feeds of feparation are fown, which may either break out in
actual rebellion or in factious divifions, whenever a war is transferred, as all wars are, to
thofe quarters.

The probability of the French government
being actuated in its conduct towards the revolted iflands by lefs liberal views than the reduced fituation of the planters demands, may
be collected, not only from the fifcal fpirit
which has uniformly prefided over the policy
of all ftates towards their colonial eftablifhments, but from the ftate of the French refources, and from the accounts of the late tranfactions in fome of the Windward iflands, more
particularly the requifitions made in Guadaloupe, if, indeed, any reliance is to be placed
on thofe ftatements.

But however enlightened its policy, and
however eafy its yoke may be, if the co-operation

tion of the planters is required in active meafures of defenfive, or, ftill more, of offenfive
warfare, we cannot expect that any thing but
difobedience and difcontent will be the confequence.

Such, then, are the probable effects of the
French colonial fyftem, and of the increafed difficulties of the planters in the revolted iflands,
in confequence of the loffes in general which
their unhappy fituation during the late years
has occafioned. But if we attend more particularly to the nature of thofe loffes, we fhall
find reafon to affent ftill more implicitly to the
foregoing conclufion. The greateft devaftation
which the rebellion has occafioned, is in the
numbers of the negroes. M. Malouet reckons, that during the firft ten years of revolt in
St Domingo, the negro population was diminifhed from five hundred thoufand to three
hundred thoufand ; that the lofs was chiefly in
males ; and that the number of children had
rapidly increafed. * Laborie, in 1797, eftimated the reduction at much more than one half
of the numbers in 1789 ; † Edwards fuppofes
it to have been two fifths of the fame numbers. ‡
All

---

* Mem. Vol. I. p. 52.

† Coffee-planter, Append. Art. X. § 12.

‡ St Domingo, cap. X. : Note to page 173.

All the plantations, therefore, muſt be extremely underſtocked ; and the firſt conſequence of a
reſtoration of tranquillity, will be the importation of a vaſt number of new ſlaves to ſupply
a deficiency fatal to the colonial agriculture.

In general, the proportion of females to the
whole number imported, has been that of one
to three. But now a much ſmaller number of
females will be required, at leaſt for ſome
time : ſo that the proportion of imported
males will be much greater than before. The
ſituation of the iſland will indeed be more favourable for breeding, from the ſuperfluity of
females. But the conſequence of increaſe from
this ſource muſt be ſlow, in compariſon of the
effects produced by the other kind of increaſe.
The yearly augmentation will be at firſt more
rapid than formerly, becauſe the births will
more nearly balance the deaths. But the treatment will be more harſh while the hands are
deficient, and the importation will be greater
than ever : ſo that the natural increaſe will be
now brought to its former level, and the proportion of Creoles to new ſlaves will ſoon be
much leſs than before. At the very firſt, the
whole will be Creoles ; but their peculiar ſituation will render them ſtill more dangerous
than if they had been imported. They are juſt
reduced from a rebellion, completely ſuccefsful

for

for a series of years, bloody beyond all former example, and, from the variety of its military operations againft all kinds of enemies, peculiarly adapted to render thofe engaged in it warlike, if not fkilful. Almoft all the men have borne a part in it. The women and children have enjoyed the fweets of freedom and idlenefs ; they have fympathized in the caufe of their hufbands and fathers. All the confiderations which before induced us * to admit the difficulty of reftoring the ancient flavery, and which have inclined many to believe it a hopelefs project, prove the difficulty of retaining the whole mafs of blacks in fubjection, more efpecially when new imports are perpetually adding fuel to the heap, and aggravated ill treatment is blowing up the fparks of the fcarcely fmothered flame. If it is uniformly found that imported negroes are dangerous in a colony, though many of them only exchange the fcene of their flavery, and all of them are kept in fubjection by irons during the voyage, and taught to regard their white mafters as beings of a fuperior order ; how much more dangerous muft thofe be, who have never known the yoke, or forcibly broken it, and who have been for years in the fituation, formerly unknown to Africans, of

mafters

---

* Book I. Sect. III. Part IV.

masters over white men and mulattoes by the right of conquest! In order to keep the new slaves in subordination, and to teach them habits of labour, as well as to disarm them by division, it has always been found necessary to distribute them among the old stock, and gradually to incorporate them with the whole mass. But now, there is no stock with which to combine the revolted slaves. They are reduced to obedience, not in small numbers and gradually, but suddenly, and all at one time ; while those newly imported are mingled with a body still less fit than themselves for the tasks and the station of servitude.

While the revolt has diminished the numbers of the negroes, and rendered new importations more necessary than ever, it has also swept away vast numbers of the whites, by massacres, by emigrations, and by disease, the constant attendant upon hard duty in the tropical climates, at least to European constitutions. *

Malouet reckons that their numbers have been reduced to one half the population of 1789, or between seventeen and twenty thousand. It seems proved, that this statement of the whole amount is above the truth ; and the effects

* Laborie's Coffee-planter, Append. X. 12.—Malouet, Mem. &c. IV. 32.—Edwards' St Domingo, cap. x. note to p. 173.

effects of the fubfequent events, with the neceffary ftruggles that muft yet be undergone before
tranquillity is reftored, will at leaft counterbalance the increafe of numbers arifing from new
fettlers.

When order is re-eftablifhed, indeed, it is
reafonable to fuppofe that a confiderable number of new fettlers will repair thither with the
ftock which may be employed in reftoring or
extending the cultivation. But not to mention
the temptations held out by thofe iflands which
have never experienced the horrors of infurrection, the acquifition which France has made of
the Spanifh part of the ifland, cannot fail to attract towards that quarter a large proportion of
thofe new fettlers. The moft valuable part of
them, thofe who remove with their families,
and with the purpofe of making the colony
their home, will certainly prefer a refidence feparated from the quarter where murder and devaftation have been naturalized, and will confider the fociety of their countrymen, when furrounded by the actors in thofe fcenes, as well
exchanged for that of the Spaniards, whofe
flaves are few in number, and, from gentle
treatment, have remained untainted with the
fpirit of infurrection. The eaftern part of St
Domingo, too, contains a vaft extent of the fineft plains perhaps in the whole ifland. The
land

land is a rich virgin foil, watered by the largeſt and moſt uſeful rivers. The acceſs from Europe and the Windward iſlands is eaſier, and the harbours are extremely convenient. Hence, we may expect that this quarter of the colony will allure ſpeculators and merchants, as well as other ſettlers, and thus prevent the old French territory from receiving a great increaſe of white inhabitants. But the partial increaſe of the whites in the weſtern diviſion where the negroes are, and not the total augmentation of whites in the iſland, is the circumſtance that muſt influence the ſecurity of the French power over the negroes ; for the two diviſions are ſeparated from each other by a difficult country, of great extent, abounding in heights and ravines and impenetrable foreſts.

The ſituation of the colony, then, whether we conſider the ſtate of the black, or that of the white population, has been rendered infinitely more precarious than before, by the events of the laſt twelve years. The tenure by which the one of theſe claſſes is held in ſubjection to the other, muſt now be weak and delicate beyond all former example. No political ſociety that ever ſubſiſted in the world, has had ſo much reaſon to deſire a ſtate of complete tranquillity and repoſe from all external danger ; none has ever exiſted ſo utterly unfit for being the ſcene of

new

new contefts ; none ever offered to its neighbours more certain pledges of pacific intentions, fhewed lefs capacity for aggreffion, or prefented to its enemies a greater number of defencelefs and vulnerable points.

The military eftablifhment which France
will certainly maintain in this ifland, muft find
ample employment in preferving internal tranquillity, and checking the feeds of new revolt
as they fpring up. It is idle to fay, as fome
writers on colonial affairs have done, that fhe
derives a formidable afpect in that quarter, from
the pretext which her colonial poffeffions afford
her, of increafing to a dangerous degree her
force in thofe parts. It is not a pretext ; it is a
real neceffity. In the Weft Indies, fhe has ample occafion for more troops than fhe can fpare
from Holland and Belgium, and the departments of the Weft, and the Italian republic,
and the protection of whatever dynafty may
happen for the time to be eftablifhed in the
Thuilleries. With all her force, fhe will find
the prefervation of her colonies, as they at prefent ftand, the moft difficult tafk which fhe has
yet accomplifhed in the career of her towering
ambition.

The remarks which have been fuggefted
by the recent hiftory of St Domingo, apply,
though with lefs force, to the prefent ftate of
Guadaloupe.

Guadaloupe. That ifland has, though in a more
flight degree, been vifited by ferious infurrections : the defect of importation fince the revolution, has checked the extenfion of cultivation,
and probably diminifhed the ftock of flaves.
There, as in St Domingo, the negroes have enjoyed the fweets of liberty, and will return with
great and natural reluctance to their former
occupations.

The conquered iflands have been exempted
from all thofe calamities, and their cultivation
has rapidly increafed. Some danger muft, however, always arife from change of poffeffion : and
we fhall afterwards have occafion to defcribe more
fully the probable effects of this event upon the
adminiftration of thofe colonies. But the queftion now turns chiefly upon the ftate of the
larger colonies, whofe fortunes the others muft
follow : and if, from the circumftances of St
Domingo and Guadaloupe, France finds it impoffible to combine military operations there,
we may reft affured that for the very fame reafon fhe will remain at peace in her other iflands.
A rupture with her neighbours, in whatever
quarter, muft be attended with danger to the
whole fyftem ; and we may reckon upon the
weaknefs or dangerous fituation of her revolted
iflands, as if it extended to thofe which the fortunes of the Britifh arms faved from deftruction.

Thus

Thus it appears, in the *firſt* place, that a
colony or remote province, in the general, is always leſs adapted than an independent ſtate to the operations either of defenſive or offenſive warfare, by the neceſſary circumſtances of its ſituation; *ſecondly*, that the peculiar circumſtances of the Weſt Indian iſlands, and the international policy of modern Europe, would render the independence of any one of *thoſe* colonies peculiarly dangerous to the reſt, and would render the colonial regimen a greater ſource of weakneſs to them than to any other eſtabliſhments of the ſame kind ; and, *laſtly*, that the ſituation of the French colonies, after ſlavery is reſtored, muſt be far leſs ſecure than that of the other Weſt Indian ſettlements, both from the peculiar circumſtances of thoſe colonies, and from the manner in which the changes have been effected. We may conclude, therefore, that the maintenance of the colonial exiſtence of the French iſlands, and of the negro ſyſtem, as eſtabliſhed before the revolution, is much leſs hoſtile to the intereſts of the other European powers, who aim at preſerving their Weſt Indian ſettlements, than the ſeparation of the French colonies from the mother country, more eſpecially if that event is attended with the independence of the negroes. We are now to conſider the probable conſequences of a

partial

partial fubjugation of the negroes, to the dominion
of France, and the interefts of the other powers
in the Weft Indies.

It cannot be doubted, that the total abolition
of flavery in any one of the fugar colonies,
and the cultivation of its territories by free
fubjects, whofe conftitutions are adapted to
the climate, would be attended with the moft
beneficial effects, and raife its comparative refources and ftrength to a very high pitch.
The labour of flaves is much more expenfive
than that of free men; and the colonies, which
fhould continue the old fyftem of cultivation,
would be deprived of all that additional force
with which the acquifition of a vaft population
of free men would arm the new-modelled fettlements.   But although the iflands are at prefent
inhabited by a race of negro flaves, they are
not poffeffed of men fit for the fituation of fubjects.   They have as yet only the bodies of fubjects—bodies animated by the minds of flaves,
in the rudeft ftate of fociety; and no power under that which called them into exiftence, could
at once transform them into men capable of
fupporting the relations required for the conftitution of a free and civilized community.   We
fhall, afterwards, in difcuffing the various plans
for the improvement of the Weft Indian fyftem,
have occafion to enter more fully into the fub-

jeᶜt

ject of the negro character ; and to demonstrate
the utter unfitnefs of thofe men for the relations of
voluntary labourers, in a regular and civilized
ftate. At the end of the prefent Section, too,
we fhall attend a little more minutely to this
matter.

But, even if the negroes already in St Domingo could be fuddenly transformed into peaceful
and induftrious fubjects, their numbers are fo
reduced, that, in order to reftore the cultivation of the ifland, and ftill more, in order to
extend it, a much quicker fupply of hands will
be neceffary than the natural increafe can afford.
While the ftock at prefent in the ifland continues free, the importation of flaves is impoffible ; and to expect induftry or fubmiffion from
Africans newly brought over, and fuddenly let
loofe, would be no lefs chimerical. Indeed, it is
not eafy to conceive how they could be brought
from Africa, as no one can have any inducement
to import a favage over whom he retains no exclufive authority after he has landed him. All
fudden addition to the number of hands, then,
is inconfiftent with the fuppofition of a community peopled by free blacks. In the mean time,
until the chains of the negroes are either firmly
rivetted, or broken for ever, the ifland muft remain in a ftate of infecurity within, which will
require the moft undivided attention of the
rulers to the maintenance of order among the
whites,

BOOK
II.

whites, and to the prefervation of external tranquillity.

But admitting, for the prefent, the poffibility
of keeping the negroes in a ftate of partial fubjection, and of forming a regular community,
confifting of free Africans for the populace
and Europeans for the higher claffes ; let us
fee what dangers the neighbouring colonies
might have to apprehend from fuch a political
eftablifhment.

It has been fuppofed by fome, * that if
France fhall fail in reftoring the ancient order
of things, fhe will have at her difpofal, a formidable body of the foldiers beft adapted to Weft
Indian warfare, and trained to military fervice,
by a feries of hazardous operations. How can
fhe fo well employ them, (it has been demand-
ed), as in expeditions againft her neighbours, at
whofe expence her turbulent fubjects will thus
be occupied with military fervice, and her dominions rapidly extended ?

As this is perhaps the moft obvious of the
dangers which can attend a partial re-eftablifhment of the French power in the revolted iflands,
and as it has, at firft fight, a very formidable
appearance, it may be worth while to examine, a
little more minutely, whether or not the alarm is
                                            real,

* See, particularly, the ' Crifis of the Sugar Colonies, '
paffim.

real, and to what extent fuch apprehenfions deferve to be entertained. .

We muft remark, in the *firft* place, that thofe
who dwell upon this topic, have greatly overrated
the difpofeable force likely to be left in the hands
of France after the fuppreffion of the rebellion
in St Domingo. The author of the ' *Crifis* '
eftimates the whole negro population at five
hundred thoufand, and the number of men able
to bear arms at two hundred thoufand. Neither the one nor the other of thefe accounts is
in any degree near the truth. We have before
fhewn, from the authority of the beft-inform-
ed writers upon the fubject, that the whole
number of negroes has been reduced to lefs
than one half during the rebellion ; and it is
evident, that the recent tranfactions in the ifland
muft have ftill farther diminifhed their force.
It is equally clear, that almoft all this extraordinary lofs muft have fallen upon the males rather than the females, and upon the young and
vigorous men rather than the infirm or the
aged. In the imported Africans, indeed, there
may be nearly the proportion of males able to
bear arms which the author of the ' *Crifis* ' has
fuppofed. But as all importation has ceafed
for twelve years, and as the blank occafioned
by deaths has in fome degree been filled up in
the natural way, and not otherwife, it is clear,
that,

that, even if as many females as males, and as
many weak or decrepit as able-bodied men, had
fallen in the troubles, the natural proportions of
the two fexes, and of the different ages, would
by this time have been reftored. The polyga-
my which prevails among the negroes might
have retarded the total progrefs of population ;
but its effect would have been the fame upon
both fexes ; and it never could have deftroyed
the relative proportions of thofe able to ferve
and thofe unfit for war. The proportion of
men fit to bear arms in any community is certainly not two in five of its whole population.
It has never been reckoned more than one in
four ; and Sir William Petty makes it only one
in fix. Admitting, then, what is evidently impoffible, that the revolt, and fubfequent reduction of the negroes, neither diminifhed their total population, nor altered the proportions of
their different claffes, the utmoft amount of
men fit for military fervice, could not poffibly
exceed one hundred and twenty-five thoufand.
But, in fuppofing fuch a body at the difpofal of
government for expeditions againft the neighbouring iflands, or for the defence of St Domingo, we muft imagine that the plantations
are to be cultivated, and the inhabitants ferved
by women and children alone ; in which cafe, it
is eafy to perceive, that the planters muft be
ruined,

ruined, and entirely alienated from the fervice of the ftate, and that the colony will no longer be worth keeping : fo that, in every view which can be taken, after making all manner of conceffions, it appears, that the eftimate upon which the alarm is founded, is exaggerated many times above the truth.

On the other hand, when we confider the multitudes who perifhed in the conteft ; when we think upon what part of the black population the lofs muft almoft entirely have fallen ; and when we take into our view, alfo, the new loffes which muft happen before a final fettlement can take place, and the manner in which thofe loffes muft of neceffity be diftributed, we fhall probably not underrate the total amount, if we conclude, that France will be unable to employ, in any military operations, more than ten thoufand negroes, confiftently with the moft moderate attention which fhe can beftow upon the planters, and the colony at large, as a valuable poffeffion.

Now, in judging of the danger to be apprehended from the ufe that a rival, or an enemy, may make of any refources, we are always to confider the point to which his own evident intereft directs him. As, in the detail of military operations, we are never to calculate upon grofs blunders in the plans of the oppofite

party :

party : fo, in fyftems of policy, we are not at
liberty to fuppofe that a neighbouring power
will commit palpable errors, and act inconfiftently with its own obvious interefts. If, then,
any fcheme propofed appears, upon a plain
and fimple confideration of its confequences,
to be diametrically oppofite to the colonial interefts of France, we may certainly conclude,
that her neighbours are more furely guaranteed
againft its effects, than if they had bound her
down by the force of treaties, or pledges, or
hoftages, to purfue a fpecified line of conduct.

It is poffible that the apprehenfions arifing
from the exiftence of a confiderable number of
warlike men in the heart of a ftate formerly the
fcene of their fuccefsful rebellion, and the defire
of annoying a formidable and envied rival, may,
for a moment, fuggeft to the rulers of France
the idea of fending forth an army of negroes
againft the Britifh iflands. But a very little
prudence will certainly incline them to confider,
whether the execution of this plan may not be
attended with ftill more alarming confequences
than any which are likely to refult from the
dangerous crifis that fuggefted the idea. The
fuccefs of the meafure can only be infured in
two ways; either the negroes, under the command of Europeans, and affifted by white
troops,

troops, may, by the regular progrefs of a campaign, conquer the enemy's troops, and reduce
his poffeffions, or they may be led againft him
as the oppreffor of their brethren, and for the
purpofe of effecting their emancipation. If ten
thoufand negroes from St Domingo, accompanied by a body of French troops, land in
Jamaica, and commence a regular campaign,
it is not eafy to fee why they may not be oppofed by the Britifh forces, with the affiftance
of a chofen body of flaves, which the Britifh
iflands will be much better able to fpare for
military fervice than the exhaufted colonies of
France. So long as the fpirit of infurrection is
not fomented among the negroes, they are uniformly found to be peculiarly adapted to the
operations of war ; they uniformly ferve with
unfhaken fidelity that government which has
levied them from the plantations. The fudden
acquifition of liberty, by the free gift of the
ftate, and the exchange of fervile drudgery,
for the comparatively eafy and honourable life
of a foldier, is a benefit of fufficient value to
fecure their loyalty : and men in this fituation are
probably better adapted to receive the leffons of
difcipline and fubordination, than thofe who have
always enjoyed the rank and privileges of free
men. They have acquired habits of implicit obedience ; and the freedom now conferred upon
them,

them, without weakening thofe habits, infpires
them with that impulfe to voluntary exertion
which they before wanted. The fituation of
foldiers is, indeed, the only one for which they
are fitted by their previous mode of life. Unac-
cuftomed to have a will of their own, or to act
with any view but that of direct obedience to
another, they are formed to make part of the
great machine which confifts of men, and moves
at the found of a fingle voice. Troops raifed
in this manner have been found ferviceable,
even againft infurgents of their own colour.
The revolted negroes of Surinam have been
frequently oppofed by bodies of flaves enrolled
for the fervice : the acquifition of freedom has
uniformly fecured their faithful obedience to
the government, and their zealous fervices againft
the liberty of their brethren. I fhall afterwards
have occafion to explain this circumftance more
particularly, when, in the Fourth Book of this
Inquiry, I come to examine the fituation of
the free negroes. If fo great reliance can be
placed upon the exertions of the negroes againft
the immediate interefts of their brethren, and
the caufe of negro freedom, it is evident that
much more may be expected from their affiftance when called out againft bodies of their
brethren, who are in fubjection to the Europeans,
and fighting folely for their caufe. Such a force
as

as the negro population could fpare from the labours of the field, would be more than a match for the embodied and half-fubdued rebels of St Domingo, accuftomed to riot in licentioufnefs, and as formidable to their employers as to their antagonifts.

But, fuppofe the expedition has been attended with fuccefs; that the negro army of France has proved victorious, without any affiftance from infurrection among the flaves of the invaded iflands, and that it returns to St Domingo in regular order, after adding a rich province to the French empire: will the admiffion of all thefe improbabilities bring us nearer to the point? It is not the nature of great fervices to lower the pretenfions of thofe who perform them. If the exiftence of the half-fubdued negroes, in the heart of the community, was fo alarming as to render fome enterprife neceffary, which might find employment for them; furely their return after victory, and victory over a European power, is not lefs to be dreaded. In order to prevent them from uniting, and renewing the infurrection, Government has feparated them from the reft of their brethren; called them off from their peaceful occupations; armed and embodied them; allowed them to conquer, and thus formed them into a military body—a feparate
clafs

clafs in the heart of the colony—a rallying
point to their fcattered countrymen, who are
free but oppreffed, and only wait for their permiffion to join them. The government has
weakened and divided its own forces by the
conqueft. Every white man that has fallen in
the expedition, or is ftationed at Jamaica, is an
irreparable lofs; while the negroes are in the
country of their fupplies, and can eafily repair the
loffes which their numbers may have fuftained.

The expedition, then, has only removed
the danger a ftep farther, in order to render
it doubly formidable; and the Europeans in
the colony have procured the fhort refpite of
a Weft Indian campaign, by the notable expedient of changing a probable into a certain cataftrophe. If, on the other hand, the negroes
are left in the conquered ifland, their confent
to this banifhment muft be obtained, and fome
means muft be difcovered to render them lefs
formidable in a country where they have conquered, than they were at home before the expedition; otherwife, the danger is only removed
acrofs the narrow channel which feparates the
one ifland from the other—an exchange, of
which we are immediately to fpeak.

But the only certain means of fucceeding in
the fuppofed enterprife, muft be fought for in
an appeal to the peculiar feelings of the negroes.

groes. In order to render their fervices effectual, they muſt be marched againſt the neighbouring ſettlement, as the ſcene where their
countrymen are ſuffering. The objeƈt of their
efforts muſt be, to liberate the ſlaves; and
the aſſiſtance of univerſal inſurreƈtion muſt be
expeƈted in ſuch an enterprife. But, after the
dominion of their old maſters has been forcibly
overturned by a ſuccefsful and general rebellion, it is not very likely that the inſurgents
will peaceably ſubmit to the controul of the invaders.

The French will have the fame work to
undertake in their new iſland, which they have
juſt performed at St Domingo; with this important difference, that their force will be divided between the inſurreƈtion to be quelled,
and the newly eſtabliſhed order to be maintained. The troops, too, by whoſe aſſiſtance the
inſurreƈtion has been excited, will ſurely prefent a more formidable aſpeƈt than they did
before they were embodied for the ſervice;
and, after the new iſland ſhall be reduced to
the fame ſtate of nominal ſubjeƈtion with the
old, it is not eaſy to imagine, that the retaining
of both in ſubordination will be an eaſier taſk
than the preſerving of tranquillity in St Domingo
alone. But if the more probable event takes
place—the complete eſtabliſhment of a negro
commonwealth

commonwealth in the conquered ifland, partly
by the exertions of the invaders, partly by
thofe of its own flaves, we fhall, in the next
Section, have an opportunity of feeing, that
the dangers of fuch a neighbourhood to all the
other colonies, are manifold and immediate.
Much more formidable to St Domingo, whofe
negroes are with difficulty held in fubjection,
will be the neighbourhood of a people of
their own race, almoft within the bounds of
the fame vifible horizon, retaining, in confequence of their efforts, a manifeft fuperiority
in every refpect, and rioting in all the fweets
of that licentioufnefs which they themfelves
have but lately loft. Without giving the rulers of France, or the local fuperintendants of
her colonial affairs, credit for any extraordinary fagacity or prudence, we may expect,
that experience will have taught them to forefee the dangers of ufing fuch a weapon as
negro rebellion, and that they will feel confiderable repugnance at renewing, in any part
of the Weft Indies, thofe fcenes which the infane councils of 1791. difplayed in their own
poffeffions. It is not to be imagined that any
thing lefs than utter defpair of retaining their
fugar colonies, will ever induce them to think
of an expedient fo full of dangers ; and while
the government of St Domingo fhall poffefs
                                    fufficient

fufficient energy to embody the negroes for a foreign fervice, the planters will never defpair of accomplifhing their fair and natural object, the reftoration of permanent tranquillity, by the complete fubjection of thofe men and the entire re-eftablifhment of the ancient order of things.

If, on the other hand, all hopes of reftoring flavery, or retaining the colonies without it, fhall be abandoned; if France fhall finally perceive that her power in the Weft Indies muft quickly expire; we need not very anxioufly inquire what conduct fhe will purfue in her laft moments. A more formidable danger than any French invafion, though affifted by free negroes and favoured by infurgent flaves, will then threaten all the neighbouring colonies— the eftablifhment of an independent African ftate in the centre of the Weft Indies. Nor does it feem of much confequence to inquire, whether the univerfal deftruction of the European name in the Charaibean Sea fhall be haftened by the machinations of a French government, or confummated by the lefs regular and fyftematic attempts of negro chiefs.

We have now been contemplating an imaginary ftate of things, which will indeed, moft probably, be the intermediate and temporary refult of the colonial crifis, but cannot be expected
ed

ed long to fubfift—the partial and nominal fubjection of the negroes, or their fubmiffion, as
fubjects, to the authority of thofe men whom
they formerly obeyed as flaves. Various circumftances, both in the fituation of the negroes
themfelves, and in that of the Europeans, concur to render fuch an arrangement only temporary, and to prevent it from being any thing
more than an intermediate ftate preparatory to a
farther and more permanent change.

There is at leaft as wide a difference between the habits of a flave and thofe of a free
fubject, as between the nature of an African
and that of a European. A flave has to learn
the difficult leffon of induftry, as different from
compulfory labour as it is from indolence and
floth. Hitherto he has only obeyed the impulfe
of another man's will; he has been actuated by
no motives but the fear of the lafh. The gift
of liberty brings with it the burden of thinking,
and willing, and planning; the tafk of providing fubfiftence for himfelf and for his family; the obligation of performing all the focial duties. The flave reftored to liberty, has
only had experience of thofe parts of the functions of a citizen, which, in themfelves, are fo
difagreeable to his nature, that nothing but
violence could have induced him to perform
them. The negroes of St Domingo have only
known

known the two extremes of flavery and rebellion ; and it is hard to fay from which of thofe
two ftates the tranfition to the rank of a free
fubject is the greateft and moft difficult.

But the negroes are not only in a ftate of
flavery : they are in a low ftate of civilization.
The induftry of a favage ; his habits of voluntary obedience ; his capacity for enjoying civil
and political rights ; and, in general, his fitnefs
for becoming the fubject of a peaceable and regular community, is, if poffible, more limited than
that of the mere flave. He has all thofe habits
of voluntary exertion and peaceable fubmiffion to
learn, which are wholly unknown to the members of barbarous tribes, and which form the
bond of union among the inhabitants of civilized fociety. The inhabitants of rude nations,
indeed, know of no medium between the extremes of fervility and defpotic fway. They
confift only of two claffes of people ; tyrants
or mafters, and flaves. Force is the only inducement to exertion, and indolence the chief
reward of wealth or power. The flave, then,
only works, and the mafter alone enjoys. But
the former does not toil for himfelf, or of his
free-will ; and the envied privilege of the latter
ftation, is to be idle and tyrannical. We fhall
afterwards have an opportunity of feeing (in the
Fourth Book of this Inquiry), that thefe remarks

marks apply, with peculiar accuracy, both to
the African tribes in their own country, and
thofe who have been tranfplanted to the European colonies in America. Enough has now
been faid, to fhow the impoffibility of expecting
any fuccefs in fo chimerical a plan as that of
forming the revolted negro flaves into a community of free fubjects, under a regular European government.

But it muft alfo be remembered, that the
peculiar fituation of thefe men in the new
community will have very little tendency to
promote their contentment and peaceable demeanour. They will form the oppreffed and
labouring part of the community ; deftitute of
property ; deprived of the moft effential political privileges ; toiling for a mere fubfiftence,
whilft others are enjoying the fruits of thofe
exertions. The clafs thus oppreffed, too, will
be united by common origin, habits and complexion ; indelibly diftinguifhed from the fuperior order by the fame circumftances ; united to the reft of the community by no common
principles or intereft ; and held in fubjection,
though not in flavery, by a handful of ftrangers. It is eafy to fee, that fo unnatural a ftate
of things cannot have a long duration ; that a
body, formed of fuch jarring principles, muft
contain within itfelf the feeds of fpeedy diffolution ;

lution ; that power, fo eftablifhed, muft quickly fall to pieces. A race of men fuch as the Africans, can only be kept in fubjection by the whites, fo long as they are in chains. ' The ' day that makes a man a flave ' (fays Homer) ' deftroys half his worth. ' The day that breaks his fetters, deftroys the whole authority and fecurity of his mafter. Whilft the flave fyftem exifts, the divifion of the negroes, the watchful eye of the overfeer, the conftant fear of the driver's lafh, may prevent the multitude from uniting and overpowering the leaft numerous clafs of the community. The mafters, though few in number, are civilized and united. Each proprietor of flaves has one conftant and fimple end in view, the preferving of fubordination, and the furtherance of work. The flaves are powerful indeed in numbers, but incapable of acting with premeditation or fkill ; and are prevented from combining, not only by the perpetual attention of the mafter, but by various circumftances in their own character and habits.

If, however, for the clofe infpection, the interefted care, and the abfolute authority of the mafter, there is fubftituted the general fuperintendance, the limited power, and the unconcerned exertions of the government, checked by the acknowledged rights of the negro fubjects,

fubjects, divided by faction, and diftracted by multiplicity of cares : it is eafy to fee how rapidly a ftill further change will be accomplifhed ; how fhort will be the duration of European property and power.

On the one hand, then, the circumftances of the negroes, and their relative fituation to the whites, will be conftantly tending to confummate the colonial revolution, by eftablifhing the complete independence, or, which is the fame thing, the fupremacy of the moft powerful clafs, and by effecting the total extirpation of their former mafters. But, at the fame time, the oppofite interefts of the Europeans will on the other hand be conftantly tending to bring about an oppofite event ; to abridge ftill more the rights of the negroes ; to reduce them to a more complete ftate of obedience ; to perfect the reftoration of the ancient order of things, upon the bafis of the flave fyftem.

Every proprietor of Weft Indian ftock will fpeedily perceive how much his profits are diminifhed by the new order of things. He will find it impoffible to recruit his ftock of negroes by new importations ; to extend or reftore his cultivation by an increafe of his ftock ; nay, even to fatisfy the demands of his creditors, or provide for his neceffary wants, out of the fcanty and capricious induftry of hired negroes.

His

His fecurity will be as much endangered as his profits, even if no jealoufy fhould arife from the inferior order poffeffing certain legal rights. Government, as well as individuals, will perceive the frailty of the tenure by which they hold the poffeffion of a fociety fo unnaturally conftituted. The efforts of individuals will all be fteadily directed to the accomplifhment of one end—the reftoration of the ancient fyftem; and government, we may be affured, will favour the attempt. The conteft, then, will be carried on quietly indeed, but unremittingly, by the fkill, the intrigues, the united intereft and combined operations of Europeans, againft the wavering and unfteady efforts of favages half fubdued, incapable of acting in concert, and united under no ruling heads. It will be carried on by the men who monopolize, not only all the talents and fkill in the community, all the influence of government, and the force of the army, but who poffefs alfo the whole of the property, and who were once mafters alfo of the perfons of the inferior clafs. It is moft probable, that a conteft fo unequal will fpeedily terminate in favour of the Europeans, and that, unlefs the oppofite event is confummated before their plans fhall have time to operate, the flave fyftem will again be eftablifhed over the revolted colonies. At any rate, it

feems

feems certain, that the partial fubjection of the
negroes, or their reduction to the ftate of a
free but fubordinate race of citizens, can only
be a temporary change, preparatory to a more
complete and permanent arrangement of things:
that there is no medium between the fupremacy and the bondage of the negroes ; between
the maftery and the extirpation of the whites :
that any other fettlement which may be made
in the mean time, muft either be a delufive fituation for the negroes, or a deceitful calm to
the Europeans : that a very fhort time will
bring about the final adjuftment, and either
deprive France of her colonies, or overthrow
the nominal freedom of the negroes.

The probable confequences of thefe two extremes to other colonies, muft be a matter of
the deepeft intereft to all the neighbouring
powers in the Weft Indies. I have already
confidered the effects which may naturally be
expected to refult from one of them, namely,
the fuccefs of the French caufe, and the complete reftoration of the colonial relations. In
the following Section, I fhall take a view of
the confequences which may be expected to refult from the oppofite event, the total failure
of France, and the eftablifhment of an independent African community in the Weft Indies.

SEC.

SECTION III.

OF THE CONSEQUENCES OF THE ESTABLISHMENT OF A
NEGRO COMMONWEALTH IN THE WEST INDIES TO
THE INTERESTS OF THE COLONIES WHICH REMAIN
UNDER THE DOMINION OF THE MOTHER COUNTRY.

THE events which have happened in the
French colonies fince the revolution, have
been fuch, as to fill every one with the utmoft anxiety as to the fate of the whole colonial fyftem. The deftruction of negro flavery
has been followed by its natural confequence,
the complete overthrow of the European power, and the eftablifhment of an independent
African commonwealth in the nobleft fettlement of the new world.

Immediately after the peace which followed
the unfortunate fucceffes of the French arms
in Europe, the attention of the new government of France was turned to the colonial affairs of the Republic. Meafures were taken
for reftoring the dominion of the Mother
Country over her revolted iflands ; and an expedition was fitted out, of a magnitude fuited
to the importance of the fervice for which it
was deftined, with that promptitude and defpatch

patch which have diftinguifhed all the operations of the Corfican Chief.

The probable confequences of this attempt
have been difcuffed in the Firft Book of this
Inquiry, where I was induced to beftow confiderable attention upon the fubject, not merely becaufe it is peculiarly interefting at the
prefent moment, but becaufe I confidered it as
part of the general queftion, and intimately
connected with the great topics of Weft Indian
policy. For the fame reafon, I am now to
difcufs particularly the confequences of the
French expedition proving wholly unfuccefsful, and of the Africans obtaining the permanent fuperiority in St Domingo ; not becaufe
this is an event which feems at prefent on the
eve of being accomplifhed, but becaufe it is an
event which at all times may be expected, and
is in fact the natural confequence of that policy, equally incautious and inhuman, by which
the Antilles have been peopled with African
flaves.

During the firft ftruggles between the different colours in the French iflands, it was the
univerfal, and very natural opinion, in the
neighbouring iflands, that the exiftence of a
negro commonwealth in thofe parts, muft be
immediately fatal to all the other flave colonies.
But the appearance of that remarkable perfonage,

age, who acquired the chief power over the new community; the fingular moderation of his views, and the inoffenfive conduct which he uniformly held towards all the neighbouring fettlements, foon difpelled the alarm with which every one had at firft been feized. To a panic much ftronger than was neceffary, there fucceeded, as is almoft always the cafe, a fearlefs confidence, not warranted by any change of circumftances. The Europeans in the Weft Indies appeared, during the reign of Touffaint, to have forgotten how much of their fecurity was owing to the peculiar habits of that fingular man, and to the length and horrors of the preceding conqueft, fufficient to fatiate even Africans with plunder and blood. It was not confidered, that, from every part of his conduct and profeffions, the negro chief appeared to refemble his countrymen in no one particular, either of his intellects, his acquirements, or his feelings; that this very circumftance of diffimilarity was, in all probability, preparing his downfal, although his life fhould efcape the variety of accidents by which he was furrounded; and that his fucceffor would, to an abfolute certainty, be a man differing from the reft of the negroes only in the greater ferocity of his nature, his fuperior cunning, and ftronger limbs. Neither was it remembered, that although

though years of bloodfhed and devaftation might fatigue the moft favage warriors, and difpofe them to enjoy an interval of repofe, yet the fame barbarians would fooner recover from their fatiety, and pant for the former fcenes of cruelty and licentioufnefs. We are now to confider, whether there be any room for the thoughtlefs confidence into which the Weft Indian proprietors have been lulled, beyond thofe accidental circumftances which gave birth to the temporary calm ; the fatigue of the ne-groes, and the peculiar character of their chief.

The events which have already taken place in the colonies prove fufficiently, if indeed any proof was neceffary, that the flavery of the Africans has had no great tendency to pro-mote their civilization, or infpire them with a relifh for the bleffings of order and regular go-vernment. The oppreffion of their mafters may have united them, and combined their ef-forts with thofe of the mulattoes to effect the extermination of the Europeans. But this end was no fooner accomplifhed, than the two par-ties attacked each other with renewed fury ; and, if a fhort time had been allowed to the conquerors, after fubduing the people of colour, there can be little doubt that they would have quarrelled among themfelves, and fplit into a number of petty barbarous ftates.

It

It is not in the nature of a rude people to
unite in extenſive political aſſociations. All ſuch unions preſuppoſe the acquiſition of conſiderable ſkill in the arts of government. At firſt, the habits of filial ſubmiſſion, reverence for age, and awe of ſuperior bodily ſtrength, retain a ſingle family or kindred in ſubjection to the head of the houſe. The imperfect union of a few families generally ſpringing from the ſame common ſtock, and kept in a partial ſubmiſſion to the oldeſt, or the ſtrongeſt and moſt cunning perſon of the tribe, forms the next ſtep in the progreſs of the ſocial union. After conqueſt or treachery has extended the partriarchal government beyond the bounds of the kindred race; by an eaſy tranſition, the regular ſucceſſion to the chief power becomes liable to interruptions from the ſame cauſes which have enlarged the territory of the tribe— violence and cunning. Still, the ſubjection of a large community to one man; the extenſion of his dominion over a multitude of ſubjects whom he ſeldom has within his ſight; the obedience of thouſands of men to the will of a ſingle perſon, neither choſen by themſelves, nor poſſeſſed of any ſuperior faculties of body or mind—indicate no ſmall proficiency in the arts of policy upon the part of the ruler, and a conſiderable progreſs upon the part of the people,

people, in the habits of abſtraction and in the peaceful arts.

After this ſkill has been acquired, and thoſe habits formed, we often meet with extenſive political aſſociations of men who are ſtill in a very rude ſtate. But the ſtability of government, and the permanent duration of extent and of power, inſeparably connected with the ſtability of a particular dynaſty in the ſovereignty of the ſtate, can only reſult from thoſe fixed ideas of hereditary ſucceſſion, which, as they are on the one hand a great cauſe of progreſſive improvement, ſo, indicate on the other hand, that a very conſiderable progreſs towards refinement has already been made. Moreover, all ſuch aſſociations of uncivilized men have ariſen from ſmall beginnings; have been gradually enlarged by the incorporation of conquered tribes; and have been ſlowly conſolidated, in ſo far as they poſſeſs any ſolidity, by the events that take place, and the habits that are ſtrengthened during a ſucceſſion of ages. It may ſafely be aſſumed as a general principle, that a multitude collected at random from various ſavage nations, and habituated to no ſubordination but that of domeſtic ſlavery, are totally unfit for uniting in the relations of regular government, or being ſuddenly moulded into one ſyſtem of artificial

tificial fociety ; more efpecially after living for a feries of years in a ftate of tumult and diforder, unnatural even to barbarians. In the moft polifhed ftates, the fudden and violent diffolution of an eftablifhed government has a ftrong tendency to produce general difunion ; and we may recollect the alarm excited in the earlier ftages of the French Revolution by the terror of Federalifm, which became indeed one of the common topics of accufation in the code of political crimes. In fact, the fudden formation of a political body has always been found the moft arduous achievement in the art of governing. The eftablifhment of the North American colonies, gradual as it was, is the inftance in the hiftory of mankind, where this has been accomplifhed in the fhorteft time. Yet thofe infant ftates were animated by political or religious enthufiafm ; united by a pofition in the midft of favage nations ; and peopled by men taken from the heart of civil fociety—fubjects for whom the moft refined politician and profound philofopher of the age was invited to legiflate. *

The free negroes of St Domingo will form a turbulent and licentious affemblage of hoftile tribes. A leader may now and then appear, whofe

* Mr Locke.

whofe fuperior talents enable him to acquire a temporary afcendant over a confiderable proportion of thofe petty ftates; but his death or affaffination will be the period of the union, and the ifland will again be divided among a number of petty chiefs.

It is a moft profound remark of Machiavel, that a commonwealth is much more to be depended upon by its neighbours and its fubjects, than a prince: and, for precifely the fame reafons, which I fhall afterwards explain more at length, a large ftate is much more to be depended upon than a fmall one, under whatever form the government may be adminiftered. The moft unftable and capricious of all neighbours muft, therefore, be a petty ftate, fubject to an abfolute prince. But the tribes of St Domingo will be fmall communities of turbulent favages, fubject to the authority of defpotic chiefs, whofe powers perpetually vary, and who fucceed each other, according to no order more regular than the caprice and violence of the human paffions. It is eafy to perceive, that fuch a government muft, beyond all others, be unfteady and changeful, utterly unfit for maintaining the regular alliance, or for preventing the depredations of its own fubjects.

From a community of this defcription, indeed, we can fcarcely apprehend any very formidable

midable combination of hoftilities againft the
other iflands. The evils which fome have
thought probable from the reftlefs fpirit of
conqueft ufually predominant in the infancy
of ftates, are, I apprehend, by no means fo
much to be dreaded as thofe which muft arife
from the fpirit of plunder. The negroes, in
their ftate of flavery, have acquired many defires, which they will ftill feek to gratify at
the expence of their fkilful and induftrious
neighbours. The love of tobacco and fpiritu-
ous liquors; the want of fire arms, and, in general, of the ufeful metals and the manufactures
of Europe; nay, the want of flaves from a-
mong their brethren, will lead them to commit perpetual depredation upon the coafts of
the neighbouring iflands. To fuppofe that
they will fupply themfelves with fuch commodities by cultivating their own territories, and
exchanging the produce of their induftry with
European merchants, is to fancy, that they
have been civilized in the late times of anarchy
and confufion; that they have acquired habits
of peaceful induftry in a few years of maffacre
and plunder.

The pofition of St Domingo is particularly
favourable to the occupations of a piratical
commonwealth. The various commodious harbours on the fouth and weft coafts, furnifh the
moft

BOOK
II.

moft advantageous ftations for annoying the outward bound trade to Jamaica and Cuba, and the veffels homeward bound, which take the windward paffage; while the fouth coaft commands the direct communication between the windward and the two moft wefterly leeward iflands. Our Weft Indian merchants well remember how feverely they fuffered by the privateering which the French, during the late war, carried on from the ports of Jacquemel and Les Cayés. In one year (1794-5), notwithftanding the ftrong naval force which we had in thofe parts to protect our trade, above thirty large veffels were captured and carried into Les Cayés. The negroes, too, at a fubfequent period of the war, attacked the fmaller veffels of the Britifh and American traders, in armed canoes; and, after maffacring the white crews, carried the fhips into their harbours. *

In a predatory fyftem of this fort, every capture muft furnifh the means of further acquifitions. The negroes, by their bodily ftrength, and their aftonifhing powers of enduring every fort of want, are admirably calculated for a feafaring life. They are employed for this purpofe in many parts of the Weft Indies. In the Bermuda

* Edwards' Poftfcript to his Hiftorical Survey of St Domingo.

Bermuda Iſlands, they are found to make as
good ſailors as the whites ; * and they were of
ſignal uſe, both as ſeamen and marines, in
the privateers fitted out from that convenient
ſtation during the American war. † The proſpect of immediate plunder will unite and mar-
ſhal ſmall bodies of men, whom it would be in
vain to think of forming into more extenſive
aſſociations by the general principles of duty,
or remote views of political expediency ; and,
in every quarter of the New World, men of
European extraction, or adventurers from Europe, are to be found, whoſe deſperate fortunes
will league them with the freebooters of St Domingo, and ſupply the deficiency of nautical
knowledge. The events which have happened
in the Weſt Indies, indeed, may teach us, that
the negroes will probably receive a more regular aſſiſtance from men leſs abandoned than
theſe. Not to mention the ready aſylum which
the towns of Jamaica always offered to the Buccaneers, and the eaſe with which thoſe pirates
found a market among fair traders, wherever
they carried their ſtolen goods ; during the heat
of the late civil war in St Domingo, the negroes were abundantly ſupplied with arms and
ammunition

* Burke's European Settlements, part VII. cap. 2.
† Governor Brown's Report.—Report of Committee
1788, part III.

ammunition by North American traders, in return for the colonial produce which they were
thus enabled to feize from the plantations, after
murdering the proprietors. *　At fuch kinds
of traffic it is needlefs to repine ; and it is e-
qually vain to expect that they fhall ever ceafe.
The genuine fpirit of commercial fpeculation
cannot exift in full force, without giving rife,
at the fame time, to evils like thefe.　The fame
unreftrained propenfity to adventure that conducted the Spaniards over unknown regions to
the conqueft of a new world, directed the depredations to which their fucceffors were afterwards expofed.　The temptation of high profits
which opened to the Buccaneers the markets
of Jamaica, led to the cultivation of the whole
Weft Indies ; and, after covering with villas
and farms the extenfive plains of St Domingo,
contributed at laft to their devaftation and ruin.

From this fyftem of piracy, to a predatory
warfare upon the coafts of Jamaica and Cuba,
the tranfition is eafy.　The trade wind, blowing
almoft without intermiffion towards the leeward
iflands, will carry the gangs of thefe new Buccaneers, in a fingle night, acrofs the narrow and
unbroken channels that bound St Domingo on
the weft ; and thefe irruptions will be made
with

* Edwards' Hiftory of St Domingo, chap. VI.

with that carelefs prodigality of life, and that
indifcriminate thirft of deftruction, which mark the military operations of barbarians. To a civilized community, indeed, eftablifhed upon folid foundations, and united in one compact body for the purpofes of regular defence, fuch an invafion would not be very formidable. But in the colonies, the enemy has a powerful auxiliary in the very heart of the fettlements, againft which his attacks are directed. The negroes of our colonies are already prepared for revolt, by the example of fuccefs which has attended the ftruggles of their countrymen on the oppofite fide of the Straits.

It is nugatory to talk of the depreffed ftate and obtufe faculties of thefe men. They are of the fame fpecies with thofe whom the mulattoes of St Domingo gained over, by the promife of liberty, in fpite of the rooted antipathy which had formerly divided the two claffes. They are not more degraded than thofe who worfhipped the Prefident of the *Amis des Noirs* as their tutelary faint: nor will the eftablifhment of a negro commonwealth in the neighbouring ifland fo far alter their nature, as to render callous to every thing affecting the fortunes of their race, the fame people who, at the beginning of the conteft, had fhowed the livelieft anxiety about the fate of the great queftion of abolition—

abolition; a queftion, in itfelf, only remotely
connected with their interefts. * There is, indeed, no direct communication between the people of St Domingo and the great body of field
negroes in the oppofite iflands : But thefe have
various opportunities of obtaining information—
from their brethren who are employed as houfe
fervants, and who thus learn the ftate of affairs
in a quarter that muft always principally occupy the converfation of their mafters—from the
artificers in the towns, whofe intercourfe with
the Europeans is more extenfive, and who are
always better informed—from the free blacks,
who, as a body indeed, we fhall afterwards
fhow, cannot difturb the peace of our colonies,
but who rank among their numbers many idle
and diffolute perfons, ready to inftruct the flaves
in what is going forward—and, laft of all, from
the negro fervants who return to the Weft Indies, after having acquired, by their refidence
in Europe as free men, a large portion of information, and imbibed many of the opinions
univerfally prevalent upon the fubject of negro
flavery. Without fuppofing, then, that the
African inhabitants of St Domingo have become infected with that rage of profelytizing
which

---

* Edwards' Hiftory of St Domingo, chap. VII.—
Petition of Weft Indian Merchants to the Houfe of Commons, March 1792.

which diftinguifhed their former mafters ; or that any meafures have been purfued in the other iflands for enlightening and exciting the negroes ; it is manifeft, from the conftitution of the communities of which they form a part, that they will have ample opportunities of information ; and, upon fuch topics, it is the fame act to inform and to intereft men placed in their fituation. Indeed, when we confider how much of the fubordination of the negroes is derived from their habitual conviction of the decided fuperiority of white men, and their conftitutional terror of oppofing them ; furely nothing can operate more immediately the deftruction of thofe feelings, and of all the force which the negro chains derive from them, than the fpectacle conftantly prefented to their eyes, plain and intelligible even to Africans, of their countrymen in the neighbouring ifland poffeffing the territory in full fovereignty ; clothed with the fpoils, and covered with the blood of Europeans.

Thus, in all likelihood the neighbourhood of a negro ftate will have prepared our flaves for ideas of independence ; and the firft incurfions of the enemy muft be the fignal for revolt. We have already noticed the extent to which the plans of all the infurrections hitherto quelled appear to have fpread. * This can

arife

---

* Book I. Sect. III. Part IV.

arife from nothing but the pronenefs of men, in the fituation of the negroes, to feek for any change. However partial, then, the depredations of our new enemy may be, their effects on the flaves will extend over the whole body. The freebooters may receive exemplary punifhment; but they will firft have communicated to our negroes the contagion for which they have been predifpofed. Nay, it is probable that no permanent footing will ever be gained by the invaders; and at any rate, that, in the beginning, their efforts will be wholly unfuccefsful. But if they ftir up the fpirit of revolt, by liberating the negroes on a few plantations before a fufficient force can be brought againft them, it fignifies little to Great Britain that her largeft colony fhould fall into the hands of the Jamaica, inftead of the St Domingo Africans, or that her planters and merchants fhould have the confolation of being murdered by their own flaves.

The fituation of Cuba is in feveral refpects lefs dangerous than that of Jamaica. The cultivated parts lye on the north-weft coaft, and muft be approached from St Domingo by the difficult navigation of the old Bahama channel. The negroes, too, though their numbers are much increafed fince the ordinance 1765, and though they bear a greater proportion to the
whites

whites than in any of the Spanish colonies, are yet far less numerous than those in Jamaica, and, like all the slaves of the Spanish and Portuguese colonists, are much better treated than those of any other European power. Were Cuba, then, to remain in its present state, it would offer few temptations to the incursions of the new community, and would probably attract little of their attention, until, by being consolidated in the course of time into one state, and subjected to a regular and efficient government, they might be in a situation to commence offensive operations upon enlarged views of conquest. The face of things, however, is rapidly improving in Cuba. In consequence of the more liberal system of policy begun in 1765, and extended under the administration of Galvez, that noble island, the largest in the new world, has, by the variety of its natural resources, attracted the first efforts of the mercantile spirit in Spain; and its cultivation has been so much extended, that in a few years its trade, instead of employing six vessels, as formerly, required no less than two hundred, and was capable of more than supplying the mother country with sugar. Various events which I have before enumerated, have contributed still more, of late, to accelerate the cultivation of this settlement.

ment. * But all thofe improvements are intimately connected with the flave trade. They
have uniformly kept pace with the removal of
the reftrictions upon the importation of negroes. The Affiento, transferred from France
to Britain by the treaty of Utrecht, had been
fucceeded by a monopoly as ftrict in favour of
a private company. The firft fymptoms of
fpeculation appeared in Cuba, after the law of
1770 had encouraged the importation of negroes at the Havanna. In fact, as the agriculture of the iflands depends upon commercial
fpeculation, and upon the employment of ftock
in purchafing hands, their improvement proceeds, not according to the flow progrefs of
population, as in other countries, but according to the amount of the ftock employed, in
proportion to which the population may be increafed to any amount. While, therefore, the
rapid importation of negroes which the improvement of Cuba requires, has been diminifhing the fecurity of the Spaniards, and while the
trade which fupports the improvement of the
ifland, and the increafed produce which is the
confequence of the extended cultivation, in-
vites the depredations of the tribes in St Domingo ; the cultivation of Cuba will foon be
extended

* Book I. Sect. III. Part II.

extended along the coafts ; and that ifland will
be placed in the fame fituation of complicated
dangers which we have already fhewn mu&
prove fatal to Jamaica ; with this difference,
that Jamaica being moft probably in the hands
of the negroes, Cuba will be expofed to a double chance of deftruction.

Yet the dread of thefe dangers, even in the
event of the negroes fucceeding completely in
St Domingo, will fcarcely prevent the importation of flaves into Cuba. It is the character of mercantile fpeculation to be clear-fight-
ed, but not far-fighted. The trader feldom
confiders any thing beyond the quicknefs and
the profits with which his capital may be re-
placed for the two or three firft times. He is
not, like the agriculturift, interefted in the prefervation of the ftate, where his capital has
been invefted in a folid form. He views a
change of fpeculation without great reluctance,
if it is not immediate ; partly becaufe he flatters
himfelf with the hopes of independence in the
interval, partly becaufe the fame fpirit which
made him change before, renders him lefs timid in repeating the rifk. The trade of planting, though connected with the foil, is yet, from
the extent of capital required in it, from the
rapidity of improvement, from the large profits
and the conftant rifk, and from the temporary
refidence

refidence which the proprietors make on their
eftates without families, while they are acquiring their fortune, much more nearly allied to
commerce than to agriculture, and promoted
by the fpirit of mercantile adventure.

But in fact it fignifies little, whether we
confider that the lofs of Cuba is likely to follow its extended cultivation, or that the profpect of fuch an event will immediately check
the prefent active fpirit of improvement. In
either cafe, the confequences are highly injurious to the interefts of Spain, ftripped as fhe
now is of her moft valuable iflands, and unable otherwife to continue the acquifition of
that colonial wealth which alone can render
her a match for the preponderating influence
of France in the Gulf of Mexico, after the refources of the Republic, withdrawn from St
Domingo, fhall have been turned to the banks
of the Miffifippi.

In the fame manner will the eftablifhment of
the negroes in St Domingo operate upon the
fafety of Porto-Rico, if the Spaniards fhould attempt to cultivate that very inferior ifland, after
failing in Cuba. Porto-Rico is indeed fituated
to the windward of the three great Antilles.
But when a community of free negroes exifts
to the leeward of a fettlement peopled by African flaves, the advantages arifing from the obftacles which the trade wind prefents to the
depredations

depredations of the former, are counterbalan-
ced by the temptations and facilities which it
affords to the defertion of the latter. The
Spanifh part of St Domingo, our own fettlements in Barbadoes previous to the fubjugation of the black Charaibes in St Vincents, and
the acquifition of that ifland by the peace of
Paris, the plantations of Jamaica before the expulfion of the Maroons, and thofe of Surinam
fince the treaty of 1762 acknowledged the independence of the revolted negroes, have all
experienced in a great degree the manifold dangers of a neighbourhood which excites the defertion of the flaves, and leaves thofe who do
not efcape, in a ftate of mind ripe for infurrection.

But further—Have we any reafon to believe
that the French will be more fuccefsful in their
Windward Iflands, than in the colony from
whence we are fuppofing them to have been
expelled by the negroes ?

I have before remarked, that the attention
of French ftatefmen having been directed almoft exclufively to the great Leeward colony,
by the events which have lately happened
there, our information with refpect to the progrefs of cultivation in the Windward fettlements is by no means extenfive or correct. I
have, however, detailed the various *data* which
we poffefs, in public documents and other four-

ces of information, for calculating the present
amount of the negro population in thofe fettlements, and the rate at which it increafed
during the time that the population of St Domingo was doubling. The refult of thefe com-
putations led us to the conclufion, that the
proportions of the different races in thofe iflands
were as unequal, and that the unequality had
been as rapidly increafing, as in St Domingo. *

But it is alfo of importance, to confider the
fituation of the free people of colour in the
Windward Iflands, fince it is to them that the
origin of the troubles in St Domingo may be
traced. The circumftances to which the rapid
multiplication of this intermediate clafs was
owing in St Domingo, muft have exifted in an
equal degree all over the French Weft Indies.
In general, a much greater proportion of the
proprietors refided in the French fettlements,
than in the Britifh and Dutch. In the French
iflands nine tenths of the proprietors lived
upon their plantations, or in the colonial
towns ; in the others not above one fifth were
fuppofed to refide. † The lazy, diffipated lives
of thefe men were fpent in amours with negreffes or mulatto women ; and as the fruits of
                                              this

---

* Book I. Sect. III. Part IV.
† Robinet, Dict. de l'homme d'etat, Art. *Colonies.*

this intercourfe lay under all the difadvantages of the mixed blood, the idea of marriage with the mothers was out of the queftion. It will always be found, where the manners of a people are in this corrupt ftate, that marriage, even between equals, falls into difrepute. In the Britifh Weft Indies we fee the confequences of concubinage with blacks and mulattoes, in the fmall proportion of white women, and the flow progrefs of the white population. In the French iflands the numbers of the whites rather diminifhed than augmented ; and the natural increafe of inhabitants, which may always be expected to arife from the cheapnefs of good land, and the paffions of a warm climate, muft be looked for, not among the whites, but among the mulattoes. Accordingly, the progrefs of the mulatto population muft be calculated, not from the numbers of the mulattoes at any particular time, but from the numbers of whites. The free negroes, on the other hand, increafe according to the progreffive ftate of the flave population. The mulattoes and free negroes, are ufually included together in the clafs of free people of colour ; and it appears, that in ten years, ending 1789, this body had, in St Domingo, much more than tripled its numbers ; whilft the numbers of the whites had rather decreafed. There is no reafon to fuppofe that

the

the people of colour were lefs numerous in the other iflands in proportion. The fame government and laws prevailed over the whole French Weft Indies ; the fame diffolute manners ; the fame want of white women ; the fame fyftem of intrigue with blacks and mulattoes. In Martinico, the free people of colour bore a greater proportion to the whites, by the enumeration 1776, than in St Domingo, by the enumeration 1779. In St Lucia, and Tobago, the proportion of people of colour was double that of St Domingo. In Guadaloupe, the proportion was a great deal lefs. But, in all the iflands, we have feen, that the cultivation and the wealth of the planters, their luxury, and the numbers of their flaves, were rapidly increafing. We may therefore infer, that the numbers, both of the free negroes and free mulattoes, were augmented in them all with great rapidity ; and that, at the epoch of the revolution, this intermediate clafs had increafed fo as to bear the fame proportion to the whites in the Windward Iflands that it did in St Domingo.

That their grievances were the very fame, we cannot entertain the fmalleft doubt. The colonial fyftem of St Domingo was common to all the French iflands. Even the flight differences which the eftablifhment of feparate
legiflatures

legiflatures have produced in our iflands, were unknown in thofe of France, where the parliaments had, as in the mother country, only the power of regiftering the royal edicts for the purpofes of publication and authentication. They were all under the immediate fuperintendance of the council of commerce, and in the department of the minifter of the marine: they were equally affected by the edicts which the King iffued in conformity to the advice of the minifter and council. The *code noire* was a general fyftem of regulations with refpect to the fubordination of the inferior races in all the iflands. The privileges which it conferred upon the people of colour, and the modifications which thofe privileges received, were the fame in all. The difcontent of the mulattoes muft have been common to this race wherever it exifted. Similarity of origin and of government muft have affimilated the manners of the whites. Subordination and grievances muft have univerfally alienated the mulattoes. Their rapid increafe in all the iflands armed them with power to refift; and it is probable, that the revolution alone, by emancipating the flaves, and eftablifhing political equality among all the claffes, prevented the renewal of the events which ruined St Domingo, in fuch of the windward fettlements as remained unconquered.

If

BOOK
II.

If, then, the natural advantages of the negroes fhould be found fo far fuperior to all the
circumftances of policy, difcipline, and union,
on the part of the French, as to render the
eftablifhment of an independent ftate in St
Domingo the neceffary refult of the conteft,
what is there in the fituation of the other fettlements which fhould prevent the negroes there
from following the example of their brethren
to the weftward? And what is there in the circumftances of the two races which fhould prevent the blacks from fucceeding in the other
iflands, as we are fuppofing them to have done
in St Domingo? The negroes of Guadaloupe
have tafted of liberty; and the French have
been attempting to reftore the yoke. The negroes of St Domingo have lived in unbridled
licentioufnefs: order has been re-eftablifhed,
and a reftoration of the yoke is attempted. In
Guadaloupe, infurrection is by no means unknown; but it has produced none of thofe effects which, in St Domingo, muft tend to
weaken the force, and reftrain the barbarity of
the negroes. It has neither glutted the fury,
nor leffened the numbers of thofe favage men.
In St Domingo, no farther danger is to be apprehended from the people of colour, at leaft
for a confiderable time: their race is at prefent almoft extinct. In Guadaloupe, the ftate
of

of morals, during the laft ten years, has been peculiarly favourable to the increafe of this race. A law has indeed proclaimed them equal with the whites ; but unlefs the convention poffeffed the power of radically altering the nature of men in the colonies, whilft at home it could not even change their political prejudices, we may be affured, that the mulattoes have continued the fame degraded and oppreffed race that deftroyed the colony of St Domingo. The *code noire* of Lewis XIV. might have faved that ifland, had the power of the Great Monarch extended to the minds and the habits of his fubjects. The fubfequent tyrannical enactments were modified in their application, by the manners of thofe in whofe favour they were made, and of thofe by whofe means they were executed. The decrees of the revolutionary legiflatures on colonial affairs, have not been more efficacious than thofe of Lewis, and have been prevented from operating the equalization of the mulattoes, by the fame caufes which formerly mitigated the fubordination of that clafs.

The conqueft of Martinico, St Lucia, and Tobago, has indeed prevented any infurrection in thofe iflands, by cutting off all communication with Guadaloupe, and enforcing ftrict difcipline, by means of a numerous army, formed

partly

BOOK
II.

partly of negro regiments, whofe attachment
to the Europeans, whether in war or in revolt,
I have frequently had occafion to notice.
When thefe iflands are reftored, and the negroes in Guadaloupe have been fuccefsful in
their efforts to throw off their yoke, it is not
difficult to forefee the termination of the
French dominion in the windward colonies.
A conqueft uniformly weakens the power of
that government which, after defeat and expulfion, regains its authority by a treaty of
peace. Every change of mafters is attended
with a change of confidential fervants and favourites ; and thofe who profited by the old
fyftem, are feldom very friendly to the new
order of things. The white inhabitants in
Martinico were by no means fo averfe to the
republican government as a few royalifts reprefented them ; and the campaign of 1793 in
the Weft Indies, as well as in Europe, fhowed
the juftice of the maxim which Machiavel has
enforced with his ufual fagacity, that much
confidence ought not to be placed in the reports of exiles. *   It can fcarcely be imagined,
that

---

* Difcorfi fopra la prima deca di T. Livio, lib. II.
cap. XXXI. ' *Quanto fia pericolofo credere a gli fbanditi.* '—
—' *Debbe adunque un principe* ' (fays he) ' *andare adagio*
' *a pigliare imprefe fopra la relatione d'un confiqato perche il*
' *più delle volte ne fe refta ò con vergogna ò con danno gravif-*
' *fimo.* '

that the Britifh government, after conquering Martinico in the following campaign, fhould treat the royalifts and the republicans in its new poffeffions with equal favour : ftill lefs can it be fuppofed, that the Britifh government fhould betray no partiality for the Britifh planters, who, in confiderable numbers, had made this ifland the place of their abode. They were enrolled in diftinct corps, and entrufted with arms : they filled the moft confidential places : they belonged, in fhort, to the conquerors ; while the other inhabitants held their property and privileges by tolerance, not by right. The reftoration of the ifland to France, is attended, of courfe, with the re-eftablifhment of the republican government, under the unmingled influence of the French inhabitants. The Englifh and the Royalifts are permitted, no doubt, if they think proper, to depart in fafety. But the colony was not merely the place of their abode ; it was the fcene of their fpeculations. They muft have fome attachment to that foil in which their capital is vefted ; becaufe they could not fell their property without confiderable lofs ; nor remove their ftock, and vary the employment of it, without fome rifk. They will remain, therefore, to repay, by fubmiffion and oppreffion, the advantages which they enjoyed under a more congenial fyftem;

fyftem; and their difcontents muft divide and weaken the new government, furrounded by people of colour and flaves.

Nor will the perils of fuch a neighbourhood tend at once to unite the different orders of the community which is expofed to them. Men are not always reconciled by community of dangers. The more immediate impulfe is generally obeyed; and fentiments of jealoufy or hatred prevent the falutary operations of that wife fear which ought to be excited by the profpect of the greater, though perhaps more diftant evils. The fame blindnefs which divides nations whofe circumftances imperioufly dictate the neceffity of making a common caufe, diftracts alfo thofe branches of the fame fociety whofe exiftence feems to depend upon a cordial and intimate union. In ancient times, that blindnefs enabled Rome to conquer the world, by fomenting divifions, and then fubduing her allies. In more enlightened ages, it has prevented the mafter principle of modern policy from maintaining the independence of the European ftates. It opened to Cortes the gates of Mexico; enthroned Pizarro in the temple of the Incas; and, after fubjecting to the Britifh fceptre the peninfula of India, will moft probably extend our dominion beyond the Ganges. It put into the

hands

hands of Katharine the balance of the north; and in the fouth annihilated the exiftence of a rich and naturally powerful ftate. It has led the tricoloured cockade over the faireft portion of Europe; and raifed up a generation of pigmy republics and kings around the common enemy of national independence. In the colonies of the great nation, the fame principle took a different direction; armed againft each other thofe whom the fear of a common enemy ought to have bound together; and taught each party madly to call in the aid of that body which, in the end, was fure to overwhelm both. We can fcarcely be fo fanguine as to expect, that the different claffes of whites in the reftored iflands will prove exceptions to fo general a rule, and unite to ftrengthen the hands of that government which muft of neceffity diftribute its favours with fome partiality. Yet the danger will be every thing but inftantaneous. The people of colour in the Windward Iflands have their paffions as well as in St Domingo. They have their grievances too, and their temptations. They will difregard the certainty of defeat by the negroes, in the event of a complete change; and, looking only to the gratification of their prefent feelings, will be callous to that fear which, in their circumftances, is the fame with wifdom.

The

The free fubjects, then, of the French colonies which are reftored by the peace, cannot
be expected to unite in one compact body, as
if no conqueft had been made, or no difference
of race had exifted. We may indeed remember the dangers which threatened our own
power in the ceded iflands, particularly Grenada and Dominica, during the courfe of the
late war, (not to mention the events of 1778
and 1779), from that animofity between the
French and Britifh fubjects which twelve years
fubmiffion to the fame mild and equitable government had not been able to extinguifh, and
which the dreadful examples then exhibited in
St Domingo could not reftrain.

It is not therefore defponding too much, to
conclude, that the French government will
find it at leaft as difficult to retain poffeffion of
the conquered iflands, as to overcome the negroes and people of colour in thofe which
have never changed mafters. Admitting, what
is evidently untrue, that the example and communication of thofe iflands which fhall have
become fubject to the negro dominion, can
produce no direct effects upon the others which
fhall yet remain to France; we may be affured, that, in thefe alfo, the very fame caufes
will confpire to overthrow her dominion; and
that,

that, after the extirpation of the whites has been accomplifhed in the more leeward of the French iflands, it will be chimerical to hope for the continuance of European influence in any of the reft.

It is now only neceffary, that we caft our eyes on the map of the Carribbee iflands, to be convinced of the immediate fall which, in this event, awaits the windward fettlements of the other European powers. If the leeward pofition of St Domingo fhall be fuppofed to have fecured Porto-Rico and the leeward Charaibean iflands, whilft the depredations and dominion of the new commonwealths were fpreading over Cuba and Jamaica, thefe are now expofed to inevitable deftruction from Guadaloupe and Martinico. In fact, the fituation of the Carribbee iflands, when expofed to fuch a neighbourhood, is much more critical than that of Jamaica, from three material circumftances.

In the firft place, they are fo fmall, that after an enemy has landed and ravaged the coafts, their defence, by the manœuvres and the ftratagems of protracted warfare, is almoft impracticable.

Secondly, they are furrounded by the enemy, upon the fuppofition that all the French iflands have been fubdued by the Africans, whereas

Jamaica

Jamaica and Cuba had only to defend one point of attack. But,

Thirdly, and principally; they are essentially weaker than the great Leeward island, by the constitution of their society, in which the disproportion of the colours is much greater.

In Jamaica, the negroes are to the whites as more than eight to one. The average proportion of the British Charaibean islands (exclusive of Barbadoes) is eleven to one: and this is divided among them very unequally; for in Antigua, within sight of Guadaloupe, the proportion is that of nearly fifteen to one; in Dominica, placed between Guadaloupe and Martinico, it is above twelve to one; and in Grenada, at a short distance to the leeward of Tobago, it exceeds the proportion of twenty-three to one. If, then, the issue of the present eventful contest shall be the establishment of the negro power in the French islands, what reason have we to hope for the British Windward colonies? The whole Charaibean chain will be overrun by the African hordes, as it formerly was by the less numerous and savage Charaibes. Barbadoes alone, from its position, from its ancient and constant establishment under the British government, but still more from its large proportion of white inhabitants (above one fourth of the negroes), may stand out for a season; but, either

overrun

overrun by the neighbouring fettlements, or deferted by its own negroes, it will, after a few
years of refpite, only enjoy the trifling confolation, of being the laft to fhare the fate of thofe
valuable poffeffions.

Similarity of fituation, produce, commerce,
and internal arrangement, have led us to confider the fettlements in Guiana as forming part
of the Weft Indian colonies. In feveral material points, however, they differ from the iflands,
and from each other. Accordingly, they may
be expected to have in fome refpects a different
fate.

Notwithftanding the attention which the
French government has uniformly beftowed
upon the ifland and neighbouring fettlements
of Cayenne ever fince the lofs of Canada, we
have already feen how extremely flow the progrefs of thefe colonies has been. The number
of negroes in 1770 was eight thoufand, according to the Cenfus, * which, however, is always
confiderably below the truth. In 1780, they
were between ten and eleven thoufand †; and
in 1794, according to the author of the ' Crifis, '
they did not exceed fifteen thoufand. ‡ The
fcarcity of negroes, arifing from bad credit
and

* Malouet, Mem. &c. II. 43.
† Neckar, Finances, tom. III. cap. 13.
‡ P. 37.

and confined capital, has been the chief caufe of the ill fuccefs which has conftantly attended the efforts of France to improve this colony. This deficiency in the importation muft have made the planters more careful of their ftock in hand, and rendered the condition of the flaves more tolerable than in the other fettlements. Accordingly we find, that their enfranchifement, in confequence of the decree of Pluviofe, An. II, was attended with none of the confequences in Cayenne, which in the other colonies it was fo well calculated to produce. After their emancipation, the negroes in general continued voluntarily upon the plantations of their former mafters; and no irregularities whatever were committed by thofe men who had thus fuddenly acquired their freedom. *

But befides the milder treatment of the flaves in general, and the greater proportion of the Creole to the imported negroes, another circumftance peculiar to the continental colonies, renders the fituation of the whites far more fecure in Cayenne than in any of the iflands. The original poffeffors of the foil exift there in confiderable numbers; and they live in the immediate vicinity of the Europeans. By an intercourfe with their civilized neighbours, uniformly amicable and mutually

* Voyage à la Guiane, &c. cap. XI.

mutually ferviceable, they have acquired many of thofe artificial wants which traffic and labour alone can fatisfy. They are thus much lefs a-verfe to exertions of induftry, than the reft of the American Indians, whom the Spanifh and Portuguefe invaders never fuffered to remain in-dependent until they fhould become accuftom-ed to voluntary labour. The French planters, in different parts of Guiana, have frequently fupplied the want of negroes by the induftry of hired Indians ; * and this refource rendered them much lefs dependent, than they otherwife would have been, on their flaves at the period of the revolution.

But the neighbourhood of the Indians has been attended with ftill more important confe-quences. As the French have conftantly and fuc-cefsfully cultivated the good will of thofe tribes, and kept them at peace among themfelves, there can be no doubt that, in the event of a rupture between the planters and their flaves, the Indians would unanimoufly take part with the former, to whom they have, upon all occafions, evinced a warm attachment ; and would affift them in fubduing and punifhing the negroes, towards whom they have, in every inftance, fhown a violent antipathy † ; a fentiment which, it may be

---

* Voyage à la Guiane, &c. cap. XVIII.
† Ibid.

be prefumed, the whites have been at no great
pains to eradicate.

From the concurrence of all thefe circumftances, it has happened, that as the emancipation
of the negroes in Cayenne was attended with no
inconvenience, fo, neither has the reftoration
of the yoke been productive of the flighteft
commotion. From the laft communications of
the French government upon this fubject, it
appears, that the flave fyftem and the flave
trade, are re-eftablifhed in this colony ; and that
the progrefs of cultivation, fo long retarded, has
of late years begun to be accelerated ; probably,
in a great degree, from the new obftructions to
the employment of capital in the other fettlements. But, if this improvement continues,
and, ftill more, if all the capital vefted in Weft
Indian cultivation fhall be forced towards Guiana by fuch a cataftrophe as we have been fuppofing in the iflands, the conftant effects of rapid improvement in flave culture muft follow ; an increafed difproportion of negroes ;
greater careleffnefs and cruelty on the part of
the mafters ; an excefs in the numbers of imported over thofe of Creole flaves ; and a rapid
multiplication of the free people of colour : fo
that, if to thefe circumftances there be added
the eftablifhment of the negroes in the Carribbee iflands, the ruin of Cayenne is not likely
to

to be fo far diftant as its fecurity during the late tumults might at firft lead us to expect.

The probable fate of Dutch Guiana will expofe Cayenne to new dangers. The Dutch, as well as the French in South America, have carefully cultivated the friendfhip of their Indian neighbours. But a variety of circumftances have concurred to prevent this alliance from fecuring the tranquillity of the Dutch fettlements. The extenfive capitals employed in Surinam, Berbice, &c. have (as we formerly obferved) * rapidly multiplied the numbers of the flaves. In 1769, they amounted to fifty thoufand ; the whites to four thoufand. † In 1777, the flaves had increafed to feventy thoufand ; ‡ and, in 1789, while the whites ftill remained about four thoufand in number, the negroes were eftimated at ninety thoufand ‖.

The treatment of thofe flaves, thus numerous and thus rapidly poured into a fettlement fo ill ftocked with whites, was infinitely more cruel in the Dutch plantations than in any other, as we have before feen: And, in their annual importation of five or fix thoufand, thofe from the Gold Coaft were uniformly preferred
by

---

* Book I. Sect. III. Part I.
† Ennery, (apud Malouet Mem. &c.) III. 190.
‡ Ibid.
‖ Voyage à la Guiane, &c. cap. X.

by that gainthirſty people, as the moſt capable
of hard work, though certainly the moſt prone
to rebellion. *

To theſe never failing cauſes of revolt and
deſertion, muſt be added, the accidental circumſtance of the Maroon negroes left in the country
by the Engliſh previous to their expulſion in
the year 1666. This body, during the whole
of the laſt century, was truly formidable to the
Dutch ſettlements. On various occaſions they
were ſucceſsful in the warfare which they perpetually waged againſt their civilized neighbours, in a regular and ſyſtematic manner.
Their numbers being augmented by natural
means, and receiving continual additions from
deſertion, they grew every day more formidable.
The peace concluded with them in 1761, was
founded ſo exactly on the baſis of equality between the two parties, that the Dutch plenipo-
tentiaries were obliged to ratify the treaty according to the African forms. † In 1772, a
war again broke out with theſe dangerous neighbours ; and the States ſent a large force for
the protection of the colony. So much was
the exiſtence of the Dutch power in America
ſuppoſed to depend upon the ſucceſs of the expedition

---

* Malouet, Mem. III. 135.
† La Richeſſe de la Hollande, cap. V.

pedition againft the Maroons, that the intrigues of the houfe of Orange were anxioufly directed towards obtaining a preponderance in the colonial affairs, by the adoption of one particular plan of military operations. For this purpofe, an officer attached to the Orange party was fent out ; the colony was divided between the contending interefts ; both parties, as ufual, endeavoured to engage the interpofition of France ; and, at laft, the Maroon invafions were checked by the eftablifhment of a permanent cordon * round the whole of the fide expofed to the Maroon fettlements.

Whilft continual preparations for warfare have repreffed and prevented the incurfions of the Maroons, the grievances of the flaves, and the increafe of their numbers, by the extended cultivation of the colony, have encouraged defertion, and rendered the neighbourhood of the infurgents as dangerous as before. The influx of Britifh capital during the late war, muft have increafed ftill farther the negro population of thofe fettlements ; and the change of mafters, and mixture of nations among the whites, will, as ufual, be unfavourable to vigorous and fecure government. The operation of the cordon muft, in one quarter at leaft, tend to prevent

---

* Malouet, IV. *paffim.*

vent all communication with the Indian nations ;
and there is reafon to believe, that the Maroons
have found no difficulty, of late years, in uniting themfelves with the natives by marriage. *

If, then, the iflands fhould be in the poffeffion of negroes, it is not eafy to conceive a
colony placed in a more critical fituation than
Dutch Guiana—furrounded, as it will be, on all
fides by independent negro ftates, and peopled
by a feeble and divided body of Europeans, mingled with a moft difproportioned mafs of flaves,
who have fo fuddenly been collected together,
chiefly from the moft ferocious tribes of Africa,
irritated by every fpecies of cruelty, and treated
with the extremity of rigid parfimony. The
exiftence of the French on the other fide of
the river Marrowni, is evidently incompatible
with the event to which fuch a combination
of difficulties and dangers will moft probably
lead.

Thus will the ruin be accomplifhed of thofe
fertile fettlements in which the race of civilized men has been diffufed, the miraculous
effects of commercial fpirit been difplayed,
and the prodigies of European arts and arms
exhibited for upwards of three eventful ages.

The favage nations of Africa, renewing a-
mong themfelves thofe horrors to which they
have

---

* Voyage à la Guiane, &c. cap. X.

have facrificed their mafters, will fpread over
the faireft portions of the New World the barbarifm that ftill covers their native deferts.
And thofe regions where, for a while, the
brightnefs of polifhed life had feemed to dawn,
will relapfe into a darknefs, thicker, and far
more full of horrors, than that which was
(fhall we not now fay?) unhappily penetrated
by the daring genius of Columbus.

───── ' *Nox atra cavâ circumvolat umbrâ.*
' *Quis cladem illius noctis, quis funera fando*
' *Explicet ? aut poffit lacrymis æquare labores ?*
' *Urbs antiqua ruit, multos dominata per annos* ₹
' *Plurima perque vias fternuntur inertia paffim*
' *Corpora, perque domos, et religiofa deorum*
' *Limina . . . . Crudelis ubique*
' *Luctus, ubique pavor, et plurima mortis imago.*'
ÆNEIS II.

BOOK

BOOK III.

INTRODUCTION.

In the laſt Book, we were occupied with the examination of the foreign relations of the members of a colonial fyſtem in general, and more particularly of the European colonies, confidered as independent of the mother countries, and viewed as forming a great federal community of fubordinate or fecondary ſtates, contiguous in poſition, and refembling each other in their origin and hiſtory.

But the mother country muſt always be affected by every thing that affects its colonies, fo long as the colonial policy is purfued by modern ſtates. A colony is, in fact, only a remote province of the empire ; but it is not on that account leſs valuable either in itſelf, or as affifting and enriching the other parts of the ſtate. This I have explained at great length in the Firſt Book.

Book.* Hence the councils of a ftate will always be more or lefs influenced by a regard to
its colonial poffeffions. The interefts of the
contiguous provinces will fometimes give way
to the fuperior interefts of the colonies ; as the
fortunes of the latter will, in moft cafes, be
made fubfervient in their turn. Not only ought
the domeftic policy of the ftate to be made fubfervient in many inftances to that of the colonies—its foreign policy fhould alfo yield in the
fame manner to the policy dictated by the external relations of the colonies. This, however,
has not often happened ; I have before fhewn †
that the quarrels of the mother country alone
are, in almoft every inftance, the caufes which
involve every part of the empire in wars ; that
the foreign relations of the colonies are almoft
always fubfervient, and poftponed to thofe of
the parent ftate ; and that, fo far from involving
her in their quarrels, they fuffer more than any
part of the fyftem by the proper quarrels of the
metropolis. Certain circumftances may, however, occur, in which it is to be prefumed, that
the policy of interfering in behalf of the colonies would be allowed by all. Thofe circumftances are chiefly of two kinds.

In

---

* Sect. I. & II.
† Book I. Sect I.

In the *first* place, the colonies of a state may
be directly attacked in such a manner as to shew
clearly an intention of insult, or to demonstrate
views of ambition in the aggressor: no nation
can possibly tolerate either, without demanding
immediate reparation and satisfaction. The
common principles of self-preservation must impel her to defensive measures; the principles
of honour must induce her to persist in op-
posing force by force, even although she would
previously have given up the invaded colonies
without any remuneration: and common feelings of justice must incline her to view such
aggressions or insults, as equally injurious, whether they are made in the remote or contiguous
provinces of the empire. In cases of this sort, no
one can for a moment entertain a doubt that
the mother country is imperiously called upon
to make war upon all the parts of the aggressor's
dominions with all her own forces. Doubts
may be entertained as to the expediency of
colonial possessions, but no hesitation can ever
be shewn upon the question of war, when the
colonies actually in her possession, are invaded.
On this point then, I shall not insist any farther.
But,

In the *second* place, a neighbouring nation may extend its colonial dominions to a
dangerous degree, by the conquest of some
third colony, or of some of the native powers;

or

or great and fudden changes may take place in the internal ftructure of its colonial fyftem, without any extenfion of its magnitude by con-queft or ufurpation; or plans may be laid for ac-quiring an extent of territory in other parts, not immediately belonging to the colonial commu-nity, yet ultimately fatal to its colonial neigh-bours in that community, if attended with fuc-cefs. None of thefe meafures can, indeed, be conftrued into a direct aggreffion ; ftill lefs into an infult upon the national honour. If you have not guaranteed the conquered power, or united your fortune to its fortunes by defen-five treaty, you cannot be faid to be imme-diately concerned in the affair ; and thofe who doubt the propriety of interfering at all in fuch cafes, will certainly deny the expediency or fuch guarantees and defenfive alliances. On the other hand, it has uniformly been the the policy of modern times to view with jea-loufy every fuch meafure of a rival or neigh-bour, and to confider each event in the inter-national fyftem, as immediately affecting all its members. After all wars undertaken upon thofe principles, it is ufual, and indeed not unnatural, for men who think war the only great national calamity, to call in queftion the foundnefs of doctrines, from which much ap-parent evil has proceeded, balanced only by
advantages

advantages of a nature too refined or remote to be perceptible to all obfervers. The fyftem of modern international policy has accordingly been called in queftion repeatedly, during the courfe of the 18th century, and at no time more vehemently arraigned, than during the eventful period in which we have lived.

I have endeavoured, in the Firft Book of this Inquiry, to fhow, that it is a narrow policy which would confider colonies as feparate and fubfervient appendages of the ftate ; that they are integral parts of the empire which is happy enough to poffefs them ; and that they ought to be confidered as fuch in all arrangements of domeftic policy. I fhall now endeavour to fhew, that the fame principle ought to be extended to the foreign policy of the ftate ; that in queftions of this nature alfo, they ought to be viewed as parts of the empire ; and that, accordingly, the queftions of interference, balance of power, alliances, guarantees, &c. ought to be decided, with refpeʄ to colonial relations, upon the very fame principles on which we may decide them with refpeʄ to the primary foreign relations of the ftate. I fhall therefore now confider, in general, the principles upon which the modern fyftem of international policy is founded, and fhall endeavour to fhow that it is effential to the ftate of modern fociety. I fhall at
the

the fame time confider the circumftances in the
natural fituation of colonies, which render thofe
principles more peculiarly applicable to fuch
eftablifhments. As the chief purpofe of this
Third Book is to fhow what line of policy is
dictated to the European powers by the prefent
ftate of the French colonies, and that ftate into
which it is probable that they will very foon relapfe, even if tranquillity fhould for the prefent
be reftored ; moreover, as this particular inquiry is intimately connected with the general queftions of interference, for the fame reafons that
the fubjects of European policy in 1792 were
connected with the fame queftions, it will appear clearly how neceffary the general inquiry
is, even for the difcuffion of this fpecial queftion.

This Book, then, divides itfelf into two
Sections.

In the Firft, I fhall explain thofe principles
upon which the modern fyftem of foreign policy is founded in the higheft reafons of neceffity and expediency, and thofe circumftances
which render it peculiarly applicable to the colonies, even if we fhould not confider them as
integral parts of the fyftem to which they belong.

In the Second Section, I fhall confider what
is the line of foreign policy recommended to the
European powers, both in the colonies, and in
                                          Europe

Europe with a reference to the colonies, by the present state of colonial affairs. This Inquiry will confist chiefly of a comparifon of the conclufions deduced in the laft Book, with thofe deduced in the Firft Section of this Book.

BOOK
III.
INTROD.

SEC-

SECTION I.

OF THE FOREIGN POLICY OF STATES IN GENERAL AND
AS INFLUENCED BY THEIR COLONIAL RELATIONS.

BOOK
III.

THE balance of power, and the general fyftem of international relations that has grown
up in modern Europe, have afforded to one clafs
of politicians perpetual fubject of ridicule and
invective, and to another clafs the conftant opportunity of defending or attacking every meafure, of difcuffing, or affecting to difcufs every
political fubject, by a reference to certain terms
of art and abftract ideas, of which it is fair to
fufpect that they little underftood the meaning
and the force.

Of thefe reafoners or declaimers, the former
fect are undoubtedly the moft dangerous. The
refinements of modern policy which have fprung
from the progreffive improvement of the human
fpecies, and have, in their turn, fecured that progrefs, and accelerated its pace, are in no danger
of being either corrupted, or brought into difrepute, by the petulance of pretended ftatefmen.
But the fophiftries and cavils which political
fceptics and innovators have founded, partly on

a

a misconception of the theory, and partly on a
miftatement of the facts, tend directly to a degradation of the fyftem in the eyes of fuperficial reafoners, and may ultimately renew a ftate of things, from which the unaffifted efforts of national heroifm would be altogether unable to redeem any one community.

The attacks of thofe men have, moreover, been extremely inconfiftent and contradictory. While, at one time, they maintain, that the idea of a political equilibrium is pregnant with every fpecies of abfurdity, and would produce, if carried into the actual affairs of nations, thofe very evils which the fyftem is extolled for preventing : at another time, they tell us that the notion is fimple and obvious ; that it arifes naturally out of the paffions of men ; that it is no refinement of modern ftatefmen, but has influenced the councils of princes and commonwealths in all ages of the world. Now—the balance of power is an unintelligible jargon, invented to cover every fcheme ; to furnifh pretexts for every act of national injuftice ; to lull the jealoufy of the people in any emergency ; or to excite their alarms upon any occafion. Now—it is ufelefs and fuperfluous ; an interference with the natural order of things ; or an attempt to effect that which would happen at any rate. Now—it is pernicious in the extreme ;

treme; the parent of war and offenfive alliances; the exciting caufe of national violence;
the watchword of ambitious princes and deftroying commonwealths; a refinement only of injuftice; and a fyftem of nothing but treachery
or caprice. It is very manifeft, without any argument, that the fyftem of modern policy con-
not be liable to all thofe accufations at once,
and that the declaimers who have ufed fuch
language with refpect to it, muft have been
talking of very different things at different
times. * But as the foreign policy of nations
was never, at any period of modern ftory, fo interefting as at prefent; as the primary relations
of ftates to each other are generally thofe which
determine their external colonial policy; and
as this whole fubject has never yet been treated
of in a general and fcientific manner, I fhall proceed, in the firft place, to offer a few obfervations upon that fyftem, which has been fo little
underftood either by fpeculative writers or practical politicians.

The national jealoufy, by which at all times
the European ftates are animated, and which
ranges them on different fides in each public
crifis, has been denominated, not a principle of
policy, but a national emotion. Nations, it is
faid,

* Note I i

faid, like the individuals which compofe them, are moved by caprice, and actuated by paffions ; excited to contention by envy and hatred ; foothed to reconciliation when exhaufted by the efforts of their enmity ; leagued in friend-fhip by the dictates of an interefted prudence ; united together by the thirft of plunder ; or combined for the gratification of fome common revenge. The principle (we are told) that has been pompoufly called the great fpring of civilized policy, is perhaps nothing more than a fyftematic indulgence of thofe natural feelings which impel the favage to attack his more wealthy neighbour, or unite rival hordes in a temporary friendfhip, when invaded by a powerful and common enemy. The policy (it is added) which we have heard extolled as the grand *ar-canum* of modern ftatefmen, and dignified with the title of a fyftem, is nothing more than the natural refult of a conflict between the defire of conqueft and love of fecurity, refined on by in-genious men, and fpun into a regular theory.

Thefe remarks are partly true, and partly unfounded. It is true, that nations are guided by human councils, and fubject, of courfe, to the paffions and caprices of men ; but it is no lefs certain, that the more regularly any fyftem of government is eftablifhed, the more will men of fober minds acquire a weight in the manage-

ment

ment of affairs ; and that the longer the art of administering the concerns of empires is practised, will prudence gain the greater afcendancy over paffion. It is true, that the dictates of feelings not always amiable, and often outrageous, are frequently, more than any impulfe of reafon, the fprings which actuate the operations of ftates ; but it is equally true, that in all animals, the paffions themfelves, even thofe moft liable to abufe and moft fatal in their effects when too ftrong, are implanted for the wifeft of purpofes ; that inftinct is the principle to which more than reafon the prefervation of life, the population of the world, and the maintenance of order in the univerfe muft be afcribed ; and that national councils may be operating what no forefight could combine, while they appear to be fwayed only by prejudice and paffion. The exiftence of rude ftates is indeed frequently preferved, and their civilization infured by the operation of principles, to affift the developement of which is the great pride of the moft learned and fkilful ftatefmen : yet, the want of this affiftance in thofe rude times, and the want of a conftant fuperintendance and controul which renders the popular feelings ufeful in one cafe, and harmlefs in another, is certainly the caufe of that inftability of national power, and thofe perpetual changes of dominion—

thofe

thofe conftant broils, and that ftate of unceafing infecurity, to which we may attribute the
many revolutions in the lot of favage communities, the frequent viciffitudes of their political
fortunes, and the long continuance of their barbarifm.

That the fyftem which we are now confidering has oftentimes been abufed, no one can deny. What human inftitution can defend itfelf
from this charge? But many of the evils
which are afcribed to the principle in queftion,
have been owing only to an erroneous conception of its nature. Many of them have arifen
from failing to carry the line of policy recommended by it, to the lengths which it enjoins;
and, in not a few inftances, thofe events which
have been deemed pernicious, would have proved altogether fatal, had they not been modified
and controuled by its influence. We are defired, with no fmall appearance of triumph, to
view the hiftory of the laft century; and to
mark the manifold wars which the balancing
fyftem produced; the various intrigues to which
it gave rife; the deftructive conquefts of which
it furnifhed the pretext; and the national cataftrophes which it could not avert. But had it
not been for that wholefome jealoufy of rival
neighbours, which modern politicians have learned to cherifh, how many conquefts and changes
of

BOOK
III.

of dominion would have taken place, inftead
of wars, in which a few ufelefs lives were loft,
and fome fuperfluous millions were fquander-
ed? How many fair portions of the globe
might have been deluged in blood, inftead of
fome hundreds of failors fighting harmlefsly on
the barren plains of the ocean, and fome thoufands of foldiers carrying on a fcientific, and
regular, and quiet fyftem of warfare, in countries fet apart for the purpofe, and reforted to
as the *arena* where the difputes of nations may
be determined? * We may indeed look to
the hiftory of the laft century as the proudeft
æra in the annals of the fpecies ; the period
moft diftinguifhed for learning, and fkill, and
induftry ; for the milder virtues, and for common fenfe ; for refinement in government, and
an equal diffufion of liberty; above all, for that
perfect knowledge of the arts of adminiftration,
which has eftablifhed certain general rules of
conduct among nations ; has prevented the o-
verthrow of empires, and the abforption of
weak ftates into the bodies of devouring neighbours ; has fet bounds to the march of conqueft, and rendered the unfheathing of the
fword a meafure of the laft adoption ; whereas, in other times, it was always reforted to in
the firft inftance.

                                           In

---

* Book I. Sect. I.

In the beginning of that century, we faw the gigantic power of France humbled by a coalition of princes, each refolved to undergo immediate lofs, and run a great prefent rifk, in order to prevent the greater chance of ruin at the diftance of a few years. In ancient times, the Stadtholder would have been more jealous of Britain or Auftria, than of France. The Great Monarch, like Cæfar, would have found a Divitiacus in the heart of the empire. By fplitting the neighbouring potentates into adverfe factions, and fighting one againft the other, he would in a few years have fubjugated the whole. No power would then have conceived that common prudence required an immediate facrifice of peace, in order to ward off a diftant peril. All would have waited quietly till the invafion came on ; then, fighting with a defperate, but an infulated valour, all would have been conquered in detail, by the ambitious enemy of Europe; and the ftory of the Roman Empire would have been renewed, when fubmiffion to foreign power, lofs of liberty, and interruption of peaceful purfuits, were no longer the phantoms of vulgar terror, or the themes of idle declamation, but real, and imminent, and inevitable calamities.

In the middle of the century, we indeed faw an ancient crown defpoiled of its hereditary provinces ;

provinces; and the neighbouring states in vain attempting to crush the new-born energies of the Prussian power. It is, however, extremely doubtful whether the principles of an enlightened policy would not have favoured the rise of a power, whose professed and natural object was the balancing of the Imperial House, and the protection of the smaller princes of the empire against the preponderating, and formerly absolute, sway of the Austrian monarchs. At any rate, admitting the other powers to have been actuated by no such principles, or to have viewed the policy of Prussia as tending to the destruction of the equilibrium, it is clear that the success of the Silesian usurpation must, according to those views, be attributed to the actual dereliction of the balancing system, and not to its inefficacy; for, both in the Silesian and in the Seven-years war, * the part of Prussia was openly espoused by some of the great powers; in the former, by France and Bavaria; in the latter, first by England and then by Russia herself. The preservation and accurate adjustment of the balance might perhaps have required some such event as the acquisition

---

* It is well known that the peace of Dresden was only a truce; that the war of 1756 owed its origin to the cause of the former contest; and that the possession of Silesia was only secured by the peace of Hubertsburg.

tion which Pruffia actually made ; but if the immediate object of the fyftem, the maintenance of the eftablifhed divifion of power, was held to be a more important confideration, it is clear that the part of Pruffia ought not to have been taken by France and Bavaria, in the one cafe, or by England and Ruffia in the other, until the ufurped dominions of Auftria had been reftored ; and then, the allies of that power ought inftantly to have deferted her, if fhe did not remain fatisfied with the fruits of their interference.

Soon after the Seven-years war was terminated, the difmemberment of an ancient European kingdom was projected, by the powers who had been moft exhaufted in the Silefian conteft, and who wifhed to indemnify themfelves for their loffes, at the expence of the Poles. The fuccefs of this iniquitous tranfaction, although it only demonftrates that the modern fyftem has not been carried to its proper length, that it is incapable of changing the nature of men, or difarming the ambition and rapacity of princes, has been always quoted by a certain fet of politicians, as an irrefragable proof of the futility and inefficacy of the great principle of modern politics. That calamitous event is indeed a fufficient proof, that the ftatefmen of Europe had for a while forgotten

ten their moſt ſacred principles; and that the
princes who did not interfere to prevent it,
were blind to their beſt intereſts. It ſerves,
therefore, to ſhow us what would be the ſituation of the world, were the maxims of ancient
times to be revived, and the ſalutary ſyſtem of
modern Europe to loſe its influence over the
councils of ſtates; but, for this very reaſon,
the partition of Poland cannot, with any truth,
be ſaid to prove the inefficacy of thoſe principles, by acting in direct oppoſition to which,
the great powers of Europe permitted it to
take place,

If, however, the policy of the neighbouring
ſtates provided no check to the injuſtice of the
partitioning powers, the influence of the balancing ſyſtem upon the conduct of thoſe parties themſelves, was productive of the moſt
important and beneficial effects. Had the ancient maxims of national indifference and in-
ſulation prevailed in the cabinets of princes,
at the criſis of Poliſh affairs in 1772, the diſ-
tracted ſtate of that unhappy country would
indeed have called in the interference of foreign force. But this interference would have
proceeded from one quarter alone. Poland
would have been overwhelmed, and its vaſt reſources appropriated, by one only of the con-
terminous powers, probably by the Ruſſian
empire,

empire, which would thus have fuddenly acquired a preponderance fatal to the reft of Europe; and, without receiving any check from the
proportional aggrandizement of the neighbouring ftates, would have been enabled to ftretch
its refiftlefs arm into the very heart of the great
weftern commonwealth. But the prevalence
of that national jealoufy, and anxious attention
to the affairs of other ftates, which is the mafter principle of the modern fyftem, prevented
the ufurpation of Ruffia, even at the moment
when fhe was actually miftrefs of the kingdom,
when fhe garrifoned the capital with her troops,
and ruled the national councils by a viceroy,
under the name of ambaffador. With all thefe
circumftances in her favour, fhe was not even
the firft propofer of the partition. Her natural
enemies, Auftria and Pruffia, actually gained a
greater fhare of the fpoil; and, inftead of being
the firft victims of her extended empire, as
they infallibly would have been in ancient
times, they have themfelves acquired, at the
fame moment, an increafe of refources, which
enables them effectually to withftand the augmented force of her power.

Although, then, it is extremely abfurd to
adduce the partition of Poland as an inftance
of the balancing fyftem, (after the manner of
the

BOOK
III.
the Pruffian ftatefmen *), it is equally ridiculous to affert, that it proves the inefficacy of
that fyftem, or to deny that the reft of Europe
has been faved by the influence of thofe principles upon the parties in the ufurpation, which
fhould have led the other great powers of Europe to prevent it.

It is fcarcely neceffary to remark, that I by no
means intend to affert any thing further than
the injuftice and impolicy of the tranfaction
upon a great fcale : at prefent, I only look to
the effects of the balancing fyftem in maintaining the independence of the weaker ftates.
The cafe of Poland appears to be one of the very
few inftances which have ever occurred, of a
nation being placed in fuch unnatural circumftances of embarraffment, turbulence, and degradation of every fort, that no change of affairs could poffibly render it worfe, and fcarce
any revolution, by domeftic violence, or foreign invafion, could fail to alter it for the better. Setting apart the high-founding phrafes
of patriotifm and national fpirit, and the feelings

* Count Hertzberg (the King's firft minifter in 1772),
in a fpeculative effay on this fubject, gives the partition as
an appofite cafe of the balancing fyftem. It was made, he
fays, ' felon les principes d'une balance dont les trois puif-
' fances partageantes etoient convenues entre elles,' Mem.
tom. i. p. 296.

ings of admiration which the very natural emotions of pity have taught us to couple with the name of Poland, it is impoffible for a foberminded obferver not to perceive, that ages of the moft debafing fervitude had utterly difqualified the Polifh boors for enjoying the privileges of free fubjects ; that a lifetime divided between unceafing tumult in public, and the revellings of a boifterous, barbarous hofpitality, had utterly unfitted the reft of the State from co-operating in the formation of a conftitution which fhould poffefs either energy or regularity ; and that the happieft event which has ever befallen the fine country of Poland, has been a difmemberment, wept over and declaimed upon by thofe who had no experience of its neceffity, or need of its benefits. Thofe benefits have moft undoubtedly been the pacification of that unhappy kingdom, by the only means which human fancy could have devifed for accomplifhing this end, without endangering the fecurity of the other powers, namely, a fair divifion of the country among the neighbouring and rival powers, and a confequent communication of the ineftimable bleffings which their ancient fubjects enjoyed under a fyftem of peaceful government and regular police.

The

The memorable events which took place at the clofe of the 18th century, it is almoft needlefs to obferve, were the immediate confequence of an adherence to the principles of the modern fyftem of international policy. The internal ftate of France would never have alarmed the neighbouring nations in ancient times. Without anxiety, they would have feen the overthrow of all regular government, the progrefs of Jacobin contagion, and the developement of thofe popular energies which armed a people, devoted exclufively to war, with refiftlefs power to accomplifh the grand object of their demagogues, the overthrow of altars and thrones, and the eftablifhment of univerfal empire. Far from combining to refift the progrefs of the new horde, they would have fplit into factions, and affifted its deftructive courfe. No efforts to check it would have been thought of, until all refiftance was too late ; nor would thofe modern Gauls have found refiftance effectual to oppofe them from the Manlius of any capitol in Europe. That this has not been the fate of every thing refined and valuable in Europe, is owing to the degree in which the maxims of the balancing fyftem began to operate their ufual effects at the very moment when the firft changes took place in France. But, that much injury has

been

been done; that many independent ftates have been humbled; that fome powers have been overwhelmed; and that melancholy changes have been effected in the diftribution of dominion, has been owing to the unprincipled ambition of certain princes, and the taint of difaffection in the people of fome countries; which have, together, prevented the modern fyftem of external policy from being followed out, and have given to the common enemy of national independence, an advantage proportioned to the neglect of thofe found and neceffary principles.

Let us hear no more, then, of the laft century, as affording arguments againft the balance of power. That eventful period in the hiftory of mankind, has been marked by the formation of vaft fchemes, which either by their fuccefs may allure, or by their failure may warn, future ftatefmen to cling ftill clofer by thofe maxims of conduct which are neceffary to the prefervation of liberty and peace.

The remarks which have been frequently made on the knowledge of the ancients in this branch of policy are for the moft part juft. Mr HUME, fo far as I know, is the firft who diftinctly ftated this point, in an effay, replete with accurate reference, and fignal acutenefs of claffical illuftration; but mingled alfo with fome injurious perverfions of facts in more recent hiftory; and with the miftatement, in one or two

points

points of the great fyftem itfelf, which he appears to treat with difrefpect. * The celebrated
paffage in Polybius, which has fo often been
quoted, † is indeed a diftinct ftatement of one
general principle in that fyftem ; and the ora-
tions of Demofthenes contain fome difcuffions
of the moft delicate parts of the theory—difcuffions which, from the events of his times, we
may be affured were but imperfectly comprehended in thofe early ages. ‡ But the number
of difcoveries, or inventions, which have been
fuddenly made in any branch of knowledge, is
fmall indeed. All the more important fteps in
the progrefs of the human mind, may rather be
termed improvements, than inventions : they are
refinements upon methods formerly known—
generalizations of ideas previoufly conceived.
By how many fmall and flowly following fteps
was the true nature of the planetary motions
brought to light? By how many infenfible gra-
dations did that theory receive its explanation,
from the great law of gravitation, which, conftantly and univerfally acting, keeps each body
in its place, and preferves the arrangement of
the whole fyftem? In like manner has that
theory of political expediency been gradually
unfolded,

---

* Effay on the Balance of Power.
† Polyb. lib. i. cap. 83.
‡ Particularly the famous fpeech for the Megalopoli-
tans ;—*paffim.*

unfolded, and its parts refined, which regulates
the mutual actions of the contiguous nations of
Europe; subjects each to the influence of others,
however remote ; connects all together by a
common principle ; regulates the motions of the
whole; and maintains the order of the great
complicated fystem. As the newly difcovered
planets are found to obey the fame law that
keeps the reft in their orbits : fo, the powers
which frequently arife in the European world
immediately fall into their places, and conform
to the fame principles that fix the pofitions
and direct the movements of the ancient ftates.
And as, even in this enlightened age, we have
not yet fucceeded in difcovering the whole extent of the planetary law, or in reducing certain
apparent irregularities of the fyftem to the common principles : fo, in thefe days of political
improvement, we have not attained the utmoft
refinements of international policy ; and have
ftill to lament the many irregularities which
continue to difturb the arrangement of the European commonwealth.

It is not, then, in the mere plan of forming
offenfive or defenfive alliances ; or in the principle of attacking a neighbour, in order to
weaken his power, before he has betrayed hoftile views ; or in the policy of defending a rival, in order to ftay, in proper time, the progrefs

grefs of a common enemy—it is not in thefe
fimple maxims that the modern fyftem confifts. Thofe are, indeed, the elements, the
great and leading parts of the theory; they are
its moft prominent features ; they are maxims
dictated by the plaineft and coarfeft views of
political expediency : But they do not form
the whole fyftem ; nor does the knowledge of
them (for it cannot be pretended that ancient
ftates were in poffeffion of any thing beyond
the fpeculative knowledge of them) comprehend an acquaintance with the profounder and
more fubtile parts of modern policy. The
grand and diftinguifhing feature of the balancing theory, is the fyftematic form to which it
reduces thofe plain and obvious principles of
national conduct ; the perpetual attention to
foreign affairs which it inculcates ; the conftant watchfulnefs over every motion in all
parts of the fyftem, which it prefcribes ; the
fubjection in which it places all national paffions and antipathies to the fine and delicate
views of remote expediency ; the unceafing
care which it dictates of nations moft remotely
fituated, and apparently unconnected with ourfelves ; the general union which it has effected, of all the European powers in one connected fyftem—obeying certain laws, and actuated
in general by a common principle ; in fine, as

a

a confequence of the whole, the right of mutual infpection, now univerfally recognifed a-
mong civilized ftates, in the rights of public
envoys and refidents. This is the balancing
theory. It was as much unknown to Athens
and Rome, as the Keplerian or Newtonian laws
were concealed from Plato and Cicero, who
certainly knew the general effects of gravitation
upon terreftrial bodies. It has arifen, in the
progrefs of fcience, out of the circumftances of
modern Europe; the greater extent and nearer
equality of the contiguous ftates ; the more
conftant intercourfe of the different nations
with each other.

We have been told by hiftorians, * that
the principle of the balance of power, was a
difcovery of the fifteenth century, made by the
Italian politicians, in confequence of the invafion of Charles VIII. Againft fuch ftatements
as this, it is perfectly fair to adduce the arguments of Mr Hume and others, who have
traced, in ancient times, much more refined
notions of policy, than any that dictated the
Italian defenfive league. It was, in truth, not
to any fuch fingle event, that the balancing
fyftem owed either its origin, or its refinement ;
but to the progrefs of fociety, which placed
the

---

* Robertfon's Charles V. vol. I.

the whole ftates of Europe in the fame relative
fituation in which the States of Italy were at
that period ; and taught them not to wait for
an actual invafion ; but to fee a Charles at all
times in every prince or commonwealth that
fhould manifeft the leaft defire of change.

The circumftances of the European ftates
have been fingularly favourable to the developement of thofe principles of eafy and conftant union, of which I formerly defcribed the
tendency to promote national intercourfe *,
and to render Europe a united whole within
itfelf, almoft feparated from the reft of the
world—a great federacy, acknowledging, indeed, no common chief ; but united by certain common principles, and obeying one fyftem of international law.

It is from thefe natural fources, through
this gradual progrefs, and not fuddenly from
any accidental occurrences in the fifteenth century, or from the cabinets of particular ftatefmen, that we muft deduce the refined fyftem
of interference, which has regulated, for fo
long a time, the councils of Europe in foreign
affairs : and we are to confider the union of
the Italian ftates againft the invafion of Charles,
merely as a fymptom of the fame progreffive
improvement,

---
* Book II. Sect. III.

improvement, which has fince taken place in the other parts of Europe.

The queftion, of the propriety of a nation interfering with thofe concerns of its neighbours, which have only a remote connexion with its own interefts, may be ftated in two different forms ;—either as a general queftion applicable to any ftate, or in its particular reference to the fituation of a nation placed in certain circumftances. Thus, many politicians, who have no hefitation in recommending the balancing fyftem to fuch powers as Auftria and Pruffia, placed in the heart of Europe, and furrounded by many other ftates of various complexions and magnitudes, are yet of opinion, that the fituation of Britain is very different ; that fhe is, by nature, infulated from the reft of Europe ; that fhe can defend herfelf againft any invafion, by means of her natural barrier and internal refources ; and that fhe ought not to facrifice the improvement of thofe refources, and the means of maintaining peace, to the vain wifh of holding the European balance, and embroiling herfelf in the ftormy politics of foreign ftates. To enter fully into the difcuffion of this great national queftion, would carry me much beyond my neceffary limits : But I cannot avoid remarking, that, fo long as Great Britain is engaged

in

in a commercial intercourfe with other nations; fo long as her infular fituation only
ferves to promote and extend thofe commercial
relations; fo long as other ftates poffefs a large
portion of fea coaft, engage in a wide commercial circle, and are acquiring a navy of formidable power; fo long as Britain interferes with
them in other quarters of the globe, where
her dominions are the moft valuable and extenfive; fo long, in a word, as fhe ftudioufly
affects the colonial fyftem of policy;—it is an
abufe of language to talk of her being feparated from the continent of Europe by the
ftraights of Dover. The tranfport of an army
by fea, is often more eafy than the march over
a confiderable tract of land. The fate of a
naval engagement is generally more quick, decifive, and dependent upon fortune, than the
fiege of barrier towns, or the forcing of moun-
tainous paffes; and the elements may, by retaining the Britifh fleets in Plymouth or Portf-
mouth, while they waft the enemy's fquadrons
from Breft or the Texel, deftroy in a moment
that bulwark to which we vainly intrufted the
national defence, and render utterly ufelefs the
whole *natural force* of the country, which, after
a change of weather, may difplay, triumph-
antly, its flags over every fea in Europe, while
the Confular legions are revelling in the plunder

der of the bank, or burning all the dock-yards in the kingdom. To fay that England may truft to her fleets, then, is to recommend a full reliance upon the chance of a fingle battle, or the event of a fea chafe; to inculcate a filly confidence in good fortune, and to counfel, that the fate of Great Britain fhould be committed to the changes of the elements, the fhifting of a wind, or the fettling of a fog. It is to her armies, that every nation, infular or continental, muft look for her fure and *natural defence*. But although it would be abfurd to recommend, that the internal refources of a country fhould be neglected, either in order to favour its naval force, or in order to commit its defence to the movements of intrigue, and the efforts of foreign policy; yet he would be an equally dangerous counfellor, who fhould advife us to neglect thofe means of preventing war, and of rendering it harmlefs when it does occur, which are only to be found in a compliance with the principles of the balancing fyftem.

When the different nations of Europe placed their whole glory in the fplendour of their warlike renown, and attended only to the improvement of their military refources, every perfon of free rank was a foldier, and devoted his life to the profeffion of arms. But, as foon as the

arts

arts of peace acquired an afcendancy, and other
fame befides that of martial deeds was fought
after, war became an object of dread, as deranging the main operations of fociety, and
expofing the national independence to unforefeen cafualties and dangers. Inftead of being
followed for its own fake, it was now only reforted to as a neceffary evil, to avoid a greater
rifk. The firft great confequence of this change
in the occupations and character of men, was
the feparation of the military from the civil
profeffions; the intrufting a fmall clafs in each
community with the defence of the reft; the
adoption of ftanding armies, by far the moft
important improvement in the art of government, with which hiftory has made us acquainted. As this great change has difarmed
war of almoft all its dangers : fo, another
change, equally important, has arifen out of
it, rendered wats much lefs frequent, and confined their influence to a fmall portion in the
centre of the Continent. The European powers
have formed a fpecies of general law, which
fuperfedes, in moft inftances, an appeal to the
fword, by rendering fuch an appeal fatal to
any power that may infringe upon the code;
by uniting the forces of the reft inevitably a-
gainft each delinquent ; by agreeing, that any
project of violating a neighbour's integrity,
                                        fhall

fhall be prevented or avenged, not according
to the refources of this neighbour, but according to the full refources of every other member of the European community; and by conftantly watching over the ftate of public affairs, even in profound peace. Such, at leaft,
would be the balancing fyftem, carried to its
full extent; and fuch is the ftate of refinement
towards which it is conftantly tending. The
divifion of labour, too, and the feparation of
the military profeffion, has been carried, by
fome of the richer nations, to a ftill greater
extent than the mere embodying of ftanding
armies. Thofe ftates, which are the moft injured by the operations of war, are alfo the
richeft in fuperfluous ftock. They have contrived a fpecies of pecuniary commutation of
war, fimilar to the commutation of military
fervice, which paved the way for the introduction of ftanding armies : they have managed
to turn off the battle from their gates, by paying lefs wealthy allies for fighting in their
caufe at a fafe diftance. The operations of
war are in this manner rendered very harmlefs, and a foundation is laid for their gradual
difufe. A few ufelefs millions, and a few ftill
more ufelefs lives are facrificed ; the arts of
peace continue to flourifh, fometimes with increafed profperity ; and the policy of prefer-
ring

ring to purchafe defeat at a diftance, rather
than victory at home—of paying allies for being vanquifhed, rather than gain the moft
fplendid triumphs on their own ground—has
been amply rewarded by the fafety, increafed
refources, and real addition of power, which
refults from an enjoyment of all the fubftantial bleffings of peace, with the only real advantages of neceffary warfare. *

I have mentioned, among the circumftances
which connect a country like Great Britain
with the politics of the Continent, the poffeffion of colonies. In fact, nothing can more
directly contribute to give any ftate an intereft
in the concerns of all its neighbours, than the
adoption of colonial policy. When a country is of moderate extent (as I before remarked), † its movements are eafily planned, and
its external policy is of a very fimple confideration. All its interefts may be perceived
at one glance ; they occupy a narrow fpace ;
are all in the fame direction ; and do not oppofe each other in different quarters. The territories, being compact and fituated in the
neighbourhood of the government, may be
eafily and promptly defended, on whichever
                                        fide

---

* Book I. Sect. I.
† Book II. Sect. II.

fide they are attacked, and however fudden the invafion may be. Offenfive operations may be carried on fingly from any point, without the danger of diverfions and reprifals in other quarters lying at a diftance and ill defended. In all thefe particulars, the fituation of a political fyftem, comprehending various and fcattered dominions, is widely different. The mother country cannot move without confidering well the pofition in which her colonies may be left. An aggreffion on a colony, in like manner, will draw the metropolis into danger. Neither, in providing for the defence of the ftate, is it fufficient, that the territories lying contiguous to the centre of the empire be placed in fecurity. The more difficult tafk remains to be performed, of fecuring the colonies—thofe points to which, in modern times, the efforts of the chief enemy are in general directed. *

We have already feen, † how much lefs adapted a colonial eftablifhment is to the operations of warfare, than a primary and independent ftate. An enemy may, by fome fudden movement, eafily make himfelf mafter of fuch a diftant part of the empire, by arranging

all

---

* Book I. Sect. I.
† Book II. Sect. I.

all his own offenfive operations in fecret, and concealing every meafure calculated to put the colonial government on its guard, until the moment that the ftorm is ready to burft. The only mode which is left of recovering this poffeffion, is an attack upon all the other parts of the enemy's dominions. But feveral cir-cumftances muft be taken into confideration, as influencing all fuch operations.

In the *firft* place, the power which has been defpoiled of its colonies by the fudden opera-tions of its neighbour, may be very inferior in refources to the aggreffor, and may find it utterly impoffible to attack him with any prof-pect of fuccefs. That power may, neverthe-lefs, be quite able to maintain its independence at home, and to fupport its place in the Eu-ropean fyftem, from the fuperior efficacy of primary government, and the advantages of a defenfive pofition. Thus, it would be ex-tremely difficult, perhaps impoffible, for France to conquer Spain by a regular invafion of the European peninfula : at all times, however, fhe has had it in her power to feize the Spanifh territories in the Weft Indies. If France had taken poffeffion of Trinidad and Spanifh St Domingo, or the Havannah, how could Spain have regained thofe valuable poffeffions by any attack upon France in Europe ?

In

In like manner, we may now (I apprehend) admit, that the conqueſt of France, by the ſingle efforts of Great Britain, is impoſſible. She has, however, generally had the ſuperiority in the colonies, both of the Eaſt and Weſt Indies : and when ſhe avails herſelf, during war, of this ſuperiority, France can never, by direct invaſion of Great Britain, hope to regain her loſt colonial poſſeſſions.

In the *ſecond* place, although the power whoſe colonies are liable to invaſion, may be a match for any one of its neighbours, and may be fully able to recover the loſt poſſeſſion by diverſion or direct attack, a combination of neighbours may be completely ruinous to its intereſts, and prevent it from attempting thoſe repriſals which might lead to a reſtitution of the conqueſts that have been made. Thus, Portugal could by no chance whatever keep any conqueſt ſhe might make from Spain in America, or from France in the Eaſt : an invaſion of her territories in Europe, would ſhake the cabinet of Liſbon, and cauſe an immediate ſurrender of the ſpoil. But, ſhould Britain unite with Portugal in Europe, to defend her againſt Spain, it is evident, that Spain might be deſpoiled of whatever colonies a ſudden movement had put into the poſſeſſion of her feeble neighbour.

For

For thefe reafons; *firft*, becaufe the ftate poffeffed of colonies may either not be a firft-rate power, and unable to ftand alone ; or may be unable to obtain reftitution by offenfive operations and reprifals, although a firft-rate power and able to ftand alone ; and, *fecondly*, becaufe a combination of rival powers may enable any ftate to extend its colonial poffeffions at the expence of a firft-rate power, which could eafily have defended or regained its colonies from any fingle enemy—it is abfolutely neceffary, that fome means fhould be reforted to for preferving diftant and expofed provinces, beyond the mere unaffifted force of the mother country. The means pointed out by the policy of modern Europe, confift in the refources of foreign policy.

If a ftate values its colonies, and is unable at all times to defend them, or to reconquer them when loft, it may, by uniting its interefts with another power placed in fimilar circumftances towards the common enemy, both immediately prevent its own lofs of territory, and in general curb the enemy's ftrength. If the colonies of Spain are feized by Britain, it would be in vain for her to contend with the force of the Englifh navy ; but fhe may call in the affiftance of France, whofe colonies and commerce are alfo expofed to the Britifh power ; whofe fituation

tuation and purfuits render her the rival of England. As the dominions of Portugal, too, lye expofed to the power of Spain, and as Portugal, for this very reafon, is an ally of Britain, Spain may make reprifals on Portugal, and by increafing, or threatening to increafe, her European territory, obtain the reftoration of her colonial dominions, from that fear of deftroying the European balance by which every European power is naturally actuated. In fact, fomething of this kind happened in the Seven-years war. The fineft fettlement in the Spanifh Weft Indies had been conquered from Spain by Britain. Spain, wholly unable to invade either the Britifh colonies or the Britifh dominions in Europe, invaded Portugal, when fhe found that even the alliance of France was infufficient to fave her diftant territories in that war, fo uniformly glorious to Great Britain. Portugal, though affifted by Britain, would probably have yielded ; but her integrity was faved by the ceffion of the Britifh conquefts in America. In like manner, the extent of the colonial conquefts made from France during the fame war, both in North America and in the Eaft and Weft Indies, and in the German war itfelf, had probably, together with the expofed ftate of Portugal, fome fhare in procuring for Spain the reftitution of her moft valuable ifland ; and tended, by diverting the force of the

Britifh

Britifh arms to thofe quarters, and preventing it from falling fo heavily upon the Spanifh colonies as it otherwife muft have done, to fave Portugal, and enable Britain to retain from the enemy whom fhe had moft defpoiled, a defireable part of the conquered territory. The conquefts made from Spain were reftored almoft as foon as they were completed. Had the victories in Canada been gained for the defence, as they were for the conqueft of a colony, their connexion with the campaigns in Germany would have furnifhed an equally appofite illuftration of our general pofition. At any rate, that conqueft was entirely of a fubordinate nature. It was undertaken for the defence of the North American colonies ; it may be reckoned almoft as much a defenfive meafure, or a meafure of reprifals, as the recapture of Gibraltar would be, or the taking of Guernfey and St Marcou. It would never have been thought of, had it not been neceffary for the prefervation of the colonies already in our poffeffion ; and it could not have been made without the aid of the campaigns in Europe. The interference of Great Britain in the affairs of the Continent, was here fubfervient to her colonial, as well as to her European interefts. America was defended, rather than conquered, in Germany. France was driven, by the fate of European campaigns, from a natural part
of

of the Britifh colonial empire, of which fhe had long kept poffeffion ; and the victories on the St Laurence would in all probability have been infufficient to transfer the poffeffion of that important territory, had France been fuccefsful in curbing the power of the King of Pruffia.

If a ftate is oppreffed by the combination or aggreffive alliance of feveral of its neighbours, nothing can be more natural, than that it fhould defend itfelf by the fame means, and feek for the means of reconquering its colonies, by making offenfive leagues againft the aggreffor with fome power, which may in its turn be expofed to a fimilar injury from the fame quarter. Thus, were a union between France and Britain to deprive Portugal of her natural ally, and to prevent her from making reprifals upon France in Europe, for the purpofe of regaining any of her colonies which France might have conquered, it would be the manifeft intereft of Portugal to feek the alliance of Spain ; and fhe, on the other hand, being expofed to a fimilar danger from the new league, would unqueftionably unite to force a reftitution of the conqueft. Auftria, too, from her European policy, would be obtained as a party to the alliance, although unconnected with the colonial interefts ; and Holland, both from colonial and European views, would certainly join the common caufe againft

a

a league, equally hoftile to all the colonial and all the European interefts of the different powers. This policy would be imperioufly dictated to Portugal and thofe other powers, by a regard for their colonies, admitting that the fingle force of each nation could refift the new confederacy at home.

But, in the *third* place, it may be for the intereft of a power poffeffing colonies, to turn its views towards foreign policy, although no immediate danger threatens any part of its own colonial dominions. If a weak neighbour is ftript of colonies, or a weak native power is defpoiled of provinces in the vicinity of your own colonial fettlements, you are not, indeed, immediately injured ; you are not even directly threatened ; but the enemy of your neighbour may attack you next ; and the conqueft of that neighbour's colony has enabled him to feize your's with refiftlefs force. To wait until the blow is levelled with this increafed force, would evidently be foolifh in the extreme : prevent the arm from acquiring fuch powers, and never truft to its ufing the new ftrength with harmlefs moderation. ' *Cui plus licet* ' *quam debet, femper plus velle quam licet.* ' This holds of the foreign policy of a ftate which has no colonial affairs to look after : but it holds doubly of one which has fuch affairs. A ftate, which has only its own defence

to

to provide for, may often truft to its internal refources, the fpirit of its fubjects, and the energy of its adminiftration, for its defence againft the increafed power that an enemy has been fuffered to accumulate. The defence of a colony or remote province is a much more difficult tafk. We have formerly feen, that fuch fettlements poffefs few of thofe refources which enable a ftate to meet new emergencies and increafed dangers with extended efforts of national ftrength, and that the keeping of the country in fubjection is always part of the difficulty attending its defence. Its fituation, then, muft be full of dangers, if the colonial power of a rival has been fuffered to acquire a fudden increafe ; or if feveral of the native ftates have been fuffered to coalefce under one government, by conqueft or otherwife ; or if fome of the other colonies have fallen a facrifice to thofe powers ; or if the colonial fyftem of a neighbouring power has been deranged, its relations to the mother country deftroyed, and an independent community formed in its place. In proportion as colonial government and refources are always lefs to be depended on than thofe of primary ftates ; and in proportion as more is left to accident and fortune and fudden movements of force or manoeuvre, in colonial warfare, than in the contefts of independent

ent ſtates : ſo ought the ſtateſman, entruſted
with the adminiſtration of colonies, to keep a
more watchful eye over the motions of all
neighbours and enemies. They have to defend a part of the empire which is naturally
feeble, and is connected with the reſt by a
fickle tenure : they ought then to ſtrengthen
and ſecure it by all thoſe ſubſidiary meaſures
ſo neceſſary to prevent any criſis from endangering the weak part. The more healthy members of the body may ſtand alone, and ſtruggle
by their native *ſtamina* againſt any unforeſeen
combination of accidents ; but the feeble
limbs need extraneous ſupport, and cannot,
without imminent danger, be expoſed to new
and critical ſituations. A body in thoſe circumſtances ought never, without abſolute neceſſity, to leave that ſtate of repoſe in which a-
lone its hopes of ſecurity lye ; and nothing but
a careful and vigilant attention to the affairs
and plans of all its neighbours, can ever prevent the neceſſity of active exertions. It muſt
not wait till the attack comes on, ſo full of
riſks and dangers ; but prevent the approach
of ſuch a criſis, by leaguing with powerful
neighbours, whoſe aſſiſtance may render the
adoption of hoſtile meaſures certainly fatal to
the enemy. It muſt conſtantly interfere in
behalf of the eſtabliſhed balance of power;
                                        muſt

muſt prevent any change whatever from taking place in any part of the ſyſtem ; and muſt not permit any neighbour to gain a dangerous increaſe of power, by ſwallowing up a weaker neighbour, leſt this change may bring on that criſis which it has ſo much reaſon to apprehend will prove fatal, and leſt the total or even partial deſtruction of this neighbour may prevent the acquiſition of his alliance and aſſiſtance againſt the common enemy.

It is almoſt unneceſſary to give examples, or to put caſes in illuſtration of theſe remarks. An acquiſition of power by Pruſſia would certainly be dangerous to the Imperial Houſe ; yet, provided that acquiſition is not made at her expence, Auſtria might probably be induced, by a ſhare of the ſpoil, as ſhe was in 1774 and 1794, to connive at a change only indirectly hoſtile to her intereſts. Although found views of policy certainly dictate the moſt vigilant attention to her rival's affairs, and the moſt unremitting care to prevent any change ; yet the effects to be apprehended from every increaſe of the Pruſſian influence, are by no means immediately ruinous to her power, or fatal to her ſafety. The vigour of her government may draw forth new reſources to meet the new dangers ; the ſpirit of her people may be rouſed, as it was in one part of the ſtate,

towards

towards Maria Therefa, by loyalty and almoft fu-
perftitious attachment to that illuftrious Houfe,
or by an extended portion of civil liberty being
wifely communicated to the mafs of the imperial
fubjects. The refources already in her poffeffion
may be economized by falutary reforms, or directed with more effect by wife changes in the
civil and military adminiftration. The ftrength
which her rival has been allowed to acquire,
may in this manner be refifted, and a ftand
may be made, until the other ftates have time
to interfere; and Britain may then be faved by
the refources of federal power, added to her
own exertions of individual force.

But if any ftate poffeffed of valuable colonies, as Great Britain, has incautioufly or ti-
midly permitted a neighbour to extend his colonial refources, or a new and independent
power to arife in the colonial fyftem; if, for
inftance, fhe has allowed France to mafter fome
of the Portuguefe fettlements; or the French
flaves or their mafters to erect in any of the
iflands an independent commonwealth, it is e-
vident that the Britifh colonies cannot be faved from ruin by any of thofe fudden exertions
which a great crifis of affairs is calculated to
call forth in primary and free ftates. A refiftance cannot be expected long enough to allow
the aid of alliance or diverfion to be called in.
In

In the one cafe, the alliance of Portugal is out
of the queftion, fince Britain did not make
a common caufe with her in the feafon of
her difficulties : at any rate, her power to affift has been either deftroyed or greatly diminifhed by the events which have happened ;
and in the cafe of a new power arifing in the
fyftem, the means of making diverfions, or
calling in the aid of alliances, are not to be obtained, for the reafons which I have formerly
explained. * It is therefore the undoubted intereft of Great Britain to prevent every increafe of power which her rivals in the colonies may attempt to obtain ; to prevent the e-
ftablifhment of any new community in that
quarter, and, in general, to maintain the aftu-
al balance of the colonies.

We have hitherto confidered the neceffity
of foreign policy to a nation poffeffed of colonies, in order to defend thofe colonies, and
prevent them from being feized by an enemy. But we have frequently had occafion to
obferve, that total conqueft is only the greateft, not the fole evil which can befal a ftate. †
Extenfive and alarming injury may be done to
a nation by unfuccefsful invafion ; and a colony

---

* Book II. Seft. II.
† Book I. Seft. I.

lony may be ruined to all intents and purpofes
by a war, which may cover the troops of the
mother country with laurels, and terminate
in the complete defence, or even in the extenfion of her colonial dominions. It is therefore
of importance to take fuch preventive meafures
as may fecure the colonies from invafion. It
will often be in the power of a ftate to avert
the war from its own fettlements, by turning
that calamity towards fome part of the enemy's dominions, or to fight two neighbours
againft each other, one of whom might have
annoyed the colonies, if unemployed. Thus,
in the fame manner that colonial territories
are highly ufeful to a ftate, by affording a
field in which war may be carried on without prejudice to the body of the nation ;
fo, the refources of foreign policy may be
called in to protect thofe colonies from the
dangers of invafion, and to turn off the attack,
or at leaft exhauft its fury in foreign contefts.
The ftates which poffefs colonial territories are
thofe which poffefs moft fuperfluous wealth,
and can beft afford to bribe or fubfidize allies.
It is for their higheft advantage fo to employ
their refources, as to fave their own territories
from invafion. Next to their European territories, their colonies call for the fame affiftance. They are indeed much more expofed
to attack from their remote pofition and in-
                                            ternal

ternal weaknefs, as well as from the wifh
which every European power has to turn the
dangers of war away from the metropolis, and
to increafe its colonial dominions. But at any
rate, a ftate pofleffed of fcattered territory
prefents more points of attack ; touches in
more parts the dominions of rivals or enemies ; and, confequently, has more need of
that policy which may enable it to avert the
dangers of actual invafion, by diverfions, alliances, and political intrigues.

We may conclude, then, that, in every
point of view, it is ftill more for the intereft
of a nation poffeffing colonies, than for the intereft of a nation compact and fituated in one
quarter of the world, to regard, with a watchful eye, every proceeding of its neighbours ;
to interfere in their concerns ; to prevent their
ufurpation ; to maintain the actual balance of
power, by checking every attempt at ufurpation or oppreffion ; to keep down the power of
rivals, by befriending the weaker ftates; and, by
acquiring a place and footing in the general
concerns of the international fyftem, to retain
the conftant power of defending all its poffeffions in the fafeft manner, and preferve that
tranquillity fo neceffary to its colonial affairs.
If the ftate in queftion is an ifland, this conclufion ftill holds ; for, whatever may be faid of

its

its foreign relations in Europe, it is not infulated in the colonies, but forms an integral part of the colonial fyftem, as much as if it were fituated in the heart of the European Continent.

Such are the general outlines of the modern fyftem, founded upon a conftant attention to the prefervation of a balance of power. The fcience which profeffes to difcufs the general principles óf this fyftem, and their particular application in detail to the actual fituation of the European powers, is, of confequence, next to jurifprudence and police, the moft important that can occupy the attention of the ftatefman. It has however been alleged, that this is an inquiry reducible to no general or fixed principles ; that it does not deferve the name of fcience ; that it depends on the caprices of a few individuals, and the variations in their views or meafures, occafioned by accidental occurrences. Mr Hume, in particular, at the very time when he recommends the drawing of our conclufions on fubjects of domeftic policy, as fine as it is poffible, adds, ' that in thefe af-
' fairs, the inferences reft on the concurrence
' of a multitude of caufes, not, as in foreign
' politics, upon accidents, and chances, and
' the caprices of a few perfons. ' * It may,
                                    however,

* Political Effays.

however, be obferved, that the very fame general arguments, fo irrefiftibly ftated by that acute
and profound writer to prove that politics may
be reduced to a fcience, † apply as well to the
foreign, as to the domeftic policy of a ftate. A
few more particular remarks on this point may
ferve to fet it in a light fufficiently ftriking ; and
to illuftrate, at the fame time, the general foundation of the ftability and expediency of the
modern fyftem.

1. All the governments of Europe have
tended uniformly, and not very flowly, towards
greater freedom and mildnefs, fince the rife of
the commercial policy of modern times, and the
general diffufion of knowledge by the art of
printing. Inftead of a collection of defpots,
actuated, in all their plans of internal and external arrangement by caprice or accident, the
fyftem of European princes is now an affemblage of deputies from the different nations,
which have intrufted them with certain powers
and commiffions for the public good. In the
execution of their truft, indeed, they are not directly accountable to any human authority ; but,
even in the ftates where no conftitutional controul is appointed to the power of the crown,
the indirect influence of a numerous and enlightened people is uniformly ftrong upon the
councils

---

† Effay III.

councils of the monarch. It is always his interest to rule by gentle and agreeable means, and to further, by every measure in his power, the prosperity of his state. This interest, though for a while it may be concealed from his eyes, or overruled by opposite passions, can never be long hidden from him; but must always, in the long-run, force itself upon his attention; and be, for the most part, the guide of his conduct. The government of the most despotic princes offers constant examples of a submission to that opinion, which can there scarcely make itself heard; and not a few instances of obedience to the voice, which, from its resistless power over divans themselves, has been emphatically called the voice of God. A check is thus provided for the violence of royal passions, and a guide or regulator for the movements of even a despot's caprice. In the free governments of modern Europe, however, the influence of public opinion is direct; the voice of the nation is acknowledged; and the will of the people is in general obeyed, the only doubt being as to the particular line of conduct which that voice and will directs.

2. As almost all princes rule by the advice of ministers, and must execute their decrees by the assistance of a great number of deputies; the connexion of those men with the people at large;

large ; their refponfibility to their country ; the
odium and perfonal danger which attaches to a
failure of any plan executed by their intervention, whether fuggefted by their councils or
not ; muft quicken their perception of every
national danger ; and embolden them to withftand, in the cabinet, any pernicious meafure
dictated by the ignorance or caprice of their
mafter. Where fo many muft thus, in fome
degree, concur in every act of the fovereign
power, and fo many are refponfible, in the eyes
of the country, for every abufe in the government, it is manifeft that the chances of wilful
mifrule, through the unprincipled caprice, or
rafhnefs, or levity, or paffions of a fingle monarch, are confiderably diminifhed ; and that
the true interefts of the country, in its relations
to foreign ftates, can only be loft fight of or
thwarted, during cafual intervals, when the minifters are utterly carelefs of popular opinion
in comparifon of their mafter's will, and the
tyrant is fo fhortfighted and fo corrupted by
his unfortunate fituation, as to defpife his beft
interefts and difregard his chief danger.

The actual refponfibility of every minifter to
the country, even in governments the moft unprincipled and defpotic ; and the fubmiffion of
the Sovereign to the will of the people, however
debafed, is proved by fo many ftriking facts of
common

common notoriety, that it is fcarcely neceffary
to ftate them in illuftration of the foregoing remarks. ' The Soldan of Egypt' (fays Mr
Hume *) ' or the emperor of Rome, might
' drive his harmlefs fubjects, like brute beafts,
' againft their fentiments and inclinations ; but
' he muft at leaft have led his Mamelukes or
' prætorian bands, like men, by their opinion.'
There is evidently fomewhat of inconfiftency
between the two parts of this propofition. For,
unlefs thofe Mamelukes and prætorian guards
were fo numerous as to command the whole
ftate, and fo feparated from the reft of the
commonwealth as to participate in no degree in
their feelings, and to be altogether unconnected
with their wrongs, it is clear, that in the long-
run they muft have been influenced by the national opinion. At any rate, although, in the
domeftic concerns of Egypt or Rome, the interefts of the two orders might be frequently
oppofed to each other, and thofe of the people
be neglected, there can be no doubt that, in the
external relations of the ftate, the two claffes
formed but one body, and the beft interefts of
the whole were the fame. The caprice of the
foldan or emperor, then, could never, for any
length of time, ftifle or difobey the voice of
thofe

---

* Effay IV. on the Principles of Government.

thofe bands whom he had to guide by their
good-will, and rule by their opinion ; that is,
by partly yielding to, and partly directing their
wifhes. In the moft defpotic governments of
the Eaft, the fury of a mob frequently obtains
a change of minifters, which is always a change
of meafures. The vizier who commands a vanquifhed army, who advifes an unprofperous war,
or concludes a difadvantageous peace, is generally bowftringed at the firft murmurs of the
mob, and his body thrown to appeafe them.
This is a facrifice made by the moft abfolute of
monarchs to the will of the moft enflaved people in the world. The power of the Grand
Signior, which lays every Muffulman proftrate
at his feet, does not extend to the enacting of
any law which might add to the taxes of the
empire. He may crufh the proudeft of his bafhaws, and fqueeze from the richeft of his officers every particle of their accumulated wealth :
he may bowftring thoufands, whom ancient
opinion and religious prejudice has taught to
believe that their lives were made for his fport :
but he dares not iffue any regular ordinance for
a fingle general impoft ; or the fame people,
who, in the ftrange contradictions of this unnatural ftate of fociety, had kiffed the axe that
was lifted againft their lives, would now raife
their

BOOK
III.
their united voice with a force powerful to fhake the innermoft receffes of the feraglio.

When Peter the Great of Ruffia wifhed to invert the order of fucceffion to the Imperial throne, from an unnatural antipathy to the Tzarowitch, whofe rights had formerly been in fome degree acknowledged, he did not think it fufficient to iffue an exprefs edict, declaring the power of the Emperor to fix upon any fucceffor that he chofe. He began, by accuftoming the minds of men to fuch an unfettled and arbitrary mode of inheritance, in cafes of private pro-perty. He publifhed a previous ordinance, ob-liging each father to bequeath his whole real property to one of his children, leaving him the choice of his heir. This fingular barbarian, notwithftanding the many vices that ftained his character, and the conftant cruelties in which his reign was fpent, had the merit of beginning the civilization of his boundlefs empire. He wifhed to raife his favage and enflaved people to the rank of men ; and the ordinance which I have mentioned, is an inftance of fubmiffion to their will, from a real or fuppofed neceffity, and from a wifh to bring about a change in their opinions. The fucceeding Tzars have ad-opted a regular mode of receiving the opinions of the moft refpectable and enlightened part of their fubjects, and of impofing a check on their

own

own authority. Upon a new and general law
being drawn up, the *ukafe* containing it is tranf- mitted to each of the *governments*, and the vice- roys may affemble the different *courts* to confi- der it. If they unanimoufly difapprove, they may prefent a *reprefentation* againft it to the fenate. The law is reconfidered, and is not obligatory on the realm, until another ordi- nance has been iffued confirming the former. *

The filly paffion for legiflation which diftin- guifhed the Emperor Jofeph II, produced ma- ny laws difagreeable to the people : and al- though the whole tenor of that weak monarch's reign demonftrates how little he was difpofed to recognize the rights of his fubjects ; yet thofe obnoxious regulations were generally abrogated almoft as foon as paffed. While he was dra- gooning the provinces of the Netherlands into a furrender of their moft facred privileges, and purpofely acting in direct oppofition to the wifhes of his conftituents in the Imperial diet, he could not obtain the acquiefcence of Auftria (where his power is abfolute by law) in a trifling and abfurd regulation prefcribing the interment of dead bodies in lime-pits : and the difcontent of that part of his empire obliged him to aban- don this idle meafure. †

3.

---

* Tooke's Ruffian Empire, vol. II. p. 395.

† Mirabeau, Monarchie Pruffienne, tom. IV. p. 472. 4to edit.

3. It muft be evident to every one, that the only reafon why the theory of international relations has been fuppofed incapable of being reduced to fixed principles, is, the apparently fmall number of men concerned in regulating the external policy of ftates. Where a great body of people are nearly interefted, and take a part in each meafure ; where their confent, advice, or acquiefcence, is neceffary to the execution of every plan, it is clear that there is always a much fmaller chance of capricious and irregular operations being carried through, than where one or two individuals only are concerned. It is a remark of Machiavel, diftinguifhed by his ufual acutenefs and profundity, that although, in matters of general difcuffion, the people are often miftaken, yet, in matters reduced to particulars, they are moft fenfible and judicious ; that the prince is much more apt to be ungrateful, both through avarice and fufpicion, than the people ; that the multitude is generally both wifer and more conftant than the prince ; and that thofe leagues or confederacies are moft to be trufted which are made with free ftates, than thofe which are made with princes. For the demonftration of thefe important and curious propofitions, both by reafoning and illuftration, I refer my readers to the
difcourfes

difcourfes of the Florentine Secretary, * more particularly the *fifty-ninth* chapter of the *firft* book, which is moft in confonance with our prefent reafonings, and contains as ftrict a demonftration of the principle, as any that we meet with in geometry, making allowance for the different nature of the evidence. † As we have feen, that in all ftates, whether free or enflaved, the regulation of public affairs is, in fome degree, influenced by public opinion, and that the moft defpotic princes are not free from its influence, either directly or through their fubordinate agents ; it may be inferred, that the principles of the Italian ftatefman are applicable, in fome meafure, to the movements of all independent communities ; and that the external, as well as internal affairs of ftates, are the more fteady, and the more reducible to certain laws, the greater the number of men is, to whofe management thofe affairs are entrufted, and the more extenfive the circle is, whofe opinion or will affects that management.

4. The relative interefts of different nations are affected by various circumftances, either unalterable,

---

* Difcorfi fopra la prima deca di T. Livio. Lib. 1. cap. 29, 47, 58, & 59.

† Cap. lix. *Di quali confederationi ò lega altri fi può più fidare, ò quella fatta con una Republica, ò di quella fatta con un principe.*

alterable, or only flowly alterable, in their relative fituation and domeftic ftate. The knowledge and comparifon of thofe circumftances,
forms the foundation of the fcience, the principles of which we are now confidering ; and
it is very evident that this knowledge muft be
of as difficult acquifition, as it is important and
practically ufeful. For, in order to have a clear
view of the foreign relations of any power, it is
neceffary to be acquainted with the circumftances, not only of that nation, but of all the
reft which compofe the European commonwealth ; to learn accurately their political ftate ;
to inveftigate their national characters and habits ; to confult minutely their ftatiftical fituation :—fo intimately is the federal power (the
puiffance federative of the foreign politicians)
blended with the internal force, and the relative pofition with the infulated ftate of any
country. The temporary circumftances of the
different powers deferve alfo to be confidered
in a practical point of view :—the court intrigues ; leading characters of the military or
political departments ; and the diftinguifhed
men in the literary world. Thefe make up, in
the great book of politics, what may be called
the chapter of accidents ; and it is a chapter
which perpetually fets all the inferences and
calculations of the other parts at defiance. Except

cept this laſt head, it is obvious that every o-
ther branch of the ſubject is general, and reducible to fixed principles: the other circumſtances
which I have enumerated are of a general and
invariable nature, or they vary ſlowly and regularly, or according to certain laws, which it is
the buſineſs of the political philoſopher to aſcer-
tain. The laſt kind of circumſtances which I
mentioned, are, indeed, more irregular, and
their diſturbing force is not denied. But, in
conſidering the effects of the former, we muſt
lay out of view thoſe deranging cauſes, as we
demonſtrate (in Dynamics) the properties of the
mechanical powers, without taking into view
the effects of friction, or the reſiſtance of the
medium in which the powers operate. In a
practical point of view, thoſe diſturbing cauſes
muſt be carefully weighed ; and to inveſtigate
them, is the buſineſs of the lawgiver, the prince
himſelf, his miniſters of ſtate, with his agents
in diplomatic affairs : in a word, of the practical politician or ſtateſman ; a character of diſtinguiſhed rank in every country, filling at once
the moſt dignified and difficult place which man
can occupy, and very little deſerving of thoſe
ill-tempered invectives which Dr SMITH has
been pleaſed to heap upon it, in a fit of peeviſh-
neſs, not unnatural to one who had ſeen how
very

BOOK
III.
very feldom this great and important character has been adequately fupported. *

That fuch difturbing caufes do exift to affect the foreign relations of every ftate, is no more an argument againft the fcience of which we are treating, than the undoubted exiftence and effects of caufes exactly fimilar in the domeftic policy of ftates is a reafon for denying (what no one now thinks of doubting) that the principles of government are reducible to a general and certain fcience. The degree of vigour inherent in any form of government—the freedom enjoyed by the people—the influence of the privileged orders upon the great engine of the ftate—all thefe are liable to be affected every moment, and are actually affected by the characters of the leaders in the different departments of the conftitution. Yet no one, fince the days of Ariftotle, has denied, that the doctrines of a monarchical, ariftocratical, and democratical government are reducible to certain general

---

* My readers will be amufed with the little piece of ill humour which this truly great man vents upon the ftatefman or politician, in the paffage here alluded to. He calls him ' an infidious and crafty animal ; ' forgetting, furely, that Cæfar, Cato, Demofthenes, Richlieu, and many others, who have made the world tremble at their names, or revere their memory, muft be ranged in this very clafs.—*Wealth of Nations*, Book iv. cap. 2.

general principles; and that the nature of government, in general, is a fubject of fcientific
inquiry.

In fact, the foreign affairs of nations are
much lefs apt to be influenced by accidental
events, than is generally imagined. The death
of a civil or military chief, who had fupported
the greatnefs of a ftate, by the vigour and wifdom of his councils, or the glory of his arms,
is feldom, if ever, a caufe of great change in
the relative importance of that country. Great
men rife in certain circumftances; they are
difciplined in particular fchools; they train up
fucceffors for themfelves; they are called forth
by certain emergencies in public affairs. This
is more particularly the cafe in great fyftems,
either civil or military—in the extenfive governments, or vaft regular armies of modern
times, all the operations of which are combined, and mutually dependent one upon another.
As thefe can only be carried on by the united
exertions of many perfons of the fame habits
and caft of talents, their fuccefs muft always
depend on the union of men whofe abilities
and experience in their arts are extenfive. If
the general or the ftatefmen falls, his place will
be filled by fome of thofe whofe talents have
affifted him in fubordinate branches of employment; and the conftant demand for merit, in a
certain department, will generally excite men
to

to apply their attention to the acquifition of
the excellence fo much wanted, and fo fplen-
didly rewarded. Great occafions draw into
public life fuch men as have long been labouring to fit themfelves for their ftation ; and new
talents, new powers, frequently fpring up in a
man's mind, when he is placed in a fituation of
preeminent difficulty and fplendour fufficient
to call them forth. The great object of every
nation fhould be, to remove every impediment
or check that may prevent fuch men from
rifing into the ftations for which their natural
or acquired faculties render them fit. Under
a free government, the reftrictions upon the
rife of real merit are much fewer than under a
defpotifm ; and the chance of preferment is extended to a much wider circle. In thofe countries, then, much lefs confequence may be attached to the exiftence, or to the lofs of a particular man. It is feldom that we meet with
Fleurys, or Turgots, or Bernftoffs, or Haffans :
But a Walpole, or a Pitt, is, happily for mankind, frequently reproduced in the courfe of
an age. Thus, the appearance of thofe illuftrious characters, in whofe hands the fates of
nations are placed, is much lefs regulated by
accident than is generally fuppofed, more efpecially in modern times and in free ftates. It
follows, that, even in that branch of foreign
policy which I have denominated the chapter of
accidents,

accidents, fome principles may be traced ; and that lefs is to be imputed to blind hazard than moft men are at firft apt to imagine. May we be allowed to hope that the time is approaching, (not rapidly, or by violent changes, but flowly and quietly, like all thofe arrangements of nature which tend to the fubftantial improvement of the fpecies), when the eftablifhment of equal rights, and rational fyftems of regular government over the whole of Europe, fhall diminifh yet farther the confequences attached to the caprices and accidental fates of individuals, and fhall reduce to complete order all the circumftances that affect the intercourfe of nations ; fo as to fubject their whole movements to certain general and invariable laws, to reduce every eccentricity of courfe, and to correct all accidental inequalities or alterations in the fyftem. *

S E C T.
I.

I have now finifhed the general obfervations that I purpofed to premife, upon the nature and firft principles of the fcience which treats of international policy.. I proceed to confider fome of the propofitions in which the doctrine of the balance of power is contained. I have, in the foregoing ftatements, infifted the more

at

---

* See the general obfervation which Mr Stewart has made upon Mr Hume's doctrine, in his very profound and elegant work on the ' *Philofophy of the Human Mind,* ' Chap. IV. fect. 8.

BOOK
III.
at large on the poſſibility of reducing the external policy of nations to certain general principles; becauſe, beſides the direct negation of
this propoſition by Mr Hume and others, it has
been very much the cuſtom of inferior politicians, and of the common run of mankind,
more particularly in Great Britain, to decry
ſuch ſpeculations as vain and illuſive; to hold
them up as objects fit only for the pedantic ſtatiſt
of Germany and Holland; and to deſcribe them
as points that ſhould be ſettled by the finical,
and too often contemptible characters, who are
generally the repreſentatives of the greateſt nations, and who have brought a ſort of ridicule
upon the very name of diplomacy. The graveſt
ſubject that can occupy the human mind (intimately connected indeed with our preſent inquiry, though not altogether of the ſame kind
with it), the *law of nations*, has been expoſed
to a ſimilar contempt. Monteſquieu himſelf,
lawyer and hiſtorian as he was, has, with his
uſual paſſion for an epigram, groſsly miſrepre-
ſented a ſubject as important and refined as
any in his own department of municipal juriſ-
prudence. He ſeriouſly explains ' the founda-
' tion of international law,' by telling us,
' that the whole ſyſtem is a ſet of obvious co-
' rollaries to a maxim in ethics—That in war
' nations ſhould do as little injury, and in peace
' as much good, to each other, as is conſiſtent
                                          ' with

' with their individual fafety. ' Without afk-
ing whether it is poffible that the author of this
witticifm fhould ever have heard of the infults
of flags, the precedence of ftates, nay, the
whole admitted caufes of juftifiable war, and
admitting that all the parts of the fyftem may
be ftrained, fo as to come under the general
propofition; we may be allowed to remark,
with great deference to fo high a name, that
fuch obfervations are extremely ufelefs and unfatisfactory; that we learn from this remark
nothing which can give the flighteft hint of the
nature of public law; that it is as inftructive
as if one ignorant of mathematics were to fay,
' the whole of this troublefome fcience con-
' fifts of obvious corollaries from a very eafy
' axiom—whatever is, is. ' In this manner
might all fcience be fimplified; and learners,
who knew what ' *corollary*' was, might be
charmed to hear, that they had but one propofition to learn and remember, and that all
the reft was ' *corollary*' deduced from it.

I truft that the remarks already ftated, will
fuffice to evince how miftaken are all fuch
views of foreign policy or international law;
that thofe fciences will appear ftrictly reducible to certain general principles, and leading
to important applications; that thofe fubjects
will be found to be highly refined and delicate,
and

and as fully deserving of minute investigation
as any within the range of the human intellect.
As we proceed, farther illustrations of these remarks will occur, to set their truth in a still
stronger point of view.

1. *Treaties* or *public pactions* are the solemn
and authentic expressions of certain agreements, which the governments of friendly or
neutral powers have entered into for their mutual advantages. In so far as refers to our present subject, they are chiefly of three kinds,
amicable, defensive, offensive and defensive. The
first are simple cessations of hostilities; the
next are agreements of mutual assistance in
case of attack from a third power; and the last
are more strict unions of interest, for the ac-
complishment of certain objects mutually beneficial. The second are seldom pure and unmingled. Many treaties bear the name of defensive, which, by secret articles, or more commonly by mutual understanding, and not un-
frequently by the express tenor of the stipula-
tions, are strictly of the third kind ; and, in
general, a paction *bona fide* defensive, has a
tendency to bring about one of the more intimate and effectual description.

The monopolizing and jealous spirit of mercantile policy, in modern times, has added to
the

the kinds of treaties juft now mentioned, a
fourth, known by the name of *commercial;* of
which the objeƈt is, to fettle a certain rate of
trade between the high contraƈting parties ; or
(what comes to the fame thing) to grant each
other certain privileges of buying and felling,
refufed to other ftates. Thefe treaties are in
every cafe abfurd ; they are meant to reftrain
that which ought in its nature to be free, and
to be regulated only by the unreftriƈted operations of private traders : they relate to fubjeƈts
in which no government ought ever to concern
itfelf : they are only tolerable when their objeƈt is the abolition of reftriƈtions formerly impofed by foolifh rulers, or gradually arifing
from the prejudices of the people.

All treaties have been expofed to the invectives and farcafms of thofe who do not duly appreciate the nature of the inftitution. They
are bits of parchment, and may be torn ; they
are made by men of peace in their clofets, and
may be violated by foldiers in the field ; they
are deeds, by which ftates affeƈt to bind themfelves, while no court of public law exifts, in
which the party failing may be compelled to
perform his part ; they are intended to check
the ambition of princes or commonwealths,
but they are to be obferved by thofe who feel
the checks, and may in a moment throw them
off.

off. ' Give me,' faid Prince Eugene, in the true fpirit of thefe reafons—' Give me,' faid the General, when he faw that his allies were flow to fulfil conventions made againft their obvious interefts, and refufing to gratify his ambition, againft their own fafety and beyond their means—' Give me a battalion of foldiers, ' they will do more than a thoufand treaties. ' If all ftates were ruled by general officers, this fentiment would indeed be accurately true. In that cafe, a corporal would be a much more important perfonage than a publicift or an ambaffador; but he would alfo be more interefting than a municipal judge or jurifconfult : for all municipal law, as well as all public law, would yield to the truncheon and the bayonet. The fame fentiment would hold good, alfo, of all fuch treaties as thofe entered into about the time of Eugene, and thofe to which he evidently alludes—treaties evidently difadvantageous to one of the contracting parties, and wholly beneficial to the others. But it happens that, in the prefent ftate of fociety, Generals receive their commiffion to act, and their orders to defift, from men ftrongly interefted in the prefervation of pacific relations; in the maintenance of the national faith ; in the exiftence of a public code, to which all parties may at all times appeal.

If,

If, by fuch declamatory arguments, it is
meant to demonftrate, that treaties will not of themfelves be fufficient to maintain peace or alliances—to preferve the independence of ftates —to infure fuccefs in war—we muft admit the pofition; for certainly no one ever imagined that an ambaffador's feal and fubfcription communicated to the fkin of a dead fheep the faculty of tranquillizing, or roufing the public mind, levying armies, gaining battles, and taking towns. One would truft more to its powers in the hands of a drummer, than of a ftatefman, to produce thofe effects. But that fuch folemn conventions as lead to treaties, fuch difcuffions as attend them in the nations contracting, fuch ratifications as finifh them, fuch ideas of pledge and form as they are uniformly fuppofed to convey—that all thofe circumftances have a moft powerful influence, cannot by any one be called in queftion, who is acquainted with the hiftory of man, or the nature of the human mind. Independent of the fpirit, indeed, with which thofe conventions are made, the mere paction is but a bit of parchment. Independent of the fpirit which extorted the Magna Charta and Habeas Corpus, thofe records of the freedom and fpirit of our anceftors would be moft unavailing to the liberties of the prefent generation. Both the one and other

other are conventional figns—legal modes of exprefling a bargain—certain folemn acts, the performance of which intimates to the world that certain intentions were perfected in the minds of the parties at the time—certain deeds, leaving a record which may refrefh the memory of the parties, and to which the party fulfilling may appeal. Neither the treaties of Weftphalia (now, unhappily, a matter of hiftory), nor the Magna Charta, can be enforced directly by the mandate of any human court, fuperior to both parties. If the circumftances which gave rife to the latter were materially altered, it would become obfolete, as the former has already become. While no material change takes place, they ftand on record before the whole world, to animate the parties contracting —to check them in their conduct on their honour and good faith—to fhew the furrounding nations what compacts have been made— and to hold up to execration thofe that break them.

The foundation of the ftability of every treaty is the mutual advantage of the parties. It is a juft remark of the Florentine Secretary, that, even after the moft unequal conteft, no peace between nations can ever be folid, by which one nation gains much more than the other. If the one gains much real good, and
the

the other only obtains fafety from total ruin,
the peace will be broken; either by the former,
as foon as her power is recruited fufficiently
to complete the work of conqueft; or by the
latter, as foon as fhe has breathed a little, and
can hope to regain her loft ground. All fuch
foolifh treaties are rather conventions of truce,
than of peace. They were one great means of
conqueft ufed by the Romans: they are rendered lefs frequent in modern times, by the
principles of the balancing fyftem.

The obfervation of Machiavel may be extended to alliances in general between nations.
Leagues, particularly thofe of a nature both
offenfive and defenfive, have generally owed
their inftability to a neceffary difunion of parties, arifing from each poffeffing views radically incompatible with thofe of the others; views,
properly fpeaking, fecondary to the main object of the convention, but more interefting
and more binding to the individual party, than
any views of the common caufe.

The remarks made above, apply to thofe
fubfidiary obligations, entered into by nations
not ftrictly concerned in the ftipulations, in
which the acceding powers guarantee the treaty or bargain to fupport the party fulfilling a-
gainft all infractions committed by the other.
Thefe are generally modified by the difpofition
of

of all parties at the time when the requifition
to perform is made to the parties guarantees.
They are the refinement of the modern fyftem
of interference.

2. The circumftances in the relative fituation of the European powers ; their proximity, their conftant intercourfe, their rivalry,
and the uniform defire that all princes have to
extend their dominions, render it abfolutely
neceffary that no one power fhould view with
indifference the domeftic affairs of the reft,
more particularly thofe affairs which have a reference to the increafe or confolidation of national refources.

For the purpofe of acquiring fuch information, the inftitution of ambaffadors has been
adopted, or of *privileged spies*, as they have
been called by witty men, with much the fame
propriety of fpeech that would mark the perfonage who fhould be pleafed to call Generals
mafter-butchers, or Judges hangmen. From the
inftitution of ambaffadors, an effential and peculiar part of the modern fyftem, have refulted
the moft important confequences—a conftant
intercourfe between the two governments ; frequent opportunities of detecting and preventing
hoftile meafures or artifices ; and ftill more frequent occafions of avoiding ruptures, by time-
ly complaint, and explanation or redrefs. The
natural

natural effects of the fyftem to which this matter has been reduced, are certainly the prevention of wars, and the fyftematizing of the grand art of pacification.

The relative influence of the national changes that happen in one part of Europe, upon the proceedings of the other parts, might be illuftrated by a variety of facts from modern hiftory. That influence feems to be wholly independent of all theory or fyftem—it is founded on natural circumftances : and I have formerly ftated feveral of thefe, particularly the hiftory of ftanding armies, and of the formation of the ftates which compofe the great national community of modern Europe. *

The right of national interference (a late refinement of this right of proportional improvement) has, like all other valuable and facred principles, been called in queftion. It has been denied, that the total overthrow of all regular government in the greateft nation of Europe ; the abolition of every falutary reftraint upon the operations of the multitude ; the erection of a ftandard to which every thing rebellious and unprincipled might repair ; the open avowal of anarchy, atheifm, and oppreffion as a public creed :—it has been denied
that

---

* Book II. Sect. III.

that the exiſtence of this grand nuiſance gave
the vicinage (to uſe Mr Burke's appoſite illuſtration) a right to interfere. Yet it is difficult
to conceive what national changes, except the
introduction of the peſtilence, could give a better right to the neighbourhood to reject all in-
tercourſe with ſo infected a maſs as France
then was. And if ſuch defenſive meaſures
were abſolutely neceſſary, it is evident that the
ſlighteſt aggreſſion on the part of this neighbour, juſtified that open war, which was ſo
loudly preſcribed by the ſlighteſt chance of its
leading to a reſtoration of order. The immenſe acquiſition of power which the French
government acquired by the revolution; the
general levy and arming that immediately took
place—would have juſtified all neighbours in
extending their reſources, upon the common
principles of the modern ſyſtem. Now, if this
increaſe of French power had taken place on
the Spaniſh, inſtead of the North ſide of the
Pyrennees; if it had been, not a ſudden augmentation of internal reſources, but an increaſe
of territory and power by conqueſt—no one
doubts the propriety of an immediate interference: nay, if this increaſe had only been in
contemplation, no one would heſitate to conſider the formation of the plan as ſufficient cauſe
for war :—So thought our forefathers at leaſt,
                                                    when

when they attacked Louis XIV. a hundred
years ago. But, what difference is there, as to
foreign ftates, whether fuch an augmentation of
power takes place at the expence of the Spanifh
branch of the Bourbons, or at the coft of the
other branch of that illuftrious houfe? whether this fudden change in the afpect of one
powerful rival neighbour is the confequence of
her foreign conquefts, or of her rapid internal
changes? whether the addition is drawn from
the pillaged provinces of Spain, or the overthrow of all the peaceful inftitutions, and the
plunder of all the wealthy orders at home?
When fuch a fudden and prodigious increafe
of refources takes place in one country, as can
only be matched by a fimilar revolution deve-
loping equal powers in the neighbouring nations, thofe neighbours are exactly in this di-
lemma ;—either they muft wade through all
manner of turbulence and danger, to the fudden poffeffion of refources fufficient to balance
this new power ; or they muft fubmit to this
new power. One mode of efcape only remains
from alternatives equally cruel : they may unite
againft this common nuifance ; they may interfere, and abate it. If France had conquered
the kingdoms of Leon and Caftile, who doubts
that Britain and Auftria might have attacked
her, though neither of them were friends of
Spain ?

BOOK
III.

Spain ? But this was not abfolutely neceffary ;
for, firft, they might have perháps faved themfelves by defenfive alliance, and the peaceable
improvement of their internal refources ; or,
fecondly, they might certainly have acquired in
Holland, or Denmark, or Spain itfelf, an extent
of territory equal to that gained by France.
But the former meafure would have been dangerous ; the latter both dangerous and unjuft.
In like manner, Britain and Auftria might have
met the crifis of their affairs, arifing from the
new and fudden acquifition of refources which
France made at the revolution. Firft, they
might have united defenfively, as ancient allies,
and worked all the while to improve their internal refources ; or, fecondly, they might have
revolutionized, and followed the French example. The firft, however, of thofe plans
would have been dangerous ; the latter, both
dangerous and unprincipled. One alternative
remained ; — a union againft the unheard-of
nuifance.

I hefitate not, then, to lay it down as a principle applicable to this extreme cafe, that,
whenever a fudden and great change takes
place in the internal ftruƈture of a ftate, dangerous in a high degree to all neighbours, they
have a right to attempt, by hoftile interference,
the reftoration of an order of things which may

be

be fafe to themfelves ; or, at leaft, to counterbalance, by active aggreffion, the new force fuddenly acquired. If a highwayman pulls out a piftol
from his bofom, fhall we wait till he loads and
prefents it, before we kill and difarm him ?
Shall we not attack him with like arms, if he
difplays fuch weapons, whether he takes them
from his own ftores, or feizes them from fome
other perfon in our fight ? * We do not attack
a neighbouring nation for plundering or conquering a third power, becaufe we wifh to a-
venge or redrefs the injury, but becaufe we
fhall be ourfelves affected by its confequences.
Shall we be lefs injured by the fame confequences, becaufe the dangerous power of doing us
mifchief is developed from receffes within, and
not forcibly fnatched from without ?

That fuch a principle as we have now been
confidering, is liable to limitations, no one will
deny: it is indeed only applicable to extreme
cafes. It would be going too far, to affert that
the right of interference is applicable to the cafe
of gradual improvement, however great, in any
nation ; nor to the cafe of that more fudden a-
melioration which national refources may receive

from

---

* The doctrine of the balance of power is deduced by
Vatell, from fimilar grounds. *Vide* Droit des Gens, Liv. iii.
chap. 3. § 44. & feqq.

from the operation of a falutary reform, or a ufeful law, or a beneficial change of rulers. I only think the right competent in cafes of fudden and great aggrandizement, fuch as that of France in 1790; and then, I maintain, that, if it endangers the fafety of the neighbouring powers, no manner of importance fhould be attached to the nature of thofe circumftances from whence the danger has originated. Indeed, it may even be fufpected, that the effential, though not always avowed principles of modern policy, would bear us out in a wider interpretation of the propofition. It would appear, that many of the alliances of ftates, formed with a view to check the growing power of a common rival, and always ending in offenfive meafures, have been formed without any pretext of violence having actually been committed by the dreaded power, or being apprehended from that quarter; and without any confideration whatever of the fource from whence this dangerous ftrength has been derived, whether from external acquifitions (the moft common cafe), or from the fudden developement of internal refources, or from the gradual increafe of national ftrength while neighbouring ftates were more flowly increafing or were lofing force. This increafe it is—this comparative ftrength, which excites the falutary jealoufy of modern councils towards neighbouring

bouring powers. The pretexts, indeed, for war, have been various ; but the caufe of fuch wars has generally been the fame. The pretext has been adopted in conformity to ancient u-fage or prejudices, or to humour the feelings of the multitude, and caufe them to take part, by working on their paffions much more pow-erfully than if the real caufe were ftated. The great maxim has generally been, ' *Obfta prin-cipiis* '—' *Venienti occurrite morbo.* ' I recom-mend it as a general watchword to all nations placed in the European community ; to thofe, more efpecially, who are neighbours of Pruffia and France ; above all, I recommend it to the greater powers of Europe, the natural guar-dians of the great commonwealth ; and to this country in particular, whofe preeminent rank among them gives her a title to interfere for others, as well as for her own immediate fafety. To her, I would addrefs a language not unknown to her children in former times— the language of the balancing fyftem :

' *Tu regere imperio populos, Romane, memento ;*
' *Hæ tibi erunt artes ; pacifque imponere morem,*
' *Parcere fubjectis, et debellare fuperbos.* '

VIRG. Æn.

3. It has been urged, as a glaring incon-fiftency in a fyftem which has for its profeffed object

object the prefervation of peace, that, according to its principles and technical language,
certain nations are denominated *natural enemies*, and others *natural allies*. A little attention
to the meaning of the propofition, in which
thefe terms are ufed, will at once demonftrate
the futility of the criticifm, and lead us to one
of the moft general and fundamental doctrines of modern international policy. It is
not meant by this phrafeology to affert, that
fome nations ought always to view each other
with fufpicion and enmity. The intention of
fuch a form of expreffion is merely to ftate a
very general, and, unfortunately, an unqueftionable fact in the hiftory of the human fpecies—
that nations placed in certain circumftances, are
uniformly found to entertain towards each other
fentiments of rivalry and animofity. The balancing fyftem prefcribes the means of difarming this bad principle in our nature of its deftructive tendency, by teaching us to confider
other nations as our natural friends, and by
making the members of each clafs unite, fo as
to act fyftematically with a view to the prefervation of national peace. A few obvious confiderations will fhow what thofe principles are,
and will comprife the more general doctrines of
the practical part of the balancing fyftem.

The circumftances which are uniformly
found to conftitute natural enmity between nations,

tions, are threefold ; *proximity* of fituation, *fimi-larity* of purfuits, and near *equality* of power. From the oppofite caufes arife the natural indifference or relative neutrality of ftates ; a reafonable *diftance*, *diverfity* of objects, and confiderable *inequality* of refources ; while natural alliance refults from the common enmity produced by a concurrence of the three caufes firft mentioned in the relations of two or more powers towards the fame third power.

But it may often happen that a ftate is involved in hoftile relations with another of which it is not the natural enemy, either from being the accidental ally of a third power primarily the enemy of this fecond ; or from being natural ally to this third power, in confequence of their common relations of enmity towards fome fourth or fifth power. Hence, indeed, arifes the intricacy, if it has any, of the balancing fyftem ; and hence the multiplied relations of each individual power with all the reft, fo that no one can be permitted to remain, for a moment, an indifferent fpectator of what is paffing in the moft remote parts of the European commonwealth. A few examples will illuftrate the foregoing propofition. Thefe illuftrations contain the theory of what is called, in practice, the European balance. The utility and application of fuch fpeculations may, like their object, be temporary and local ; the principles are of all times and

and places; they are regular, fixed, and general.

In conformity to the propofition above enun-
ciated, France is faid to be the natural enemy
of Great Britain. Thefe ftates, feparated by a
narrow channel, are of fufficient relative ftrength
to be mutually formidable ; the one, by the extent and compactnefs of her territory, and by
her large and ufeful population ; the other, by
her immenfe wealth, the defence afforded by
her infular fituation, and the myriads of her
fleets which cover the ocean. They are both
engaged in fimilar purfuits ; becaufe the circumftances of their fituation are fimilar. The
ifland, however, is more adapted to commercial
occupations, by the genius of her inhabitants,
the nature of her produce, and the extent of
her fea-coaft ; from whence has refulted a habit
of application to manufactures, navigation, and
trade, and, in confequence, fuperior fkill in the
arts, and greater extent of trading capital. The
other country, eminent alfo in thofe points of
view, is, however, fo far inferior to the ifland,
that her attention has, for above a century, been
conftantly directed to emulate fo valuable a fuperiority ; while Britain, finding herfelf deficient in direct power to fway the continental
ftates of Europe, otherwife than by intrigue and
gold, has returned France the compliment of
attempting

attempting to beat, on her own element, the natural miſtreſs of the European continent. From this reciprocal inferiority, and conſequent emulation, has ariſen that ſpirit of rivalry, which will, it is to be feared, permanently alienate from each other, the two nations moſt formed to love and eſteem each other; beſt adapted to entertain cloſe and profitable relations of commerce; and able, by their union, to ſecure the laſting peace, and ſway uncontrouled the ſceptre of the civilized world. Unhappily the natural paſſions of the people, and the ambition of their rulers, have taught both to ' bear no ' brother near the throne; ' to ſuffer no equal in trade, in arts, or in learning; and to divide, by their irreconcileable enmity, the other powers in the ſyſtem of which that enmity has become the corner ſtone.

Holland, from her proximity to Britain, her extenſive commerce, and her ſplendid reſources of national wealth, would have been our natural enemy, had France been out of the queſtion. But as Holland lay ſtill nearer to that ambitious power, with whoſe purſuits ſhe interfered at leaſt as much, not to mention the jealouſy excited by her democratic government and Calviniſtic religion, it became her intereſt to league with the enemies of her formidable neighbour. Accordingly, in all the wars of the two laſt centuries, Holland has been

found

found on the fide of England, with only two exceptions;—the impolitic conteft of Charles II. when he was in the pay of France, and the jealous enmity of Holland in the end of the American war, as anomalous in Dutch politics, as the war of Charles had been in the hiftory of Great Britain. After the peace of 1782, the breach was kept open, chiefly by the fucceffes of the republican party, until the year 1787; when, by one of the moft fkilful and fuccefsful interferences in continental affairs, which the balancing fyftem has ever accomplifhed, the Stadtholder's power was re-eftabilfhed, French influence deftroyed, and the Dutch reftored to their natural alliance with England.

The prefent alliance of the French and Batavian republics is obvioufly no anomalous cafe: it is in every refpect the refult of a conqueft, retained, as it was made, by the force of arms and the influence of factious intrigue. The day is perhaps not diftant, when even the prefent flight appearances of national independence will be thrown off, and the abforption of the United Provinces into the modern empire of the Franks, be (fhall we fay?) the laft great facrifice to the fweeping principle of ' *Arrondiffement*,' one of the moft fignal inventions of the 18th century.

Next to France, the greateft power on the continent of Europe refides in the Houfe of Auftria,

Auſtria, from the union of its hereditary dominions in Hungary, Bohemia, Auſtria, the frontier
provinces, and the late acquiſitions in Poland
and the Venetian territories, with the Imperial
crown, which confers an authority, chiefly of
indirect influence, over the princes of the empire. The hereditary loſſes of this power in
the late war, have on the whole been trifling;
but ſhe has loſt much in the power of ſwaying
the affairs of Italy, much of her influence in the
Germanic affairs, and ſtill more of relative force,
by the aſtoniſhing increaſe of France, and the
augmentation alſo of Pruſſia (her natural rival
in Germany), to one or other of whom, or their
dependants, has accrued every thing loſt by Auſtria. After all, the Auſtrian power is great
and formidable. It would be the greateſt and
moſt formidable in Europe, were its extenſive
territories ſomewhat more compact, ſo as to derive full advantage from their central poſition;
were it to acquire a ſmall addition of ſea-coaſt
in the Adriatic, ſo as to have eaſier vent for its
numerous and coſtly products in the foreign
markets; were its vaſt reſources called forth
and wielded by a better formed government, or
a wiſer race of ſtateſmen, ſo as to take every advantage of the fineſt climates, richeſt mountains,
moſt fertile valleys, and greateſt variety of hardy
ſubjects; and, more eſpecially, were its armies,
the

the firſt in the world, organized upon a better
plan, ſo as to place at their head younger leaders:
Were theſe advantages (the moſt of which may
be acquired) added to its immenſe natural reſources, Auſtria might be deemed the firſt power
in Europe, and dreaded by all her neighbours
as reſiſtleſs in the ſcale.

The circumſtances which render Auſtria the
natural enemy and counterpoiſe of France, render her alſo the natural ally of Britain, and the
great continental ſupport of the Britiſh influence
in Europe. In proportion to the enmity between
thoſe leading powers, this natural union between
Britain and Auſtria has always been more or leſs
cloſe, ſince the ſeparation of the Spaniſh from
the Auſtrian branch of the houſe. It has experienced only one remarkable intermiſſion, and
that a ſlight one, during the peace-loving admi-
niſtrations of Fleury and Walpole. In the war
which ſucceeded the fall of Walpole's miniſtry,
France ſiding with the Bavarian Emperor, England naturally took the part of the Empreſs-
Queen, at that time almoſt cruſhed by the union
of her enemies. The ſingular alliance of 1756,
the *chef-d'œuvre* of Kaunitz, and, according to
the French politicians, the greateſt error France
ever committed, deranged, for a while, the natural relations of the continental powers. Britain was not thrown out of amity with Auſtria;
but

but Auftria, ceafing to be the enemy of France, ceafed alfo to be the ally of Britain. Yet ftill, it is worthy of remark, that the affiftance given by us to Pruffia during the Seven-years war, in confequence of France fiding againft Frederic II. *, was pointed, not againft Auftria or Ruffia, his two moft formidable enemies, by checking whom we could at once have faved him, but againft our natural enemy alone, to our defire of oppofing whom, Pruffia owed the aid fhe received from us.

Practical ftatefmen, as well as fpeculative writers on political fubjects, have been much divided in opinion upon the foundnefs of that policy which dictated to the French government the adoption of Kaunitz's fcheme of alliance. The moft enlightened politicians in the reigns of Louis XV. & XVI. have loudly decried that fyftem, as deftructive to the military, as well as the federal power of France: they have attributed to the treaty 1756, and the confequent military operations of France during the Seven-years war, not only the immediate

---

* Vide Hift. de la Guerre de Sept-ans, vol. I. cap. 1. where that Prince himfelf details the reafons that induced him to undertake the war. One of thefe was, the certainty of both England and France not taking the fame fide; whence, he could count on the affiftance of one of thofe powers.

mediate lofs of men and money at that crifis, all for the benefit of Auftria, without any good to the concerns of France ; but alfo the fubfequent aggrandizement of the Auftrian houfe, already too powerful, by the exhauftion of Pruffia, and the valuable acquifition of territory from Poland, the natural ally of France and fcene of French influence, whofe deftruction they have not hefitated to impute to the Auftrian fyftem. The advocates of the alliance, on the other hand, without denying the loffes experienced by France during the war, and the ftill greater evils arifing to her from the Polifh cataftrophe, have afcribed thofe confequences to the maladminiftration of French affairs in the Seven-years war, and during the whole interval between the peace of Hubertfburg and the Revolution. They have maintained, that the wifeft policy which France could poffibly have adopted, was, the fecuring of a long peace by an alliance with her natural enemy. They have argued this point upon much the fame grounds as thofe chofen by the defenders of Walpole and Fleury; and contended, that no danger whatever could have arifen to France from the alliance of 1756, if the adminiftration of her domeftic affairs had been as wife and energetic as the management of her foreign relations at that æra.

It

It appears to me (although I cannot now enter into the difcuffion), that the doctrine of the former clafs of ftatefmen, with a few limitations, is by far the foundeft. All the benefits of repofe might have been gained by France, although fhe had never entered into the defenfive treaty of 1755, or the fubfequent conventions of 1756 and 1757. The chance of France being attacked, was chimerical. By whom, but Auftria or England, could fhe poffibly be annoyed? If by the former, of courfe the defenfive treaty was abfurd: if by the latter, clearly Auftria could never affift her; fince the Britifh forces would only attack by fea, or by a littoral warfare, or in the American and Eaft Indian colonies. But Auftria was liable to attack from that power which had defpoiled her of her fineft provinces a few years before. Befides, the object of the treaty turned out to be (according to the remarks on conventions which we formerly made), not defenfive, but offenfive. France was in fact to affift Auftria with 24,000 men to recover Silefia, and humble the houfe of Brandenburg, or difmember its dominions. After the war broke out, the ftipulation was forgotten; that is, the terms were changed, as is very commonly the cafe; and, inftead of 24,000, France fent 100,000 men, to be defeated by the Britifh and Pruffian armies.

armies. How could fhe poffibly gain by fuch
an object, though completely fuccefsful in at-
taining it ? She was fighting for Auftria, conquering, without reimburfement or reward,
for her profit, and, if defeated, fharing her
loffes. *

The vicinity of Spain to France, their diftance from the reft of Europe, and the compactnefs of their territories, which renders
them, as it were, parts of one great peninfula,
might have rendered them natural enemies,
had not Holland and Britain been fituated in
much the fame predicament, with refpect to
France, on the north. Befides, the infulated
pofition of Spain, joined to her great inferiority of ftrength from political and moral caufes,
makes her naturally dependent on her powerful neighbour. But, above all, the feparation
of the Spanifh from the Imperial crown and
the Auftrian dominions, and the confequent
difputes between the courts of Vienna and
Madrid about the dominion of Italy, have
thrown Spain into the arms of the natural enemy of the houfe of Auftria. I do not enumerate, among thefe caufes, the family compact, which fo clofely united the two branches
of the houfe of Bourbon, or the blood rela-
                                        tionfhip

* Note K k.

tionſhip which was the caufe of that convention. Thoſe circumſtances may have drawn
cloſer the natural ties of alliance between
France and Spain : but, ſtill, they are to be
viewed as accidental and ſubordinate. If it
was the evident intereſt of Spain to depend on
France, and of France to rule over Spain, the
death or marriage of one of the reigning
branches, could never for a moment have prevented the union of the nations. The laſt-
will of Charles II. indeed, ſet all Europe in
arms, to break this formidable union. But
does any one imagine, that had Alberoni ſucceeded in ſtealing this document, the other
powers would have ſhut their eyes on the
ſtrides which Louis was making to obtain dominion over Europe by playing off Spain a-
gainſt Auſtria ? Or, had the combined enemies of that ambitious prince been prudent e-
nough to accept of the terms extorted by his
humiliation, and terminated the Grand Alli-
ance-war at Gertruydenberg ; can any one
ſuppoſe, that the union of the two natural allies, thus apparently broken, (for Louis' offers
went to this length), would have ſubſiſted leſs
cloſe and compact at the next criſis of European affairs ?

　　To ſuch as believe that all great events depend more on chance than principle, and de-
ſpiſe

fpife all general reafonings on the train of human affairs, I would recommend one or two obvious confiderations. Did the alliance of 1756 maintain indiffoluble the unnatural union of the two powers? Or, has the diffolution, with every cruel aggravation, of the marriage which had been intended to cement that temporary alliance, prevented peace and feeming amity from fubfifting between the murderers and the neareft blood relations of the ill-fated Antoinette? Has not one of the various means tried by Spain to regain that power over her feeble neighbour, which the Bragança revolution (1640) overthrew, confifted in always endeavouring to have a Spanifh princefs on the Portuguefe throne? And yet, has that prevented her from feconding her policy by open force, and attacking the throne which fhe had immediately before filled with her royal offspring? Or, to come ftill nearer the prefent difcuffion, was not the family compact diffolved in 1793, under circumftances of complicated infult and violence to every branch of the houfe of Bourbon, as well as of imminent danger to the moft defpotic and bigotted government in the weft of Europe? And have the ancient politics of the Spanifh cabinet in any refpect varied, in confequence of all thofe perfonal confiderations, and grand occurrences? No. After a few months

months of languid co-operation with the combined powers (from the expectation of crush-
ing the infant republic), as foon as Spain faw
that the new ftate could ftand alone againft
foreign attacks, and had fome chance of fur-
viving the revolutionary ftorms, fhe inftantly
returned to her natural policy, and refumed
her alliance with France; that is to fay, fhe
refigned all her family regards, the confequences of which had once alarmed all Europe; facrificed much of her trade; expofed
her fea-coaft to the troops and fleets of England; rifked and loft her fleets by fighting the
battles of France; and put the very exiftence
of her weak-handed government to the fevereft
trial, by a free intercourfe with republicans
and regicides—by acknowledging and receiving into her capital a Jacobin emiffary with his
crew. In a word, the Spanifh branch of the
Bourbon line is as clofely united, or rather as
fubmiffively dependent on the ufurper of that
throne which the fifter branch once filled, as ever
it was during the proudeft days of the French
monarchy. In return for his homage, the
haughty Sovereign of the two Indies is pleafed
to receive for his fon, from the French Chief, a
crown patched up of the Italian fpoils, taken
from the natural enemy of Spain. The fervice

vice performed, and the boon granted, are e-
qually illuftrative of our general principles.

The internal ftate of Portugal and her relative pofition to foreign powers are equally
fingular and worthy of our attention.   A petty
ftate, thinly inhabited by a lazy and uncultivat-
ed people ; governed by a fucceffion of weak
princes, and in general by minifters as ineffi-
cient; fubject to a conftitution effentially vici-
ous in church and ftate ; the ark where prieft-
craft and hierarchical tyranny have found a
fhelter amidft the flood of liberal opinion that
has fpread over the Weft of Europe ; ruined
and depopulated at home by the moft cruel
and fhortfighted policy which defpotifm and fu-
perftition combined could invent: Portugal has,
for feveral ages, been reduced to a ftate of weaknefs which muft have long ago rendered her
an eafy prey even to Spain, had not her fituation with refpect to that neighbour, and the
danger fhe thereby incurred of being fwallowed
up, and augmenting the federal influence of
France, rendered her the natural ally of Britain.

It is indeed worthy of remark, how exactly the foreign connexions of this power, always naturally dependant, have varied according to the circumftances of Auftria and Spain,

and

and their relations to France and Britain. At
the revolution, which, in 1640, feparated Portugal from Spain, and placed the Houfe of
Braganca on the throne, France was at war
with both the branches of the Houfe of Auftria, and was accordingly the firft to acknowledge the independance of Portugal, whom
fhe defended during the firft twenty years of
the war of the *Acclamaçion*. When France and
Spain were pacified by the treaty of the Pyrennees in 1660, and the latter turned her whole
force againft Portugal, the weaker power would
have fuccumbed, had not France protected her
underhand, and enabled her to make the peace
of 1667. During the fame war, the policy of
Cromwell, his enmity to Spain as well as his
alliance with France, induced him alfo to fide
with Portugal; and he obtained the treaty of
1654, the moft advantageous treaty of commerce that England ever concluded. This,
however, was the only time that Europe ever
faw the phænomenon of Portugal in alliance
with both France and England. The protec-
tor's treaty raifed Colbert's mercantile jealoufy.
This was increafed by the marriage of Charles
II. with the Infanta of Spain; and the acceffion
of Philip V. to the Spanifh throne, by uniting
Spain to France, and oppofing her to Auftria,
fixed Portugal as our natural ally, and determined

BOOK III. mined alfo her alliance with the Imperial
Houfe. In 1703, fhe joined in the grand alliance, and granted to Britain what has been
thought by many an advantageous treaty of
commerce, and was certainly confidered as fuch
at the time by both parties. * In this firm
union fhe has ever fince continued, and has
been repeatedly fupported by Britain in her
difficulties—probably faved from entire ruin,
particularly in the Grand Alliance war, the war
1762, and the late conteft. The events of
the laft of thefe wars have undoubtedly affected the balance of Europe; and Portugal
has been peculiarly expofed to the power and
to the influence of the New Republic aided
by its natural ally. How long fhe may be
fuffered to continue, even in a ftate of nominal
independance; how long her great ally may
be able to fupport and protect her; how long
her rulers may be pleafed to ftruggle againft
every difadvantage natural as well as political
on this fide of the Atlantic, whilft the fair and
extenfive dominions of South America lye open
to their occupancy; it is not within my province (although it were in my power) to inquire.

I might now proceed to trace the relations
between the Italian ftates and the Tranfalpine
powers

* Note L l,

powers to the right and left of the Rhine ; between the Porte and Ruſſia, or the Porte and
Britain or France : the connexions between the
three powers ſurrounding the ancient and diſ-
membered kingdom of Poland ; the mutual relations of the Northern Crowns. All theſe juntos
of ſtates form ſeparate aſſemblages, of particular
intereſts ; ſmaller ſyſtems, influenced internally
by the ſame principles, and connected by the
ſame law with the general maſs of the European
community. I have, however, gone through
the chief points in the mutual relations of
the great powers poſſeſſing American and Eaſt
Indian colonies. The mutual relations of thoſe
ſecondary ſtates which form the different colonial ſyſtems, depend upon ſimilar principles, and
are regulated in the ſame manner. It would be
needleſs to give any particular example of thoſe
relations at preſent : In the next Section we ſhall
meet with abundance.

In the mean time, I truſt it will be admitted, that enough has been ſaid to ſhew, that, in
practice, as well as from theoretical conſider-
ations, this important ſubject is capable of being
reduced to ſyſtematic arrangement, and to fixed,
general principles. I have now only to conclude this general ſketch, with repeating, in a
form ſomewhat different, the propoſition which
at the outſet I propoſed to demonſtrate.

It

It appears that, by the modern fyftem of foreign policy, the fate of nations has been rendered more certain; and the influence of chance, of the fortune of war, of the caprices of individuals upon the general affairs of men, has been greatly diminifhed. Nations are no longer of tranfient or durable exiftence in proportion to their internal refources, but in proportion to the place which they occupy in a vaft and regular fyftem; where the moft powerful ftates are, for their own fakes, conftantly watching over the fafety of the moft infignificant. A flourifhing commonwealth is not liable to lofe its independence or its profperity by the fate of one battle. Many battles muft be loft; many changes muft concur; the whole fyftem muft be deranged, before fuch a cataftrophe can happen. The appearance of an Epaminondas can no longer raife a petty ftate to power and influence over its neighbours, fuddenly to be loft, with the great man's life, by fome unforefeen victory at Leuctra. In the progrefs of freedom, knowledge, and national intercourfe, this great change has been happily effected by flow degrees; it is a change which immediately realizes the advantages that every former change has gained to mankind; a ftep in his progrefs, which fecures the advancement made during all his previous career; and contributes, perhaps more

than

than any other revolution that has been brought about fince the invention of written language, to the improvement and magnificence of the fpecies.

Let ftatefmen, then, reflect on thefe things; and, in the prefent awful crifis of affairs, let them often ponder upon the principles which fhould direct their public conduct. Without neglecting the increafe of their internal refources, by wife regulations, and gradual improvements of the civil and military conftitution of the countries entrufted to their care, let them conftantly look *from* home, and remember, that each ftate, more efpecially if poffeffed of colonial territories, forms a part of the general fyftem, liable to be affected by every derangement which it may experience; and, of neceffity, obliged to truft for its fafety, and for the maintenance of its colonial power, to a concurrence of other caufes befides thofe which domeftic policy can controul. ' *Non arma neque thefauri regni præfidia funt, verum amici : quos neque armis cogere, neque auro parare queas; officio et fide pariuntur.* ' Sal. Jugurth. *

---

* Note M m.

S E C-

SECTION II.

OF THE RELATIVE INTERESTS OF THE DIFFERENT EU-
ROPEAN POWERS AS WELL IN THEIR COLONIES AS
IN OTHER QUARTERS ON ACCOUNT OF THEIR COLO-
NIAL RELATIONS.

BOOK
III.

HAVING, in the foregoing Section, laid
down, at great length, the general principles
which ought to regulate the international policy of ftates, with refpect both to their primary
and their colonial circumftances, the following
Inquiry will embrace chiefly the leading points
in the application of the principles to the actual
ftate of the European colonies in the Weft, and
to their connexion with the other parts of the
world. It will confift rather of an exemplifi-
cation of our general views, than a full and
minute detail of all the circumftances that influence the mutual relations of the different
powers in confequence of their colonial interefts. I fhall begin with the circumftances
which are proper to the actual pofition of affairs in the colonial fyftem—and fhall then difcufs the interefts of the European powers in a
colonial

colonial point of view, with regard to certain S E C T.
changes which may happen in European af- II.
fairs.

PART I.

OF THE INTERCOLONIAL RELATIONS OF THE EUROPEAN
POWERS, AS INFLUENCED BY THE POSITION OF AF-
FAIRS IN AMERICA.

FROM attending to the deductions contained
in the Third Section of the First Book, and to
thofe contained in the Second Book, feveral
practical inferences muft already have forced
themfelves upon the reader.

In the *firft* place—I endeavoured to fhew,
that, from the natural fituation of Holland in
Europe, her colonies are of infinite importance
to her profperity, of much more importance
than thofe of any other European power; that,
from the prefent ftate of things in the Spanifh
and Scandinavian peninfulas, the diftant fettlements of the nations inhabiting thofe vaft tracts
of various territory, are an object of very fubordinate importance; that to both France and
Britain their colonies are of great importance,
of

BOOK
III.
of an importance every day increafing; but.
that, in almoft every point of view, the colonial
trade and agriculture are of much more importance to the wealth and power of France, than
to the wealth and power of her natural rival.
In judging concerning the probable conduct of any nation in a given combination of
circumftances, it is chiefly, and in a government perfectly free it would be almoft folely,
neceffary * to inquire, what is the line of conduct recommended by the obvious interefts of
the ftate. Sometimes, however, more efpecially in countries fubject to a defpotic government and far behind their neighbours in political improvement, a lafting prejudice may
affect the tone of public meafures, and a uniformly erroneous fyftem of policy may be long
perfevered in, until it has become interwoven
with the character and fixed fundamental principles of the national councils. Sometimes,
though more rarely, even in the freeft ftates, a
popular prejudice derived from accidental occurrences or from the ignorance and falfe
views of lefs enlightened times, may retain the
public councils in a courfe of great and obvious
error. If I might be fo bold as to hint at fuch
an example, I fhould not fcruple to give the
Britifh

---

* Book III. Sect. I.

Britifh prejudice and confequent political ftruggles in favour of the rock of Gibraltar, as an
inftance of falfe policy perfifted in by a wife
government, from deference to the loud voice
of a people remarkable as well for high fpirit as
for good fenfe, until it has become a point of
national honour, and has for this reafon acquired a real and folid importance in the mutual relations of Britain and Spain. Inftances
of uniform and fatal prejudice in the political
fyftems of abfolute governments, are to be
found in a melancholy variety and number;
moft frequently in the domeftic policy of thofe
ftates, and fometimes in that branch of their
domeftic policy which forms the fubject of this
Inquiry. A very obvious example is furnifhed
by the colonial hiftory of Spain and Portugal.
The large fums uniformly received from South
America by the cabinets of Lifbon and Madrid,
have ftrongly attracted the attention of all the
rulers of both countries to colonial affairs, and
have given the poffeffion of America a falfe importance in the eyes both of the monarchs and
of the people. Many years will in all probability elapfe before thofe nations fhall have brought
themfelves to admit even the idea of their exiftence feparated from their rich colonial fettlements; and it is not unlikely that the fineft
provinces of the mother countries would be facrificed

crificed by the fovereigns of the Indies, with
the full concurrence of their fubjects, in order
to preferve the diftant realms from which thofe
high-founding titles are derived.

In judging, then, concerning the probable
conduct of thefe powers in any colonial crifis,
it is not fufficient that we fhould eftimate the
real value of their American fettlements, which
is unqueftionably great ; but we muft alfo take
into the calculation, that much higher value
which they have thus acquired in the eyes of the
parent ftates, from ancient prejudice, national
fpirit, and political ignorance. We cannot, becaufe the Brazils and Peru are really of much
lefs effential importance to Portugal and Spain,
than the Weft Indian iflands are to Britain and
France, conclude, that any meafures tending to
endanger their colonies, would be more readily
purfued by the courts of Madrid and Lifbon,
than by thofe of London and Verfailles. A crifis
which fhould end in the univerfal feparation of
the colonies, though it would certainly injure the
profperity of thofe different powers in very unequal proportions, would moft probably be e-
qually dreaded by all; and the meafures fuggefted with a view to prevent fuch a crifis, would
be as readily adopted by thofe ftates to whofe
prejudices they appealed for their fupport, as by
thofe whofe real and folid views of policy all concurred in the recommendation.

                                        In

In comparing the fituation of Britain with that of France, we find the prepoffeffion in favour of colonial eftablifhments equally ftrong, but much better founded in the former than in the latter country, inafmuch as the difmemberment of her empire would be much more fatal to her wealth and power. We may therefore conclude, that France will be the laft power in Europe to relinquifh the plans of colonial policy ; that fhe will conftantly and feduloufly avoid all meafures which have a plain tendency to deftroy her colonial fyftem ; and that, unlefs fuch infane councils as thofe of the revolutionary times fhall again fway her public affairs (a cataftrophe not to be reckoned upon), fhe will never think of gratifying her ancient fpirit of rivalry or animofity against Britain, by purfuing fuch fteps as muft far more irreparably injure herfelf than her neighbour. It is furely the plain intereft of France, and confiftent with her prejudices as well as her intereft, to maintain that ftate of things which renders her territorial fuperiority over Britain as great as poffible, and brings her wealth and maritime refources as nearly as poffible on a level with thofe of her powerful and opulent rival. To abandon her colonies, becaufe by fo foolifh and cruel a ftep fhe may ftrip Great Britain of her fettlements alfo,

would

would be as ridiculous a piece of national fpite,
and as obvioufly ruinous, as if Britain, in order to diminifh the territory of France, were
to make a treaty, giving up to fome third
power all her dominions except the Ifle of
Wight, provided France gave up to fome o-
ther power an equal number of fquare miles.
It would be a fort of policy fimilar to that
which fhould incline France to fet her whole
fleet againft the fleet of Britain, with orders
to engage defperately, fo that fhip for fhip
might be funk or burnt. Such conduct in a
nation is exactly analogous to thofe eccentric
actions which mark the deranged moments of
individuals. And as no one in trade, or in faction, or in private communication, fquares his
behaviour by the expectation that his neighbours will act like madmen (however much
he may lay his account with experiencing their
faithleffnefs and cunning), fo, no ftate needs
ever purfue meafures framed with a view to
counteract fchemes which can refult from nothing but national infanity in a rival or enemy,
however much all ftates ought to act as if
their neighbours were influenced folely by regard to their private interefts. It will therefore be always a fufficient guarantee to Britain
againft any line of policy of which fhe may
dread the adoption on the part of France, if it
can be fhown that fuch a line of policy will be
                                        more

more hurtful to France than to her. We fhall
even have a fufficient fecurity, in common cafes, againſt any meaſures which are proved to
be equally detrimental to the two powers.
Such guarantees, in fact, are the beſt that we
can poſſibly expect to obtain. Wherefore, if
it has been ſhown that any ſyſtem of colonial
policy would bring about the ſeparation of the
French ſettlements, we have the moſt complete
fecurity againſt its adoption. We need only
dread thoſe ſchemes, which, whilſt they do not
materially injure our rival, are ſeriouſly detrimental to our own influence or wealth. But
fince meaſures of this defcription, for fimilar
reaſons, may always be expected, they ought
conſtantly to be guarded againſt, as if they
were hanging over our heads, and were actually in a train of preparation.

In the *ſecond* place, I have endeavoured
to ſhew, * that no meaſures can be deviſed
more effectual for the deſtruction of all the
colonies, than the eſtabliſhment of negro independence in any one of them ; that, of
all the colonies, the French are moſt expoſed to danger ariſing from this quarter ; and
that the inſurrection of the Britiſh, or Spaniſh, or Dutch ſlaves, would, to an abſolute

---

* Book II. Sect. II. & III.

lute certainty, bring about their fupremacy in the fettlements where they formerly laboured in chains. It can never be fuppofed then for one moment, that, in any event, France fhall endeavour to overpower her colonial neigh-bours by the affiftance of the negroes, unlefs fhe finds her colonial affairs utterly defperate; and in that cafe, as I before remarked, it fig-nifies little what her conduct may be, as a much greater and more inevitable cataftrophe awaits all the flave colonies, from the deftruc-tion of thofe whence the French fhall have been expelled.

We cannot therefore admit the fairnefs of any view of the fubject, which reprefents the reftoration of tranquillity in the French iflands, whether, by a total or partial fubjection of the infurgents, as dangerous to the other colonies, from the chance that France may then invade them, and fucceed through the help of infurrec-tion. We muft be fatisfied that fuch a conqueft would inftantly bring on her own ruin in the Weft Indies; and we need not fear that fhe will ever adopt fuch expedients in order to humble her enemies, or increafe for a few mo-ments her own nominal power. It may indeed be faid, that in the American war, France, con-trary to her own moft obvious interefts, took the part of the North American colonies againft
Britain.

Britain.   But, befides that a repetition of fo ac-   s e c t.
knowledged a blunder is not to be fuppofed, †   II.
we may remark, that the dangers of that policy
were far lefs confiderable than thofe of the meafure which we are now fuppofing.   For, in the
firft place, the colonies of France did not lye
expofed to thofe of Britain in North America.
In the next place, the dangers to be apprehended from the growth of North America as an independent ftate, were furely very diftant and
trivial, compared with thofe inevitable calamities which the progrefs of negro rebellion muft
ever bring along with it, and of which France
has already had fo bitter a tafte.   Had the
planters of Jamaica and Barbadoes thought of
rebellion, it may be imagined that they would
have received little aid from either Holland,
France, or Spain, fo long as Surinam, St Domingo, and Cuba, were fubject to the Dutch,
French, and Spanifh governments.   Still lefs
would they have met with a favourable reception
in Amfterdam, Paris, and Madrid, had they
propofed to execute their purpofes by the aid of
their liberated flaves.   Leaft of all would their
application for affiftance have been fuccefsful,
had it been made in the prefent day, when
the maffacres of Guadaloupe and St Domingo
are frefh in the recollection of every European
                                                court,

---

† Note N n.

court, and are the perpetual theme of terror to
all whofe property or refidence lies in flave colonies. It is not therefore a thing to be taken
into the calculation, that the re-eftablifhment of
tranquillity, by whatever means, in the revolted
iflands, can affect the fecurity of the neighbouring colonies, by enabling France to purfue offenfive meafures againft them, with the affiftance either of free negro fubjects, or of negro
infurrection.

3. It has been proved, * that any meafures
which can be devifed for the reftoration of
tranquillity in the revolted iflands, however
fuccefsful, muft leave the colonial refources
of France fo exhaufted, and her power there
fo unftable, as to render the flighteft movement, even of regular warfare, moft pregnant
with dangers. Nothing, then, but abfolute neceffity can ever tempt her to facrifice a ftate of
peace, in which her only chance of exiftence
lies, for all the dangers and uncertainties of
Weft Indian warfare. Her refources, too, are
little adapted in that quarter for new efforts,
admitting that fhe fhould be fearlefs of the refult ; and it may be prefumed that the mother
country is herfelf fomewhat exhaufted by the
late conteft, expenfive and bloody in an unexampled degree. What better fecurity for pacific

---

* Book II.   Sect. II.

fic conduct can any ftates poffibly have, than that their natural enemy or rival is in a fituation of weaknefs and exhauftion, which muft render all attempts to conquer or plunder abortive, and in a ftate of internal confufion or half-quelled tumult, which muft render every fuch aggreffion a ftep to abfolute ruin? I demand, if the poffeffion of her treafures, and armories, and dock-yards, would furnifh ftronger pledges of pacific conduct, or greater fecurity againft any effects of a rupture?

4. I have fhown * that a colony is, in all circumftances, a lefs formidable neighbour than a primary and independent community; that, of all colonies, thofe in the Weft Indies are the weakeft and leaft formidable neighbours; that they are the colonies which would be moft improved in ftrength by a feparation from the parent ftates; and that, of all the Weft Indian colonies, the French are not only the weakeft, but are the fettlements which would be moft improved in refources by being feparated, in whatever way, from the mother country. Since the relation of colonial dependence, then, is a caufe of weaknefs, its continuance is always to be favoured by each power belonging to the fyftem, and the independence of any one member of that fyftem is uniformly to be dreaded as fatal, both

to

---

* Book II. Sect. I. & II.

to the dependence of the reft, and to their fafety from hoftile aggreffion. In general, therefore, we may conclude, that it is the intereft of
every power poffeffing colonies, to league with
whatever parent ftate may be annoyed by colonial
rebellion, and to affift its colonial neighbours,
even if they fhould be its natural rivals or allies,
in crufhing all revolt, and preventing the independence of the colonial infurgents. No affiftance in troops, or treafure, or fhips, can be
thrown away, that is directed to prevent fuch a
cataftrophe. The principles of modern policy
evidently require, that every exertion fhould
be ufed to prevent a change immediately fatal
to the fecurity of the national or colonial fyftem. If a colony is lefs dangerous to the fecurity of its neighbours than a primary ftate,
the independence of that colony is an event
as much to be dreaded, and as vigoroufly to be
refifted by thofe neighbours, as the conqueft
of any of the petty powers in the European
commonwealth. The motive to refift the change
is the fame in both cafes. If France conquers
Bavaria, fhe becomes a more dangerous neighbour to Auftria and Pruffia, than France and
Bavaria were when feparate. Auftria and Pruffia, then, to prevent this, will forget their
mutual animofities, and defend Bavaria ; nay,
Pruffia will defend Bavaria, although that
power is the ally, or rather the dependant of
                                        Auftria,

Auſtria. In like manner, if a free ſtate in St Domingo is more dangerous to the Britiſh iſlands than a colonial eſtabliſhment in that iſland, Britain is called upon, if ſhe values her colonial intereſts, to aſſiſt France in preventing the riſe of ſuch a free ſtate. She thus aſſiſts her natural enemy, but ſhe does not make the ſituation of that enemy better than before : ſhe only prevents a change hurtful to both.

This inference is evidently of a very general nature ; it is applicable to all colonial ſyſtems, and to revolts of every kind. But it applies much more forcibly to the ſituation of the Weſt Indian colonies, which are more liable than any others that have ever been planted, to be affected by a change of government, and by being ſeparated from their parent ſtates ; moſt of all does it apply to the mutual relations of the French colonies and the other ſettlements, from the peculiar circumſtances which I have fully explained in the civil and political ſituation of the former. While, then, the circumſtances of thoſe iſlands preclude all poſſibility of their being dangerous as colonies after tranquillity ſhall be reſtored, the ſame circumſtances would render them moſt formidable neighbours as independent ſtates. The other powers of Europe, therefore, but more eſpecially Holland and Britain, are imperiouſly

called

called upon to affift France in all her meafures
for reftoring the colonial ftructure of her fettlements. Without abating any thing of that
national jealoufy with which thofe two powers
ought always to view their great rival—nay, in
confequence of the very principles which recommend this jealoufy in European affairs,
they ought, without any hefitation, to unite
with her to prevent all revolt and all eftablifhment of new powers in the Weft Indies, if
they value the balance of the colonial fyftem
and the poffeffion of their own colonies, incompatible with any change which fhall emancipate
the rich fettlements of the French Republic.

5. Although all fuch changes in the colonial relations of the different members which
compofe the Weft Indian fyftem, muft be dangerous to the others which remain dependent,
and muft deftroy the colonial balance, I have
endeavoured to fhow, that fome changes of this
kind would be infinitely more hazardous than
others. By tracing the probable confequences
of the negro independence in any of the iflands,
more particularly in the French fettlements,
where that calamity feems moft to be apprehended, I attempted to demonftrate, in the
Third Section of the Second Book, that the
eftablifhment of a free negro commonwealth in
any

any part of the fyftem, would be the moft dangerous event that could poffibly happen to the
other iflands, and would inevitably and fpeedily
be followed by the extirpation of all the white
colonifts—the univerfal dominion of the Africans over the Weft Indian fettlements. The
negroes, then, are the enemy moft to be dreaded in America by all Europeans; they are the
natural foes of thofe white men who are diftinguifhed from them by indelible marks in body,
and by marks almoft indelible in mind. The
hoftility has originated in every fpecies of cruelty and oppreffion on the part of the moft civilized but leaft numerous clafs ; it has been
cemented by length and variety of injuries ; it
has been occafionally inflamed by reciprocal ferocity, and barbarous revenge, on the part of
the favages ; it is rendered perpetual by all
thofe events and habits of animofity, and by
thofe effential marks of natural diftinction. With
fuch a power as the New Black Republic, no
European colony can form a league againft any
other European colony, or any other negro
ftate. The negroes are alike hoftile to all who
have been mafters of Africans ; to all who are
civilized and white. In oppofing them as enemies, after their independence has once been acknowledged, the Europeans have almoft every
difdavantage to contend with ; and all idea of
a peace with fuch men muft be chimerical—a
mere

BOOK
III.

mere truce with the wild leaders of favage
tribes, whofe numbers furround and overwhelm
the handful of their weak and polifhed enemies. If any power, then, deferves the name
of a natural enemy, it is the negro commonwealth ; a ftate with which no other power can
live in amity, or form an alliance ; a ftate e-
qually hoftile, and radically hoftile, to all its
neighbours. If any crifis can call for vigorous
meafures of prevention, it is that which may
terminate in the eftablifhment of fuch a power—
a power which, if once fuffered to breathe alone
and independent, muft overwhelm every thing
within its grafp. If the European powers value
their colonial poffeffions, it becomes them to
unite againft this tremendous enemy ; to forget
all rivalry, and join in oppofing the progrefs of
this inevitable calamity ; to interfere, at all e-
vents, and abate this unexampled nuifance. *

6. Hitherto we have only confidered the effects of the changes which we have been fuppofing to take place, upon the interefts of
the European powers, in a colonial point of
view. Some of the changes that may be imagined, can indeed affect thofe colonial interefts
alone. The extenfion of any one colony at
the expence of its weaker neighbours, and the
emancipation

---

* Book III. Sect. I. (Vol. II. p. 262.)

emancipation of any colonial eftablifhment from
its dependence on the mother country by the
efforts of the European colonifts, can only affect the power of the other parent ftates over their
colonies, by bringing about the conqueft or e-
mancipation of the other colonies. The only termination of fuch a crifis, will be the univerfal independence of the colonies, or a great extenfion of
power—the acquifition of univerfal colonial fovereignty to one or to a few of the European powers.
Of both thefe cataftrophes, I have already explained the probable confequences to the commercial relations of the ftates, formerly fupreme
over the emancipated or the conquered fettlements. * A mutual trade will ftill fubfift, in
the one cafe, nearly as before ; in the other,
modified by the colonial policy of the conquering power. But effects, widely different indeed, will attend the more formidable cataftrophe of negro fupremacy being eftablifhed
over the Weft Indian Archipelago. It is manifeft, that all commerce with thofe rich and fertile fettlements will now be at an end. All the
capital vefted in the Weft Indian trade will be
inftantly thrown out of employment, and that
which is fimilar in colonial property will of courfe
be buried for ever : all the cafh employed in colonial loans will be either loft, or fuddenly forceed
back

* Book I. Sect. I. & Sect. II. Part I.

back upon the European market : all the loſſes
of the planters will be immediately ſhared by
their European creditors and correſpondents :
all circulation of population and wealth to thoſe
parts of the world will at once be terminated :—
not to mention the leſs important conſideration
of private diſtreſs ; leſs important, only becauſe
it is of a leſs laſting nature. An univerſal earth-
quake or deluge, which ſhould at once blot out
thoſe fertile regions from the face of the phyſi-
cal globe, is not ſo much to be deprecated as
the lamentable cataſtrophe which ſhould abſorb
them in negro dominion, and deſtroy their exiſtence as a civilized quarter of the globe.

It is needleſs to add, that the total loſs of
thoſe ſettlements as colonies, or their complete
ſubjugation by any one European power, are
bleſſings to every party concerned—bleſſings
ſurely to the very Africans themſelves, compared with the annihilation of the European
name in the Charaibean Sea. Admitting, what
I have demonſtrated to be falſe, that all the
dangers are real which ſome ſpeculative men
have apprehended from the reſtoration of the
French colonial power ; admitting, what is evidently chimerical, that the aſſiſtance, ſo ſtrongly recommended to be afforded the French government in the Weſt Indies, would ſtrengthen
its hands at our own expence ; and, to put the

matter

matter in its ftrongeft light, admitting that every
aid which Britain lends to her, is an expence
and a danger embraced in order to ftrengthen
our natural enemy, ruin our whole colonial
fyftem, and eftablifh the univerfal fovereignty
of France over the Weft Indies :—what is all
this, in a political, a commercial, or a moral
point of view, but wifely and humanely choof-
ing the leaft of two evils, and giving up what
we can do without, in order to prevent a fhock,
from which, although all feelings of humanity
fhould be laid afide, it is difficult to conceive
that the mercantile refources of Great Britain
herfelf could recover ? France would, indeed,
be more affected than even Britain by fuch a
fhock; in other words, we fhould have little to fear
during our adverfity from the direct attacks of the
French government. But, befides the dangers to
be apprehended from other powers unconnected
with America, and from thofe colonial powers fo
much lefs involved in the calamity than the two
nations hitherto the arbiters of European affairs
—are there no dangers in domeftic confufion ;
no chances of ruin and revolution in commercial failure ; no evils in national bankruptcy,
which may render the political independence of
France and of Britain, little worth maintaining, and which either of thofe great ftates
would feel but little alleviated by the melancholy

choly reflection, that they were common to
both?

It is natural that the prejudice fhould be
ftrong in this country againft any clofe alliance,
and much more againft any active affiftance to
an enemy whofe power in Europe we have
had fuch reafon to dread, and of late years to
lament. However clear the reafons may appear in favour of the fyftem of policy propofed,
and however definite the line between aiding
France in the colonial fyftem, and favouring her
pretenfions to univerfal power in the European
commonwealth, it is eafy to perceive, that he
who fhall argue the queftion upon the grounds
above expofed, and recommend the practical
conclufions to which the reafonings in the laft
and in the prefent Book of this Inquiry appear
to lead, will have a great weight of popular
prejudice to combat, and a variety of powerful
declamatory topics to refift, from many refpectable quarters. It is by no means my intention to propofe any thing but the utmoft
vigilance towards our natural enemy in every
part wherein the two countries are contiguous,
and may interfere. In the colonial, as in the
European fyftem, her boundlefs and conftant
ambition may be fatal to the balance. Let us
endeavour, by every precaution which jealoufy
and political forefight can fuggeft, to keep her
influence

influence within due bounds, in that as in every
other part of her extenfive empire. But let all
thofe precautions be regulated by circumfpec-
tion, as well as prompted by alacrity, left the
meafures adopted for the purpofe of avoiding a
danger on one fide, may throw the fum of affairs
into much greater and more irreparable diforder
on the other. Let a union againft French aggreffion be cultivated with all the European powers
who can maintain the relations of amity, and
bind themfelves by the faith of treaties. But
let not the very firft principles of modern policy
be violated, by permitting the colonial power of
any European ftate, even of France herfelf, to
be annihilated, and annihilated too by the
common enemy of all Europeans.

And furely, if it is neceffary to ufe fuch arguments, popular topics may well be found in the
ftate of colonial affairs, to ftrengthen the conclufions which plainer and more valid deductions
have eftablifhed, and to convince thofe whofe
paffions muft be inflamed before they can liften
to the voice of reafon. Admitting every thing
that can be urged againft the policy of affifting
France, and thus enabling her to retain her
American dominions, do the lives and properties of thoufands of our countrymen in thofe
parts claim no regard, that we fhould for a moment entertain the idea of facrificing them to

a

BOOK a mean defire of needlefsly ruining our rivals
III. in a quarter where they cannot materially hurt
us, merely becaufe the cataftrophe will injure
ourfelves in a fomewhat fmaller degree? ' It
' is the finfulleft thing in the world, ' (fays an
author not very blameable for excefs of tender
feelings) ' to forfake or deftitute a plantation
' once in forwardnefs ; for, befides the difho-
' nour, it is the guiltinefs of the blood of many
' commiferable perfons. ' *

It is indeed no common fate to which the European fettlements in the Charaibean Sea will be
left, if their parent ftates defert them by fuffering
the French negroes to triumph in St Domingo.
It is not to the peaceable yoke of fome civilized
nation, nor the quiet transference of dominion
by treaty or conqueft, nor the miferies of long
contefted invafion by regular troops, nor the
hardfhips of blockade and famine, nor even
to the anarchy of Jacobin law. The worft of
thefe calamities, which may be dreaded from
the preponderance of France in the colonial fyftem, is nothing compared with the warfare of
the African labourers. Hordes of blood-thirfty
favages, intimately acquainted with every corner of the planter's houfe, every retreat into
which his family may be driven, every crevice
in the whole country ; mad with unnatural
rage againft all that deviates from the fable
hue

* Bacon's Effays, p. 164. edit. 1800.

hue of their own ferocious brethren ; pouring
over each fpot where European life exifts ;
fcattering on all fides, not deftruction, for
that would be mildnefs, but every exquifite
form of ingenious torment ; only ftopping,
in moments of fatiety to lay afide the fword
for the torch, and, in the intervals of mercy
alone, exchanging torture for murder; march-
ing againft the parent with the transfixed body
of his butchered infant as a ftandard ; facrificing the weaker fex to their brutal luft, amidft
the expiring bodies of hufbands and kinfmen ;
and enacting other deeds of fuch complicated
horror, that it is not permitted to the pen of
a European to defcribe or to name them—
thefe are a few features of the picture which
wretched eye-witneffes have given us of negro
warfare ; and it is to fcenes like thefe that we
fhall inevitably expofe thoufands of our countrymen, if we facrifice the fecurity of the Europeans
to gratify either a foolifh jealoufy of our rivals in
the Weft Indian commonwealth, or a ftill lefs ex-
cufeable tendernefs for the barbarians who have
unhappily been poured into the French iflands. *

With the greateft fympathy, then, for the
unmerited fufferings of the unfortunate negroes ; with unmingled deteftation of the odious traffic to which they owe all their wrongs,
and

* Edwards' Hiftory of St Domingo, chap. VII,

and the Weft Indian colonies their chief dangers; the confiftent friend of humanity may be
permitted to feel fome tendernefs for his European brethren, although they are white and
civilized, and to deprecate that inconfiftent
fpirit of canting philanthropy, which in Europe is only excited by the injuries or miferies
of the poor and the profligate, and, on the
other fide of the Atlantic, is never warmed but
towards the favage, the mulatto, and the flave.

It appears, therefore, on the one hand, that
the greateft of dangers to the Weft Indian community lies in the fuccefs of the negroes, and
that the reeftablifhment of the old fyftem in the
French iflands can alone infure the permanent
fuperiority of the Europeans, either there or in
the other colonies. Nothing but the fubdivifion
of the negroes, and their fubjection to the power
of mafters armed with abfolute authority, can
prevent them from acquiring that afcendancy
to which divided fuperiority in numbers and
ftrength naturally and invariably leads. On the
other hand, I have endeavoured to fhew that
the complete fuccefs of the French Weft Indian
policy, while it removes for the prefent all the
dangers of our fituation, can never arm the republican government with power to overthrow
the colonial balance. But, even if fuch a derangement of the fyftem was the neceffary confequence of the reftoration; we may fairly affert,

fert, that the welfare of all the European colonies, and of the parent ftates fo far as their interefts depend on colonial affairs, is intimately
connected with the fuccefs of the republican
arms, unlefs it fhall be faid, that a total extirpation, or expulfion, or fubjugation of the white
inhabitants is a lefs awful cataftrophe than the
univerfal eftablifhment of colonial fupremacy
by any one European power. The interefts of
all the whites in the Weft Indies are one and
the fame. The negroes are truly the Jacobins
of the Weft : They are the anarchifts; the ter-
rorifts; the domeftic enemy: Againft them it
becomes rival nations to combine, and hoftile
governments to coalefce. If, according to the
principles formerly detailed, † Pruffia and Auftria felt their exiftence to depend on a union
againft the republican arms in Europe, (and
who does not lament that their coalition was
not more firm and enlightened ?) a clofer alliance is imperioufly recommended to France,
and Britain, and Spain, and Holland, againft the
common enemy of civilized fociety, the de-
ftroyer of the European name in the New
World. If, according to the obvious confequences of the fame principles, as formerly deduced, all neighbouring nations are juftified in
providing for their felf-prefervation, by interfering in the internal affairs of any one member

of

† Book III. Sect. I.

BOOK
III.

of the great national community who may eftablifh a ftate of things hoftile to their domeftic
peace and independence ; by the fame rule,
would the neighbours of any large colonial eftablifhment, where the negroes fhould be fuddenly
let loofe and permitted to raife an independent
ftate, be juftified in uniting to attack both mafters and emancipated flaves, until the intolerable
nuifance was abated, and the ancient order of
things reftored. *

In the actual cafe, however, this interference is not called for. The French government of the prefent day, different from
that of 1792, is neither hoftile to the domeftic
tranquillity of the neighbouring ftates, nor to
the fecurity of their colonies, however dangerous the power of the republic may be in Europe. In the firft ftage of the revolution, it
belonged to their peace in the Weft Indies as
well as in Europe, to ftep forward and take part
with one faction againft another in the management of the domeftic affairs of France—with
the planters againft the infane councils of the
republican government in the colonies, as with
the royalifts againft the anarchical principles of
the Jacobins in the mother country. At prefent,
the powers which compofe the Weft Indian
fyftem, are only required to affift the ftrenuous
efforts of the French government in the revolted iflands, as they would be called upon in
Europe

---

* Book III. Sect. I.

Europe to aid the regular government of France, were the Jacobins once more to fpread themfelves over the country, and to threaten an immediate reftoration of the reign of terror.

Let us then at once adopt that fyftem which our common interefts clearly point out. Let us not ftartle at a found, and fhrink back from the name of a French alliance, at leaft in the Weft Indies. Let us remember, that we are in thofe parts expofed to a common enemy, whofe yoke would be incomparably more fevere than the dominion of Jacobinifm itfelf; whofe ftrength is more to be dreaded than the boafted army of England or the Grand Monarch of the feventeenth century in the plenitude of his power. And as the aggrandizement of Ruffia would drive us, however unwilling, into an alliance with France, even in Europe: fo, let us make a common caufe with her where fhe cannot endanger our fecurity, where we are threatened with a foe more terrible than Tartars and Coffacks. It is to be hoped that the French troops may themfelves fucceed in the great enterprize committed to their charge, becaufe, in that cafe, their conqueft will be more eafily retained. But if they fhall ftand in need of our affiftance, let us recollect, that in fubfidizing the colonial treafury of France, we are preferving that trade which fupplies our fleets with feamen, and pours millions into our exchequer; that the troops which may be fent to affift the government of

St

BOOK III. St Domingo are fighting the battles of our own
colonies, and defending from the ineffable horrors of negro warfare, one of the faireft portions
of the habitable globe.

PART II.

OF THE EXTERNAL RELATIONS OF THE EUROPEAN POWERS IN DIFFERENT QUARTERS AS INFLUENCED BY THEIR COLONIAL INTERESTS.

WHEN a ftate poffeffed of colonial eftablifhments is drawn into any quarrel with its neighbours, every part of its territories may become
the theatre of warlike operations, and all the
branches of the empire muft neceffarily take
part in the conteft, whatever may be the origin
of the difpute. We have already feen how
much more frequently the colonies are expofed
to the evils of warfare than the mother country,
although they are very feldom the caufe of the
rupture. * If, however, a war fhould be undertaken on account of the remote provinces, the
contiguous diftricts muft of courfe bear their
fhare of its burdens, and the mother countries
may thus, on account of their colonial interefts,
be

* Book I. Sect. I.

be engaged in war with each other, in Europe S E C T.
II. and in the colonies at the fame time. This is one of the neceffary confequences of extenfive and remote poffeffions, and forms an effential part of the very idea of a political union.

It will indeed happen, in the great majority of cafes, that the interefts of the colonies are made fubfervient to thofe of the other provinces, which are generally more extenfive, and always more valuable. Thus, while the whole empire will inevitably be plunged into an obftinate war for the advantage or honour of the metropolis, the colonies may often fuftain injuries, or receive infults, of which a flight explanation or acknowledgement will be admitted as a fufficient reparation. Accordingly, I have already * fhown how very fmall a fhare the colonial interefts have had in producing thofe contefts which conftantly recur to divide the European powers, after a fhort interval of peace recruits their forces and treafures. It does indeed almoft always happen, as I have formerly obferved, † that when any neceffity for reparation of injuries, or any change in the balance of power, is attended with a transference of dominion in confequence of a decifive war, the territories given up as indemnities obtained by right of conqueft, are taken from the colonial eftablifhments

* Book I. Sect. I.　　† Book II. Sect. II.

ments of the humbled nation, becaufe every ftate naturally wifhes to retain, firft of all, its contiguous provinces, and to make both the calamities and the effects of war fall as much as poffible on thofe remote diftricts, which, from their diftance, are too much undervalued. It would, however, be extremely erroneous to conclude from thence, that the acquifition of thofe dominions was the object of the war on the one fide, or their defence the motive of refiftance on the other. While the campaigns of Germany or Egypt may have led to no other change in the relative pofition of the belligerent powers, than the transference of fome ifland in America or fome factory in the Eaft Indies, it neither follows that the maintenance or the change of the colonial balance was the object of the war, nor that the change or the prefervation of colonial dominion is the only purpofe to which the fuccefs of the hoftile operations has been fubfervient. If the party whofe diftant territory has been defended, had not infured fuccefs by carrying on the war in every quarter, new aggreffions in the nearer parts of the empire would have been the confequence. If the ftate whofe victories, in various regions, have procured an enlargement of colonial dominion, had failed from confining the war to the colonies alone, its honour would not have been preferved

ed or raifed ; its name and influence in the fyftem, always proportioned to the total, rather
than to the partial fuccefs of a war, would not
have been extended ; it would not have thus
far diminifhed the power of a natural rival ;
and, on the next rupture, it would have wanted
all thofe means of intimidating the enemy, which
are acquired by exhibiting proofs of military
greatnefs in whatever quarter of the world.

But although the colonial interefts of a ftate
are thus fecondary and fubfervient, it will frequently happen, that the fituation of affairs in
thofe fyftems where the diftant territories are fituated, may call for a facrifice on the part of
the mother country, and a temporary fubmiffion of her own interefts to thofe of the colonies. I have already pointed out * thofe general
cafes where fuch an appeal to the principles of
modern policy is confiftent with ftrict prudence,
and have illuftrated this pofition by a reference †
to the prefent ftate of affairs in America. The
fafety of valuable poffeffions, as well as the honour of the nation, may often call for active
meafures of precaution, or of vengeance on the
fpot, altogether dictated by colonial views. The
fame views may fometimes be extended fo far
as to prefcribe the moft vigorous interference
with

---

* Book II. Introd.   † Ibid. Sect. II. Part I.

with the conduct of foreign ftatcs, if it tends
mediately to operate the deftruction of the colonial balance, and affect the fecurity of our own
poffeffions or thofe of our allies.

Thofe nations which poffefs no colonies of
any value (Sweden and Denmark for example), can never be called upon by any danger,
even by the direct violation of their colonial
property, to plunge their contiguous provinces
into a ftate of war, for the purpofe of preferving the benefits derived from fuch inconfiderable fettlements. The whole value of the territory loft by any fudden aggreffion of a neighbour, will not be fufficient to compenfate the
expence and danger of recovering the poffeffion, and revenging the infult. Yet, even thofe
colonial dominions can never be given up to
the forcible attack of an enemy, without fuch
an injury to the honour and name of the mother country, as muft diminifh her influence
at home, injure the fpirit of her people in
all future negotiations, and weaken her federal power in all future European wars. That
ceffion then of a ufelefs territory (admitting
the colonies to be in any cafe ufelefs), which
ought not to be deemed any evil in a commercial or financial point of view, fhould uniformly be refufed to forcible aggreffion ; although, after the honour of the nation is faved
by

by retaliation, and after fome equivalent is procured, it will never be wife for the government
to adjuft matters very fcrupuloufly, by nicely
comparing the revenge with the infult, or the
indemnity with the lofs fuftained.

But the name and honour of a nation cannot be immediately affected by fuch changes
as only tend indirectly to endanger the fafety
of its diftant fettlements, or ultimately to fhake
the colonial balance. Thofe ftates, therefore,
which poffefs colonies of inconfiderable value,
can never be called upon, by the principles of
found policy, to interfere in the affairs of their
European neighbours, for the purpofe of preventing the adoption of any line of conduct
only remotely dangerous to the colonial fyftem
in which they have fo trifling an intereft. Thus,
although the fupremacy of France in the Weft
Indies would be highly dangerous to every
other power poffeffed of colonial territory; and
although that fupremacy would be a very natural confequence of a compact between Britain
and France transferring to the latter Jamaica
and Barbadoes; what could be more ridiculous
than that Sweden and Denmark fhould endeavour to unite Ruffia with them in order to prevent or annul the bargain? It would clearly
be nothing more than common prudence in
Sweden and Denmark to affift France (as we
have

have already feen) in quelling the infurrection of her flaves, becaufe the danger arifing from fuccefsful negro rebellion is immediate to every white colony. It would be equally neceffary for thofe ftates to arm in all parts, and to avail themfelves of the refources of federal power, if unjuftly attacked in the colonies, becaufe their honour and name would demand this, and becaufe the certainty of retaliation in every quarter is the great check to fuch aggreffions in a fyftem which, like that of the colonies, is not properly balanced of itfelf. But if nothing fhort of war could prevent the projected change, it would never leffen the name, or ftain the honour of either Denmark or Sweden, to allow France peaceably to acquire the decided fuperiority in a quarter where their power is at any rate fo trifling, and to truft for their defence in the laft refort to their fubfequent exertions when attacked, and to the refources of foreign policy—even although in the end thofe ftruggles and alliances fhould fail to fave the colonies, or to obtain exact reparations and indemnities. Still lefs reafonable would it be for powers thus circumftanced, to hamper their European policy with colonial confiderations in matters more remotely connected with colonial interefts, fuch as thofe which I fhall immediately point out; or to fuffer the circumftances of their trifling fettle-

ments,

ments, however nearly affected, to ſtand in the
way of any amicable arrangements ſubſervient
to the proſperous management of their foreign
affairs in the great national ſyſtem. The peculiar difference between a remote and contiguous
province conſiſts in this—that whereas the latter, however trifling in itſelf, muſt at all e-
vents be retained as a part of the empire directly neceſſary to keep the whole together,
the former is disjoined from the reſt, and although a component part in every other reſpect,
yet is only indirectly ſubſervient to the exiſtence
of the whole body ; and may therefore be ſacrificed in ſuch emergencies as would otherwiſe
endanger the contiguous members of the ſyſtem. The caſe of Sweden and Denmark, with
reſpect to colonial affairs, is one in which the
trifling value of the diſtant ſettlements will always render the probable ſacrifice preferable to
the loſſes and dangers of hoſtilities undertaken
from motives of extreme precaution, and dictated by the view of preventing changes only
ultimately dangerous to the colonial balance.

But widely different is the ſituation of thoſe
powers which poſſeſs colonies of great intrinſic
value as important parts of their dominions
and rich mines of commercial wealth. In various points of view, their conduct muſt be regulated by a regard to their diſtant, as well as
to their contiguous provinces. An invaſion of
their

their colonial territory is, next to an invasion of
their European dominions, the event most to
be dreaded, even although unsuccefsful, and,
if poffible, to be averted by all the refources
of federal power. The attack, when made, is
to be repulfed and revenged, not merely from
a regard to national honour, but from a confideration of the real value of the poffeffion which
is at ftake. All the means which the cautious
and longfighted views of modern policy can fuggeft, muft be put in practice to remove every
danger that may arife in any quarter to the colonial balance ; becaufe fuch rifks, though indifferent to the name and honour of a ftate,
lead to a cataftrophe fubftantially hurtful, perhaps ruinous—the lofs of an important branch
of the national territory, the difmemberment
of the empire. To prevent changes only ultimately dangerous to the colonial fyftem, or
even to obviate the effects of arrangements that
may lead to fuch changes, the whole influence
of the mother country fhould be called forth ;
that influence which her internal refources and
her colonial poffeffions have confpired in be-
ftowing, and which will no longer be her's, even
in affairs ftrictly European, if fhe fhall be fo
blind to her beft interefts as to neglect all the
meafures neceffary for keeping her fcattered empire together.

It

It is eafy to imagine a variety of cafes, in
which changes may be effected, of the nature which I have juft now defcribed. By amicable contract between two powers naturally allied, a transference of colonial dominion may take place. Such was the compact by which France fold to Sweden the only ifland which fhe poffeffes in the Weft Indies. Had this ifland been of great importance, and had the tranfaction been reverfed, fo dangerous an increafe of colonial power to the French dominions would have called for the determined interference of the neighbouring ftates, as much as if a fimilar compact had transferred to France a part of the European continent.

By a treaty of peace, terminating either a general or a partial European warfare, a fimilar transference of colonial territory may be effected. In the one cafe, all the powers poffeffing colonies will be confulted, as having an immediate intereft both in the pacification and in the colonial fyftem. In the cafe of a partial treaty, fuch as that which confolidated the whole of St Domingo under the French dominion, it becomes the other powers to interfere, according to the principles of modern policy. * If the matters at ftake in Europe be not more important than the colonial interefts, it becomes all parties to join againft the new ftipulation,

* Book III. Sect. I.

pulation, regardlefs of the fides which they had
efpoufed in the previous part of the conteft.
If, on the other hand, as was the cafe at the
peace of Bafle, the fate of colonial affairs is of lefs
moment than the European interefts ftaked on
the conteft, the colonial powers are called upon,
by the partial treaty which has taken place, to defer their oppofition until the end of the European
difpute, and then to introduce the confideration of
the change that has happened, into the difcuffion of the general pacification ; or if the fortune
of war has unhappily confined their influence, as
has been but too much the cafe in the inftance
which we are contemplating, their colonial interefts require that they fhould defer their oppofition to a more favourable opportunity,
when their ftrength fhall be recruited, and the
eyes of the powers, whofe defertion from the
common caufe has produced all the evil, fhall
be opened to their real honour and advantage.
Such ought to be the conduct of the powers
poffeffing Weft Indian colonies, in the prefent
ftate of affairs. The great increafe of territory
which France has acquired in the iflands, is indeed rendered lefs dangerous than it otherwife
would have been by the augmentation of the Britifh dominions in the neighbourhood ; and the
change has attracted lefs attention than it ought
to have done, from the diftracted ftate of the
whole

whole French colonies in thofe parts. But as it is for the evident advantage of the other colonies, nay effential to their exiftence, that the French fettlements fhould be reduced to a ftate of order ; and as, in the event of their pacification, the vaft force of the newly acquired dominion will far more than counterbalance the increafed power of Great Britain, it certainly becomes the other powers to aid her in attempting to reftore the colonial balance, before the complete fubjugation of St Domingo and its augmented cultivation fhall have rendered it a formidable neighbour. I have already * ftated the greater probability of St Domingo becoming foon independent of the mother country, in its prefent united ftate, than in its former ftate of divifion. This circumftance, and ftill more the reftoration of Louifiana to France, forms an additional reafon for an interference, in which the United States would moft probably bear an important part. And it furely deferves fome confideration, that Spain, engaged only as a fecondary party in the great European conteft, fhould not only have paid fo great a fhare at home, but fhould have entirely furnifhed the equivalents in the Weft Indies. The fame remark applies to Holland in the Eaft : So that,

in

* Book I. Sect. III. Part IV.

BOOK
III.
in the colonies, as well as in Europe, the fame
melancholy reflection muſt ſtrike every one who
contemplates the events of the late memorable
conteſt. The great powers who began the war,
and who were the principals in it from beginning to end, received all their indemnitieś, and
equivalents, and *douceurs*, from thoſe leſſer
powers who had only an indirect concern in the
origin of the conteſt, and were dragged into it
unwillingly. The defeats, both of Auſtria and
Pruſſia, were paid for by Venice and the German
princes. The victories of France were, in Europe, recompenſed by the ſpoils of Germany and
Italy. In the colonies, Spain and Holland alone
were ſtripped of their fineſt territories, in order
to reward the ſucceſſes of the French and Britiſh arms. The time is certainly not yet arrived, in which the balance of Europe and of
the colonies can be readjuſted, and the violation of public equity repaired. Unfortunately,
the ſpoil has been ſhared by almoſt all the great
powers of Europe; and thoſe who have received an inadequate portion, will not, it is probable, be inclined to make reſtoration, until the
ſacrifice is found neceſſary, as a preliminary
to the meaſures that may be preſcribed by the
wiſh to ſtrip thoſe whoſe ſhare has been dangeroufly great.

Nor

Nor can we expect that the colonial power
of France will receive no farther augmentation
at the expence of her vaſſal allies, if her preponderance in European affairs ſhall remain as
formidable as it now is. If the other powers of
Europe ſhall continue as blind to their intereſts
as they have hitherto been, and ſhall ſuffer the
New Republic, recruited during the preſent interruption of hoſtilities, to domineer over ſo large
a portion of the continent under the name of
protecting and befriending it ; what ſecurity
is there to thoſe ſtates which retain their independence and poſſeſs valuable colonies, that
new gifts and ceſſions of colonial territory ſhall
not follow thoſe which we have been conſidering, and pave the way for the immediate acquiſition of ſupreme power ? In Europe, it may be
enough for France to ſway the continental balance, by the aſſiſtance of the ſubordinate powers whom ſhe uſes as tools, while ſhe allows
them to retain their ſeparate names and ficti-
tious independence, without running the riſk
of the internal diſunion and the oppoſition from
without, which always attend the eſtabliſhment
of unwieldy empires. She gains as much real
power as ſhe can retain over the deſtinies of the
world, by ruling Holland, and Italy, and Switzer-
land, and Spain, through the medium of their own
governments. But in order to turn the Dutch and
Spaniſh

Spanish colonies to her own use, the actual poffeffion of them muft be transferred. This is the
only way in which the advantages, whether political or mercantile, peculiar to colonial eftablifhments, can be ufurped; and we can fcarcely doubt, that the temptations held out by territories fo rich in natural and acquired refources
as thofe of Holland and Spain both in the Eaft
and Weft, will be a fufficient inducement to the
ambition and the national avarice of France to
reftore her colonial profperity in America; to
extend her influence in the Indian ocean; to
recruit her exhaufted treafury; and to revive
her commerce and her navy—all at the expence
of an ally who has more territory than fhe can
cultivate, and a vaffal who dare not murmur,
although her capital were to be facked by the
republican troops.

It is only by interfering in the immediate
concerns of France, Holland and Spain, that
Britain and Portugal can prevent a cataftrophe
fo ruinous to their interefts immediately in the
colonies, and ultimately alfo in Europe. By
fubfidizing other powers lefs directly concerned
in fuch arrangements, and by reviving that falutary jealoufy of the French power in general,
which has for fome years been lulled or terrified
into a ftate of reft, a check may be given to
fuch meafures as muft in the mean time deftroy
the

the whole balance of the colonial fyftem, and in the end complete the fupremacy of the great republiç over the European commonwealth.

The ftates which poffefs territories in the Eaft Indies, are certainly expofed to fewer dan-gers from the fide of Europe, than from the o-perations of the native powers. Yet, even from Europe, fome danger may be apprehended. The extenfion of Ruffia towards the fouth and eaft, and the feeble ftate of the princes to the north of Indoftan, feem to have filled the am-bitious mind of Katharine II. with plans for accomplifhing her darling objeɛt, the extenfion of the Ruffian commerce, by an invafion of the rich provinces that now form the great eaft-ern wing of the Britifh empire. To thofe who refleɛt upon the feeble tenure by which, at the peace of Kainardgï, the Britifh dominions in India were held, ·the bare mention of fuch a fcheme as that attributed to Katharine, will not fuggeft any contemptuous ideas. Since the con-vention with Ruffia put an end, at leaft for the prefent, to all fears from that quarter, the fortunes of the Britifh arms in the Eaft have no doubt placed our dominion in a very different fituation, by the extinɛtion of our great natural enemy in the peninfula. But ftill, many of the native powers poffefs a force, which, if united, might prove dangerous in the extreme. They all retain their jealoufy of England ;

England; and, upon half enlightened politicians, it would not be difficult for European
councils to prevail, even if their real interefts
were not (as they unqueftionably are) inimical
to the exiftence of the Britifh name in the Eaft.
From France and her allies, they have no profpect of affiftance, at leaft according to the prefent diftribution of colonial force. From the
wealthy and populous ftate on the eaftern fide
of the Bay of Bengal, they may expect the
moft cordial co-operation. The fame falutary jealoufy of Europeans, which has fteadily
prevented them from intruding into the Bur-
man territories, and dictated to the natives
a line of policy that might do honour to
more enlightened ftatefmen, would certainly
induce that prudent people to co-operate
in checking the progrefs of a nation, from
whofe increafe nothing but deftruction can a-
rife to all the Indian ftates. A Ruffian invafion, then, would be moft probably fecond-
ed by the Eaftern powers, to whom the ruin
of the Britifh interefts, though effected by
the introduction of a new European tribe,
would ftill be highly advantageous.

Befides, it fhould be remembered that Ruffia
is by no means fo far removed from thofe fcenes,
as to render the efforts of her own individual
force contemptible, or the plan of conquering
India by direct and feparate invafion, chimerical.

cal. From Aftracan to the northern frontier of Indoftan, the diftance is not greater than from St Peterfburg to thofe plains where Suwa-roff defeated one of the fineft armies in Europe ; and the affairs of government in Siberia and Kamtchatka are managed by communication with the metropolis, although the diftance is nearly twice as great as that of Calcutta from the Gulf of Finland, and the route incomparably more difficult. If the Britifh empire in the Eaft has been acquired by all manner of intrigues, rather than by force, and fupported partly by the fame means, partly by armies fent from an immenfe diftance ; will it be impoffible for Ruffia to difpute the prize, partly by the aid of thofe ftates whofe paffions and interefts confpire to alienate them from the firft great intruders, and whofe jealoufy muft now be increafed, and their union cemented, fince the defeat of their chief ally ; partly by the force of thofe armies who may in fo fhort a time march from Aftracan, a ftation peculiarly adapted to become the depôt of an armament, from its maritime fituation, its own importance, and its eafy communication with the heart of the empire ? Is it then a chimerical fear that makes us tremble at the confequences of that fyftematic ambition, which may pour into the peninfula a well equipped army of a hundred thoufand men, fingularly adapted

apted to Eaftern warfare, and fhake the Britifh power in provinces remote from the feat of
empire, peopled by a difunited mafs of inhabitants, retained in fubjection, as they were conquered, by the force and cunning of a handful
of men ; furrounded by powerful ftates, ready
to promote any change that may weaken the
Europeans, and give them the chance of free-
ing the great Indian commonwealth from thofe
formidable intruders who have fo long revel-
led in its fpoils ? An invafion, although unfuccefsful on the part of Ruffia, might have the
moft fatal confequences to the Britifh power all
over Indoftan. Such an attempt muft be
viewed as a calamity which it becomes Britain
to avert by every exertion. Her naval power ;
her influence in continental affairs ; the force
of her treafures ; her intereft with allies ; in
fhort, all the refources of modern policy muft
be exerted in Europe, to prevent the great
northern power from attempting a blow, of
which the ultimate fuccefs and failure are almoft indifferent to the fate of our Eaftern empire, provided it is levelled with a force at all
adequate to the magnitude of the occafion. *
In the mean time, an equal jealoufy fhould be
entertained of any encroachments which Ruffia
may

* Note N n.

may attempt on the fouth. She lately added to her dominion, if common fame may be credited, a confiderable province of the Perfian empire ; and her encroachments on the Turkifh dominions deferve unremitting attention, as well on account of their ultimate confequences to the colonial fyftem, as on account of their immediate effects upon the adjuftment of the European balance.

I fhall now take an example of a remote caufe, which may, by a lefs obvious and apparent procefs, operate the deftruction of the colonial fyftem in the Weft, and affect more immediately, though not fo dangeroufly, the colonial dominions fituated in the Eaft Indies.

During the laft years of the eighteenth century, by far the moft eventful period in the hiftory of the human fpecies, a fcheme was put in execution, by the revolutionary rulers of France, which appears to have been frequently in the contemplation of the ancient Government. When the colonial power of the republic in America had been almoft extinguifhed, the foundation of a new and invaluable colony was laid by the fudden conqueft of Egypt. The unparalleled achievements of the Britifh arms, towards the end of the war, reconquered to it the Turkifh empire. But it is almoft needlefs to obferve, that for many years before the

French

BOOK
III.
French expedition, the Porte had ceafed to have
any real power over this fine province ; * that the
unexpefted victories of the laft campaign have
not in any degree reformed its domeftic adminiftration ; that it lies as much expofed as
before to the armaments which France may a-
gain fit out from her Mediterranean coaft ; and
that a convention between the Porte and the
Republic, dictated by alarm or obtained by
the promife of affiftance againft two powers
the natural enemies of both, may peaceably
transfer a poffeffion almoft totally ufelefs to its
prefent mafters. It is of fome importance to
confider the natural confequences of an event
fo extremely probable, to the interefts, firft of
the Afiatic, and then of the American colonial
fyftems.

I. The moft obvious danger, but, I apprehend, by far the leaft formidable that can arife
from the eftablifhment of any European colony in
Egypt, is the rifk of invafion to which the Eaft
Indian fettlements may be expofed. As France
is the power moft likely to attempt the eftablifhment of a colony in Egypt, and as fhe is
undoubtedly the moft able to derive advantage
from this acquifition, we fhall, in general, take
for an example the cafe of Egypt becoming
a French colony ; a cafe already for nearly three
years fully realized.

I.

* Note O o.

1. In attacking from this quarter the Britifh S E C T. fettlements on the Malabar coaft, France will II. poffefs many very obvious advantages, from the near neighbourhood of her new colony. The communication between Alexandria and Marfeilles is much eafier and fhorter than that between the capital and the frontier provinces of fome European ftates ; between St Peterfburg, for inftance, and the Ruffian provinces on the Black Sea. The average paffage to Alexandria is fifteen or twenty days ; and from thence to Suez is only a journey of a week. It is poffible, with favourable winds, to defpatch a courier from Paris, who fhall pafs through Egypt ; deliver his inftructions to the colonial government eftablifhed at Cairo ; carry on advices to the expedition fitting out at Suez or Coffeir on the Red Sea, and proceed with defpatches to part of the armament arrived at Surat on the Malabar coaft, in fifty days. *
But admitting the average to be ten weeks, how much fhorter is this than the time taken by a quick-failing veffel to reach Bombay from Britain ?

It muft, however, be remarked, that the route, though fhort, is almoft entirely by fea.

So

* Maillet, (Ed. de Mafcrier), Part. III. p. 200.—
Ricard, III. 43.—Niebuhr, Voyages, I. 205, 228, 248, & 356. (French edit. in 4to.)

So long as Britain retains the decided naval
fuperiority in Europe, the communication between France and her new colony is commanded by Britifh cruifers. The fame remark
applies ftill more ftrongly to the communication between Egypt and India. A powerful
fleet, ftationed on the Malabar coaft, may always cruife off the Straights of Babelmandel,
or in the Channel itfelf, or in the Red Sea,
of which the navigation muft be ftill more dangerous to a large fleet of tranfports than to a
fquadron of the line. Befides, the veffels neceffary for the expedition muft be conftructed
in the colony, where for many years fhip-
building cannot be expected to flourifh ; or they
muft be brought round by the Cape, and confequently expofed to the Britifh fleets. The
navigation of the Red Sea, too, in every
part extremely bad, is impracticable for large
veffels within eighty leagues from Suez. * It
muft alfo be remembered that no part of the
world is more fubject to regular and ftrong
monfoons than the Indian Ocean and the Red
Sea ; and, what cannot fail to hamper any expedition fitted out from Egypt with very great
difficulties, the direction of the wind varies in
different parts of the paffage at the fame time.
Thus, during the fix months of northerly monfoon

---

* Econ. Polit. et Diplom. (Encyc. Method.) II. 254.—
Note P p.

foon in the Red Sea, the foutherly monfoon S E C T.
II. prevails in the Indian Ocean. *

After the dangers of the firft coup de main, therefore, are over, (and in modern times fuch fudden fhocks have feldom or never any effect), the Bombay government, affifted by the fqua-dron which the neighbourhood of Egypt will conftantly render neceffary in the Indian Ocean, may be expected to provide fufficiently for the defence of that fettlement.

2. There can be no doubt, that, from its aftonifhing fertility, and advantageous pofition, Egypt, under a colonial government, will foon acquire immenfe wealth; and that the exten-five population which it actually maintains, and the ftill larger number of inhabitants which it may eafily fupport, added to its other refources, muft render it a formidable neigh-bour to the fettlements on the Malabar coaft, the moft inconfiderable of all the Britifh co-lonies in the Eaft. But the dangers to be apprehended from this improvement of Egypt, are far from being immediate. To mention on-ly one circumftance—The population of the country, though much greater than that of the Bombay eftablifhment, is made up of fo many
different

---

* Capper on Winds and Monfoons, p. 68. 72.—Bruce, I. 431.—Note Q q.

BOOK
III.
different nations, in fuch a low ftate of civilization, fo refractory and difunited, that for many
years the colony will be very ill adapted to
encounter the rifks of a ftate of war; and, at any
rate, muft truft for its defence and government
entirely to the troops of the mother country.
It can only, then, ferve as a point from whence
India may be attacked, by ferving as a depôt
or paffage for French troops, while it offers every
where the moft vulnerable points to attract an
effectual diverfion from the enemy. When, on
the other hand, the refources of the colony
have been augmented and its inhabitants difciplined and enlightened by the progrefs of
civilization, it will become, as an ultimate object, an invaluable poffeffion. Its ftrength and
profperity being derived from commerce, its
inhabitants will naturally be averfe to war, and
more particularly to war with fome of their
beft cuftomers. If the mother country fhould
force it on to hoftilities, fhe will probably meet
with refiftance; and the amicable intercourfe
may thus be continued between Egypt and
Indoftan, to their mutual advantage, in fpite
of the mother country's ambition.

3. The fhortnefs of the paffage between the
Malabar coaft and Suez, has often induced
fpeculative politicians to imagine that the ancient

cient communication between Europe and India might be revived with advantage, not only for the purpofe of conveying intelligence, but alfo for the purpofes of commerce. It has therefore been imagined, that the nation poffeffed of Egypt may deprive Great Britain of her Eaft Indian trade, and monopolize the wealth of the Eaft, by joining the Mediterranean with the Red Sea, or by making Egypt an entrepôt for the Afiatic merchandize.

Upon this point it may be remarked, in the *firft* place, that the communication between the Indian ocean and the Mediterranean, even admitting the poffibility of joining the Red Sea with the Nile or the Mediterranean by means of a canal, would be extremely tedious and inconvenient for the courfe of mercantile tranfactions. A fwift failing veffel, of fmall bulk, fit for beating to windward and for avoiding rocks and fhallows, might eafily carry defpatches down the Red Sea, at times when no fleet of merchantmen could encounter the monfoons. The meffenger intrufted with them could, without difficulty, perform his journey through Egypt in a week, either by the Nile and the canal, or by land carriage, while repeated difficulties would neceffarily occur to retard the progrefs of laden boats and caravans. I fpeak not of the dangers which valuable merchandize muft

run,

BOOK
III.

run, in the prefent unfettled ftate of the country, from the various tribes of banditti that infeft both the river and the deferts; or of the many difficulties and vexations arifing from the pofitive inftitutions fupported by the Porte and the Beys, for the purpofes of legal plunder. * Admitting that all thefe impediments to the communication fhall be abolifhed, as fome of them certainly muft ceafe with the prefent order of things, there are ftill various phyfical obftacles to the projected communication, which muft for ever diminifh, perhaps deftroy, the fuperiority of this route in point of fhortnefs. The fame veffels which navigate the Mediterranean cannot afcend the Nile, and crofs the defert in the canal. The goods muft therefore be all unloaded at Alexandria. The canal and river boats can never encounter the tempefts and fwell of the Red Sea and Indian Ocean. Another loading will therefore be neceffary at Suez, although the river boats fhould be able to navigate the canal. Hence the lofs and expence of two additional loadings and unloadings muft be deducted from the profits of the cargo; and the delay occafioned thereby muft be added to the total length of the paffage. Moreover, unlefs

---

* Note R r.

lefs a prodigious number of veffels are employed
in this trade, the goods muft often pay for two
veffels inftead of one; fince it will frequently
happen, that the empty veffels cannot immediately receive a new freight. The profits, too,
of the confignees in Egypt muft be taken into
account; or, if the goods are accompanied by
fupercargoes, their wages come to diminifh the
total gains. Laftly, however fhort the voyage
may be, it cannot be undertaken at all times, on
account of the monfoons. Niebuhr fays that a
fkilful voyager may go from Suez to India and
back again in a year, by taking advantage of
the half-yearly wind. * But if the winds blow
half-yearly, it is clear that two voyages may be
made in thirteen months. Still it will not be
poffible, after making every allowance, to perform the voyage from Europe to India oftener
than twice in the courfe of eighteen months.
This will clearly appear from the following
ftatement.

The moft advantageous time of failing from
Marfeilles, will be the middle of June. Suppofe that the average time taken in tranfporting
goods from thence to Suez is fix weeks (it cannot poffibly be rated lower, when we confider
the

---

* Defcript. de l'Arabie, p. 303.

BOOK
III.
the double loading and unloading) : The mer-
chandife is fhipped at Suez in the beginning of
Auguft, and is immediately carried down the
Red Sea by the northerly monfoon. In a
month it arrives at the Malabar coaft, and is
unfhipped : A new cargo, we fhall fuppofe, is
taken in, and ready to return with the firft
foutherly monfoon ; it arrives at Suez in the
beginning of November, and at Marfeilles about
the middle of December. Now, in however
fhort a time a new cargo may be fhipped, it
cannot fail fooner than the middle of February,
otherwife it would have to wait at Suez for the
northerly monfoon, which begins in April. The
veffel will arrive at Bombay in May, and muft
wait there till October for the foutherly monfoon. It will therefore not return to Marfeilles
until the middle of December, which is juft
eighteen months from the failing of the firft
cargo.

The expence of thefe two voyages will undoubtedly be fomewhat fmaller than that of the
Cape voyages, which might be performed in
the fame time. But the expences of loading,
the canal and river expences, the commiffion
or fupercargo's wages, the extraordinary tear
and wear of veffels in the Red Sea and Straits
of Babelmandel, together with the inutility of
thofe fhips during the months when they are
not

not employed, and the idlenefs of the crews during the greater part of that time, may be confidered as almoft fufficient to balance fo trifling an advantage.

But it is not by any means probable that the communication between the Mediterranean and Red Seas will be fo eafy as we have fuppofed. The junction of the Nile with the Gulf of Suez by a canal, has been frequently projected; and we are even told that in ancient times it was effected. That it was more than once attempted, there can be no doubt; but the impracticability of fuch a fcheme is now almoft placed beyond a doubt. This arifes, not fo much from the old opinion, of the level being higher in the Red Sea than in the Mediterranean, as from the nature of the ground through which the cut muft neceffarily pafs. The diftance between Cairo and Suez is above one hundred and five Englifh miles by the caravan track, according to Niebuhr; * according to others, one hundred and fifty miles; + it is above feventy miles in a ftraight line. The canal cut muft certainly be one hundred at the very leaft; and the whole of this route is a fandy defert, where the foil is perpetually fhifting with the

---

* Voyages, tom. I. p. 175.

+ Econ. Polit. et Dipl. (Encyc. Method.) II. 254.

the wind, and where no foundation can be obtained for conftructing works of any kind. ‡
Befides, although the natural level of the Red
Sea and Mediterranean may be the fame, the
effect of a wind of uncommon violence, that is,
the half year's monfoon, or, as fome have called it, the nine months monfoon, blowing all
the waters of the Indian Ocean through the
Straits of Babelmandel, muft be to raife their
level, and drive an irrefiftible current through
the Gulf of Suez. This, of itfelf, would render the canal impracticable, even although the
experiment fhould be tried, as it once was, by
cutting from Suez due north, fo as to join the
Red Sea with a fmall river that runs into the
Nile a few miles below Cairo, or by cutting
ftraight through the Ifthmus. The manifold
inconveniences, too, of an inland navigation
through a defert, deferve to be confidered, admitting the poffibility of forming the cut. All
thefe inconveniences would either be of fuch a
nature as to damage the goods tranfported, or
to increafe the expence of carriage, by the re-
pairs neceffary for the canal, and the diftance
from whence it would be neceffary to tranfport
every article of confumption required for the
perfons

---

‡ Econ. Polit. et Dipl (Encyc. Method.) II. 254.—
Volney's Egypt and Syria, I. 210.

perſons and cattle employed on its banks, or in
the boats. We may therefore conclude, that the communication between Europe and India through Egypt, cannot be facilitated by any internal navigation ; and that, in addition to all the expence and delay formerly enumerated as the neceſſary attendants of ſuch a ſcheme, there muſt be reckoned the coſt and time required for a new loading and unloading at Cairo, together with the conſignee's profits, and the riſks and charges of a journey acroſs the deſert. From all that has been ſaid, I am inclined to infer the impoſſibility of gaining any important advantage, in point of eaſy and expeditious mercantile communication with the Eaſt, by the poſſeſſion of Egypt.

It may farther be obſerved, that the ſtatements above detailed with reſpect to the winds, clearly prove the abſurdity of ſuppoſing that ſuch a communication would be ſhorter or eaſier to France than to any other maritime country. The only difference between the navigation of the Marſeilloiſe and the Newcaſtle veſſels is, that the former would be a few weeks in the year longer at reſt than the latter. They would both make the ſame number of voyages in the year ; and, conſequently, if a free trade were allowed to India through Egypt, the diſtant nation would be able to derive as much advantage

vantage from it as the nation poffeffed of the colony, and fituated in its immediate vicinity.

But, in the *fecond* place, admitting the certainty of all the advantages which have been expected from the communication with India by the Ifthmus of Suez; and admitting that France, in poffeffion of Egypt, fhall monopolize the carriage of Eaft Indian commodities; it is evident that this change muft be as beneficial to Great Britain, to the other confumers of Afiatic produce, and to the colonies themfelves, as to France. The fuperior cheapnefs and fhortnefs of the new route will be the caufe of the preference given to the French carriers; and, like any of thofe natural or acquired advantages which confer upon particular nations fuperior fkill in one branch of trade or manufacture, the poffeffion of Egypt will be a benefit, not only to the French, but to their cuftomers. The advantages derived from it will thus be mutual, like the advantages which once rendered the Dutch the carriers and brokers of Europe, and thofe which render the Englifh the chief manufacturers. The goods of Eaft Indian growth or fabric will be tranfported cheaper and better to England and Holland, though not in Englifh and Dutch veffels; the agriculture and manufactures of the colonies will therefore be promoted; and the capital
formerly

formerly employed in carrying the colonial merchandize to the mother country will be employed either in fupplying the new demands of
the colonies, occafioned by the improved communication, or in preparing manufactures to
meet the demands of the French market, extended by the increafed wealth of the country,
and deprived of a ready fupply by the quantity
of ftock withdrawn to the carrying trade.

A fimilar obfervation may be applied to that
view of the fubject which would lead us to apprehend danger from our natural enemy becoming mafter of the wealth and ftrength of
Egypt, in fo far as its refources are likely to be
augmented by its mercantile connexion with the
Eaft. There cannot indeed be any doubt that
the pofition of Egypt is extremely favourable to
all the branches of commerce, as its foil and climate are admirably adapted to the raifing of raw
produce; that it will foon become the moft valuable colony in the world ; and that one of the
branches of trade which will contribute effentially to its wealth, is the traffic with India. In
itfelf, therefore, this fplendid acquifition will
be of incalculable advantage to France ; and,
from its fituation in the immediate neighbourhood of Europe, as well as from its influence
upon the relative power of the mother country,
it is a change well calculated to roufe the jealoufy

oufy of all the other ftates. But, at prefent, we are only contemplating the probable effects of the acquifition upon the colonial fyftems ; and, however much Egypt immediately, or France confequentially, may gain by the commerce of the Eaft, the advantage muft neceffarily be exactly equal to the Indian ftates or the colonies with which the trade may be carried on, and confequently to the European ftates poffeffing thofe Afiatic colonies.

Were the Eaft Indian commerce of Britain and Holland laid open to the whole capital which could be drawn into it, the neighbourhood of fuch a colony as Egypt muft foon become, under the government of France, would be, of all changes that could happen, the moft beneficial, both to the Indian colonies, and to the mercantile interefts of the parent ftates as connected with thofe colonies.

From its pofition, Egypt will be the natural entrepôt of the Indian merchandize; from its wealth, it will offer, in itfelf, a moft extenfive market for every thing which is raifed or manufactured in Afia. From the nature of its produce (as we fhall immediately fee), it will interfere fo very little with the commodities raifed in the Eaft, that no great or fudden fhifting of colonial capital or induftry will be the confequence of Egypt being improved to the uttermoft ;

uttermoſt ; and from the peculiar fertility of this country in all ſorts of grain, it will afford a ſure reſource to the natives of the peninſula, ſo often liable to the miſeries of extenſive famine. To the colonies, then, and in like manner, to the conſumers of colonial produce, the neighbourhood of this great entrepôt for Eaſtern merchandize, will be as advantageous as the corn-merchant is to the farmer and conſumer of grain, or the retail dealer to the manufacturer and uſer of wrought goods, or the merchant importer in the mother country to the colonies and conſumers of colonial produce; while the market and the ſupplies which ſo rich and populous a country will afford, cannot fail incalculably to promote the wealth of the colonies in the firſt inſtance, and ultimately to augment the riches of the mother country alſo.

There is indeed no doubt, that ſome of the ſtock formerly employed in carrying Eaſt Indian goods, muſt now be ſhifted to another occupation. Part of that ſtock, inſtead of bringing them round the Cape, with a ſlow return of profits, will now bring them from India to Egypt, and from Egypt to Europe, with a much quicker return. The competition of Egyptian and French capital will unqueſtionably throw out another part of the capital formerly veſted in the Indian trade. But this is
only

only a confequence of the free commerce which
we are fuppofing to be eftablifhed, and which
would produce the very fame effects on the
traffic, as is at prefent carried on by the Cape.
It is unneceffary to prove that this fhifting of
capital, flowly effected, can produce only good
confequences to the mother country, and confer upon the colonies the fame benefits as if a
vaft capital were gradually poured into their
agriculture, manufactures, and commerce.

If it be fuppofed that the prefent fyftems of
monopoly fhall continue in the Afiatic colonies, the colonies and the parent ftates will
have to lament all that additional lofs to which
they will now be fubjected, comparatively fpeaking, by being excluded from a fhare in the vaft
additional benefits fo likely to flow from a free
trade with their new neighbours. But this neighbourhood will not on that account occafion any
real lofs, either to the colony or the mother
country. Things will remain actually in the
fame ftate as before the eftablifhment of the colony in Egypt. If, however, the abfurd policy of
the other ftates poffeffing Eaft Indian territories,
fhall drive the new rulers of the colony to feek
for fettlements among the native powers on the
coafts of the peninfula, or among the iflands of
the Indian ocean, or to attempt, by treaty with
thofe powers, the extenfion of the fettlements
already

already obtained, or to extend their commercial relations with the Afiatics, whofe purfuits
may in no fmall degree be new-modelled by
the intercourfe of the merchants belonging to
the new colony ; then, the fupport of the prefent Eaft Indian monopolies will be a matter of
much greater difficulty than it hitherto has
been. In fpite of England and Holland, the
merchants of the French colony will obtain
abundance of Eaft Indian goods, and will be
able greatly to underfell the Eaft India Companies in every market, although thofe bodies
fhould reform their grofs abufes, trade as eco-
nomically as individuals, and be contented to
take the loweft, inftead of the monopoly profits.
Thus, befides the great difficulty of preventing a
contraband trade, mutually lucrative, from being
carried on between Egypt and their fettlements
in India, the companies will have to ftruggle
againft the ftill greater difficulty of preventing
a contraband trade equally gainful from being
carried on in Europe. In order to fupport the
exclufive privileges of thofe corporations, the
legiflatures of the refpective countries will be
obliged to new-model all their reftrictive laws ;
and it may probably be found that a new code
of cuftom-houfe law will be inadequate to check
fuch a fyftem of fmuggling as muft be engendered both in Afia and Europe, by the temptations

tions of aftonifhing profits, and to maintain the
exclufive privileges of the trading corporations
for any profitable purpofe. The contraband
trade in Swedifh teas carried on fome years a-
go, notwithftanding all the efforts of the Englifh Eaft India Company to check it, muft be
frefh in the memory of every one ; yet, compared with the new contraband, of which we
are now fpeaking, that traffic was trifling indeed.
In fhort, it is fcarcely poffible to figure the continuance of fuch trading companies, after the
Egyptian colony fhall have been firmly eftablifhed. The influence of thofe bodies will
probably prevail, fo far as to obtain the fupport
of their refpective governments, until the evil
becomes too great for any legiflative remedies.
The end of fuch commercial nuifances will
then be allowed to approach, when no efforts
of ftate can prevent the cataftrophe ; and, according to a feature but too common in the character of human councils, the nations which
have been fo effentially injured by thofe deftructive fyftems of monopoly, will at laft be
forced to relieve themfelves from the evil, in
confequence of external events beyond the
fphere of their controul. It is not eafy to a-
void wifhing for any change, even a change,
favourable to the power of France, which may
gradually but effectually blot out from the
colonial

colonial policy of Europe all remains of commercial monopoly and company government. *

In a mercantile point of view, then, the
powers poffeffing Eaft Indian colonies have nothing to apprehend, but much to hope for
their diftant fettlements, from the improvement
of Egypt and its fubjection to a regular and
efficient government. In a political point of
view, thofe colonies have little to dread from fuch
a change. A little more vigilance will be required, a larger fleet and a higher eftablifhment
of land forces will be neceffary in time of
war ; but no real danger can ever arife from
this quarter, to the prefent fyftem of colonial
power in the peninfula and Afiatic iflands.
Still lefs need any apprehenfions of this nature
be entertained from the eftablifhment of an
independent and primary government in Egypt,
fuppofing fuch an event to be at all poffible in
the prefent circumftances of that country. The
new power will never regard India as a fcene of
conqueft, whilft Arabia, Syria, and the Archipelago remain unfubdued. It is only the relations which fubfift between France and the
parent ftates of the Indian colonies, that could
ever render the project of invading the peninfula a matter of ferious confideration. In a
commercial point of view, it will not make any
difference whether the improvement of Egypt

is

* Note S s.

is effected by foreign conqueft, or by the efforts
of an independent and civilized government
eftablifhed upon the ruins of the Ottoman and
Mameluc power. In either cafe the confequences muft be equally beneficial to the colonial interefts of all the European powers poffeffed of Afiatic dominions.

II. I come now to confider that view of the
fubjeft which is apparently very remote and
fanciful, but in reality prefents to our attention
the moft important and ferious confiderations—
the probable effects of the fubjection and improvement of Egypt upon the Weft Indian
colonies of the European powers. There can
remain no doubt whatever in the mind of any
perfon who examines the natural refources of
Egypt, that the cultivation of this noble province, by an induftrious race of men, will be
attended with the immediate defolation of the
whole Charaibean iflands, from Cuba to Trinidad, and of the continental poffeffions of the
Europeans along the Weft Indian coaft of South
America.

1. Let us attend, in the *firft* place, to the prodigious extent of fertile land which has all been
at different times, in a ftate of high and eafy
cultivation in Egypt, and let us compare this
with

with the whole cleared and cultivated Weft Indian territory.

The Delta and the fertile parts of the country adjoining it on the Canopic and Tanitic branches of the Nile, form a vaft plain, of a figure fomewhat triangular, or rather a fector of a circle, whofe arch extends from Tana to Alexandria, and whofe radius is a line drawn from Cairo to Cape Berelos. As the chord is about one hundred and forty Englifh miles, and the radius about one hundred and ten, the whole area cannot contain fewer than eight thoufand feven hundred fquare miles. The lakes Abufiche and Menzale are indeed included in this fpace, as well as a fmall portion of defert to the weft of the canal Bahre: But this is nearly balanced by the cultivated land belonging to Lower Egypt, and not comprehended in the portion which we have been confidering. However, we fhall fuppofe that all thefe deductions, together with the fpace occupied by the river, amount to about a twelfth part of the whole, and we fhall eftimate the fertile part of Lower Egypt at eight thoufand fquare miles, or five million one hundred and twenty thoufand acres.

Upper Egypt, or the Said, contains, in proportion to its extent, but a fmall diftrict of fertile foil. It is, in fact, one vaft defert, through which the Nile runs in a winding valley of no great breadth. This valley is the only fertile

part

part of the whole territory; and its extent cannot be computed with any tolerable degree of
precifion. We may however obferve, that the
length of a ftraight line drawn between the two
extremities of the valley Affuan, and Cairo, is
about five hundred and fifteen Englifh miles,
or, allowing for windings, fix hundred miles.
The greateft breadth is about twenty-five, near
Benifuef ; and it grows gradually narrower and
narrower to its fouthern extremity at Affuan,
where it is only feven or eight miles broad. If
we call the average breadth feventeen miles, we
fhall certainly keep much within the truth ;
and this hypothefis gives ten thoufand two hundred fquare miles for the fuperficies. But to
this muft be added the rich diftrict of Faioum,
by far the moft fruitful part of the whole country. Befides feveral other fertile fpots not comprehended in the valley, Faioum contains, of
itfelf, between five and fix hundred fquare
miles. So that, altogether, the cultivated part
of the Said cannot poffibly be rated at lefs than
eleven thoufand fquare miles, or feven millions
forty thoufand acres ; and the whole fertile territory of Egypt muft of confequence be above
twelve millions of acres, at the very loweft
computation. *

Let

---

* Savary, tom. I. let. 1. tom. II. let. 3.—Ricard,
III. 433.—Danville & Niebuhr's maps.

Let us compare this with the extent of territory at prefent cultivated in the Weft Indies, in order to fupply the demands of the European market.

The number of acres in cultivation in the ifland of Jamaica, in 1787, was one million fifty-nine thoufand ; and the exports from thence were valued at two million one hundred and thirty-fix thoufand four hundred and forty-two pounds. As the total exports from the Britifh Weft Indies during the fame year were ftated at five millions two hundred and fixty-five thoufand one hundred and two pounds, and as many of the iflands contain far more fruitful foil than Jamaica, we may fafely conclude, that not above two millions fix hundred and nine thoufand eight hundred and forty-five acres were in cultivation. The reports of the French Chambers of Commerce to M. Neckar, give the exports for the year 1788 confiderably lower, *viz.* four millions one hundred and fifty-feven thoufand five hundred pounds : fo that, according to this eftimate, the cultivated land would only amount to about two millions of acres ; but we fhall take the higheft computation.

The number of cultivated acres in the French iflands was four millions twenty-four thoufand fix hundred and fixty, according

to

BOOK
III.
to the average of Jamaica produce, which,
for almoſt all thoſe fine territories, is a great
deal too low. In the Spaniſh iſlands, the number of cultivated acres was ſeven hundred and
forty-five thouſand eight hundred and eighty-
three ; and in the Dutch colonies of Guiana,
about eight hundred and fifty thouſand, according to the ſame very low average : ſo that we
may compute the whole cultivated land in the
Weſt Indies at eight millions two hundred and
thirty thouſand three hundred and eighteen ;
or, allowing for the trifling ſettlements of Sweden and Denmark (the laſt of which has only
ſeventy thouſand acres meaſured out for cultivating), we may call the total eight millions
three hundred thouſand acres, ſuppoſing all the
land to be of the ſame indifferent quality with
that of Jamaica. *

Thus it appears that there is in Egypt
nearly half as much more of fertile land as
there is in all the parts of the Weſt Indies
which the demand for colonial produce has
cauſed to be cleared, even if we ſhould ſuppoſe

as

---

* Edwards' Weſt Indies, vol. I. p. 185—230. &
II. 385.—Barré de St Venant, Colonies Modernes, I
chap. X.—La Richeſſe de la Hollande, tom. I. p. 334.—
Ricard, III. 676.—Catteau, Tableau des etats Danois,
tom. II. p. 320.—See alſo Book I. Sect. III. of this
Inquiry.

as much of the Weſt Indian ſoil to have been
uſed for raiſing this produce, as would be neceſſary were the whole territory of an inferior
degree of fertility. Let us now ſee to what
uſes the Egyptian ſoil may be turned.

2. The wonderful fertility of Egypt in all
ſorts of grain, is too well known to require
any deſcription. The only remark which it
is neceſſary to make, is a correction of the vulgar exaggerations that have been grafted upon
the real account of its fruitfulneſs. Inſtead of
one, two, and three hundred fold, the common
return is twenty-five and thirty, and ſometimes
as much as fifty for one. But theſe crops are
the produce of the moſt careleſs huſbandry in
the world. The indolent Copt ſcarcely takes
the pains to ſcratch the rich earth on which
he liſtleſsly ſpills his ſeed-corn; and in four
months his harveſt is reaped. Another ſuc-
ceeds in the ſame year; and in ſome favoured
diſtricts, particularly of the Delta, where a-
bundance of water can be procured, the ſoil
yields no leſs than three crops to thoſe lazy
and unſkilful cultivators. The ancient cultivation of Egypt, indeed, when it was the gra-
nary of the Roman empire, or the country in
which Ptolemy Philadelphus amaſſed a treaſure
of one hundred and ninety millions, or the
conqueſt

conqueſt from which the Arabs drew a revenue of three hundred millions of crowns, cannot now be perceived. Thoſe innumerable canals by means of which the precious ſupplies
of the river were diſtributed, and thoſe reſer-
voirs which aſſiſted the induſtrious natives in
œconomizing that treaſure, have for the moſt
part been neglected ſince the decline of the
ſtate under the Saracen dominion. But,
though choked up and ruinous, the works
may without much difficulty be repaired.
The ſoil ſtill preſents the ſame ſoft ſubſtance
to the ſpade, and the ſame materials for the
kiln, that formerly enabled the Ptolemies to
excavate the entire channel of the river, and
raiſe the ſtupendous mountains of architecture
which alone, of all human works, ſeem capable
of reſiſting the injuries of time. The ſand
that in many places lightly covers the ſur-
face of the country, ſcarcely conceals the ancient furrows over which it has been permitted to ſpread ; and all Egypt offers to the cul-
tivator thoſe tempting proſpects of exceſſive returns which have allured Europeans to clear
the thick foreſts of the New World, with this
ſtriking difference, that its fineſt ſoil is every year
renewed, enjoying the perpetual advantages of
the virgin ſtate which only once belong to the
American plains, while the labour of the cul-
tivator

tivator who firſt ſows a field, is no greater than
that of his ſucceſſors who repeat the ſame operation. *

The quantity of grain at preſent raiſed in
this favoured territory cannot be aſcertained
with preciſion. But it is enough to obſerve,
that bad as the Egyptian huſbandry is, the very
ſmall part of the community, who may be rather ſaid to reap the ſpontaneous fruits of the
river and ſoil than to till the ground, abundantly ſupply the whole population of nearly four
millions of perſons, feeding chiefly on grain
and vegetables, beſides exporting a great part
of the grain required by the inhabitants of Con-
ſtantinople, and the whole of what is conſumed
in Arabia. It may eaſily be imagined, then,
with what eaſe a ſmall part of the twelve millions of acres which according to our computation form the fertile territory of Egypt, may
be appropriated to raiſing the ſupply of grain
required for the ſubſiſtence of the community,
while

---

* Suetonius in Veſpaſiano.—Plutarch. in Antonio.—
Hiſtory of Eaſt Indian Trade, apud Harris's Collection,
Vol. I. p. 419.—Maillet, (Edit. Maſcrier) Part. I. p. 14.
—Ricard, tom. III. p. 433. & 443.—Sonnini, Voyages
en Egypte, chap. XXVI. & XLVIII.—Savary, tom. I,
Let. 1. ; tom. II. Let. 3. 18. ; tom. III. Let. 2.—Vol-
ney's Egypt, vol. I. p. 55, 67.—Eton's Survey of the
Turkiſh Empire, chap. VII.

while the part now employed in raiſing grain
for exportation, and the ſtill greater portion
laid waſte by abſolute neglect, is devoted to the
raiſing of more valuable commodities.

We have thus found our proviſion grounds
and pens, to uſe the language of the Weſt Indian agriculture, and in an abundance ſo great
as to preclude the neceſſity of importation, under which almoſt all the American colonies labour. Let us ſee if we cannot diſcover alſo the
plantations.

3. From the narratives of various authors,
ancient and modern, more particularly of thoſe
travellers who have viſited Egypt, and given
us a deſcription of their route, with no other
vſew than to gratify their own or their reader's
curioſity about the antiquities of the place, we
may gather, that every article of Weſt Indian
produce, except coffee, flouriſhes with peculiar
felicity on the banks of the Nile.

The great Weſt Indian ſtaple, the ſugar
cane, appears to be indigenous in Egypt. It
has been raiſed there in all ages, ſometimes in
very conſiderable quantities, and always from
feed. Its culture is attended with no difficulty,
and trifling expence. In Faioum, more eſpecially, it grows in abundance, and almoſt ſpon-
taneouſly. Although the natives are but little
                                        acquainted

acquainted with the culture of the plant, or
the fubfequent preparation of the commodity,
they manufacture a confiderable quantity. All
the fugar ufed in the feraglio at Conftantinople
is made in Egypt; and the peculiar excellence
of its quality is a fufficient proof that the cultivation of the cane might be there carried to
any degree of perfection. It is in fact to all
appearance natural to the fpot ; whereas in the
Weft Indies there is every reafon to believe
that it is exotic. We muft remember, too,
that the fugar lands in Egypt would produce
exactly twice as much as thofe in the American
iflands, although the foil were in itfelf only
equally fertile : for in the Weft Indies the cane
pieces muft be allowed to lye fallow every al-
ternate year, whereas the foil of Egypt is annually renewed. But, for this very reafon, the
ground in Egypt muft be incalculably more
productive, and muft have, for fugar culture,
and the other branches of planting, as well as
common hufbandry, the perpetual advantages
which belong to a virgin foil.

Flax and cotton are articles of Egyptian
growth ; and only require a little care and fkill
to render them equal to what they anciently
were, when the linen and cotton cloths of Egypt
were proverbially noted for delicacy and dura-
bility. The exquifite dyes which are brought

to

to fuch perfection by European induftry and art in the new world, need fcarcely be looked for among the Copts and Turks. So much of the value both of cochineal and indigo is owing to the mode of preparation, that we may confider them as the growth rather of a certain ftate of fociety than of a particular foil. Neverthelefs, there can be no doubt that both the infect which furnifhes the materials of the one fabric, and the plant which produces the other by the intervention of one of the moft delicate and uncertain proceffes in the whole circle of the arts, are to be found in their natural ftate in Egypt; and are even ufed by the natives as dyes, after a rude and inefficacious preparation.

Several of the moft valuable fpices and perfumes, not to be found in the Weft Indies, as caffia, myrrh, gums, frankincenfe, &c. are indigenous in Egypt; the pimento and others might without doubt be eafily introduced; and no country is fo favourable to the growth of the filk-worm.

Coffee, we are told by fome authors, has never been cultivated with fuccefs in Egypt, although repeatedly tried. Others, however, have pofitively denied this; and have argued, with great appearance of probability, that a plant by no means delicate, requiring very little care, and flourifhing in the worft of thofe foils which produce

produce the other West Indian staples, may be
expected to thrive in a country so very favourable to all those articles ; more especially as, in
the neighbouring territory of Arabia, the finest
coffee in the world is raised in prodigious a-
bundance : and in Syria, which closely resembles Egypt in its physical character, coffee can
be raised to a degree of perfection that rivals
the famous produce of Arabia. A country
perfectly flat, is not indeed favourable to the
growth of this valuable fruit. In the Delta,
therefore, we can scarcely expect its culture
to succeed ; but in the Said, on the sides of
those hills between which the valley of the
Nile lies, we can hardly doubt the possibility
of bringing this branch of planting to as great
perfection as that which attends the scanty exertions of the cultivators on the other side of the
Red Sea. It has in general been remarked
of the Egyptian soil, that it is not favourable
to exotics, unless their culture is introduced
gradually and carefully. We may be allowed
to suspect, then, that the experiments, upon
the failure of which Maillet and others have
asserted the impossibility of raising coffee in
Egypt, were not fairly tried.

If, however, all the other articles of value
which I have enumerated, shall be raised in
such abundance by the colonists of Egypt, it
signifies

fignifies little whether or not this one remains
an exception. The neighbourhood of Arabia
will amply fupply the deficiency; the coffee
planting of that rich territory will be promoted
and reduced to a fyftem by the demands of
the new colony; and if the European traders
refort to Egypt for all the other commodities
which they formerly received from the Weft
Indies, they will alfo ufe the colonifts as mid-
dlemen in the coffee trade, while Egypt will be
as much benefited by becoming the emporium
of this produce, as by raifing and felling her
own ftaples. At this day, the Mocha coffee,
fo much prized all over the world, bears a
much higher price than it ought, in confequence of the various taxes raifed upon the
tranfport, and the reftrictions laid on the exportation, by the governments of the countries
where it is produced and of thofe through
which it muft be carried; fo that the article
which at Mocha cofts only from fourpence to
fixpence per pound, cofts at Cairo no lefs than
from one fhilling and threepence to one fhilling
and tenpence, or even two fhillings and a penny, and at Marfeilles about half a crown. *

4.

---

* Bruce's Travels, vol. I. p. 81.—Volney's Egypt and
Syria, vol. I. p. 220. & 229.; and vol. II. p. 318.—Mail-
let (edit. Mafcrier), Second Part, p. 15.—Savary, tom. I.
Let

4. For the manufacture and tranfport of all S E C T.
the articles which have been enumerated, Egypt _{II.}
poffeffes natural conveniences by no means enjoyed by the Weft Indian colonies. Abundance of
cedar and palm trees are to be had, of a nature
admirably fitted for the tool. It has however
been found fo much more profitable to ufe the
foil for other purpofes, in the beft times of this
province, that timber has generally been imported. As the cultivated country all lies near
the river, of which the navigation is eafy, and
as various ftreams interfect the valley to join it,
the ufe of machinery, and the tranfport of
goods by water carriage to the ports of fhipping, where the hill joins the fea, muft of courfe
afford ineftimable conveniences to the planter
and manufacturer. Befides, the level nature
of the whole territory and the aftonifhing fecundity of all the domeftic animals are circumftances equally favourable at once to the eafy
communication between the different diftricts,
and to the erection of machinery wrought by wind
or draught. Here are produced, too, in unrivalled

Let. 1. & 5.; tom. II. Let. 3.; and tom. III. Let. 4.—
Sonnini, Voyages en Egypte, chap. XXXI. & XLVIII.
—Niebuhr, Voyages, tom. I. p. 116. 117. id.—Defc. de
l'Arab. p. 127.—Commerce (Encyc. Method.) tom. III.
p. 790. Ricard, tom. III. p. 439. Eton's Survey, Appendix, Art. I.

led abundance, fome articles of fignal fubot-dinate ufe in various branches of manufacture, particularly natron, faltpetre, and fal ammoniac. I have already noticed the adaptation of the foil, both for eafy excavation, and for the manufacture of bricks and earthen ware.

5. The climate of Egypt has been fuppofed by many to be as unfavourable to animal life, as it is genial to the productions of the foil; and one author, remarkable for a general and un-meaning fyftem of invective, has declaimed a-gainft it as the worft under which the human fpecies has been permitted to live. * There is however, every reafon to believe that thefe prejudices are wholly unfounded, and that we fhould come much nearer the truth, were we to beftow upon the climate of this country praifes equal to thofe which all mankind have agreed to heap upon its foil.

The extraordinary fecundity of all animals on the banks of the Nile, has been repeatedly defcribed, both by ancient and modern writers. This circumftance, of itfelf, forms a ftrong prefumption, if not a fufficient argument, in favour of the wholefomenefs of the air. The prejudice againft Egypt on account of the frequent difeafes

* Pauw fur les Chinois & les Egyptiens, *paffim*.

eafes of the eyes to which its inhabitants are
fubject, has of late years been removed by the
fatisfactory explanations of the moft intelligent
travellers ; and it now appears that this malady,
fo long a reproach to the climate, owes its origin in fact to the cuftoms of the people, their
conftant ufe of hot-baths, the weight of clothes
which they wear round their heads, and their
fondnefs for the practice of fleeping in the open
air, expofed to the chilling dews of night, after
the heats of the day have opened all their pores.

The plague, too, has been fuppofed by many * to be indigenous in Egypt. Yet nothing
can be more certain, than that in ancient times
it was unknown to the induftrious cultivators
and merchants of this province ; and there is
no doubt that it has often been confounded
with other maladies. The true caufe of thofe
putrid difeafes which fometimes prevail on the
banks of the Nile, muft be fought for in the
habitual uncleanlinefs of the inhabitants refpecting every thing but their bodies ; the dirty clothes
which they always wear, even after fteeping
themfelves for hours in boiling water ; the uncommon filthinefs of their ftreets at all feafons
of the year ; the innumerable pools of ftagnant
water which they never think of draining or
filling up. As for the plague, it is now proved
beyond

* Eton's Survey, chap. VII.

BOOK
III.

beyond a doubt, that this difeafe is always of
foreign growth ; and has never, except after a famine, been hatched even in Cairo itfelf, where
nine hundred thoufand inhabitants are heaped
together in a dirty, confined, and moulder-
ing city. But, notwithftanding its conftant
prevalence in fome parts of the Ottoman empire, and generally at Conftantinople, the communication between Alexandria and thofe infected quarters is never for one moment ftopt.
No regimen or fyftem of health laws is adopted.
Indeed, in the whole extent of the Grand Signior's dominions, there never was a fingle act
of quarantine performed. The univerfal belief
of the Turks in predeftination, and their utter
ignorance of medicine, both prevent any means
from being purfued to check the progrefs of in-
fection, and preclude all chance of a cure being
effected, or the difeafe being eradicated, until
the natural courfe of the feafons brings relief.
How abfurd, then, is it to accufe the climate
of engendering a malady which feems to be
courted by all the efforts of the people, with
the entire concurrence of their rulers ?

No fituation in fact can be more falubrious
than that of Egypt; a level plain expofed to the
fea breeze, with no forefts or hills to obftruct the
freeft circulation of air ; a perpetual vegetation
of the plants moft adapted to purify it ; and a
conftant flow of water through all parts of the
country

country increafing the motion and coolnefs of the atmofphere. Accordingly, there can be no doubt that the encomiums beftowed on the falubrity of the Egyptian climate by all the ancient authors, are in themfelves juft, and perfectly applicable to the prefent circumftances of the country. In no part of the world do we meet with fewer prevailing difeafes; in no ftate have the numbers of mankind multiplied more rapidly, and kept pace more exactly with their induftrious exertions, than in Egypt during the better days of its government and manners. The natives are not affected by the moft violent heats of the fun, fcarcely even by expofure to the effluvia of their ftagnant pools, or to the Khamfin wind, which occafionally blows during fix or feven weeks of the year, and is the only unfavourable attendant of the Egyptian climate. The moft violent efforts of bodily fatigue are borne with eafe and fafety. Even the culture of rice, which in every other country is the moft unwholefome of all occupations, is in Egypt attended with no manner of inconvenience or injury to the health. *

It

---

* Volney's Egypt and Syria, I. 67. 202. 244. & 255.
—Savary, tom. III. Let. 1.—Maillet, (edit. Mafcrier) Part. I. p. 14.—Sonnini, Voyage en Egypte, chap. XXVI, XXXI.

It is evident, then, that the climate of the new fettlement will be found as far fuperior to the climate of the Weft Indian colonies, as the fertility of the foil and the facility of cultivation. But, even if the difference in point of climate were wholly in favour of the old colonies, it is not certain that this circumftance would occafion any obftruction to the improvement of the leaft wholefome territory. On the contrary, we fee conftant examples of health being facrificed, without hefitation, to the profpect of wealth; and the moft deadly climates in the world have not been able ferioufly to retard the cultivation of thofe regions which prefent to the adventurer the irrefiftible temptations of cheap and rich land. It is worthy of remark, that the greateft population and wealth which can be found in any European ftate of equal extent, are collected in a diftrict labouring under the moft unwholefome of the European climates; and that the colonies which have accumulated the moft fplendid treafures in proportion to their extent, have been thofe of the Dutch in Java and Guiana, fubject to the moft peftilential atmofphere that is breathed by men on the whole furface of the earth : So feeble an influence have the greateft of all dangers on the minds of men, if placed at a little diftance, and fet in oppofition to the ftrong paffions of avarice or ambition!

We

We have feen how favourable the ordinary
ftate of the climate in Egypt is to animal as well as vegetable life. It enjoys another very effential advantage, in being free from thofe de-ftructive hurricanes and earthquakes which fo often prove deftructive both to the wealth and the lives of the Weft Indian planters. * This circumftance gives the new fettlement a decid-ed fuperiority over the old colonies in point of capacity for improvement ; a fuperiority which cannot be compenfated, like the common ad-vantages of a wholefome atmofphere, by the daring fpirit of adventure fo conftantly difplay-ed in thofe remote fcenes of induftry and for-titude.

Indeed, the general circumftances of climate affect (though much lefs confiderably) the rich-es as well as the comforts of any fettlement, by their influence upon the progrefs of population ; but of this we are to fpeak in the fequel.

6. The fituation of Egypt gives it as decided a fuperiority over the American colonies, as its great fertility, its favourable climate, and terra-queous diftribution. It is placed almoft in the immediate neighbourhood of the market which its various and plentiful produce is adapted to

fupply,

---

* Volney, I. 262.

BOOK III. fupply. The diftance between Alexandria and Marfeilles, is not greater than that between the Baltic and the northern ports of France. Italy is not fo far from the Egyptian coaft, as the fouth of England from Bourdeaux. The Turkifh empire is fcattered round this fine province; Conftantinople itfelf not being more than five days fail from Alexandria. The navigation of the Mediterranean is in general eafy and fafe, except at the equinoxes, when ftormy weather prevails in the weftern parts of the fea. The run is almoft clear from Italy, France and Spain; it may be made at any feafon. *

The harbours on the coaft of Lower Egypt are not now very good; but they were once the fineft in the world. The port of Alexandria, for example, is almoft choked up by the mud which the river brings down, and by the ballaft which all veffels have for many ages been allowed to difcharge into the water. As this change, however, is entirely owing to the indolence of the government and inattention of the police, the activity and fkill of Europeans will eafily reftore things to their former ftate, and open once more the great harbour of Egypt to the commerce of the world. The other ports on the

_____

* Capper on Winds and Monfoons, p. 78.—Ricard, III. 438.

the coaft are by no means in fuch a ftate of dif-
repair ; and fome of them are excellent. †

It is evident, then, how much more advan-
tageoufly than the Weft Indies, Egypt is fituated in point of diftance for the tranfport of
its produce. Inftead of a fix or eight weeks
voyage, the Egyptian commodities will only
have to pay for a voyage of two or three ; a
voyage not liable to the dangers of the tropical
hurricanes, the delays of regular winds, and
the numerous rifks of foul channels and narrow ftraights. This advantage alone, even if
the price of the goods at the ports of fhipping
were the fame, would be fufficient to drive out
of the European market every article of Weft
Indian growth which could be raifed in Egypt.
It deferves alfo to be noticed, that the trade
may be carried on at almoft any time of the
year to and from Egypt, both from the ftate
of the population and the diftribution of profeffions, as we fhall immediately fee, and from
the variety of feafons in different quarters at one
time. The harvefts being retarded or accelerated according to the fituation of the land with
refpect to the water, which is the univerfal
fpring of fertility, a fucceffion of crops may be
procured by the difpofition of the canals and
fluices—a fucceffion which is indeed in fome
refpects natural to the country, without any
contrivance,

---

† Ricard, III. 436.—Volney, I. 7.

contrivance, from the various pofition of the grounds.

7. The laft, but in every refpect by far the moft important advantage, which the new fettlement will poffefs over the American colonies, yet remains to be confidered—the ftructure of the fociety.

The population of Egypt has indeed been gradually decreafing fince the Saracen conqueft. With the reign of Omar began that dynafty, which, during a courfe of ages, was employed in defolating the conquered territory, and in fpreading the fame devaftation over the provinces that yet remained free. The Ottoman power, which fucceeded the Caliphat, carried ftill farther every principle of intolerance and barbarity in government and in religion, adding, in all its operations, to thofe bad qualities that marked the Saracen rulers, the feature of extreme and infectious ignorance. Under the complicated miferies which Egypt has for centuries been doomed to fuffer from conqueft, infurrection and civil war, almoft naturalized in thofe fruitful regions, it is no wonder that the traces of her ancient glory fhould be almoft worn away, and the numbers of her inhabitants greatly reduced. It is no fmall proof of her various capacity and
                                        natural

natural refources, that fhe ftill can reckon fo
many as four millions of fouls. *

This large population is indeed of a mixed
and impure conftitution. The moft numerous
clafs are the Arabs ; men not remarkable for
their induftrious habits ; but, in general, defcribed as bearing a moft refpectable character †. I fpeak not of the Bedouins, who belong properly to the defert, nor of the Fellahs
or Arabs of the villages on the river. Both of
thofe claffes are inconfiderable, compared with
the Arabs who are employed in an imperfect
fort of agriculture. The Bedouins, engaged
rather in the occupations of fhepherds, are, like
all tribes devoted to the paftoral ftate, not the
innocent Arcadians fung by poets and canted o-
ver by philanthropifts, but robbers and butchers.
The Fellahs are for the moft part pirates or
thieves. The agricultural Arabs, on the other
hand, are generally a people of fimple lives,
remarkable for honefty and good faith, for o-
bedience to their patriarchal chief, and valour
in defence of his caufe. It muft be admitted,
that thefe qualities are at leaft the rudiments
of a good national character ; and if the diffen-
fions which have fo long torn the country to
pieces, with the total want of all but military
law,

---

* Note T t.   † Savary, tom. III, let. 2.

law, have divided thofe tribes naturally peaceful, armed them againft each other, and
cramped their habits of induftry, it is furely
no great conceffion to allow that the pacification of the country, the eftablifhment of a regular and vigorous government, the accurate
allotment of land, and the introduction of thofe
new wants which are natural to polifhed fociety,
will revive the more quiet and natural induftry of
the Arabs, reclaim them from habits of military
exertion, and afford to the ftate the full benefit
of their characteriftic good qualities. I do not
maintain that fuch an improvement will take
place as fuddenly as the new government may
iffue ordinances, or even as rapidly as the eftablifhments fo decreed can be inftituted : But I
contend, that the improvement of the Arabs may
be expected to proceed with no common degree
of celerity ; that men in their fituation will be
eafily reftored to orderly habits ; and that the
firft fruits of the political change will be an
increafed induftry on the part of the people.
They are not, they never have been flaves,
never even in a political relation to the government, much lefs in domeftic bondage to
the authority of a mafter.

They have not, then, thofe principles and
habits to acquire which are wanting in men born
to flavery, and broken down or eradicated in
men made flaves by capture. They are in a very
different

THE EUROPEAN POWERS.

different situation from the negroes, of whose character and powers we have elsewhere treated. Their labour is indeed defultory, or rather languid; but it is voluntary—it is induftry. The political changes which a new order of things muft introduce, will be fufficiently powerful to operate a fpeedy extenfion and confirmation of thofe habits already acquired, and to develope more fully principles whofe exiftence is unqueftioned.

After the Arabs, who form two thirds of the whole population, the Copts deferve to be confidered. They are the proper Egyptians; defcendants of the fubjects over whom the Ptolemies and Cleopatra once reigned. The character of thefe men, too, is reprefented as refpectable; and one circumftance of no fmall importance diftinguifhes them from the Arabs, to whom, in fome other refpects, they are inferior—they are all Chriftians. The defects to which their political circumftances have rendered them liable, flowing from the fame caufes, are fimilar to thcfe which I have noticed in the habits of the Arabs, with this difference, that the Copts have not the martial qualities fo characteriftic of the other people. They are more accuftomed to peace, and more fubjected to the controul of oppreffive and barbarous rulers. They are probably more induftrious

BOOK III. duſtrious than the Arabs; and they are ſaid to have at bottom a great natural fire of character. * Such are the materials of which the new community is fundamentally to be conſtructed. The handful of Turks and Mamelucs deſerve no attention : they will probably be exterminated in the ſtruggle which may precede a conqueſt of the country ; if not, they muſt be ſunk in the common maſs.

From theſe particulars it may be inferred, that the general qualities or capacities of the materials of civil ſociety, juſt now deſcribed, are favourable to the plan of government which a European dynaſty will certainly adopt ; and that a ſufficient number of cultivators, that is, of day-labourers, will not be wanting to perform the ſimple and eaſy operations of Egyptian agriculture, in the new form which it muſt immediately aſſume ; while the ſtewards, overſeers, upper ſervants, teachers, clerks, and moſt of the mechanics, will be brought over from the mother country.

It is not, then, by ſlaves brought from a diſtant country, and ſcarcely reſembling their maſters in any one particular, that the new colony will be cultivated. A numerous body

of

* Volney, I. 202.—Savary, tom. III. let. 2.

of hardy and active peasantry will soon be formed, enjoying the freedom granted by the mild forms of European government, working for the maintenance of their families, and rewarded by the enjoyment of pleasures, comforts, and political privileges. The African slave trade, it is most fervently to be hoped, will never find admittance into this promising system, from the temptations which very low prices and abundant supply of negroes hold out. The government which we are supposing to obtain the rich possession, will surely remember the fates of the French slave-masters in America, abolish at once the trifling commerce in men, which at present subsists in Egypt *, and prefer a struggle with some small additional inconvenience or delay, to the contemptible and transient advantages that may be obtained at the risk of ultimate ruin.

We may conclude, then, that the structure of the new colony will be firm and pure ; as well adapted to sustain all the shocks to which it may be exposed, as any colonial establishment can possibly be; closely united to the mother country, both by commercial or casual intercourse of inhabitants, interchange of population, and respectable public character ; and more especially connected with it by the proximity of its situation.

---

* Sonnini, chap. XXXVI.

BOOK
III.
fituation. In all thefe effential particulars, it will have a manifeft advantage over every American colony ; and they are circumftances affecting the wealth, as well as the political importance and relations of a remote province. But, above all, Egypt will be cultivated by a numerous body of free and hardy men ; labour will bear its ordinary price ; the produce will be raifed at an expence trifling indeed when compared with that of the Weft Indian negroes * ; and it will be manufactured into its moft refined forms, with the fame facility as in Europe, fince labour will be nearly as cheap. This free peafantry will cultivate the moft fertile region on the face of the earth, with every convenience for manufacturing their raw produce and tranfporting their wrought goods ; with a conftant facility of felling their commodities at home,

* We may remark the important confequences of employing hired labour, in the prices of Afiatic fugars, which are raifed entirely by free hands. In Cochin, the great fugar market of the fouth of Afia, the fineft fugar is fold for lefs than a penny the pound, (De Poivre, Voyage d'un Philofophe, p. 89.) Although the truth of this fact is no manner of argument in favour of the emancipation of the negroes, or the culture of the Weft Indian colonies by free hands ; a purpofe to which fome zealous and worthy men have attempted to apply it, (Clarkfon's Effay, part II. chap. I. § 3.—De Poivre, p. 90.) ; yet it proves clearly how much cheaper Egyptian produce will be raifed by free men, under a favourable climate, and in an excellent foil.

home, and with a conftant demand for them from
Europe and Afia. The goods thus raifed in the
moft frugal manner and in the moft luxuriant
abundance, will be collected into depôts by the
wholefale merchant and manufacturer ; a clafs
of men who will not be wanting in the new
colony, as they are in the defective fociety
of the Weft Indies. They will be tranfport-
able at all feafons, fubject only to the additional expence of a fhort, fafe, and eafy voyage to the confumer.—And thofe are the commodities with which the Weft Indian planters have to fupport a competition! Is it
fanciful to affert, that every cane-piece which
is holed in Egypt, muft neceffarily lay wafte
two in the Antilles? and that the tropical
colonies of the New World muft be defolated, by the rapid operation of irrefiftible
powers, exactly in proportion to the revival of
induftry and fkill in the moft ancient theatre of
human exertion ? The cultivation, that is, the
conqueft of Egypt by a European ftate, or its
improvement by an enlightened and independent
government, muft be as inevitably fatal to the
exiftence of the European name in the Charaibean Sea, as the eftablifhment of a negro commonwealth ; with this difference, that the latter
cataftrophe will, in all human probability, work
its effects by force and flaughter, while the
former event will defolate the Weft Indies by

a

BOOK III. a peaceful though fudden operation. The one is the violent, the other the natural death—the true *euthanafia* of the old colonial fyftem.

Such appear to be the confequences, firft to the Afiatic, and next to the American colonies of the European powers, which muft neceffarily flow from the improvement and cultivation of Egypt, in whatever manner that event fhall be brought about. It remains to take a curfory view of the policy dictated by the colonial interefts of the different ftates, with refpect to the combinations which may accelerate fuch confequences as thofe that have juft now been paffed under review.

We have feen, that to the Afiatic colonies nothing but good can arife from the improvement of Egypt, whether under an independent government, or under the colonial dominion of any one European power. But the Afiatic colonies are of much lefs importance to the parent ftates than their American fettlements. The abfurdity, then, of facrificing the exiftence of the latter, to the partial improvement of the former, is abundantly obvious : and we have feen, that nothing lefs than the annihilation of of the Weft Indian colonies, by far the moft important part of the American fyftem, can refult from the improvement of Egypt, whether it is effected by an independent or by a colo-

nial

nial regimen. It appears manifeft, then, and at firft fight altogether unqueftionable, that the improvement of Egypt is an event to be deprecated, and if poffible prevented by all the European ftates which poffefs colonies in the Weft Indies. But a little farther attention to the fubject, may perhaps lead us to modify this conclufion in feveral important particulars.

A great diftinction muft be made between the improvement of Egypt as a colony of fome European power, and its improvement as an independent ftate. Let us, in the *firft* place, confider the general confequences of the defolation of the Weft Indies, whether caufed by the eftablifhment of an independent government in Egypt, or by the efforts of fome power unconnected with the European community, or by the victories of fome European power.

The improvement of Egypt can only deftroy the Weft Indian fyftem, by enabling a new fet of planters and merchants greatly to underfell thofe of the Weft Indies. All the confumers of Weft Indian produce, therefore, muft be great gainers by the change. Thofe only can lofe who are immediately concerned in the plantation trade, who have removed to the Weft Indies for the purpofe of felling their labour dear, who have invefted their ftock in the purchafe of land, or who have lent their capital to perfons engaged in the Weft Indian agriculture.

agriculture. All thefe claffes of men will be
ruined by the change ; the labourers will be
forced to remove elfewhere, the proprietors
will lofe all their ftock, and the creditors all
that part of their capital which they had lent
to the proprietors. But the merchants-im-
porters of colonial produce will gain by the
new arrangement. They will trade to Egypt
inftead of the Weft Indies. The returns of
their capital will be quicker, though their profits will be a little lefs ; the rifk will be confiderably diminifhed ; and the cheapnefs of the
Egyptian produce will increafe the demand for
it. The manufacturer of goods formerly ufed
in the colonies, will alfo gain by the change,
inafmuch as the new market will be much
more extenfive than the old.

The general interefts of manufacture and
trade will gain in like manner ; for a portion
of the capital formerly employed in the more
expenfive traffic will now be fet free by the
diminution of the prices ; and the cheaper the
confumer purchafes that produce, the more money will he have left to purchafe other articles.
The general interefts, then, both of the mercantile and confuming part of the community,
will reap great and folid advantage from this
new diftribution of colonial property, whether
that fhall be effected by France, Spain, or Holland,

land, or by fome independent government e-
ftablifhed in Egypt, or by fome power unconnected with Europe. On the other hand, the interefts of the
Weft Indian colonifts, and of thofe concern-
ed in the agriculture of the iflands, will be
ruined ; the mother countries will lofe all the
advantages, political and commercial, which
they formerly derived from purfuing the fyftem
of colonial policy, and which I endeavoured to point out in the Firft Book of this Inquiry. All the capital embarked in colonial
fpeculations and loans will of courfe be funk ;
but the new capital conftantly accumulated,
which would naturally have fought for employment in the Weft Indies, will now be employed either in the remaining colonies, or in
the new community. Different nations will
evidently fuffer in very different degrees by the
change. Holland, whofe colonial policy is of
moft importance to her, and whofe Weft Indian colonies bear a greater proportion to her
whole colonial dominions than thofe of any
other power, will be moft of all injured. France
will probably fuffer next, admitting that fhe is
not miftrefs of Egypt ; after her Britain ; and
then Spain, whofe interefts will be very little
affected : while Portugal can fcarcely fuffer at
all by the change. It happens, however, that
all the powers which poffefs Weft Indian territories

ritories of confiderable importance, poffefs alfo
other colonies both in Afia and America, except
Holland, whofe remaining colonies lye in Afia
and Africa. The fcene of their colonial profperity will therefore be changed by the new
arrangement; and inftead of cultivating the
Weft Indian iflands, they will improve North
and South America, Africa and Afia, after adopting thofe reforms, and introducing that liberal fyftem of provincial policy, which the
lofs of their fineft fettlements muft ftrongly recommend.

It is not eafy to form any comparative eftimate of the advantages and difadvantages likely to arife from any event, fo as to balance the
one againft the other, when the benefits are
altogether of a commercial, and the injuries
are both of a commercial and political nature.
All the benefits which can refult to the ftates
of Europe from the improvement of Egypt,
are of a nature ftrictly commercial or œconi-
mical; they end in the faving or the increafe
of the national capital. The loffes to which
this event will unqueftionably fubject the ftates
poffeffing Weft Indian colonies, are partly
commercial, and partly political. It may be
poffible to compare the commercial loffes with
the gains likely to refult from the change;
and there can be little doubt that we fhall be
inclined to ftrike a balance favourable to the
change

change in this refpect, if we take into the account
the vaft extent of the confumption of colonial
produce, now reckoned amongft the prime neceffaries of civilized life ; the fmall amount of
the capital employed in raifing that produce,
compared with the capital employed in circulat-
ing and in purchafing it for confumption ; and
the vent which remaining colonies will ftill afford to the future accumulations of ftock. On
the other hand, admitting that an overplus remains in favour of the new arrangement confidered as a mercantile benefit, this balance,
confifting entirely of commercial profit, cannot
be compared with the remaining lofs attendant
upon the event, and compofed entirely of political inconvenience or injury. The wealth of
France and Britain, for example, may, upon
the whole, be increafed by the change which
fhall deprive them of their Weft Indian colonies. But thofe colonies, confidered as an integral part of the French and Britifh dominions,
are productive of various advantages to the o-
ther parts, befides contributing to augment
the national capital. Thefe have been enumerated in a former part of this Inquiry, * and they
cannot properly be compared with any pecuniary confiderations. They therefore remain to
induce an oppofition on the part of Britain and
France to any plan which may improve Egypt at
the

---

* Book l. Sect. I.

the expence of the Weft Indies. Perhaps, too, the total clear gain in point of wealth which is to be expected from the improvement of Egypt, may receive a great diminution from the fuddennefs of the change. The fhock which the credit of the mother country is likely to experience from fuch an event as the rapid deftruction of the Weft Indian colonies, and the injury which the whole fyftem muft receive from a fudden change in the employment of part of the trading ftock, are evils of a ferious nature in all communities of modern ftructure. Joined to the political inconveniences and injuries before mentioned, thefe circumftances will probably be deemed, by all the European powers, to afford fufficient reafons for deprecating, and if poffible preventing the improvement of Egypt, in whatever way that event may be brought about.

But let us confider, in the *fecond* place, the relative confequences which may be apprehended from the lofs of the Weft Indian colonies, if it is accompanied with the eftablifhment of a European power in Egypt. There is, in this cafe, no difficulty whatever. A fingle glance muft convince us, that this mode of improving Egypt is in the higheft degree hoftile to the interefts, political as well as commercial, of every other European power befides the one to whofe lot Egypt

may

may fall. It is evidently hoftile to the commercial interefts of Europe, inafmuch as the poffeffion of the colony puts the whole produce under the power of one trading nation. Admitting that, for the purpofe of more rapid improvement, a free trade fhall be allowed at firft, then the Weft Indian iflands are laid wafte, and a monopoly continues in the hands of the power poffeffing Egypt ; the colonial produce will therefore be fubjected to imports, taxes, duties, and all the regimen of the fifcal fyftem, excited by the jealoufy of rival traders and hoftile governments. But the poffeffion of the new fettlement is ftill more dangerous to the neighbours of the mother country, from the immenfe addition which it muft fuddenly beftow on her refources. Whilft all her neighbours have loft their Weft Indian colonies, fhe alone has acquired one of importance equal to the whole colonial fyftem, placed almoft in the vicinity of her contiguous provinces, and immenfely valuable, not only as a fubftitute for all the Weft Indian fettlements, but as an emporium of Eaft Indian and of European trade.

This noble province will unite all the advantages of a colony, in a higher degree than they have ever exifted elfewhere, with moft of the benefits arifing from a great extenfion of the proper boundaries of the parent ftate. The poffeffion of

Egypt

Egypt muft of neceffity derange the European balance. After deftroying the colonial fyftem of the Weft, the keys of the Nile will probably beftow the decided fuperiority in the arbitration of European affairs upon the nation which fhall be permitted to keep them, as they anciently threw the fupreme power over the deftinies of the Roman empire into the hands of the firft pre-tender who was happy enough to feize them.

It is unneceffary to point out more explicitly the conduct which thefe confiderations dictate to every European ftate, but more efpecially to thofe poffeffing American colonies. In a merely colonial view, it appears that the poffeffion of Egypt by any enlightened power, however bene-ficial to the Afiatic colonies, is ruinous to thofe of the Weft Indies, and that the colonial in-terefts of all the other powers are oppofed to fuch a revolution. In a more general point of view, fuch a revolution is to be deprecated as fatal to the European fyftem ; and the dread of it will be efteemed at all times a fufficient reafon for vigorous coalition againft the ftate whofe views may be directed towards this quarter, fo long as the different members of the great commonwealth retain that fpirit, equally prudent and honour-able, which has fo often faved the whole fyftem from deftruction.

Let

Let us apply thefe remarks more particu- larly to the event which was in fact accomplifh- ed during the late war—the conqueft of Egypt by France. The difficulty and expence in which the French Weft Indian adminiftration has for fome years been involved, appear to fome more than a match for the whole benefits of the colonial policy. It is even thought that fuch compli- cated difadvantages cannot long be borne, and that the negroes muft foon obtain the fupreme power in the French iflands. I have endeavoured to fhow * that this conclufion is not warranted by the circumftances of thofe fet- tlements ; but it has all along been admitted that the ftruggle by which the colonial exift- ence of the republic muft be maintained is one of no common difficulty and hazard. If, then, the poffeffion of Egypt fhall transfer all the be- nefits of the Weft Indian fyftem to a Mediter- ranean colony, with various additional advan- tages which the old fettlements never poffeffed, it is fair to conclude, that the Weft Indies will be abandoned by France at the very moment of her obtaining a quiet footing in the new pro- vince. Long before an independent govern- ment could fo far improve the Egyptian terri- tory

---

* Book I. Sect. III. Part IV.

tory as to underfell and lay wafte the Weft Indian colonies, the eftablifhment of negro fuperiority in the French iflands will defolate the
whole fettlements in the Archipelago. The ca-
ftrophe, then, which we have been contemplating †, will be moft fuddenly accomplifhed by
the eftablifhment of the French yoke in Egypt.
This is, in every refpect, the mode of improving that country moft hoftile to the colonial interefts of the European powers.

In like manner we may, from this point of
view, eafily perceive new inducements to affift
France in her ftruggle againft the Weft Indian
flaves. If her affairs in that quarter grow defperate, fhe has only one way of retrieving her
colonial exiftence ;—fhe muft ftake her commercial profperity on the acquifition of Egypt,
and prepare for making a ftrong effort in that
quarter with the remains of her colonial troops
and treafure, and the flower of her European
forces ; fhe will of courfe abandon her Weft Indian poffeffions at the outfet of the ftruggle, both
in order to fave the continued expence of the
war and government, and alfo in order to make
a diverfion by means of the revolted negroes,
who will now be fighting her battles as effectually as they before fupported their own
caufe.

In

---

† Book II. Sect. III.

In every point of view, therefore, two inferences may be drawn from all that has been
faid. We may with certainty conclude, that
the colonial interefts of the European powers
dictate the neceffity of aiding France in the
Weft Indies, and vigoroufly keeping her out
of Egypt; and that the European interefts of
thofe ftates dictate the neceffity of purfuing the
fame conduct in the Weft Indies, as well as in
Egypt. The acquifition of Egypt is directly
hoftile to the European fyftem, and indirectly
deftructive of the colonial fyftem. The continuance of the French power in the Weft Indies, is directly effential to the colonial fyftem,
and indirectly favourable to the balance of Europe, from its tendency to prevent the ftrong
efforts which otherwife muft be made againft
Egypt.

The fuccefs of the French arms during the
late war, and the blindnefs of fome European
powers to their beft interefts, render it not impoffible that France may fucceed in the attempt which we are now conceiving her to
make. May not fome meafures be purfued
with the view of continuing a kind of balance
fuited to the new order of colonial policy which
muft in the fuppofed event be introduced?
May not Britain, for example, obtain a fimilar
fhare of the Turkifh empire? The rich and
extenfive

extenfive province of Syria, in little more than
in name a part of the Turkifh empire, is in
many refpects a more valuable acquifition than
Egypt itfelf. The pofition is not altogether fo
convenient, nor the territory fo well diftributed, nor the foil fo inexhauftible in confequence
of perpetual renovation : But the fertile territory is twice as extenfive ; the harbours are
more convenient and numerous ; the climate
is ftill more variegated and falubrious ; the
growth of animals wild and domeftic more a-
bundant ; and the fertility of the land in vegetable productions if poffible more rich and various. Befides affording every fpecies of ufeful
grain in prodigious plenty, the climate and foil
of Syria are admirably fitted for the culture of the
fugar cane, the cotton and tobacco plants, the
indigo and coffee trees, the vine and the olive,
not to mention the cochineal infect and filk-
worm, which thrive in great perfection and a-
bundance. Even under the worft conceivable
fyftem of adminiftration, almoft all of thofe valuable articles are at prefent raifed in great
quantities, without any thing more than the
moft contemptible exertions of induftry and
fkill. In its ruined and defolated ftate, Syria
produces a revenue of nearly one million three
hundred thoufand pounds Sterling ; and its population,

pulation, rapidly diminifhed by a long fuccef- S E C T.
fion of execrable meafures in every department II.
of government and police, is ftill reckoned at
two millions three hundred and five thoufand
by Volney, whofe eftimates are in other inftances
greatly under the truth. †

If this rich and delightful region were added
to the Britifh empire, the acquifition of Egypt
by France would be in every refpect harmlefs,
and in many points of view advantageous. The
Afiatic colonies would be faved from every
chance of annoyance, whilft all the advantages
formerly pointed out as likely to refult from the
improvement of Egypt, would now in a manifold proportion attend the joint cultivation of
Egypt and Syria. The general interefts of the
European powers, and of Britain as well as
France, would be promoted by the abundant
production of colonial produce in its cheapeft
form. The Weft Indian fyftem would indeed
be overturned ; but on its ruins there would be
raifed a more folid and valuable colonial ftructure, a new fyftem, in which France and England

† Volney's Egypt & Syria, vol. II. p. 318. 359. 363.
& 364.—Ricard, III. 421.—Geographie (Encyc. Method.)
III. 318.—Econ. Polit. & Diplom. (ibid.) IV. 297.—
Commerce (ibid.) III. 784.—Eton's Survey, p. 292.—
Harris's Collection, II. 841. *et feqq.*

land would be mutually poifed. The dangers
that might fo fairly be apprehended to the European balance from the conqueft of either province by one power, would now be rendered
nugatory by the equal and oppofite acquifitions
of the two great natural enemies whofe quarrels
divide the European fyftem. The Turkifh empire would, indeed, apparently be difmember-
ed ; and a certain defcription of politicians
would lament the fates of the Ottomans, as
they once wept over the deftinies of the Poles.
But furely no fuch change could render the Sy-
rians, Copts and Arabs, lefs happy than they
at prefent are in their political circumftances ;
whilft any beginning of enlightened government
muft be the dawn of national improvement,
civilization and civil enjoyment to all thofe unfortunate tribes of men. The lovers of humanity,
too, might juftly rejoice in the execution of the
project here fketched, as the dawn of a happier
day to a vaft portion of the human fpecies. The
downfal of the odious traffic which has always
been intimately connected with the Weft Indian
fyftem, is the neceffary confequence of the propofed partition ; and if there were no farther argument from general topics of philanthropy, this
furely would deferve our attention, that it is
not eafy to clofe our ears againft any fcheme,
of which the neceffary confequence muft be,
the

the inftantaneous abolition of the African flave S E C T. II. trade.

I do not here enter at greater length into thefe fpeculations. The fubject is in its nature very much mingled with conjecture and hypothefis. I have ftated the moft material facts, and attempted to point out, both the probable confequences of the events which are fo confidently expected by many politicians, and the peculiar difficulties which attend the different branches of this Inquiry. Some of the conclufions which I have now drawn, appear to follow with fufficient certainty from a comparifon of thofe facts with the principles formerly eftablifhed. The reft, together with other inferences which may be purfued on this fubject, I leave to the difcernment of the reader.

BOOK

BOOK IV.

INTRODUCTION.

In the Firſt Book of this Inquiry, I explained the relations between colonies and their mother countries ; that is, the internal ſtructure of the fyſtem compoſed of colonies and a parent ſtate. In the Second Book, I proceeded to deſcribe the relations between different colonies ; that is, the ſtructure of the fyſtem compoſed of various colonial eſtabliſhments ſituated in the ſame part of the world. In the Third Book, I conſidered the relation between different powers as influenced by their colonial intereſts ; that is, the effects produced by colonial relations upon the ſtructure of the great national fyſtem which we denominate the European Commonwealth. I now proceed to the laſt object of Inquiry, the

Domeſtic

Domeſtic or Internal Colonial Policy of the European powers ; that is, the arrangements of colonial adminiſtration contrived with a view to
promote the happineſs of the ſettlements, and
to preſerve their dependence upon the mother
country.

As the great objects of all domeſtic policy are the preſervation of domeſtic tranquillity, the repulſion of foreign invaſion, and the
promotion of national wealth (which is in many reſpects alſo the foundation of the two former objects) : ſo, the great ends of the internal
adminiſtration of colonial affairs are the increaſe
of wealth, and the ſecurity both of the colonial
government and the power of the mother country from all the efforts of external and internal violence. This branch of the Inquiry,
therefore, divides itſelf into two general heads,
the commercial and the political adminiſtration
of the colonies. Under the former head, are
comprehended all laws relating to trade, agriculture and manufactures, in ſo far as thoſe
may be modified by the ſubordinate predicament
in which the ſettlements are placed. Under
the latter head, are comprehended all laws relating to the ſecondary government eſtabliſhed
in the colonies, their military as well as civil affairs, and their dependence upon the parent
ſtate.

This

This is the general claffification which is
fuggefted by the circumftances common to all
colonies whatever ; but the peculiar ftructure
of fociety in the American fettlements is of
fuch a nature, as to prefent a feparate and preliminary object of fpeculation. The flave fyftem has now become fo radically incorporated
with the colonial fyftem, as to form an effential part of it, and to affect immediately and
powerfully every branch of internal adminiftration, whether commercial or political. Before
we can proceed to difcufs a fingle meafure connected either with the wealth, the government,
or the defence of the American colonies, it is
abfolutely neceffary to examine the grand feature which diftinguifhes thofe fettlements from
every other, and extends its influence fo widely
over the whole fyftem, that no arrangement of
policy can be adopted without a conftant reference to the peculiar conftitution of the colonial
fociety. This fubject, then, is in itfelf complete,
and is by far the moft important that can occupy our attention in confidering the great
weftern branch of the modern colonial fyftem.

The domeftic policy of the Afiatic provinces
being adapted entirely to the ftate of conquered countries, does not properly fall within the
plan of this work. The detail of the internal
adminiftration of the American colonies prefents fo wide a field of difcuffion, that I do not
intend

intend at prefent to enter into it, farther than
is neceffary for the difcuffion of the preliminary
fubject. The domeftic policy of colonial eftablifhments is indeed the part of our general
fubject which is the leaft intricate and the
moft completely underftood. The principles
of national policy upon which fuch inquiries
reft, are fufficiently comprehended by all inquirers in modern times. The only difficulty
which incumbers the difcuffion, arifes from the
ftructure of the colonial fociety in America,
and from feveral particulars hitherto mifunder-
ftood in the general fyftem of colonial policy.
Thofe errors I have attempted to remove in
the Firft Book of this Inquiry; and, after I
fhall have finifhed the confideration of the Negro Slavery, which forms the fubject of this
Book, the remaining part of the Inquiry,
which I propofe to omit, can prefent no material difficulty. It will confift of a few eafy
corollaries from the principles laid down in
the three firft Books, and from thofe which I
am now about to explain.

The complicated iniquities and the manifold difadvantages of the flave fyftem, have for
feveral years called the attention of European
ftatefmen to the correction of abufes fo flagrant, and the remedy of evils fo pregnant
with danger to the fum of colonial affairs.
Various expedients have been propofed during
the

the wide difcuffion which thofe momentous queftions have excited. Some zealots have contended, with an inexcufeable thoughtleffnefs, that the crimes of thofe whofe avarice has transferred the population of Africa to the Weft Indies can only be expiated by immediate emancipation of the flaves. The councils of fuch fanatics have unhappily been adopted and carried into effect by one of the moft enlightened nations in the world ; and we have frequently had occafion to view the confequences of thofe infane meafures in the courfe of this Inquiry.

Others have propofed an abolition of the traffic which has been the original caufe of the evil. But they have differed among themfelves as to the time and mode of effecting this object.

The abolition of the flave trade, however, does not feem, in the opinion of many, to be a fufficient remedy for the dangers of our colonial fyftem at the prefent day. Several fchemes have therefore been brought forward with a view to provide fuch remedies as the urgency of the occafion appears to call for. Of the plans fketched out with this view, the moft important are thofe which recommend an amelioration of the condition of the negroes, and a gradual change in their hard lot. It has been fuggefted by many, that fettlements not yet cultivated may be peopled by free negroes ; and the moft fanguine hopes have been entertained of the falutary confequences

of

of fuch a fcheme. The poffeffion of a great extent of wafte lands, highly fitted for the purpofes
of Weft Indian agriculture, ftrongly recommends to every trading nation any project
which may facilitate the clearing and peopling
of the defert, without the danger and expence
attendant upon the old fyftem. Any plan, too,
which comprehends the idea of free negroes,
or includes the word, is peculiarly adapted to
accord with the feelings of thofe worthy perfons
who are fo keenly alive to the fufferings of the
Africans in a ftate of bondage. It is natural,
therefore, that the fchemes to which I allude
fhould be well received, and even eagerly embraced, before a fufficient interval is allowed for
fober examination. The topic has been lately
renewed by fome ingenious and virtuous men of
this country. It is faid to have found a favourable reception amongft a certain clafs of practical politicians, and, if common fame may be
trufted, it has for fome time occupied the attention of men high in the public confidence. It
has at various times, too, been canvaffed, both
by the fpeculative inquirers, and by the ftatefmen of other nations. It appears to have
been a favourite idea of the virtuous and philofophical Turgot, as well as of others connected with him in affairs ; and a project was
completely prepared about the time of his memorable adminiftration, for conducting the cultivation

tivation of French Guiana upon the principles
of the free negro fyftem. *

The projects to which I am here alluding, are
dangerous in the extreme. They have all the dangers and defects of puny half-meafures ; they offer no remedy to the great evil ; they lull the
attention of men during thofe critical moments
when a real cure might be effected by bolder fteps.
They give the interefted advocates of the prefent
order of things a plaufible pretence for affecting
to concede on their part, and claiming reciprocal conceffions from the other party. They afford the falfe friends of the abolition an opportunity of deferting a ftrong hold which they do
not wifh to fee defended, and of occupying a
middle ground fafe only to themfelves. In politics, the bold and decifive meafure is generally
the fafeft in the end ; though it requires ftronger nerves to attempt it, and a more capacious
mind to perceive its fuperior wifdom. In the
prefent great queftion, the bold and decifive
line of conduct is either immediate abolition,
or a fteady perfeverance in the fyftem now eftablifhed. Paltry and timid minds would fhudder
at the thought of mere inactivity, as cowardly
troops would tremble at the idea of calmly waiting for the enemy's approach. Both the one
and the other haften their fate by reftleffnefs
and foolifh movements, inftead of boldly ad-
vancing

* Note U u.

vancing to the charge, or firmly awaiting the onfet.

I purpofe, therefore, in the *firſt* place, to examine this very interefting queftion ; to prove, from the moft fimple and obvious confiderations, the inefficacy and impoffibility of the plans propofed ; and to fhew, that the dangers of the new order of things intended to be eftablifhed by fuch fchemes would be fo great, as to render their utter impracticability a real blefling. This will form the fubject of the Firft Section. In the Second Section, I fhall proceed to confider the means of ameliorating the ftructure of fociety in the flave colonies, and of averting the dangers which impend over the whole fabric, from the preponderance of the inferior claffes, their low degree of civilization, and the fuccefles that have, in fome of the colonies, attended their efforts to revenge themfelves upon their fuperiors.

The difcuffion of thefe topics will complete the general and preliminary view of Weft Indian policy, which alone I purpofe, at prefent, to embrace in this Book, and will comprehend the examination of all thofe queftions connected with the flave fyftem, which have not been confidered in the foregoing Books. An inveftigation of the remaining fubjects that fall under the title of Domeftic Colonial Policy muft be deferred to a future opportunity.

S E C-

SECTION I.

OF THE FREE NEGRO SYSTEM, OR THE POLICY OF
CULTIVATING THE COLONIES BY MEANS OF FREE
NEGROES.

IT has been remarked a thoufand times, that
the defires and wants of man in a rude ftate
are few and eafily gratified. The chief exertion to which neceffity impels him, is the procuring of food; and his hunger is no fooner
fatisfied than he finks into the luxury of repofe. When the natural fertility of the foil
affords him fpontaneoufly a regular, though
fimple and perhaps fcanty fupply, and the unvaried ferenity of the climate precludes the neceffity of covering or fhelter; the powers of
his mind become languid and feeble ; his corporeal ftrength decays; and he regards as the
greateft of all evils any occupation that calls
for mental exertion, or is attended with bodily
fatigue; while this indolence in its turn enables him to fubfift on a much fmaller portion
of food, than is required to fupport a life of activity and labour.

Thus, the original inhabitants of America were aftonifhed at the voracity of the
Spaniards,

Spaniards, who, probably from the fame caufes, are the moft temperate people in Europe : and while the neceffaries of life were
fo eafily procured, the conquerors found it utterly impoffible to overcome the conftitutional
repugnance to labour of every kind, which
they perceived in their new fubjects. Before
they had recourfe to an expedient which they
knew muft in the end prove ruinous, the fyftem of *repartimientos*, every trial was made to
call forth voluntary induftry : But they foon
difcovered that men, who had no defires to
gratify, would not fubmit to work ; and that
no fear of diftant evil, nothing but the lafh of
a mafter, could conquer the rooted averfion
with which habit had taught the Indian to
view every purfuit that required active exertion. Even after the plan, fo fatal to the inhabitants of the New World, had been adopted,
the humane zeal of Las Cafas brought its impolicy and injuftice repeatedly under the review both of Ferdinand and Charles. The fubject was inveftigated by Ximenes, with his ufual boldnefs and ability : the minifter was overcome by the arguments of the ' Friend of the
' Indians : ' commiffioners of the moft undoubted integrity and talents were appointed
to inveftigate on the fpot, the whole merits of
this great queftion, with powers fuitable to the
importance of their office ; but the refult of
their

all their inquiries led to the fame conclufion, that the emancipation of the natives muft be the fignal for an univerfal ceffation of induftry ; and the Spanifh government had not fufficient virtue to embrace this alternative. Towards the latter part of Charles's reign, the confequences of the fyftem were fatally experienced in the rapid extermination of the Indians. Anxious if poffible to preferve fo large a portion of his American fubjects, the Emperor, with that quicknefs of decifion which too often marked his councils, proclaimed their immediate and unconditional emancipation. Still it was found that their induftry and freedom were incompatible. The alarm was inftantly fpread over the whole Spanifh colonies : Peru, for a while loft to the monarchy, was only reftored by the repeal of the obnoxious law : the quiet of New Spain was preferved, by a combination of the Governor and the fubjects to fufpend its execution : and all that the power of the Spanifh government has hitherto been able to effect, confiftently with the profitable cultivation of its American poffeffions, is the eftablifhment of certain humane regulations, tending to mitigate the neceffary fervitude of the Indians.

The negroes, though in a lefs degree, are nearly in the fame circumftances with that unhappy race, to whofe bondage and toils they

BOOK
IV.

they have been doomed to fucceed. Born in
a lefs genial climate, and compelled to procure their fuftenance by fomewhat greater exertions, they are not content with fo fmall a
portion of food, and view with lefs horror the
labour of providing it. But beyond this their
induftry does not extend. Like all favages,
they are incited to exertion only by immediate
neceffity. If you talk to them of conveniences,
and comforts, and the delights of activity,
you fpeak a language which they have not yet
learnt to comprehend ; and the idea of a pleafure which muft be purchafed by toil, prefents
to their minds a contradiction in terms. Were
they, indeed, allowed to remain in their own
country, the influence of thofe defires which
fpring from local attachment, the ties of kindred, and the intercourfe of more civilized men,
might by flow degrees awaken thofe appetites,
and create thofe artificial wants, which alone
can excite regular and effective induftry. But
if fuddenly removed to a milder climate and
a more plentiful foil, with their original repugnance to exert more labour than neceffity prefcribes, it is not to be imagined that any thing
except the power of a mafter can prevent
them from finking into the ftate of liftlefs inactivity, which feemed to be the natural condition of the Indians. *

Accordingly,

* Park's Travels in the Interior of Africa, Chap.
XXIV.—Wimpffen's Letters, No. XV.

Accordingly, the negroes who have been tranfported to America, are uniformly found to be totally deficient in active induftry. That thofe who continue in a ftate of flavery fhould exhibit the appearance of an indolence which nothing but the immediate terror of the lafh can overcome, is perhaps more the confequence of their degraded condition, than of their uncivilized ftate. But the want of activity is not confined to the flaves. The free negroes in the Weft Indies are, with a very few exceptions, chiefly in the Spanifh and Portuguefe fettlements, equally averfe to all forts of labour which do not contribute to the fupply of their immediate and moft urgent wants. Improvident and carelefs of the future, they are not actuated by that principle which inclines more civilized men to equalize their exertions at all times, and to work after the neceffaries of the day have been procured, in order to make up the poffible deficiencies of the morrow : nor has their intercourfe with the whites taught them to confider any gratification as worth obtaining, which cannot be procured by a flight exertion of a defultory and capricious induftry.

The flaves, indeed, who are forced to labour during the whole week for their mafters, fhew fome fymptoms of application in cultivating their own provifion-grounds on the

holidays

BOOK
IV.
holidays allowed them. But the moft indolent of men, if pufhed into activity for the advantage of others, will naturally continue their exertions, at leaft for a fhort time, when they are themfelves to reap the fruits of the additional toil; and the voluntary labour for their own profit, during the little interval of liberty, may become tolerable, by forming a contraft to the unrepaid and compulfory fatigues, in which by far the greater part of their days are fpent. In fact, even under thefe favourable circumftances, the flaves in our Weft Indian iflands allot but a very fmall proportion of their free time to the work for which they are with certainty to be recompenfed, by gains that no mafter ever interferes with. Out of the fix days per month (befides accidental holidays) which are allowed them in Jamaica, for the cultivation of their grounds, the more induftrious do not allot above fixteen hours to this employment. *

But from the accounts which have been received of the free negroes, it appears that their induftry is ftill more fparing. Of their invincible repugnance to all forts of labour, the moft ample evidence is produced in the Report of the Committee of Privy Council in 1788. The witneffes examined upon Queries 37. & 38. from all the Britifh iflands, concur

---

* Edwards' Weft Indies, Book IV. chap. 5. [note.]

cur in this ſtatement. It will be ſufficient to refer more particularly to the evidence from Jamaica and Barbadoes. In the former ſettlements, Meſſrs Fuller Long & Chiſholme ſtate, that free negroes were never known to work for hire; and that they have all the vices of the ſlaves. The Committee of Council of the iſland, beſides corroborating this aſſertion, add, that the free negroes are averſe to work for themſelves, except when compelled by immediate neceſſity. Mr Brathwaite, the agent for Barbadoes, affirms, that if the ſlaves in that iſland were offered their freedom on condition of working for themſelves, not one tenth of them would accept of it. Governor Parry ſtates, that the free negroes are utterly deſtitute of induſtry; and the Council of the iſland adds, that from their confirmed habits of idleneſs they are the peſts of ſociety. *

The accounts which foreigners have given us of the ſame claſs of men in almoſt all the other colonies, agree moſt accurately with the ſtatements collected by the Committee of Privy Council. M. Malouet, who bore a ſpecial commiſſion from the French government to examine the character and habits of the Maroons in Dutch Guiana, and to determine whether or not they were adapted to become hired labourers, informs us, that they will only work

one

---

* Report 1788, part III.

one day in the week, which they find abundantly
fufficient, in the fertile foil and genial climate of
the New World, to fupply all the wants that they
have yet learnt to feel. The reft of their time is
fpent in abfolute indolence and floth. ' *Le repos*,'
(fays he) ' *l'oifiveté font devenus dans leur etat fo-*
' *cial leur unique paffion.* ' * He gives the very
fame defcription of the free negroes in the
French colonies. † Although many of them
poffefs land and flaves, the fpectacle, he tells
us, was never yet exhibited of a free negro
fupporting his family by the culture of his
little property. ‡ All other authors agree in
giving the fame defcription of free negroes in
the Britifh, French, and Dutch colonies, by
whatever denomination they may be diftinguifhed, whether Maroons, Charaibes, Free blacks,
or Fugitive flaves. The Abbé Raynal himfelf,
with all his ridiculous fondnefs for favages,
cannot, in the prefent inftance, fo far twift the
facts according to his fancies and feelings, as
to give a favourable portrait of this degraded
race.

Such are the men by whofe voluntary labour
it is propofed to clear the thick forefts of the
New World, and to cover its boundlefs favan-
nahs with plantations and pens. Nor does it
feem to be of much confequence, in this view
of

---

* Mem. fur les Colonies, V. 121.
† Ibid IV. 141.   ‡ Ibid V. 127.

of the matter, whether the new ftock of negroes is imported at once from Africa, or purchafed in a ftate of flavery from our old fettlements. Thofe who had been flaves, either in the European plantations, or the kingdoms of Africa (efpecially the former), would from habit be more prepared for labour, and more fkilful in performing work, than free men in a rude ftate, who had never experienced the hardfhips of fatigue. The Whydah negroes, in their own country, are for the moft part in a ftate of bondage, and their lands are in much better cultivation than thofe of the other tribes. Accordingly, in the Weft Indies, they are uniformly preferred to all others for docility, quietnefs, and fubmiffion to the mafter. * The Kòromantees unite to greater bodily ftrength a more fierce and untameable difpofition : but fuch of them as have been flaves in Africa, are obferved to apply with greater alacrity and effect to field labour, † and are on this account preferred by the Dutch planters to all others. ‡ Thefe habits of induftry, however, have been formed by the conftant dread of punifhment ; no principle lefs powerful can maintain them ; and they muft ceafe with the mafter's authority to which they owed their exiftence.

This

* Edwards, b. IV. c. 3.   † Edwards, ibid.
‡ Book. 1. Sect. III. Part I.

This has been clearly eftablifhed by the view which has already been taken of the free negroes in our old fugar colonies. But ftill more chimerical would be the expectation of any voluntary exertion of induftry in Africans newly imported from a ftate of freedom in their own country. Is it to be fuppofed that thofe men, carried directly from their native fands and deferts to the New World, will at once feel wants and acquire habits to which they were formerly ftrangers? In our old colonies, it is found neceffary to teach the newly imported flave the difficult leffon of induftry by flow degrees, by the example of others to whofe care he is committed for inftruction, and by the conftant application of the driver's lafh. In the Portuguefe fettlements, this courfe of difcipline is ftill more feduloufly attended to ; and, that it may begin fooner, the flave fhips are partly manned with Brazil negroes. But, in the Weft Indies, the fame uncivilized men are fuddenly to become diligent and quiet labourers, eager for employment and ready to be taught, able to fhake off with their fhip irons all their ancient habits of liftlefs indolence, and anxious to divert their thoughts from brooding over their misfortunes, by fubmitting to a life of active exertion, with that cheerful refignation which is the moft valuable growth of a refined and philofophic age. I greatly fear that thefe

projectors

projectors truft a little too much to the effects of
the middle paffage upon thofe unfortunate men.
I muft be allowed to fufpect, that, in order to
people Trinidad and the other unfettled colonies with negroes who will work for hire, they
muft difcover a new race of Africans induftrious in their own country, or invent fome method of operating inftantaneoufly upon the tribes
already known, an enlargement of defires and
a change of habits, which, in the natural progrefs of human fociety, is the flow produce of
many fucceeding ages.

Voluntary labour for hire, that exertion
which we denominate induftry, however fimple
it may appear to us who are accuftomed to it,
is neverthelefs a refinement wholly unknown
among the favage tribes of Africa. All travellers agree in this ftatement of the fact. The
numbers who are either born or made flaves in
that continent, are faid to exceed thofe of the
free inhabitants in a threefold proportion. There,
as in the Weft Indies, the bondfmen form the
labouring part of every community. In Africa,
as in our colonies, that unnatural ftate of fociety
exifts in full perfection, which feparates the toil
from the enjoyment of its fruits. No fuch thing
as a man working for another, from the inducement of hire or reward, or from any voluntary
bargain, was ever heard of in that continent.
Nothing, then, but compulfion can there effect

that

BOOK
IV.

that divifion of labour and reward which is fo repugnant to natural juftice. Thofe who have no flaves, work juft long enough to fupply their neceffary wants, or hire the flaves of others if they can afford it : thofe who have flaves of their own, never think of labouring themfelves.*

It would appear then, that, with refpect to the habits and qualities of the negroes, the moft hopelefs of the two fchemes for extending the Weft Indian cultivation, is that which confifts in direct importation. But befides the objections already urged againft the more circuitous method of procuring negroes, there are others fo infuperable as of themfelves to render its adoption impoffible.

After a refidence in our iflands fufficient to train and feafon the negroes, they muft have formed local attachments ftrong enough to make tranfportation in a high degree painful. Accordingly, in the penal code of the flave laws, banifhment occupies the next place to death. Still more cruel would fuch an exchange be to the Creole negroes, for whom, as moft valuable, the demand would be greateft. And as the place of all who are exported muft be fupplied by frefh importations from Africa, a double cruelty and injuftice would thus be committed.

---

* Park's Travels in the Interior of Africa, chap. XXI, & XXII.

committed. Befides, the fecurity of the old colonies would be manifeftly injured by fuch conftant drains of their feafoned hands, and fo great an influx of new and unbroken flaves; while the inhabitants of the new fettlements would have their profits, already much lefs than thofe of flave proprietors, ftill more diminifhed by being forced to buy their negroes, not at the African price, nor yet at that which new flaves fetch in the Weft Indian market, but at the ftill higher rate which the old planters muft demand for flaves already trained to work. This additional expence, firft, from the double paffage, next, from the difference between the labour of the negroes feafoned in the iflands, and the labour of thofe firft feafoned and then tranfported, and, laftly, from the extra profits of the Weft Indian planter, would operate at the very period of cultivation, already fufficiently necumbered with coft and difficulty, and would effectually difable the planter, who fhould adopt the new fyftem, from entering into competition with his brethren in the old colonies : not to mention the impoffibility of preventing a contraband trade with the coaft of Africa, where the temptation would be fo ftrong, and the means of concealment fo eafy; in extenfive countries abounding in harbours, and thinly peopled with men more or lefs engaged in planting, and in-

terefted

terefted in conniving at abufes of this fort. Suppofe it were required to people Trinidad in this
way, the foreign fettlements in the Weft Indies
and America would be at leaft as unfit to fupply the demand as our own, except perhaps
Brazil, which is favourably fituated, and is enabled, by the extent of the Portuguefe poffeffions in Africa and the fhortnefs of the middle
paffage, to import flaves at a much cheaper rate
than any other colony ; but, then, the Portuguefe laws ftrictly prohibit re-exportaion, doubtlefs, in order to keep up the proportion of Creole
negroes ; and as, in various inftances, they
watch over the rights of flaves, it is evident
that goods of this defcription would be of all
others the moft difficult and expenfive to fmug-
gle.

We may conclude, therefore, that the only
practicable method of tranfporting a population
of negroes to Trinidad, or the other unculti-
vated colonies, is the direct importation from
Africa, while, unfortunately, the people thus
procured, are leaft of any adapted to the fituation of free labourers, which they are required
to fill.

But, admitting for a moment that capitalifts
acquainted with the nature of the bufinefs could
be induced to fpeculate in the way recommended, let us confider the probable confequences of
the

the plan fucceeding, and fee whether the very
fame dangers might not refult from filling the
fettlements with emancipated exiles, that are fo
juftly to be apprehended, from the more practicable and fcarcely lefs humane fcheme of allowing the flave trade to be introduced in its
full extent.

In the *firft* place, as it is granted on all
hands that the cultivation by free negroes will,
for fome years at leaft, be more expenfive than
the old method, both from the price of their
labour in addition to their purchafe-money, and
from the inferior efficacy of their voluntary induftry ; fome compenfation for this difference
muft be given, and a ftrong temptation held out
to induce planters to employ their capital in a
fpeculation againft which fo many violent prejudices may be expected at firft to prevail. If
any allurements can be found fufficient to counteract thefe ; if, for example, as has been propofed, * government fhall freely grant the crown
lands to cultivators ; and if the inducement of
faving the original purchafe-money fhall be
ftrong enough to outweigh the confiderations of
fubfequent expence and rifk ; it is moft probable that the balance will only need to be turned, in order to preponderate as much the other
way.

---

* Crifis of the Sugar Colonies, let. IV.

way. The fpirit of adventure delights in fudden movements, and when once excited, generally runs into extremes. In the New World,
at leaft, it has always been of an infectious nature ; and a fpeculator who is led aftray by its
flattering influence, feldom wants companions
either to partake of his fuccefs or to fhare his
ruin. If the general effects of large capital, and
the character of Britifh traders, left us any room
to doubt that they are as fufceptible of thefe
impulfes as the firft invaders of America ; the
whole hiftory of our fugar iflands, but ftill more
the eagernefs with which Britifh capital was
poured into the Dutch colonies during the late
war, might convince us of what we have to expect, fhould any means be adopted for opening
a paffage to the rich and virgin foil of Trinidad. The inftant that the obftructions to the
new fcheme are removed, we may reft affured, that no bounds will be fet to the enter-
prifing fpirit of monied men. If the engine is
once put in motion, its velocity will be prodigious. The arguments which convince, or the
profpects which allure one planter, will fpread
their influence to many ; and in a very fhort
time the few white inhabitants of the ifland
will be furrounded with multitudes of free negroes, far more fuddenly collected, and probably in greater numbers, than the flaves who cul-

tivate

tivate the moft populous of our ancient poffeffions.

Now thefe fwarms of barbarians, thus rapidly introduced, are indeed to be all free.

Before examining what, in their fituation,
muft be the meaning of this word (whofe found
feems to have ftrangely mifled fo many writers
and orators on the colonial queftion), let us
confider under what circumftances the importation is made. So great and fudden an increafe
in the demand for negroes, muft produce extraordinary exertions on the part of the African
flave merchant and his providers. The ftock of
thofe who poffefs flaves will foon be exhaufted ;
the number of thofe condemned for crimes will
remain nearly the fame as before ; the deficiency muft be fupported by an increafe of the
only other means of procuring negroes, war and
pillage. * It is eafy to perceive, that the tract
of country whofe inhabitants are moft fierce and
contentious, will be neceffarily reforted to. The
peaceful natives of Whydah will furnifh but a
fmall part of the additional fupply. The ferocious inhabitants of the Gold Coaft, eafily roufed

to

---

* In the language of moft of the African nations, what
we call war is diftinguifhed by the name of the ' *Great Pil-*
' *lage* ; ' a metaphor (fhall we call it ?) peculiarly defcriptive of the hoftilities of thofe people, and not altogether in-
expreffive of the contentions carried on in fome other parts
of the world.

to hoſtilities congenial to their diſpoſitions, will
recruit the holds of our ſlave ſhips, and form a
large proportion of the quickly increaſing population of the new ſettlements. Can it be imagined, that tribes of ſavages thus torn from their
native country, ſuddenly deprived of that unre-
ſtrained freedom which was the pride of their
roaming lives, loaded with chains, and crowded
into a nauſeous dungeon, tranſported to a diſtant
region by a ſtrange race of men, known to them
only by their cruel rapacity—Can it be imagined, that immediately on the words of emancipation being pronounced, they will become
peaceful ſubjects of their oppreſſors, and voluntarily ſubmit to an authority unſupported by
force?

We know, that in all colonies where the
ſtrict ſubordination of ſlavery exiſts, the newly imported negroes are carefully diſtributed a-
mong thoſe whom time has habituated to the
yoke; and any rapid increaſe of numbers is
dreaded as the forerunner of rebellion. In almoſt all negro inſurrections, the new ſlaves
have been the chief inſtigators * ; and thoſe
from the Gold Coaſt have generally been found
the moſt difficult to tame, and moſt prone to
rebellion. † Yet our iſlands have been ſlowly
peopled;

* Long's Hiſt. of Jamaica, vol. II. p. 444.
† Edwards' Weſt Indies, b. IV. c. 3.

peopled ; and time has always been given for
uniting the unbroken negroes with the general
mafs. In the beginning of the laft century, the
average imports from the Britifh Weft Indies a-
mounted to feven hundred thoufand pounds. In
the middle of that century, this average had only increafed to a million and a half; and at the
end of the century, it was under five millions,
including the produce of Trinidad and the
iflands ceded by the peace of Paris, and notwithftanding the diminifhed fupply occafioned
by the ftate of the French Weft Indies, and the
diverfion of capital from North America in
confequence of the war. The increafe of the
whites, too, bore fome proportion to the importation of flaves. In 1734, the negroes of Jamaica amounted to upwards of eighty-fix thoufand ; the whites to feven thoufand fix hundred
only. In 1768, the former had increafed to a-
bout a hundred and fixty-feven thoufand ; the
latter to feventeen thoufand : And in 1791,
the negroes amounted to two hundred and fifty
thoufand, while the whites had increafed to
thirty thoufand, of whom eight thoufand eight
hundred were feamen, and fix thoufand three
hundred bore arms in the militia. The vaft
importations into St Domingo during the ten
years previous to the contentions between the
whites

whites and the people of colour, facilitated in all probability the defigns of thofe who excited the negroes to infurrection. While the numbers of the whites had rather decreafed, * the ftock of negroes had rifen from two hundred and fifty thoufand to four hundred and eighty thoufand, including thofe employed in domeftic fervice and town occupations, who were of courfe as numerous in 1779 as in 1789, that is, about forty-fix thoufand. The field negroes, then, were confiderably more than doubled. † Yet even in St Domingo, there was a large population of flaves born in the ifland, with whom thofe newly arrived might incorporate. In Trinidad and the other new fettlements, there is not even this foundation to build upon. Every thing muft be begun anew. Swarms of negroes muft be poured in, with only the few proprietors of plantations to keep them in fubjection, and to ftand between them and plunder.

But the *freedom* of thefe unfortunate men is, according to the principles upon which the project appears to have been formed, fufficient to difarm them of all defigns hoftile to the fecurity of the whites. Let us for a moment confider the fituation in which this freedom will place them.

It

---

* Necker, Adminift. des Finances, tom. I. chap. 13.
† Rapport à l'Affemblée Legiflative 1792,

It is propofed that the planter fhall have a preferable right to purchafe the labour of the negroes
whom he imports, and this right of preemption
is defcribed as an additional encouragement to
fpeculation. But it is manifeft that this is not
merely a gratuitous encouragement ; it is a neceffary part of the plan. No man could ever
be found foolifh enough to buy or import negroes, if, upon their landing, another might reap
the profit of the fpeculation, by hiring them for
his own ufe. It is therefore not an arbitrary
regulation added for the farther encouragement
of cultivation, but an effential ingredient of the
fyftem, that the importer or purchafer öf a negro fhall have the fole right to his labour for a
term of years, at a rate of wages fixed by law.
This is called by the projectors, particularly by
the author of the *Crifis*, ' the known relation of
indented fervant ; ' and the fancied analogy
feems at firft to give the fcheme a more feafible
afpect. But it fhould be remembered, that indented fervants in the North American colonies
were always men accuftomed at home to labour
for hire ; driven from their country by want of
employment, or the profpect of greater wealth,
and eager to find work in the new world. They
were, therefore, exactly in the fituation from
which the greateft exertions of induftry might
be expected, whether for profit or for hire ;
and

BOOK IV.

and there was no occasion for coercion to prevent them from being idle. The free negroes,
on the other hand, muft be forced to work;
and accordingly, it is farther admitted, that mafters fhould have the power of inflicting moderate
chaftifement. It is very clear, that the two
modes of exciting induftry, punifhment and
hire, are utterly incompatible. They appeal to
different principles, and give rife to oppofite habits. Befides, it is not eafy to conceive a fyftem
of regulations which fhall prevent this power,
neceffarily entrufted to the plan*er over his fervant, from degenerating into the tyranny of the
mafter over his flave.

But, at any rate, admitting the poffibility
of drawing a line between the two relations,
it is evident that two orders of men will be
formed in the fettlements : the Whites, poffeffing all the land, entrufted with the whole
civil power, clothed with domeftic authority :
and the Blacks, whofe lives are fpent in poverty
and fubjection ; toiling for mafters whom they
confider as a different race of beings, and in
whom they recognize the enemies that tore
them from their country. Between thefe two
orders there can exift no bond of union but
that of force ; they are the oppreffors and the
oppreffed. Similarity of complexion and fitu-
tion will conftantly unite the one againft the
other ; and there will be no intermediate clafs,

at

at leaſt for a ſeries of years, to ſoften the tranſition, to hold the balance, or to connect the
two claſſes to together. The White will always
view the Black as a being of an inferior order,
bought with his money, depending on him for
ſupport, and born for his uſe. In all the colonies of the Europeans in the New World,
the colour is made the ſtandard of diſtinction ;
and by its different ſhades the approaches to a
ſtate of equality with the whites are regulated. *
Nor is it of much conſequence, whether we
conſider the diſadvantages attached to negro
blood, as having originally been the cauſe, or
the reſult of the contempt which the difference
of colour excites. The preſent race of planters, who are to found the free negro ſyſtem,
labour under the prejudice, from whatever
cauſe it may have ariſen ; and he who ſhall
ſuperintend the eſtabliſhment, may poſſibly find
it ſomewhat difficult to change the nature of
theſe men. Nay, ſhould he ſucceed in finding,
or creating a new generation of white proprietors, half the work would ſtill remain. The
Africans, too, muſt undergo a radical change :
they muſt be enlightened with the ideas of ab-
ſtract philanthropy, and inſpired with the ſenſe
of general expediency, and the love of order. In
ſuch circumſtances, it is idle to talk of laws and
regulations. Men muſt firſt be found ready to
obey,

* Wimpffen's Letters, p. 63.

obey, and to conform. Manners and circumftances are independent of pofitive inftitutions.
They prefcribe bounds to the decrees of defpotifm, and give laws to the legiflator in the
plenitude of his power. It will be vain to
think of fecuring the privileges of the negro
vaffal, fo long as the hand of nature has diftinguifhed him from his lord, and the circumftances of his fituation have given his brethren
the fuperiority in numbers as well as ftrength.
The magiftrate, however appointed, will generally be inclined towards the caufe of his fellow Chriftian ; and fhould he even be impartial,
how is the negro to adduce his evidence? The
mere circumftance of flavery, is not the only
reafon for rejecting the teftimony of the Blacks
againft the Europeans, in the American colonies. The diftinction of race ; the radical difference of manners and character ; the perpetual oppofition of interefts, as well as prejudices ; the inefficacy of oaths in the mind tempted by paffion, uninfluenced by religious impreffion, and a ftranger to the dictates of honour,—thefe are the circumftances which render a negro's teftimony utterly inadmiffible a-
gainft a white man ; and they would mark the
fituation of the vaffal as decifively as they now
do that of the flave. We muft therefore expect that abufes, beyond the knowledge of any
                                            conftituted

constituted authority, would soon affimilate the S E C T.
villenage of Trinidad, &c. to the flavery of our
old poffeffions ; and that there would refult from
the new fyftem, a ftate of fociety tainted by
radical evils, beyond the reach even of parliamentary legiflation. The modifications of flavery eftablifhed by law in favour of the negroes,
would, without rendering their fituation much
more tolerable, give them far greater opportunities to difturb the peace of the colony. Actuated by the fame *efprit de corps*, which even
under the whip of the driver has fo often broken
out into revolt, and given rife to plans concerted
with wonderful prudence and unanimity, in
fpite of all the regulations by which, in the
organization of the old colonies, they are feparated from each other ; the vaffal of Trinidad would be free from many of thofe obftacles which the flave fyftem throws in the
way of infurrection. The laws, for inftance,
which prevent flaves from poffeffing horfes,
fire-arms, and ammunition ; thofe which re-
ftrict their powers of locomotion, and thofe
which prohibit them from meeting for the purpofes of recreation, are utterly inapplicable to
the condition in which it has been propofed to
place the negroes of the new fettlements, if it
is intended that there fhould be more than a
nominal difference between the projected fyftem and the one at prefent eftablifhed.

It

BOOK
IV.

It is eafy, then, to fee the refult of all this. The planters, knowing that by law their vaffals have certain rights, will ufe their power over them with far lefs moderation than if they lay wholly at their mercy. The negroes, on their part, finding how nugatory their conftitutional privileges become, in the particulars moft effential to their happinefs, and united by every tie which can induce men to make a common caufe, will avail themfelves of the few advantages of which their fuperiors cannot deprive them, and will at once revenge the injuries of their race. From every view of the fubject, therefore, we are led to the fame conclufion, that, admitting the plan to be practicable, its confequences muft be fo inevitably fatal, that we are eafily reconciled to the profpect of the various difficulties which cannot fail to prevent its adoption.

But, it will be faid, the magnitude of the change produced upon negroes by their emancipation, has been proved by the example of the free negroes in all the European colonies ; and more particularly by the unfhaken fidelity of thofe flaves who have been taken from field work, and entrufted with arms, fometimes in the midft of rebellion. The univerfal prejudice of our colonifts againft fuch troops will be overlooked , and the hiftory

tory of the revolts in Surinam, of our own
black corps, and in general of the free negroes
in the different colonies, will be appealed to as
proofs, that the dangers of our fituation arife
from the bondage in which the bulk of this
unhappy clafs of men are kept. Thefe facts it
is by no means my intention to difpute ; but
I apprehend that a little reflection will fhew
how imprudent it would be to draw from them
any inference in favour of the fcheme now
under confideration.

There is perhaps no principle more univerfal in its influence over the mind of man,
or more confpicuous in its effects on his conduct, than the defire of being diftinguifhed a-
mong his fellows. The eagernefs of individuals to better their condition, is indeed one
of the moft powerful of the fprings by which
the great machine of fociety is moved. But
the love of diftinction feems to be the moft
univerfal criterion, by which they judge of the
comparative advantages of different fituations ;
more efpecially in a rude ftate, where comforts
and luxuries are little prized. This defire, it
is evident, directs itfelf in relation to the clafs
to which we ourfelves naturally belong, and
at which our envy or jealoufy is always pointed. The fortunes of thofe who are removed
to a great diftance, either above or below us,
have

have no power to raife fuch emotions. All
our ideas centre in our own order. Thus, it is
not among the polifhed ftrangers who vifit his
coaft, but among his kindred tribes, that the
favage warrior pants to fignalize himfelf; and
where the principles of policy are fo imperfectly underftood, the aid of the foreigner is cheer-
fully accepted againft a rival horde.

This is the very principle that attaches the
free negroes in the Weft Indies to the party of
the Europeans. A flave, born or trained to
fervitude, courts the favour of his mafter, becaufe it diftinguifhes him from his fellow flaves.
After he has obtained this mark of diftinction,
he naturally takes the fide of his mafter, partly becaufe his comrades view him with diftruft,
and partly becaufe his relative importance is
connected with his mafter's fafety. In like
manner, the flave who has obtained his liberty,
views this honourable diftinction, not with a reference to other freed men whom he refembles
in every thing, or to Europeans whom he
fcarcely refembles at all, but to the great body
of flaves by whom he is furrounded, and to
whofe clafs he once belonged. The free negroes form in each fettlement a fmall body
naturally related to the bulk of the inhabitants,
but proud of the diftinguifhing circumftance
which raifes them above the common level.
They

They are as it were the privileged order in the
African community. As the nobles in the European monarchies have for the moft part rallied round the throne, fince the commonalty became an order independent of their authority: fo, the free negroes have generally joined the whites, in their refiftance to the great body of enflaved blacks. They are as much interefted in preventing a univerfal emancipation, as the ariftocracy of a well regulated kingdom would be, in oppofing a fyftem of levelling, or a plan for conferring on the lower orders all the privileges of nobility.

So long, then, as the free negroes bear a very fmall proportion, both to the Europeans and flaves, the former may always count upon having their affiftance againft the latter. This is happily the fituation of all our Weft Indian poffeffions, and of thofe parts of the United States where flavery is tolerated. In Barbadoes, they are not much more than the twentieth of the whites, and fcarcely the fixty-eighth part of the flaves. In Jamaica and Dominica, where they are moft numerous, their proportion (including the large body of free people of colour) to the whites in 1790, was that of one to three, and to the flaves that of one to twenty-five; and thofe negroes who have at different junctures been armed, both in our own and in the Dutch colonies, bore a

ftill

ftill fmaller proportion to the body of the
people.

If, however, we fuppofe that the numbers
of the free negroes are fo much increafed as
to equa thofe of the whites, the cafe is materially altered. By degrees they will confider
themfelves as on a level with thofe who were
once their mafters. Being always lefs induftrious and wealthy, they will view the European proprietor with envy. Idlenefs, difcontent and indigence will give birth to projects
of plunder; and the ftate of degradation in
which they have been held by the whites, will
add a mixture of revenge. Accuftomed now
to regard the European more than the flave,
and fufficiently ftrong to fancy that they can
manage the latter, and keep their ground againft
either, they may poffibly form the dangerous
fcheme of attacking the whites, and of calling
in the affiftance of the enflaved negroes.

Unhappily this is no longer a matter of
fpeculation. The devaftation of the fineft colony in the world was produced by thefe very
means. The rebellion in St Domingo was begun by the free people of colour, who were
nearly equal to the whites in number, and
kept by them in the fame ftate of inferiority
and oppreffion in which the free negroes are
all over the Weft Indies. It fhould feem,
then, that fome danger is to be apprehended
from

from the free negroes, even in the iflands where the bulk of the community are enflaved. Accordingly, the policy of our colonies has watched over this intermediate order of men with a jealous eye. Various laws have been made to prevent too great an increafe of their numbers, to enforce their fubmiffion to the whites, and to limit their influence in the community. In Antigua, * St Vincent, † and the Virgin Ifles, ‡ they are obliged to chufe a white man for their patron. Unlefs they have landed property, they cannot become freeholders, and are incapacitated from poffeffing more than eight acres of land. If they ftrike the meaneft white fervant, they are to be fummarily and feverely whipped ; whilft a white who ftrikes a free negro or mulatto is only to be bound over to the next feffions, and punifhed at the difcretion of the juftices. In the Bahamas, ‖ there is a heavy tax upon all free negroes or mulattoes who come thither ; and in Barbadoes ¶, the evidence of a flave is received againft them. In what light they are viewed by the colonial jurifprudence of France, we may gather from the following paffage of the *Code Noire;* a fyftem of laws diftinguifhed for nothing fo much as its extreme mildnefs towards the negroes. ' *D'ailleurs, les*
                                        ' *negres*

---

* Aɛt 1702.   † Aɛt 1767.   ‡ Aɛt 1783.
‖ A.ɛt 1784.   ¶ Aɛt 1739.

' *negres en general font des hommes dangereux ;*
' *prefque pas un de ceux auxquels vous avez ren-*
' *du la liberté qui n'en ait abusé, et qui ne foit*
' *porté à des exces dangereux pour la focieté.*' *
But if fuch are the dangers to be apprehended
from a body of free creole negroes, gradually
formed in old eftablifhed colonies, where the
whites and flaves are numerous ; what muft be
the fituation of the new communities, when, in
confequence of the plan now propofed, they fhall,
in the fpace of a few years, be peopled with freed
and imported negroes, in numbers and ftrength
far exceeding the whites, bound to them by no
defire of diftinguifhing themfelves from a furrounding multitude of flaves, or of uniting a-
gainft an enemy equally formidable to both ?

In St Domingo, the influence of manners
foftened the rigour of the laws againft the free
people of colour ; they were connected with the
whites by the ties of blood ; and the property
which they poffeffed defended them ftill farther
from oppreffion. In the new colonies, the manners will be ftill more fevere than the laws upon
the free negroes quite unconnected with their
oppreffors ; and, long before they can acquire
the protection of property, matters will have
come to a crifis. In St Domingo, the flaves
formed

---

* Edit. 1762, 31 Mars & 5 Avril.

formed a third party, to whom indeed the mulattoes appealed, but whofe affiftance could not
be procured without much difficult management, and whofe fubjection to the whites afforded them an opportunity of moderating, in many
parts of the ifland, the violence of the combined
attack. In the new colonies, the vaffal negroes
will have no fuch fteps to take ; the contagion
will fpread at once ; and the Whites have no
auxiliaries to whom they can appeal. * The
pofition of St Domingo to the leeward of the
other French colonies, enabled the vigorous government which was eftablifhed there to throw
in very feafonable fuccours. Admitting (to
take the inftance of our own colonial affairs)
that our ifland eftablifhments could afford relief
to Trinidad, the cataftrophe will probably be
over before a fingle tranfport can reach the
Gulf of Paria. After the French in St Domingo

---

* It is, indeed, propofed that government fhould take into
its pay a certain number of the imported negroes ; and the
author of the ' *Crifis* ' more particularly remarks, that they
will be faithful from their gratitude to the power that has
delivered them from flavery, and will delight in the honours
of a military life. But, in the *firft* place, government, fo
far from emancipating them, has only carried them off from
their own country to a Weft Indian garrifon ; and, *fecondly*,
when flavery is abolifhed, we find that military fervice is a
fevere punifhment to field negroes.—*Vide* Touffaint's Proclamation.

BOOK
IV.
go had been fubdued, the two great claffes of men whom common enmity had united, inftantly turned their arms againft each other, with a rage ftill more exterminating than that which had marked their combination. Both parties, now, pretended authority from the Republic, and in both armies the Whites acquired fome influence. An opportunity was thus given them to undermine their enemies, to reconcile the conquering party, and to put in motion all the powers of intrigue, by which ill cemented alliances of half-civilized men may be quickly diffolved. But in Trinidad and the other fettlements organized upon the fame plan, our vaffals will form one united band, bent on the extermination of the European name, unfit for any union or compromife by which the whites may retain a footing, and, after having expelled the planters, capable only of renewing, in the moft favoured quarters of the New World, thofe fcenes of favage life to which their forced intercourfe with Europeans will rather have increafed their attachment. Then will Trinidad, more particularly, be to all the Carribbee iflands that windward fire which we have before proved that the Leeward fettlements would experience in the negro commonwealth of St Domingo; with this only difference, that its inhabitants, lefs civilized and totally unacquainted with the arts of peace, will devote

themfelves

themfelves to the extirpation of the Europeans
in thofe feas.

' *Sufpecta majoribus noftris fuere ingenia fer-*
' *vorum, etiam cùm in agris, aut domibus iifdem,*
' *nafcerentur, caritatemque dominorum ftatim ac-*
' *ciperent. Poftquam verò nationes in familiis*
' *habemus, quibus diverfi ritus, externa facra,*
' *aut nulla funt, colluviem is tam non nifi metu*
' *coercueris.*' *

I have thus rapidly attempted to fketch a
few features of the picture which the experience
of the paft holds up for the inftruction of thofe
who may be inclined to fport with negro emancipation. And if the examples already furnifhed in that quarter of the globe which is to be
the theatre of the new experiment, are not in
all their details applicable to the cafe which
may arife from the profecution of the propofed
fcheme, we may conclude, that thefe inftances
fall infinitely fhort of the dangers with which it
is fraught. But when the various infurmount-
able difficulties attending this new and untried
fyftem are fully confidered, we can entertain no
ferious apprehenfions of its being carried into
effect. The old, and impolitic, and iniquitous, but
practicable, and, I really believe, lefs dangerous
mode of colonization, will probably be reforted

to.

─────────────────────────
Tacitus, Annal. lib. XIV. cap. 44.

to. The dominion of the cart-whip re-eſtabliſh-
ed over the ancient ſettlements of the weſtern
Archipelago, will be extended to the more ſe-
rene regions of the Oroonoco and the Miſſiſſip-
pi, where the traffic of human fleſh will be in-
terrupted by no avenging ſtorms, and the avarice of Europeans may for yet a few genera-
tions wallow in the blood-ſtained ſpoils of African labour ; until, in the fulneſs of time, the
great event, which has for ages been ſlowly preparing, ſhall be accompliſhed ; and the African warriors, gradually civilized in the fruitful
iſlands of America, ſhall obtain quiet, and, may
we not add, rightful poſſeſſion, of thoſe plains
which have been cultivated by the toils and ſuf-
ferings of their fathers.

SECT.

SECTION II.

OF THE NEGRO SLAVE SYSTEM, OR THE PRESENT
STATE OF SOCIETY IN THE SLAVE COLONIES, AND
THE MEANS OF IMPROVING IT.

The remarks which have been made upon the character and habits of the negroes, both in the laſt Section, and in the former Parts of this Inquiry, ſeem to ſuggeſt certain concluſions of a very poſitive and definite nature with reſpect to the internal ſtructure of the ſlave colonies.

It may be obſerved, in the *firſt* place, that all attempts ſpeedily to change the ſtate of ſociety in thoſe ſettlements by legiſlative enactments, are if poſſible ſtill more ridiculous, and, if attended with any material conſequences, ſtill more dangerous than ſimilar endeavours made ſuddenly to new-model communities of the ordinary texture.

In the *ſecond* place, we may remark, that however deficient in civilization, the negroes are evidently capable of acquiring thoſe wants and deſires which are the ſeeds of induſtry ; that they are endowed with powers, not only of body but of mind, ſufficient to render their improvement

ment and high refinement a matter of abfolute
certainty under a proper fyftem of management ;
and that there is nothing in their nature peculiar or diftinguifhing, which renders them a feparate clafs, or places them beyond the influence
of the paffions and principles common to all the
reft of mankind in certain ftages of fociety.
Through the whole of this Inquiry, I have argued every queftion relating to the negroes, upon the fame general grounds which are ufed to
inveftigate the hiftory, or determine the probable
fates, of other rude nations. All the facts with
which we are acquainted, concur to juftify a
mode of reafoning pointed out by the cleareft
analogies ; and the greateft errors have been
committed by politicians, both in fpeculation
and in practical arrangements, from the fundamental and vulgar prejudice of confidering the
Africans as a peculiar race, to whom general
views do not apply. The Africans, in fact, as
clofely refemble every other rude people in their
characters and habits, as in their circumftances.
When enflaved their characters and habits are
modified by the change of fituation ; and they
become fimilar to all rude tribes placed in a
ftate of bondage. When wife and liberal regulations mitigate the hardfhips of their lot, a door
is opened for their gradual improvement and
progrefs in civilization, according to that general

ral principle of advancement which feems to be an effential part of the human character, and which always works its effects in the moft obvious manner, unlefs when ftifled by abfurd or wicked inftitutions.

We may remark, in the *third* place, that the mixed breed of mulattoes in the flave colonies does not render the ftructure of the fociety anomalous. On the contrary, thefe men are fubfervient to many ufeful purpofes. They are in fome refpects fuperior to the negroes ; as, in civilization and mental endowments. In bodily ftrength and adaptation to the circumftances of the tropical climate, they are almoft on a level with the pure African breed. They are uniformly attached to the Whites, in thofe colonies where cruel rigour on the part of the government has not alienated them, or their numbers rendered them formidable. They form, together with the free negroes, an intermediate clafs of men, connecting the other two, however imperfect the link or however fudden the gradation may be, compared with thofe uniting principles which knit and mould the more curioufly arranged fabrics of European and Afiatic fociety. It is entirely from the influence of manners, and of pofitive inftitutions, that the people of colour have uniformly been held in a flate of degradation, and even claffed with the free negroes.

The

The exiftence of flavery is the great caufe of thofe manners and inftitutions. The free mulattoes are tinged with a hue which is almoft the charaƈteriftic of degradation and bondage in the eyes of Weft Indians. They are related by blood to the vileft portion of the fociety ; they are of the fame race with many who yet obey the cart-whip : while no white man can name a brother in chains. They are, moreover, from the ftate of morals among the Whites (the immediate effeƈt of the flave fyftem), almoft univerfally the fruits of illicit and vulgar amours ; they owe nothing to their mother but life ; and are, in their turn, facrificed to the brutal paffions of the common tyrants. It is evident that thefe circumftances which diftinguifh the mixed race in the colonial fociety, are altogether the confequences of the flave fyftem, and of the ftate of manners which that fyftem has produced. They prefent, therefore, no formidable obftacle to the legiflator who would, by gradual and prudent meafures, reform the corrupted mafs, and lay the foundations of a more natural arrangement in the focial union, by cautioufly but firmly applying the axe to the root of the evil, and undermining the inftitutions that have grown up in defiance of all juftice and policy.

The fame remarks apply with equal precifion to the free negroes, who indeed refemble

femble the mulattoes in their moral and political circumftances. And as the ftate of
fociety among the Whites themfelves is evidently affeated in the moft material degree by
the fame fyftem of inftitutions which fo peculiarly diftinguifhes the tropical colonies of
America *, we may with confidence conclude, that the whole fabric of colonial fociety
has naturally arifen out of the circumftances in
which legiflative enactments originally placed
thofe provinces ; that it prefents no infuperable
difficulties to the wifdom of enlightened re-
formers ; that it may receive complete and radical amelioration from the gradual abolition
of the noxious and artificial eftablifhments
which have been formed by the meafures of
former ftatefmen.

In the *fourth* place, there can be no doubt
that the climate of the Weft Indies renders the
labour of negroes effential to the cultivation of
the foil. It is only in their corporeal qualities
that thofe men are fundamentally diftinguifhed
from the reft of the human fpecies. They ex-
cel all the other races of mankind in hardinefs,
agility, and ftrength of limbs ; in the capacity
of fuftaining the moft galling fatigue and pain ;
in the faculty of enduring labour under every
fort

* Book I. Seat. I.

BOOK IV.

fort of privation, and all kinds of annoyance ;
above all, in that quality which chiefly diftinguifhes the human body from the bodies of
the lower animals, the power of fubmitting
with eafe to every change of feafon, and ad-
apting the corporeal habitudes and functions,
with fafety and alacrity, to all the varieties of
climate. From the firft difcovery of America
to the prefent time, the experience of every
day in thofe fultry though fplendid regiens, has
proved, that neither Europeans nor their defcendants are capable of enduring fatigue in the
burning climates of the fouthern colonies. To
the negro, all climates and foils are the fame.
He thrives as well in thofe marfhes whence the
heat of the vertical fun exhales every noxious
vapour, and engenders all the multifarious
forms of animal and vegetable poifon, as in
the happieft vallies of the old world, where the
breeze, the fhade, and the ftream, temper
the genial warmth of the moft ferene and fra-
grant air. As long, therefore, as the colonies
are cultivated, the population muft confift of a
mixed and variegated tribe. The great object
of the legiflator is the improvement of that
ftate of fociety, and that fyftem of manners,
which have arifen from the neceffary introduction of diftinct races of men, differing from
each other in civilization, in bodily qualities,
                                              and

and in political privileges. The only plan
which can be admitted into our thoughts muſt proceed upon the principle of new-modelling the preſent ſtructure of ſociety, and retaining at the ſame time all the parts of which it is compoſed. I have endeavoured to illuſtrate, by a few general obſervations, the poſſibility of accompliſhing both theſe ends. I ſhall now attend more particularly to the means which are ſuggeſted for the attainment of this purpoſe, by the nature of the principal evils which in the preſent ſituation of things call ſo loudly for correction.

I. The firſt and the greateſt of thoſe evils, the radical vice of the whole Weſt Indian ſyſtem, is, beyond all doubt, the oppreſſive treatment of the negro ſlaves. It requires very little argument to prove, that the quantity of work which may be obtained from a labourer or drudge, is liable to be affected as much by the injurious treatment that he receives, as by the idleneſs in which he may be permitted to indulge. Where this drudge is a ſlave, no motive but fear can operate upon his diligence and attention. A conſtant inſpection is therefore abſolutely neceſſary, and a perpetual terror of the laſh is the only preventive of indolence. But there are certain bounds preſcribed even to

the

the power of the lafh. It may force the unhappy victim to move, becaufe the line of diftinction between motion and reft, action and
repofe, is definite; but no punifhment can
compel the labourer to ftrenuous exertion, becaufe there is no meafure nor ftandard of activity. A ftate of defpair, not of induftry, is the
never-failing confequence of fevere chaftifement; and the conftant repetition of the torture only ferves to blunt the fenfibility of the
nerves, and difarm the punifhment of its ter-
rors. The body is injured, and the mind becomes as little willing, as the limbs are able to
exert. Bad food, fcanty fupport of every kind,
conftant expofure to the extremities of the
weather, muft weaken the ftrength and exhauft
the conftitution even of a Creole negro. Want
of reft, which thofe men can bear, or appear
to bear, with miraculous indifference, muft ere
long wear them out. Both their bodies and
their minds muft fooner become incapable of
labour than thofe of voluntary workmen, who
have conftantly before them the ftrongeft poffible motives to activity; and whilft complicated ill ufage is rapidly deftroying the lives of
the fufferers, it muft evidently diminifh the
productive powers of the exertions which the
furvivors continue to make.

It

It may therefore appear fomewhat fingular,
that the melancholy hiftory of the American colonies fhould prefent fo unvaried a picture of cruelty and oppreffions, when nothing can be more manifeft than the immediate and grofs impolicy of fuch conduct. Thofe who are always confident in mens honefty as long as their direct and fpecific interefts draw them to the paths of integrity, may find fome reafon, in the annals of Weft Indian cultivation, to believe that the caprice and folly of human nature is fcarcely inferior to its depravity; and that, inftead of following the dictates of humane feelings or eonfcientious principles, in oppofition to the temptations of felf-love, there feems to be fome rooted predilection for vice and cruelty fo ftrongly implanted in the human breaft, as to predominate altogether over the united temptations of virtue and intereft. Certain it is, that the mafters of flaves have in all ages indulged their worft appetites and moft ufelefs caprices, at the expence of thofe very interefts, to further which the flaves were purchafed; and that, in order to gratify thofe momentary gufts of paffion, they have fyftematically given up the beft and eafieft means of purfuing the great objects of their whole lives.

The facts which have repeatedly been laid before the world, prove to a demonftration the
truth

truth of thefe remarks. It is eftablifhed beyond all doubt, that the moft unprofitable
plantations are not always thofe of which the
foil is unfruitful or incommodioufly fituated,
but uniformly thofe which are cultivated by
negroes fubjected to a cruel and ftingy fyftem
of management ; that the moft laborious duty
is performed by the beft fed and moft indulged
flaves ; that the more nearly the negro is permitted to approach the condition of freedom
in his enjoyments, his privileges and his habits,
the more alacrity does he fhew in performing
the tafk affigned to him. Yet, in fpite of this
uniform experience, fo few experiments have
been tried of the mild and profitable fyftem of
management, that thofe plantations into which
it has been introduced are pointed out as remarkable. The exception to the general rule
is not found in that eftate, of which the proprietor prefers the commiffion of cruelty and injuftice, to the purfuit of his evident advantage ;
but in that eftate, of which the owner purfues
the eafieft and moft profitable fyftem of management, notwithftanding its moral rectitude.
There appear, then, to be certain bad principles inherent in the human heart, certain blind
paffions and movements of caprice, which conftantly impel men, in certain circumftances, to a

line

line of conduct as obviously inconsistent with their interests as repugnant to their duty.

The ill treatment of the negroes is as unfavourable to the manners of the colonial society, as it is prejudicial to the wealth of the settlements. The negroes are deprived of all opportunities of individual improvement ; all chance of gaining a part of that civilization, in the midst of which they are placed ; all possibility of acquiring industrious habits, so incompatible with the constant exertion of cruelty and unjust oppression. Where they are allowed certain indulgences, and gradually made to feel their own importance and reap the rewards of voluntary labour, by receiving certain privileges connected with property, and being permitted to work for the increase of their own *peculium*, we may expect the foundation to be laid of those industrious principles which are the great cause of human improvement, and form the bond of civilized society. The more cruelly and unjustly any dependent order of men are treated by their superiors, the more debased will all their sentiments become. Where fear is the only motive of action, or the great and predominant feeling in the mind, it soon absorbs every other principle, and moulds all the habits of thought to its own degrading form. Where caprice is mingled

gled with tyranny, the principle of implicit o-
bedience becomes ftill more corrupting. No
general rules of conduct can be followed. The
body of the wretched flave becomes a mere
machine, actuated in all its movements by a
power placed at a diftance from it. The bad
paffions of the mafter too, pollute, by the mere
force of example, the flave who is fubject to
them and can eftimate their full extent. It
is partly from this caufe that the fervant or the
beaft of a flave, is of all animated beings the
moft wretched.

The oppreffive treatment of the negroes is
equally prejudicial to the manners of the whites
themfelves. We have formerly had occafion
to trace this effect of the negro fyftem in its
ftate of abufe ; and to remark the injuries a-
rifing from thence to the extent and value, as
well as to the character of the white population. *

But the moft fatal of all the confequences
which refult from the corruptions of the flave
fyftem, are thofe that immediately affect the
fecurity of the colonies. We have often had
an opportunity of contemplating the effects of
cruel treatment upon the fidelity of the negroes
in the different fettlements. In ftrict conformity to thofe general principles which the
beft writers upon the human character have
                                                  fo

* Book I. Sect. I.

fo fuccefsfully explained, and in broad defiance of all the abfurd affertions, fo confidently made by the apologifts of the Weft Indian policy, it has been proved, by the united teftimony of all the authors whofe opportunities of information are moft extenfive, that the pronenefs of the negroes to revolt, is in precife proportion to the cruelty and parfimony of their mafters. The hiftory of the Dutch colonies, contrafted with that of the Spanifh and Portugueze fettlements, * and (I fear we may add) the hiftory of the Spanifh and Portugueze fettlements, contrafted with that of all the others, furnifhes abundant proofs of this ftatement, in itfelf fo extremely probable, that it requires fcarcely any fupport from experience to gain belief. In all rebellions, the plantations where the flaves were treated with moft indulgence, have fuffered the leaft from the fury of infurrection; and, on the contrary, thofe eftates have generally been the hotbeds of the rebellion, or the firft objects of its attack, where the overfeer was cruel, and the mafter avaricious or needy; where, of confequence, the flaves were hard-worked, fcantily provided with neceffaries, and feverely or unjuftly punifhed.

The

---

* Book I. Sect. II, parts I. II. & III.

    The inefficacy of mild treatment, in fpite
of all thefe facts, has been afferted with a degree of confidence, more perhaps the refult of
mercantile prudence, than of entire conviction
on the part of thofe whofe interefts have led
them to fupport the flave fyftem. As a fpecimen of the manner in which this important
branch of the fubject has been difcuffed, by
perfons of the defcription juft now mentioned,
I fhall ftate the argument of Mr Edwards, ad-
duced in his Hiftory of St Domingo ; a work
certainly containing much valuable information, but conceived in a temper of mind very different from that in which the moft dignified fpecies of compofition ought to be undertaken ; and apparently written more with
the intention of making an appeal to popular feelings againft the caufe of the abolition,
than with the defign of impartially record-
ing the moft interefting feries of events that
has been difplayed in the annals of the negro race. I fhall quote the argument in Mr
Edwards's own words. It is introduced under
the form of an anecdote, after a variety of in-
finuations urged in the fame impofing difguife.
‘ The largeft fugar plantation on the plain,
‘ (fays our author, in his defcription of the
‘ firft infurrection at the Cape, *) was that of
‘ Monf. Gallifet, fituated about eight miles
                                        ‘ from

* Chapter VI.

' from the town, the negroes belonging to
' which had always been treated with fuch
' kindnefs and liberality, and peffeffed fo many
' advantages, that it became a proverbial ex-
' preffion among the lower white people, in
' fpeaking of any man's good fortune, to fay,
" *il eft heureux comme un negre de Gallifet,*' (he
' is as happy as one of Gallifet's negroes). M.
' Odeluc, the attorney or agent for this plan-
' tation, was a member of the General Af-
' fembly; and being fully perfuaded that the
' negroes belonging to it would remain firm
' in their obedience, determined to repair
' thither, to encourage them in oppofing the
' infurgents; to which end he defired the af-
' fiftance of a few foldiers from the town-
' guard, which was granted him. He pro-
' ceeded accordingly; but on approaching the
' eftate, to his grief and furprife, he found all
' the negroes in arms on the fide of the re-
' bels; and (horrid to tell!) *their ftandard*
' *was the body of a white infant, which they*
' *had recently impaled on a ftake.* M. Odeluc
' had advanced too far to retreat undifcover-
' ed; and both he and a friend that accom-
' panied him, with moft of the foldiers, were
' killed without mercy. Two or three only of
' the patrole efcaped by flight, and conveyed
' the

‘ the dreadful tidings to the inhabitants of the
‘ town. ’

The following extract from Mr Clarkfon's
‘ *Effay on the Impolicy of the Slave Trade*, ’ *
will probably furnifh, in the firft place, a fatisfactory explanation of the ftatement thus confidently given by Mr Edwards ; and in the next
place, a commentary upon the general fidelity
of the latter gentleman's narrative. ‘ In the
‘ ifland of St Domingo is an eftate which has
‘ experienced a fimilar change. The owner
‘ confidered himfelf as the father of his flaves ;
‘ he never haraffed them with exceffive labour ;
‘ he fed and treated them fo well, and fo
‘ mild and gentle was his government, that it
‘ became a proverb, “ As happy as a flave of
“ Gallifet. ” Thus treated, their increafe was
‘ rapid. About fifteen years ago he died. The
‘ prefent proprietor has fince adopted a differ-
‘ ent fyftem. His flaves continually decreafe,
‘ and he lofes by the change of management. ’

It may be obferved, that this narrative of
Mr Clarkfon, publifhed in 1788, long before
the rebellion, is introduced among twenty-five
other facts collected, as we are told in the pre-
face, from authentic information obtained by direct communication with St Domingo. † The object

---

* Part II. chap. I. fect. I.   † Page 1,

ject of thofe ftatements is entirely different from
the purpofe for which I have ufed the authority, as will appear to any one who reads the above quotation. It is in every refpect highly probable, that the ftatement of the total change of management is correct. Now, Mr Edwards did not publifh the firft edition of his work on St Domingo till eight years after this narrative had been given to the world by Mr Clarkfon. I am very much miftaken if he does not mention Mr Clarkfon's writings in the courfe of his work ; at any rate, it is abfurd to fuppofe that he could be ignorant of them ; and as the paffage which I have extracted is among the arguments urged by the reverend author upon the moft important branch of the whole fubject—the poffibility of keeping up the flave ftocks without importation—it is to be feared that Mr Edwards could fcarcely have omitted to perufe it. But whether he did fo or not, the charge which I am under the neceffity of grounding upon the collated paffages, is equally fatal to the credit of Mr Edwards's general ftatements. Of the narrative given by Mr Clarkfon, the truth is beyond a doubt ; and it is difficult to fay whether the rafhnefs of Mr Edwards's affertions, admitting him to have been ignorant of the real fact, or his want of fidelity, fuppofing him to have read the other account, throws the greateft ftain

upon

upon his chara&er as an hiftorian. After the
eafy explanation which the real ftatement of the
tranfaction affords, it would be credulity indeed
to truft the other anecdotes of a fimilar ftamp,
which Mr Edwards has paraded in his rapidly
compofed and ill-digefted performance. What
conclufion, for inftance, can we draw, with any
degree of fafety, from the ftory of the poftil-
lion, who, in the rebellion, was the firft to attack and butcher a mafter that had treated him
with marked kindnefs ? * Poffibly here, as in
the former inftance, a true narrative of this affair, reconciling the whole to the common order
of occurrences, may have been publifhed eight
years before Mr Edwards wrote his book. Still
lefs dare we follow our author in drawing fuch
general conclufions againft the efficacy of gentle
treatment, as are contained in the beginning of
the anecdote in page 100. (edit. 1801.) He
does not fcruple to infinuate, that this folitary
inftance of fidelity and attachment forms an exception to the whole condu& of the negroes
during revolts. †

Such is the rafh or uncandid mode of argument adopted by thofe who would prove, what
nothing but the ftrongeft evidence can ever eftablifh—that the negroes are in their nature diametrically

* Chap. VI.   † Note V v.

metrically oppofite to all the reft of mankind; that
kindnefs and compaffion for their misfortunes
meets with no return of fidelity from their ftubborn
hearts ; that thofe acts of gratuitous beneficence
which attach all other races of men to their fuperiors, only ferve to alienate the favage African, in whom favours and indulgences produce
nothing but the blackeft ingratitude and perfidy. No one can entertain the flighteft doubt
upon this fubject, after cafting his eye over the
ftatements which I have given in the Third
Section of the Firft Book, borrowed chiefly
from writers whofe antipathy to the negroes is
extreme, and whofe works abound in the moft
abfurd allegations againft the character of that
race. It is fufficient to mention the teftimony
of M. Malouet, who, with all his attachment to
the flave fyftem, and all his violent prejudices
againft the negroes, * has laid down, in the
moft unqualified terms, the very propofition
which I have been maintaining, and fupported
his general opinion by a variety of facts that
came within his perfonal knowledge. † ' *Quelle*
' *jouiffance*,' (fays he, after defcribing the good
treatment experienced by the flaves on fome
eftates in Surinam) ' *pour un maitre fensé et*
' *humain*

---

* Mem. fur les Col. tom. V. *paffim*.
† Ibid. V. 152. III. 116.

BOOK
IV.

' *humain de fe procurer ainfi la recompenfe de fa*
' *juftice : car les habitans dont je parle ont dans*
' *leurs atteliers une population nombreufe, font*
' *cheris de leurs efclaves, et n'eprouvent jamais*
' *les defordres du marronage : leurs propres ne-*
' *gres exterminent les Marrons quand ils vien-*
' *nent chez eux.*' This fact, it muft be remembered, is ftated with regard to the colony
which of all others has fuffered moft conftantly
from negro rebellion and defertion, and which
has been, more than any other, the fcene of domeftic cruelty and oppreffion.

We may conclude, then, that the maltreat-
ment of the negroes directly and uniformly pro-
motes the fpirit of infurrection, and that gentle
treatment of that unhappy race is as effentially
neceffary to the fecurity as to the opulence of
the flave colonies.

II. Next to the bad treatment of the negroes, the greateft defect in the Weft Indian
fyftem, is the large proportion which the imported Africans bear to the whole black population.

It requires no argument to prove that the
newly imported flaves muft be infinitely more
dangerous to the peace of the community than
thofe who have been born in the iflands. Whether the Africans, partly ftolen, partly purchafed

chafed (if there can be fuch a thing as buying
human beings with a price), were originally free or enflaved in their own country, it is manifeft that the forcible tranfportation of thofe men is a mifery not eafily defcribed, and their exile an affliction which muft embitter the reft of their lives; and furely the difference of climate, and the exchange of a life of indolence for one of moft fevere labour, is a fufficient grievance in itfelf to infpire them with the utmoft averfion for their new fituation, even if their banifhment had been voluntary. Although we fhould admit every abfurd affertion which has been made with refpect to the entire felicity of the flaves in the Weft Indies, we muft be convinced that this picture of happinefs can only apply to the lot of Creoles ; for the blifs of a ftate of Paradife or Elyfium forced upon a fentient being againft his will, amounts exactly to a contradiction in terms.

Accordingly, what we might expect has uniformly happened ; the imported negroes have been the firft to promote rebellion, and at all times the moft refractory and difcontented flaves. To keep them in order, as well as to teach them work, all the refources of the cruelty that forms the main fpring of the flave fyftem, have been exhaufted. And even this feverity of itfelf is infufficient ; for it has been found neceffary to incorporate the newly arrived Africans with
the

BOOK
IV.

the old ftock by degrees; never filling a plantation
with too great a number of the former, and dif-
perfing them carefully among the latter, for fecurity and difcipline. Notwithftanding all thefe
precautions, the fpirit of adventure has always
proved fufficiently ftrong to increafe very rapidly the numbers of the new hands. In proportion as the facilities of the African trade
have been great, and the capital turned to the
colonial agriculture extenfive, the iflands have
been filled with hordes of native Africans, until,
in fome cafes, the numbers of bad fubjects were
fo much and fo quickly augmented, while the
neceffary proportion of the Creoles was of courfe
decreafing, that extenfive and fatal rebellion
has been the lamentable confequence. As the
large ftocks, fmall profits, and pecuniary incum-
brances of the Dutch planters, have rendered
their flaves remarkable for bad treatment, and
continual though partial infurrection or defertion, the unexampled rapidity with which the
French colonies were peopled during the ten
years previous to the Revolution, produced, in
all the fineft parts of thofe fettlements, fo fatal
a difproportion between the two kinds of negroes, as has fhaken the whole Weft Indian
fyftem from its foundation, and rendered its exiftence a matter which many enlightened men
rather wifh for than expect. The hiftory of
the French colonies furnifhes as fatal a leffon

of

of the evils arifing from the difproportion of
Creoles to imported flaves, as the hiftory of the Dutch fettlements exhibits a picture of the evils arifing from the habitual feverity and op-preffion of the mafters.

The effects of the rapid importation are certainly more extenfively fatal to the fecurity of the community which is thus peopled, than the confequences of cruel treatment. But I have mentioned the latter as the greater im-perfection of the two, from its prejudicial ten-dency to the wealth as well as to the fafety of the colonies. The difproportion of Creoles can-not be faid to injure the opulence of the planters. The work performed by new flaves, is no doubt much lefs confiderable than that which is per-formed by Creoles or feafoned flaves: their num-bers, too, are more rapidly thinned, both from the neceffary ill ufage they receive, from the change of climate, and from the influence of mental diftrefs, as well as unufual bodily fa-tigue. But thofe loffes are only comparative; they only prevent the total amount or produce of fervile labour from being fo great as it would be were the negro population equally extenfive, and all compofed of natives. The rapid importation of flaves, with all its dangers to the fecurity of the colonies, is, on the whole, beneficial to their wealth, by enabling all the
capital

capital of the planters to find an immediate
and profitable employment, although, certainly,
the profit would be greater were it poffible to
employ the fame capital in purchafing a ftock
of Creoles. It may, however, be obferved, that,
in the long-run, the fecurity of the iflands muft
furnifh the fureft meafure of their opulence,
and that, in a confiderable number of years,
the caufes which moft endanger the internal
peace of the community, may be reckoned the
moft detrimental even to the wealth of the proprietors. In the mean time, the fecurity of
the fyftem is of fo much more confequence to
both the mother country and the body of the
colonies, in comparifon with the increafe of
wealth (however difproportionate thofe confiderations may be in the eftimation of individuals), that the commercial benefits arifing
from the rapid importation of new flaves, can
in no fenfe of the word compenfate for the
grand evils which flow directly from the fame
fource. And we may confidently ftate this as
one of the chief defects in the ftructure of
Weft Indian fociety.

Such, then, are the two great flaws in the
prefent ftructure of the American colonies.
And to any one who fhall confider the matter
with tolerable impartiality, it muft appear manifeft, that both of thefe evils have their origin
in

in the power which the Weſt Indian planters
enjoy, of increaſing to any amount, and in any
given time, their ſtock of hands.

The cruel treatment of the negroes ariſes
evidently from the eaſe with which the ſtock
can be kept up by purchaſe. If a man cannot
buy cattle, either from want of money, or from
the dearth or want of the article, he will breed.
Although this plan muſt immediately dimi-
niſh his profits, he will alſo be careful of the
lives and health of thoſe beaſts which he already poſſeſſes. This change will be effected
in the ordinary œconomy of live ſtock, by the
failure of caſh, or the ſhutting up of the market. But a much greater change will be produced by the ſame circumſtances, upon that ſort
of management, if management it can be called, which conſiſts in working out certain kinds
of cattle, by ſcanty feeding and hard labour ;
upon the plan, for example, which certain
poſtmaſters adopt, of purchaſing old horſes, and
replacing the price with a tolerable profit, by
feeding the wretched animals as cheaply as
poſſible, and forcing them to run as long
and as often as their limbs can ſupport them.
The want of a market muſt either inſtantly
put a ſtop to this iniquitous trade, or reduce its extent to a very narrow compaſs.
And ſuch is preciſely the trade of the negro
proprietors

proprietors in the European colonies! We are informed, that fo long as a flave market exifts, men find their profit in working out a certain number of their flaves, and fupplying the blank by purchafe, rather than by breeding. If this deteftable crime (I will not infult Liverpool, Briftol, and London by calling it a trade) is really attended with gain, as it certainly is but too congenial to the paffions and habits of flave-drivers, we can never expect to fee its termination, while the poffibility of perpetrating it fubfifts. But it fignifies little to our general argument, whether this iniquity is really gainful or not; nay, whether it exifts or not. The general cruel treatment of the negroes cannot be denied. Even they who have moft zealoufly defended the flave fyftem, have admitted, that the oppreffions of the negroes call for redrefs, however much thefe men may have differed from their antagonifts upon the nature of the remedy.

This cruelty of ufage, then, is an undeniable evil in the ftructure of the colonial fociety, and produces all thofe confequences which we have lately been contemplating. Nor can it ever be expected to difappear, while the paffions of men remain as blind as they hitherto have been; while their prefent interefts, or the gratification of their caprices, prevents them from purfuing their

real

real advantage; and while they retain the
means of gratifying their paſſions or whims by
throwing away a little money.

The evils of the oppreſſions, too common
all over the colonies, are no doubt felt by thoſe
very men who are guilty of them. The evils
of the ſudden importations, ſo dangerous to the
ſafety of the ſyſtem, are alſo ſuch as muſt in
the long-run fall upon the importers. But
although both thoſe lines of conduct affect the
ſecurity of the colonies, and although the former affects alſo the wealth of the individual
planters, it is evident that, according to a principle too extenſive in its operations upon the
conduct of men, the apparent and immediate
is preferred to the real and ſubſtantial good;
and often the indulgence of ſuch bad paſſions as
do not in the moment of excitement ſeem to
be expenſive, is purſued at the riſk of deſtruction, and with the certainty of future loſs. It
is unneceſſary to offer proofs that ſuch is the
natural frailty of man; a frailty from which
few of his plans are exempt, and which all
moraliſts and divines have united in deploring.
It is in vain to believe that the intereſt alone
of Weſt Indian planters will ever lead them to
that line of conduct which is really the moſt
advantageous. It is abſurd to expect that
men will ever be ſo much reformed as to ſeek
the

BOOK IV.

the path to enjoyment or wealth which is moſt circuitous, becauſe it is moſt eaſy and beneficial in the long-run. But it is truly ridiculous to affect a belief, that this improvement will begin upon the ſpot where the evil has firſt originated, and has been confirmed by habit, and to twiſt our necks into groteſque and fantaſtic poſtures, by way of looking towards the Weſt Indian plantations for this viſionary reformation of the human character. ' Where it is ' mens intereſt to act in a certain manner, we ' may be aſſured they will follow that intereſt. ' True—but it muſt be a near, a diſtinct proſpect of intereſt in which we ſhould confide. If the view is either dimmed by diſtance, or obſcured by paſſion, let us not reject the policy which enjoins that nothing ſhould be left to the acute viſion and prudent choice of the perverſe and ſhort-ſighted animal we have to deal with. In the caſe of the Weſt Indian ſlave-market, to recommend that things ſhould be left to their natural courſe; to maintain, that reſtrictive laws are unneceſſary for inducing men to purſue their own real good; and that interfering with their private plans may be detrimental to the public good, is a groſs and intolerable perverſion of the moſt liberal and enlightened principle in modern policy. It is as contemptible a ſophiſm as the argument of

any

any enthufiaft who fhould infift upon the annihilation of all criminal jurifprudence, and recommend the method of reforming the world,
by leaving every man to difcover that his trueft
happinefs lies in the paths of virtue. Such arguments are furely as ridiculous, when applied
to fupport the freedom of negro importation
in the Weft Indies, as if they were ufed to
bring the decalogue or the gallows into difrepute.

The only effectual method of preventing
the cruel treatment of flaves, and deftroying
the dangerous mixture of imported Africans,
confifts in cutting off that fource which truly
feeds the paffions, and caprices, and fhort-
fighted wifhes of the planters. A conftant check
muft be found out, which fhall at every inftant arreft the arm of the tormentor, by fetting before his face, in diftinct and near profpect, the immediate and irreparable deftruction of his ftock, as the neceffary confequence
of cruel treatment. An arrangement muft be
contrived, which fhall habitually lead the flave-
driver to reflect, that not the eventual, but
the certain and inftantaneous defolation of his
eftate, muft be the confequence of oppreffive
and cruel deportment towards the fole fupporters of his wealth. The planter's habits of
thinking may thus be, by fome fure means,
moulded

moulded into a steady form, and his conduct
adapted to the interests, now rendered immediate, of his estate and live stock. Nothing
must be entrusted to that fear of insurrection,
so natural to all the colonists, but so much divided and frittered down by being shared with
the whole community, as to exert no perceptible influence on the actions of the individual,
when opposed by passion, or caprice, or tempting
views of personal advantage. The disproportion-
ate admixture of imported Africans must be prevented, by the only means which can prevent
or in the least degree check it, the positive and
definite measure of cutting off the supplies of
slaves, and thus forcibly restraining the avarice
as well as the cruelty of slave-holders. The only
plan, then, which can prevent the effects of the
slave system,—the only method which can be
devised for stopping the cruelties that irritate
the negroes to rebellion, stunt the growth of
colonial opulence, and taint the body of colonial society,—the only resource which can be
appealed to, for securing the advances already
made in cultivating the West Indies, and for
preventing the increase of the most fatal malady that ever threatened any political system
with sudden dissolution,—the measure formerly
pointed out by every consideration of sound
policy, and now enforced by the most obvious
                                             demands

demands of a menacing and awful neceſſity, is the Total Abolition of the Slave Trade. Every conſideration of found policy, every view of expediency, every call of urgent neceſſity, now concur in this recommendation.

The queſtion of abolition, though one of the moſt momentous that ever occupied the attention of men, is extremely ſhort and ſimple. The whole argument is confined to a very narrow compaſs. If we look to the nature of the traffic, its *unneceſſary* enormities are ſufficient to make us forget the firſt great and eſſential objection which may be urged, that it is not a trade, but a crime. We find that it is a crime of the worſt nature, radically planted in the depths of injuſtice, branching out into various new forms of guilt, prone to entwine with manifold acceſſory pollutions not inherent in the ſeed, terminating in every ſpecies of noxious produce which can blaſt the ſurrounding regions, and taint the winds of heaven. The men, then, who would perſuade us to cheriſh ſo monſtrous a production, becauſe they have given it a name borne by the moſt ſalutary and nutritious branches of the ſocial ſyſtem, are ſurely guilty of a mockery to our common ſenſe, ſtill more intolerable than any inſult to our feelings. We can never ſtop to argue with them, or to hear the prepoſterous applications which they make of principles peculiar

culiar to things of a nature effentially different
from this. We cannot allow fo great an out-
rage upon the common forms of fpeech, as the
defence of a glaring iniquity, by an appeal to
views that belong to the great fource of wealth
and virtue—the commercial intercourfe of mankind.

The arguments which have been engrafted
on this moft falfe view of the great queftion,
are if poffible ftill more abfurd.   Many of
them confift in grofs miftatements of facts, either completely proved by the evidence ad-
duced on the fide of the abolition, or fo tho-
roughly well known, that no evidence of their
exiftence was deemed neceffary by the enemies
of the flave fyftem.   Some of thofe topics are
drawn from the narroweft views of mercantile
policy, and the moft infulting appeals to the
bad paffions of mankind.   Others are deduced
from abfurd ideas of natural law or revealed religion, and fupported by allegations which were
inftantaneoufly proved to be falfe.   To enter
into any analyfis of thefe arguments, or of the
fhort and fatisfactory anfwers which they have
received, would be very unneceffary, after the
fhort and fimple procefs of reafoning by which
we have been led to conclude in favour of the
abolition.   Such a difcuffion of the queftion is
now no longer requifite.   All views of the expediency

pediency of the meafure have yielded to the ftrong and unanfwerable conviction of its neceffity, with which the events of the laft ten years have infpired every impartial ftatefman. It is upon this high ground that I wifh to reft the final difcuffion of the queftion ; without, however, prefuming to infinuate that any reafons whatever can be paramount to thofe plain notions of juftice (humanity is not an appropriate term), which muft in all the councils of a great and honourable nation, be of themfelves the ruling principle of decifion. The argument of neceffity is only introduced to fupply the place of the arguments formerly drawn from expediency. That which I muft be bold to call the fundamental point, the folid and refiftlefs argument, is the appeal to the common principles of juftice.

Although, however, I do not mean to enter into the difcuffions which formerly occupied mens minds upon this queftion, before the teft of experience had furnifhed us with unanfwerable arguments ; yet may it not be ungrateful to record a very few of the affertions made by the fupporters of the flave fyftem, as a fpecimen, for the information of thofe who are not accuftomed to wade through the mafs of ephemeral matter, in which the difcuffion is to be found.

1. For

1. For the moſt outrageous violation of moderation in this argument, the moſt ludicrous
and hyperbolical extravagance in defence of
the ſlave ſyſtem, we muſt look to the writings
of the French coloniſts. They have actually
maintained, that the negro trade is the only
means of civilizing the interior of the great A-
frican continent ; that the natural conſtitution
of the negroes is utterly repugnant to the climate in which they are born ; that they muſt
be tranſplanted to the milder regions of the new
world, and civilized by main force. The illuſtration or analogy by which this truly ſingular
argument is elaborately ſupported, preſents us
with an abſurdity if poſſible more flagrant. It
is maintained, that if the Mexicans (who it
ſeems were alſo born in a climate incompatible
with their conſtitutions) had enjoyed the advantages of tranſplantation like the happy negroes,
we ſhould not have witneſſed the total extinc-
tion of their numerous race : and this is called
the evidence of experience in favour of the ſlave
trade. I am confident that every reader will
be aſtoniſhed, when he obſerves the name of
Barré St Venant cited as the author of ſuch arguments. The above ſtatement is almoſt a literal tranſlation from his words ; and although
M. Malouet diſapproves of the extent to which
the argument is puſhed, his approbation of the
general principles of M. Barré is unqualified,
                                                    and

and he explicitly fupports the other congenial
theme of his countryman, the only part of this
argument which has found its way into Great
Britain, that the negroes in the Weft Indies are
much happier than the European peafantry. *
But will the reader believe that a ftill more flagrant infult has been offered to the common
fenfe of mankind in purfuing the fame topics?
Will it be conceived, without actually refer-
ring to M. Barré's words, † that he imputes the
origin of the flave trade among the Spaniards,
entirely to their liberal views of benefiting mankind, their rational plans of promoting the happinefs and civilization of Africa!

‘ *On auroit de la peine* ’ (fays he) ‘ *à croire*
‘ *aujourd'hui, que ce fut par un motif d'huma-*
‘ *nité que les Efpagnols allerent, les premiers*
‘ *en* 1503, *chercher des negres à la côte d'A-*
‘ *frique, pour fupplier les foibles Mexicains dans*
‘ *le travail des colonies. Voyant que les peuples*
‘ *conquis etoient trop foibles pour fupporter le*
‘ *travail dans leur pays natal—Voyant enfuite*
‘ *que les negres, placés fous un ciel brulant, refide-*
‘ *roient mieux fous un climat temperé — Voyant*
‘ *enfin que, de tems immemorial, l'efclavage exiftoit*
‘ *en Afrique avec des caracteres plus hideux que*
‘ *dans*

---

* Barré St Venant, Col. Mod. chap. V. VI. & VII.
—Malouet, Mem. fur les Colonies, tom. IV. p. 77. & 84.
See alfo ‘ Memoire fur l'efclavage des Negres, ’ in tom. V.
† P. 40.

‘ *dans aucune autre contrée, ils crurent leur rendre*
‘ *un bon service de les retirer de leurs repaires,*
‘ *pour en faire des laboureurs.* ’

After this, we are not surprifed to find our
author exprefs a fort of regret that France was
fo long of following this glorious example, and
then exultingly enumerate the bleffings of the
flave trade.

‘ *Ce n'eſt que cent vingt ans après que les*
‘ *François les imiterent.*

‘ *Cette tentative a fertilisé une partie du nou-*
‘ *veau monde ; elle a donné de nouvelles jouiſſances*
‘ *à l'ancien ; bien conduite elle auroit aggrandi la*
‘ *proſperité des deux hemiſpheres.* ’ *

He may doubtlefs derive fome confolation to
his patriotic feelings of regret, from the confideration that his countrymen, though late, have
been fuch ftrenuous and fuccefsful imitators of
the Spanifh philanthropy. †

2. The fame men who have afferted that
the negroes are happier in the Weft Indies than
in their own country, and enjoy more of the
comforts of life than the peafantry of Europe,
might well be expected to deny all the allegations of bad treatment which have been fo often
brought againft the planters, as well as the flave-
traders.

---

* P. 40.   † Note W w.

traders. In Britain, where this queſtion under-
went the moſt ſolemn and ample diſcuſſion, the
friends of the ſlave ſyſtem had every opportunity of bringing forward all their proofs. The
firſt debates which took place were introduced
by the ſlave-carrying bill ; and the moſt remarkable circumſtance attending this diſcuſſion, was
the groſs prevarication of the witneſſes brought
forward by the opponents of the meaſure. The
ſlave trade abolition bill was oppoſed with equal
zeal ; and the difficulties under which its advocates laboured in adducing their proof, muſt be
evident to every one who reflects that, from
the very nature of the caſe, almoſt all the witneſſes had neceſſarily an intereſt in concealing,
or modifying, or perverting the truth, in ſo far
as it was unfavourable to the planters and ſlave-
traders, while almoſt every one of the witneſſes
brought forward in exculpation, were immediately concerned in the charges, being in fact the
very parties accuſed. Notwithſtanding this, any
perſon who ſtudies with tolerable attention that
invaluable maſs of information which the Committee of 1789 have collected in their Report,
muſt be convinced, as the Houſe of Commons
were, that the whole caſe of the petitioners was
clearly made out. As a ſpecimen of the manner in which their opponents attempted to vin-
dicate the planters from all charge of cruelty,

I

I fhall tranfcribe a paffage from Sir William
Young's Tour to the Windward Iflands. This
tour appears to have been undertaken during
the greateſt heats of the negro queſtions ; and
the account of it publiſhed by the traveller (who
was one of the chief oppofers of the abolition)
feems to be given to the world, with the precife
view of biaffing the public mind, in favour of
the gentle treatment of the Weſt Indian flaves.
It is publiſhed in the fame volume with Mr Edwards's Hiſtory of St Domingo, and to all appearance for the fame purpofe.

The very firſt day that the touriſt lands in
the Weſt Indies, he delivers the refult of his
obfervations upon the ſtate of the flaves ; denies
that they appear to be abject and humble ; a-
fcribes to them the greateſt pride and felf-im-
portance ; compares their manners and wit to
thofe of the Roman flaves, nay to thofe of the
flaves pourtrayed by the Roman dramatiſts,
who were of courfe much more refined in
their characters and converfation than the ori-
ginals in real life *. Such accounts, to fay
the leaſt of them, furely prove a great deal
too much ; and the fame remark might have
been applied to the following paffage, had we
not poffeffed a more pofitive contradiction of
                                             the

* Young's Tour, *apud* Edwards's Weſt Indies, vol. III.
p. 262.

the conclusion drawn from the facts contained
in it.

' I particularly noticed every negro whom I
' met or overtook on the road. Of these I count-
' ed eleven who were dressed as field negroes, with
' only trowsers on ; and adverting to the evi-
' dence on the slave trade, I particularly remark-
' ed that not one of the eleven had a single mark
' or scar of the whip. We met or overtook a
' great many other negroes, but they were dress-
' ed. Passing through Mr Greathead's large
' estate, I observed in the gang one well-look-
' ing negro woman, who had two or three
' wheals on her shoulders, which seemed the
' effect of an old punishment. ' * But even
this solitary exception to the general good usage
of the slaves our tourist explains away ; for he
afterwards says, †

' Never passing a slave without observing his
' back, either in the field, or on the road, or
' wenches washing in the rivers, I have seen not
' one back marked besides that of the woman
' observed before on Mr Greathead's estate (in
' whom I may be mistaken as to the cause),
' and one new negro unsold at Kingston, who
                              ' found

* Young's Tour, *apud* Edwards's West Indies, vol. III.
p. 267.
  † Ibid. p. 280.

BOOK
IV.

' found means to explain to me that he was
' *fumfumm'd* (flogged) by the furgeon of the
' fhip, and he feemed to have had two or three
' ftrokes with a cat. '

Now, unfortunately for all this induction of
facts, we meet with the following note by Mr
Edwards, upon the paffage firft quoted. *

' In the Weft Indies, the punifhment of
' whipping is commonly inflicted, not on the
' backs of negroes (as practifed in the difcipline
' of the Britifh foldiers), but more humanely,
' and with much lefs danger, on *partes pofte-*
' *riores.* It is therefore no proof that the ne-
' groes whom Sir William Young infpected had
' efcaped flagellation becaufe their fhoulders bore
' no impreffion of the whip. This acknowledge-
' ment I owe to truth and candour. '

The praife of candour we cannot award to
this note, becaufe Mr Edwards was the firft
publifher of this tract, and becaufe every man
who knew any thing about a Weft Indian plantation, would of himfelf have inftantly perceived the unfairnefs of the inference from
the facts—an inference which, on Sir William's part, may only have been ignorance,
but on the part of Mr Edwards muft have
been falfehood. It is fcarcely neceffary to
add,

* Young's Tour, *apud* Edwards's Weft Indies, vol. III.
p. 267.

add, that the favourable account of the negro
punifhment in this note, is as falfe as the al-
lufion to Britifh military difcipline is infidious.
But the fubftance of the note is valuable, becaufe
it furnifhes an authentic refutation of the Effay upon negro happinefs, which runs through
Sir William's whole narrative. What truft
fhall we repofe in the portraits of this artift,
when he paints to us the wit, honour, pride,
contentment, gambols, mirth and comforts of
the flaves, after we have found him fo fuper-
ficially acquainted with the œconomy of Weft
Indian property? Nay, what confidence can
we place in the negative evidence of the other
great Weft Indians, when we find one of the
moft wealthy, intelligent, and refpectable members of this body, fo ill informed, or fo duped by
his fubordinate agents? It may farther be remarked as a fingular circumftance, that Sir
William Young fhould not have added fome
retractation of his general affertions in the laft
edition (1801) from which I quote. He is
himfelf the editor after the death of Mr Edwards; and he publifhes the text with his
friend's notes, exactly as he had written it at
a time when, it is to be hoped, he was utterly
ignorant of the miftatement he was giving to
the world.

3. It

3. It is fcarcely credible, that men fhould have been found abfurd enough to defend the fyftem of negro flavery upon abftract principles. I have, however, given one fpecimen of this mode of argument from the writings of the French planters. The Britifh planters and their a-gents have fallen confiderably fhort of their foreign brethren in this line of abfurdity : but fomething of the very fame nature may be met with in the tenor of their reafonings. They have maintained, that in all ages flavery has ex-ifted ; that a worfe kind than that of the negroes was known to the moft celebrated nations of antiquity ; and that Chriftianity itfelf approves of the inftitution. If Parliamentary Reports may be trufted, thofe arguments were brought forward in a very elaborate fpeech, delivered by the agent for Jamaica in the Houfe of Com-mons, when the abolition was firft debated. To all fuch appeals it may be anfwered, that they are partly nugatory, partly falfe, and partly im-pious. The defence of negro flavery, by a refer-ence to its antiquity, is nugatory ; for what an-tiquity can juftify a crime ? The affertion, that the lot of the enflaved negroes is lefs hard than that of the Roman and Greek flaves, is com-pletely falfe. The appeal to the Gofpel in its behalf, is, I devoutly believe, moft unauthorifed by any *dictum* in that bleffed difpenfation. But

if

if fuch a *dictum* fhould be found in the Sacred
Writings, its total repugnance to the whole fpirit of the fyftem, is a fufficient proof of its being interpolated. If, on the other hand, its in-
terpolation be denied, I hefitate not to declare,
that there is an end of all rational faith in
Chriftianity ; for what can more decifively dif-
prove the divine origin of any fyftem of belief,
than its inculcating or fanctioning the flavery of
the Weft Indies ?

4. The ground which the advocates of the
flave trade occupied, in order to meet the arguments of expediency, was in many refpects
as extravagantly high as that upon which they
built their defence of its humanity and juftice.
A traffic, which at the utmoft never employs
more than five thoufand feamen, has been called the pillar of the Britifh navy. A traffic
which deftroys more failors in one year, than
all the other branches of trade put together
deftroy in two; a traffic which is in fact
the grave of our ableft feamen, has been extolled as their beft nurfery. A commerce,
in which a million and a half Sterling was
never employed at any time, and which is,
beyond any other, fubject to vaft rifk and
unavoidable flownefs of returns, has been defcribed as the grand pillar of the Britifh commerce. The moft extravagant falfehoods have
been

BOOK
IV.

been blazoned forth to fupport thofe allegations. But for a full refutation of them, I refer my reader to the Report of the Committee
1788, if indeed any anfwer is neceffary ; for,
admitting all that can be faid in favour of the
traffic, either as a nurfery of feamen or a
fource of mercantile opulence, if the immediate confequence of continuing the trade muft
be the lofs of the colonies, or their total derangement as a valuable poffeffion, furely every
argument of this nature, in favour of the flave
trade, turns with increafed force againft the
end for which it was advanced, inafmuch as
the lofs of the African trade will fall with
redoubled and fatal effect upon the national
profperity, when, by a fhort delay, the traffic
has grown in importance, and has drawn along
with it another branch of commerce infinitely
more valuable and extenfive. Although the
abolition were not to prevent our total deftruction in the Weft Indies, it is evidently advantageous if it only divides the lofs, and prevents
the fhock from being felt all at once. The
capital employed in the flave trade, will eafily
find other employment in the trade of African
commodities, or, if that opening is infufficient, in the other branches of foreign trade.
It is a capital returned more flowly than any
other, and with greater rifk : it is, therefore,
peculiarly adapted to find its way into the
diftant

diftant branches of commerce, as, for inftance, the Eaft Indian trade, which we may be al- lowed to hope will ere long be opened. If the flave trade were to be abolifhed only with the downfal of the colonial fyftem, (admitting that to be inevitable which would moft pro- bably be prevented by the immediate aboli- tion), then two capitals would at once be thrown out of employment inftead of one, and a much greater fhock given to the national credit. It is unneceffary to obferve, that when a nation lofes any branch of commerce or ma- nufacture, in which it has long been engag- ed, the neceffity of fhifting all the capital fo employed, is only dangerous in proportion to the fuddennefs of its occurrence.

But we are told, that if the Britifh were to abolifh the flave trade, the French and Dutch would take it up. This is indeed a contemp- tible fophifm; and fuch I will call it in fpite of the high names which have fanctioned it. For, in the *firft* place, if Britain fubftantial- ly abolifhes the trade, fhe muft prevent the importation of flaves into her colonies from whatever quarter. The fhare of the Britifh flave trade, then, which can fall to France and Holland, will only be that part which Britain formerly carried on for the fupply of the French and Dutch fettlements; a part of no confiderable magnitude, and liable

every

every day to be diminifhed by the increafe
of commerce, or the alteration of trade-laws
in France and Holland. But, in the *next*
place, may not the fame argument be ufed in
France and Holland to oppofe the abolition?
It has in fact been employed by the French
and Dutch colonifts exactly in the fame terms : *
So that a trade of iniquity and fhame is to be
fupported to all eternity, becaufe each of the
parties engaged in it may fay, that the others
might continue it! The ufe of the fame argument at the fame time by all the parties, is a
complete demonftration of its abfurdity. Surely in the feafon of peace, fome communication
might be opened between the different powers
engaged in colonial affairs, and union of views
effected upon fo important a fubject.

We may alfo remark, that if the African
traders of Britain were to give it up, and if part
of the capital employed in other countries were
to flow towards the blank fpace left by Britain,
as much of the Britifh capital, transferred from
the trade, would find immediate employment
in fupplying the demands of thofe other countries, as could fill the blank occafioned there
by the new arrangement. But all fears of our
ftanding alone in this great meafure are ground-
lefs. We have been the chief traders, I mean,
the

---

* Malouet, Barré St Venant, &c. &c.

the ringleaders in the crime. Let us be the firſt to repent, and ſet an example of reformation. It becomes the dignity of Great Britain to take the lead, and to truſt that her example will be followed. No great reform has ever taken place in one part of the international and intercolonial ſyſtems, without a ſimilar change being ſoon effected in all the other parts ; * and the meaſure which is adopted in order to prevent the ruin of the Britiſh colonies, will ſurely be imitated by the other ſtates, whoſe colonies are expoſed to ſtill more imminent dangers from the ſame quarter.

5. The laſt view of the queſtion, to which I ſhall allude is, that of the conſequences apprehended to the Weſt Indies from the abolition. It is ſaid, that the negro population cannot be kept up without importation. A full refutation of this aſſertion may be found in various parts of the preceding pages. But the matter reſts on plain and undeniable facts. The official Reports from the different iſlands, have clearly proved the poſſibility of breeding a ſufficient number to ſupply all the blanks occaſioned by deaths, and even to increaſe the ſtock in the natural way. † And he who would ſee

a

---

* Book II. Sect. III. & Book III. Sect. I.

† Report 1789.—Reſolutions laid before the Houſe of Commons 1791.

a complete view of all this argument, founded
upon facts of infinite variety, and unqueſtion-
able authenticity, may conſult the very diſtinct
and comprehenſive ſtatement of Mr Clarkſon,
in his ' *Eſſay on the Impolicy of the Slave Trade* ; '
a work replete with ſound ſenſe, diſtinguiſhed
by temperate views of a queſtion ſeldom diſcuſſed in ſo calm a ſpirit, and abounding with
ample information upon the whole details of
this extenſive ſubject. *

Let us, then, conſider to what the arguments of commercial expediency amount, admitting that the continuance of the traffic is
not inconſiſtent with the exiſtence of the Weſt
Indian ſyſtem. The only claſſes of men who
can be affected by the meaſure, are the African
traders in the mother country, and the proprietors of plantations which have been purchaſed with the view of extending their cultivation. The European traders may eaſily find
employment, in the other branches of domeſtic
and foreign commerce, for that capital which
the

---

* It is unfortunate that we have no full account of the
ſplendid oration delivered by Mr Pitt, upon the great diſcuſſion of the ſlave trade. If we may judge from the ſpeci-
mens publiſhed of that performance, it muſt have been one
of the moſt maſterly efforts of his unrivalled genius, diſtinguiſhed at once by the higheſt perfection of eloquence, and
by a clearneſs of reaſoning amounting to the preciſion and
rigour of geometrical inveſtigation.

the ordinary traffic with Africa does not ab-
forb. At any rate, their number and importance deferves little confideration ; and the i-
dea of indemnification to them for the lofs,
would be as abfurd as if all the merchants of a
country were to demand public aid, becaufe
the public meafures of juftifiable hoftility excluded them from foreign markets ; or all the
monopolifts of a certain branch of traffic, were
to require a compenfation for the lofs of that
commerce which the wifdom of the Legiflature
fhould lay open to all.

The other clafs of perfons injured, are only
fubjected to the want of what they might o-
therwife have gained, or at the utmoft to a
trifling inconvenience. They ftill poffefs an e-
quivalent for their purchafe-money. If they
are not fatisfied with the flow accumulation by
means of natural increafe, they may fell again,
and remove their ftock to another channel.
They cannot now fulfil their expectations of
acquiring a rapid fortune by clearing the land,
becaufe the price of negroes will rife, or rather, for fome years, there will be no poffibility of purchafing flaves. But this is no
real or abfolute lofs which can juftify their demands of an equivalent. Suppofe that the
Britifh Cabinet were difpofed to annul the
Methuen treaty ; would it be neceffary firft
to confult all thofe merchants who, on the
faith

faith of it, had removed to Portugal, or fettled a correfpondence with that country, or vefted their ftock in French wines, or bought woollens to fupply the market of Lifbon? Or, fuppofe that the Eaft Indian monopoly were abolifhed, would the holders of India ftock have a claim for indemnification; or would the capitalifts, who had laid out their money in fhares of Eaft India veffels, or in loans to captains and traders, have a right to demand compenfation? But thefe cafes are much more favourable to fuch claims than the one which we are confidering. Suppofe that a number of capitalifts have vefted their ftock in the three *per cents.* at the end of a long war, from the full confidence that the value of the funded property will in a few months rife twenty or thirty *per cent.*; if the national honour is infulted, muft all thofe ftockholders be indemnified for their probable difappointment, before a war can be proclaimed? Or muft the King's crown be endangered, his people defpifed, his flag buffeted, his ambaffadors fpit upon in every court or Jacobin *coterie* throughout Europe, becaufe the proclamation of a juft and neceffary war would prevent the ftockholders from realizing all their golden dreams, founded upon the laft treaty of peace? And can any ftain be fo deep on the honour and the

character

character of the country, as the fupporting of a traffic founded in treachery and blood? Can any meafure attended with partial lofs or difappointment, be in its effence more juft and neceffary than the immediate wiping out of fo foul a pollution? Can any policy be more contemptible than that which would refufe its fanction to fuch a meafure, for fear of difappointing thofe men who had arranged their plans with the hopes of fattening upon the plunder of the public character and virtue? —' *Habet aliquid ex iniquo omne magnum exemplum, quod contrà fingulos utilitate publicâ rependitur.* ' *

We have already feen how neceffary for the prefervation, as well as the improvement of the American colonies, the great meafure of abolition is proved to be by the whole hiftory of the Weft Indies, and more particularly by the events of the laft twelve years. But the immediate advantages, in point of wealth, which muft flow from that meafure to the proprietors of flaves, deferve alfo to be noticed. They form a fufficient counterpoife to the difappointment, which thofe planters may experience from being deprived of the power to extend their cultivation at pleafure. The value of every flave
already

---

* Tacitus, Annal. XIV. cap. 44.

already in the iflands will of courfe rife incalculably, as foon as the line is drawn and the
farther fupply ftopped. The abolition of the
African trade will produce the fame augmentation in the value of the ftock on hand, that the
deftruction of the Golconda mines would upon
the value of the diamonds already in the European market. This will be the natural recompenfe to the planters for the inconvenience
arifing from a limitation of the fupply. Particularly, it will be favourable to thofe iflands
or plantations which have for fome time ceafed
to import, and have wifely kept up their ftock
by breeding.

Such are the chief arguments that have been
brought forward by the advocates of the flave
fyftem, and fuch are the anfwers to which they
eafily yield. I muft repeat once more, that the
plea of neceffity is now the ftrongeft fupport of
the meafure, next to the paramount confideration of its juftice. The arguments above detailed and anfwered, only deferve our attention as
tending if poffible to ftrengthen conclufions to
which we have been led by a more fhort and
eafy procefs. They furnifh, too, a curious fpecimen of the fundamental weaknefs of the caufe
which they are employed to uphold; while the
fuccefs of fuch reafonings, in fuch a caufe, e-
vinces how lamentably eafy it is to perfuade
mankind, by the moft ridiculous and extravagant

gant topics, of propofitions the moft outrage- S E C T.
ous to every natural feeling of humanity and
juftice, when thofe propofitions are connected
with an apparent intereft.

From this unfatisfactory view, let us turn to
a more pleafing profpect, and figure to ourfelves
the probable confequences of that great meafure which fo many reafons of juftice, of expediency, of overruling neceffity, concur in prefcribing to the European powers. The land-
fcape it is true exifts but in fancy ; yet is it not
ungrateful fometimes to refrefh the mind by the
relief of contemplating thofe pictures which depart from nature only in the too favourable co-
louring of the human figures, and the Arcadian
beauties of the fcene wherein they are pourtrayed. Before indulging in this view, let us ftop
for a little to confider in what manner the fundamental change of colonial policy muft be effected.

It appears very manifeft that the mother
country alone is competent to effect the abolition of the flave trade. No affembly compofed
of planters, and fitting in a flave colony, will
ever, to the end of time, think for one moment
of abolifhing the trade. Can we expect it ?
Can we blame the perfons compofing fuch bodies for their obftinate adherence to that fyftem
which ancient habits and prejudices, and the
zeal

zeal of fome worthy but intemperate men in attacking them, and the conduct of others fig-
nalized by a mad and unprincipled love of
change, have all confpired to render venerable
in the eyes of every Weft Indian ? We might
as reafonably hope to fee the poor-laws of England amended by a parifh veftry, or a profitable
war terminated by a board of commiffaries and
general officers, as to obtain the abolition of the
flave trade from the colonial affemblies. If every found reafon did not concur to teach us the
folly of entertaining fuch hopes, we might be at
once convinced by a fingle confideration. How
many independent legiflatures are there in the
Weft Indies ? Let it be admitted that a few
colonies relinquifh the trade ; can it be fuppofed that every other will join them, when the
partial abolition in one quarter renders the continuance of it more profitable to the reft ? Yet
if any one refufe to concur, the fame doctrines
of colonial fupremacy muft render the forcing
of the meafure upon that one, as unjuftifiable as
the univerfal violation of the colonial rights.
In fact, the colonial affemblies and the planters
have fpoken very plainly upon thefe matters,
and given us a full view of what may be expected from their deliberations on the abolition.
To go no farther back than the year 1799, the
petitions of the Britifh Weft Indian iflands to
                                        Parliament,

Parliament, contain the moſt open and explicit avowal of the rooted determination of the planters and aſſemblies to ſupport the ſlave trade for ever, as an integral part of the colonial ſyſtem. The tenor of theſe addreſſes, whilſt it ſhews the duplicity of many previous declarations and arguments, at once evinces the abſurdity of truſting the moſt trivial branch of the diſcuſſion to the colonies ; and, that any one ſhould have been found thoughtleſs enough, after thoſe declarations, to propoſe leaving the whole matter to the deciſion of the planters, would be aſtoniſhing, upon any other queſtion than the preſent.

It is not my intention at preſent to touch the ſubject of colonial government. But, to thoſe who maintain the rights of colonies in ſuch queſtions as that of abolition, let it be a ſufficient anſwer to ſtate the eſſential ſubordination of all colonial eſtabliſhments in the diſcuſſion of the moſt important imperial affairs. We have formerly noticed this diſtinguiſhing feature in the conſtitution of all ſeparate and diſtant provinces *. Does the ſlave trade intereſt the colonies more than the queſtion of peace and war, which ſo often recurs ? and is any colony ever conſulted on ſuch a diſcuſſion ? When we hear the friends of the ſlave trade maintain that the
abolition

---

* Book II. Sect. I.

BOOK
IV.

abolition can only be determined by the colonifts, and then recommend to the colonial governments this meafure which they oppofed at
home, we plainly perceive a grofs inconfiftency.
They do not confine their oppofition in the mother country to a denial of her jurifdiction ; they
oppofe the abolition upon the merits of the cafe :
yet, in the colonies, they affect to fupport the
meafure alfo upon the merits. * This is a fair acknowledgement that they are infincere, either in
their defence of the fyftem at home, or in their
defence of the abolition in America. When we
confider that they are themfelves colonifts, it is
not difficult to determine from which of their
fpeeches their real opinions and wifhes muft be
taken. They do not wifh to fucceed in their
defence of the abolition ; they do not expect it.
The compofition of the colonial affemblies is a
fufficient fecurity to them againft all the effects
of their mock efforts. They are only oppofing
the whole meafure of abolition in a roundabout,
uncandid, and treacherous manner.

1. The abolition of the flave trade muft, as
we have already feen, greatly ameliorate the
ftructure of fociety in the Weft Indian colonies.
Every man may now be left to purfue his own
interest

* Edwards, vol. II. & Hift. of War in St Domingo :
Conclufion.

interest in his own way. Few will continue fo
infane as to maltreat and work out their flock,
when they can no longer fill up the blanks occafioned by their cruelty, or their inhuman and
fhort-fighted policy. A great increafe of wealth,
and a rapid augmentation of the negro population, will be the confequence of this milder fyftem ; for every proprietor of flaves will attend
to the breeding, as the only method by which
his ftock can be recruited, or his cultivation extended. The fecundity of the negroes may be
gathered, not only from their hiftory in Africa, but ftill more ftrikingly from the eftimates
given in the Report of 1787, by which it appears, that, under all forts of bad treatment,
their numbers were kept up naturally in almoft all the iflands. * The effects of a milder
treatment may eafily be fuppofed ; and if facts
are neceffary to defcribe thofe effects, we may
refer to the ftatements of Mr Jefferfon, in his
celebrated work on Virginia. The experience
of the United States has diftinctly proved that
the rapid multiplication of the Blacks in a natural way, will inevitably be occafioned by pro-
hibiting their importation. †

In

---

* See a fuccinct ftatement of this fact in the Refolutions
of 1791.

† Notes on Virginia, Query 8.

In a very few years, all the negroes in America will be Creoles, and all the masters will
treat them with kind indulgence for their own
fakes. The two great dangers arising from bad
spirits will be removed ; the labour of the negroes will be more productive, and will resemble
in some degree the industry of free men ; the
negro character will be improved ; the manners
of the other classes will also be ameliorated ;
the non-residence, so much to be lamented at
present, and the want of women, so fatal to the
colonial character, will gradually wear out ;
the structure of West Indian society will more
and more resemble that of the compact, firm,
and respectable communities which compose the
North American states.

2. It will now only be necessary that the legislature should farther interfere with the plans
and actions of the people, in so far as certain
topical irregularities may still arise from the bad
passions of individuals, and in so far as indirect
encouragement may be given to operations or
schemes evidently beneficial to the whole society.

All those subordinate arrangements are better left to the colonial legislatures. After the government of the mother country has abolished
the African trade, they are fully competent to
take all the steps that may be necessary for improving

proving the fyftem. They are precifely in the fituation which infures the adoption of wife meafures;
they are compofed of men immediately interefted in the purfuit of that very conduct which
the good of the fyftem requires. All the individuals who form the affemblies, are concerned
in the prefervation and increafe of the negro
ftock; in the improvement of the whole colonial fociety; in the gradual reformation of the
general fyftem. They are feparated from their
brother colonifts only by that election which
confers upon them the power of watching o-
ver the common good, and impofes on them
the duty of inveftigating the means whereby
it may beft be attained. For the fame reafon that it would be in vain to expect from
fuch men the great meafure of abolition, it
would be foolifh to defpair of obtaining from
them every affiftance, in promoting thofe fubordinate fchemes, which may conduce to the
amelioration of the colonial policy. Of their
fuperior ability to devife and execute fuch meafures, we cannot entertain the fmalleft doubt.
They are men intimately acquainted with every
minute branch of colonial affairs, and accuftomed, from their earlieft years, to meditate upon
no other fubjects. They refide in the heart of
the fyftem for which their plans are to be laid,
and on which the fuccefs of every experiment
is to be tried.

The

The general queſtion of abolition may eaſily be examined at a diſtance. All the information that is neceſſary for the full diſcuſſion of it has already been procured by the mother countries of the different European colonies. Its connexion with various intereſts not colonial, renders the provincial governments incompetent to examine it, even if their intereſts and prejudices left them at liberty to enter upon a fair inveſtigation.

But the details of the ſlave laws require more minute and accurate acquaintance with an infinite variety of particulars, which can only be known to thoſe who reſide upon the ſpot. To reviſe the domeſtic codes of the colonies, would be a taſk which no European government could undertake, for want of information, and for want of time. Any Parliament, Council, or Senate, which ſhould begin ſuch a work, would find it neceſſary to give up legiſlating for the mother country, in order partly to mar, and partly to neglect the legiſlation of the colonies. Let this branch of the imperial adminiſtration, then, be left to the care of thoſe who are themſelves moſt immediately intereſted in the good order and government of the diſtant provinces, and whoſe knowledge of local circumſtances, of thoſe things which cannot be written down in reports, nor told by witneſſes, is more full and practical.

The

The queftion of abolition is one, and fimple ; it
is anfwered by a yea or a nay ; its folution requires no exercife of invention. The queftions of regulation are many and complex ; they are ftated by a ' *quomodo* ; ' they lead to the difcovery of means, and the comparifon of meafures propofed. Without pretending to difpute the fupremacy of the mother country, we may be allowed to doubt her omnifcience ; and the colonial hiftory of modern Europe may well change our doubts into difbelief. Without ftanding up for the privileges of the colonies, we may fuggeft their more intimate acquaintance with the details of the queftion, and maintain, that the intereft both of the mother country and of the colonies, requires a fubdivifion of the labour of legiflation ; a delegation of certain duties and inquiries to thofe who are moft nearly connected with the refult, and fituated within the reach of the materials. When the abolition fhall have rendered all the planters more careful of their ftock, and more difpofed to encourage breeding, the only tafk for the colonial governments will be, to regulate the relative rights of the two claffes, to prepare the civilization of the fubordinate race, and to check thofe cruelties which may ftill appear in a few inftances of individual inhumanity and impolicy.

3. The

3. The great object of the colonial go‑
vernments as a body, and of their members as
individuals, will be the encouragement of fome‑
thing like voluntary induftry. The humane
treatment of the flave; the granting him con‑
fiderable latitude of indulgence by flow de‑
grees; and, above all, the encouragement of
breeding, will probably effect this great ob‑
ject. With the rearing of a family may be
coupled fome of thofe liberties which the prof‑
perity of the children requires, and which the
ftrength of parental feeling renders fafe. The
admiffion of the flave to certain privileges of
property, has produced the happieft effects in
our colonies, even under the ancient policy.
But I have already pointed out the effects of
the rigorous flave fyftem, in preventing many of
the good confequences which would otherwife
refult from this cuftomary indulgence, equally
politic and humane. Little voluntary labour is
in fact performed by the flaves during their days
of reft, even on their own grounds, in confe‑
quence of the hard treatment which they expe‑
rience all the reft of the week in working for
their drivers. * But the new fyftem will draw
from this, and other fources, the moft falutary
confequences. In order to appreciate the pro‑
bable effects of the great and fundamental mea‑
fure

---

* Book IV. Sect. I.

fure in this point of view, let us for a moment
caſt our eyes over the ancient hiſtory of that
quarter of the world in which we live, and contemplate the origin of that ſociety which is now
ſettled in ſuch a compaƈt, regular, and beautiful
fabric.

In ancient times, a great part of the population of the moſt poliſhed ſtates was the perſonal
property of the reſt. Thoſe ſlaves were chiefly
captives taken direƈtly in war, or purchaſed from
other warlike nations who had obtained them
in this way. The conſtant hoſtilities which at that
time divided the people of all countries, rendered this a very fruitful ſource of ſupply. During the riſe of Athens and Rome, accordingly,
when many foreign nations were by rapid ſteps
conquered, and when others, ſtill unſubdued,
could ſell the perſons of their weaker neighbours, there was never any ſcarcity of men in
the great ſlave markets. The cruelty of the
treatment which thoſe unhappy men experienced, was proportioned to the eaſe with which
they were procured ; and we have already remarked how intolerable their lot was among the
very people who called every foreigner a Barbarian. As war became leſs common, and the
arts of peace were more cultivated, this ſupply
of ſlaves of courſe decreaſed ; and when the
Roman empire, tottering under its own weight,
could think of nothing leſs than new conqueſts,

there

there was an end of importing flaves. Accordingly, with the progrefs of real civilization, but
ftill more with the diminution of wars and conquefts, was introduced a milder fyftem of domeftic government, a greater humanity towards
the flaves, and a more careful attention to breeding, when the ftock could neither be kept up
nor increafed by other means. The laws added
their fanction to this falutary change, which no
laws could of themfelves have wrought. The
rights of flaves came to be recognized, the conduct of the mafter to be watched, and the practice of emancipation to be encouraged. By degrees, the flaves were incorporated with their
mafters, and formed part of the great free population, which was rather mixed with, than
fubdued by, the Goths.

The conquefts of the great ancient ftates,
and the purchafes which they made from petty
tribes always at war, may be compared with the
flave trade carried on by the modern ftates of
Europe : and the pacification of the Greek
and Roman commonwealths—their inability either to conquer or buy—may be compared with
the abolition of the African trade ; or (if fuch
a thing were poffible without the abolition) with
the civilization of the great theatre upon which
this trade is carried on.   Making allowance for
the difference of race, the confequences of the
abolition

abolition upon the manners of the planters and
condition of the flaves, aided by the regulations
which the colonial legiflatures will adopt, but
which they never either would or could effect
without the abolition, will form exactly the
counterpart of the change introduced, by the
ceffation of conquefts, into the domeftic manners and œconomy of the ancients, affifted and
enforced by the alterations of their pofitive laws.

To the flavery of the ancients fucceeded the
bondage and villenage of their Gothic conquerors. But the difference between the two was
marked and important. The Greek and Roman flaves were imported ; the Gothic flaves
were the peafantry of the country, and born on
the fpot, unlefs during the wars which accompanied the firft inroads of the northern tribes.
Accordingly, we find no parallel between the
rigour of the ancient and of the modern flave
fyftem ; and a foundation was laid in this effential difference, for a much more rapid improvement of the whole fociety than took place in
Greece or Rome, notwithftanding the fuperior
refinements of the claffic times. The flave firft
became attached to his mafter, not as his perfonal property, but as part of his ftock, and
aftricted to the foil, to ufe the language of the
feudal ages. By degrees, the mutual interefts
of the lord and his villeins, in the progrefs of
national

national improvement, operated that important
change in the ftate of manners, out of which
the modern divifion of ranks, and the privileges
of the lower orders, have arifen in the civilized
quarters of the European community. Firft,
the villein obtained the ufe of the land to which
he had been annexed, and of the ftock in which
he had been comprehended, on condition that
a certain proportion (generally one half) of the
produce fhould belong to the lord of the land
and proprietor of the ftock. This great change,
one of the moft fignal of thofe events which
have laid the foundation of human improvement by degrees too flow for the obfervation of
hiftorians, was owing entirely to the mafter difcovering how much his intereft was connected
with the comfort of his flaves ; how neceffary
it was to treat well that race whofe toils fupported the community in eafe, and whofe lofs
could not be repaired ; how much more profitable it was to divide with the vaffal the fruits of
his free and ftrenuous exertions, than to monopolize the fcanty produce of his compulfory
toil. As foon as the right of property, and the
fecure enjoyment of the fruits of labour were
extended to the vaffals, the progrefs of improvement became conftant and vifible. The proportion of the fruits paid to the lord was diminiſhed according to an indefinite ftandard ; the

peafant,

peafant, having been permitted to acquire property, provided his own ftock, and obtained the
power of changing his refidence, and commut-
ing the nature of his fervices. By degrees, the
rent came to be paid in money, according to
the number of competitors for a farm ; and they
who could not farm land themfelves, fold their
labour to others for a certain price or maintenance. Laftly, the legiflature fecured the leafe
of the farmer with the fame certainty that it fecured the property of the landlord, and recognized the one as well as the other for ufeful and
independent fubjects.

A fimilar progrefs will moft probably be the
refult of that abolition, in the fuppofition of
which we are indulging. That this idea is not
chimerical, the confideration of a few facts,
very little known, in the hiftory of America,
may convince us.

The peculiar circumftances in the fituation
of the Spanifh and Portugueze colonies of
South America, have already partially operated fome of thofe happy effects which we may
expect from the abolition of the flave trade.
The high price of the negroes in the Spanifh
fettlements, partly from abfurd regulations of
trade, partly from the deficiency of the Spaniards in the practice of commerce and naval affairs, caufes that want of hands which would
prevail in its full extent, were the African
trade

trade ſtopt. Both in the Spaniſh and Portugueze colonies, the great proportion of the Indians to the whole population, has inculcated
(as we have already ſeen *) the policy of gaining over the negroes, by all means, to the
White cauſe, in caſe of any ſtruggle with the
more powerful claſs. From theſe circumſtances, and partly no doubt from the peculiarly
indolent character of the coloniſts in thoſe
parts, there has ariſen a much better ſyſtem of
treatment than any other European colony can
boaſt of. The firſt conſequence of this ſtate
of things has been, the conſtant ſecurity of the
Spaniſh and Portugueze ſettlements from all
riſks of negro rebellion. Other views of intereſt have conſpired to confirm and extend
this ſyſtem of mildneſs and equity towards the
ſlaves ; and the Legiſlature has not failed, by
every prudent interference, to aſſiſt the inferior
race in the acquiſition of rights and privileges.

Thus we meet with many very ſingular
analogies between the hiſtory of the negroes in
South America, and that of the villeins or
bondſmen of Europe, in the earlier feudal times.
All the gold and jewels in Brazil have, for
many years, been collected according to the
ſame plan that the feudal lords adopted for
the purpoſe of quickening the induſtry of their
vaſſals.

---

* Book 1. Sect. III.

vaffals. The mafter fupplies the flave daily with a certain quantity of provifions and tools, and the flave is obliged to return a certain quantity of gold or jewels, according to the nature of the ground. Every thing that remains over this ration, the negro keeps to himfelf, were the balance to be millions. The gold mines of Popayan and Choco in Spanifh America, are wrought in the very fame way. The fineft pearl fifheries in South America, thofe of Panama for example, are in the hands of negro tenants as it were. Thefe are bound to give a certain number of pearls every week. The negroes in the towns are allowed to hire themfelves out to fervices of different kinds, on condition of returning to their mafters a certain portion of their wages : the reft they may fpend or hoard up for their own ufe. The profligate avarice of the Spanifh women, in fome parts of the continent, has imitated this fpecies of trade. The negreffes are permitted to proftitute themfelves, and acquire money from their paramours or keepers, provided they pay to their miftreffes a certain part of their infamous gains, for having the ufe of their own bodies. *

After a flave has in any of thefe various ways acquired property, he endeavours to purchafe his

* We are told that the fame difgraceful practice prevailed alfo in the French iflands.—Wimpffen, Let. XXX,

his freedom. If the mafter is exorbitant in his demands, he may apply to a magiftrate, who appoints fworn appraifers to fix the price at which the flave fhall be allowed to buy his freedom. Even during his flavery the behaviour of the mafter towards him is ftrictly watched : he may complain to the magiftrate, and obtain redrefs, which generally confifts in a decree, obliging the mafter to fell him at a certain rate. The confequences of all thefe laws and cuftoms are extremely beneficial to the Spanifh and Portugueze power in America. While the flaves are faithful and laborious, the free negroes are numerous, and in general much more quiet, ufeful, and induftrious, than in the other colonies. Moft of the artificers are of this clafs ; and fome of the beft troops in the New World are compofed entirely of negroes, who by their own labour and frugality have acquired their liberty.*

It is hardly neceffary to remark the ftriking analogy between the ftate of the Spanifh and Portugueze negroes, and that of the European bondfmen, at a certain period of their progrefs towards liberty. We find the fame gentlenefs

* Report of Committee 1789, part VI.—Townfend's Travels, vol. II. p. 382.—Ricard, III. 635.—Hiftory of Brazil, *apud* Harris's Collection, vol. I.—Campomanes, Educaçion Popular. tom. II. p. 172. & note.—Raynal, Hift. Philof. III. 270.—D'Ulloa's Voyages, tom. I. p. 31. & 129.

tlenefs of treatment, the fame protection from the laws, the fame acknowledgement of rights, the fame power of acquiring property, granted to the American flave, which prepared the complete emancipation of the European vaffal. In fome particulars we obferve another ftep of the fame-progrefs ; for in many parts the negroes are precifely in the fituation of the *coloni partiarii*, or *metayers*, of the feudal times. In one refpect the negro is even in a more favourable fituation : his *reddendo*, (if I may ufe the expreffion), is fixed and definite : all the overplus of his induftry belongs to himfelf. The metayer was bound to divide every gain with his lord. The former, then, has a much ftronger incentive to induftry than the latter had. As this difference, however, arifes, not from the progrefs of fociety, but from the nature of the returns themfelves, eafily concealed, and with difficulty procured : fo, in fome other refpects the negro is not in fuch favourable circumftances. But the great fteps of the procefs of improvement are materially the fame in both cafes. Both have, in common, the great points of a bargain between the mafter and flave ; privileges poffeffed by the flave, independent of, nay in oppofition to his mafter ; the rights of property enjoyed by the flave, and the power of purchafing his freedom at a juft price. This refemblance, in

circumftances

circumftances fo important, may fairly be ex=
pected to render the progrefs of the two orders
alfo fimilar. In the negro, as in the feudal
fyftem, we may look for the confequences of
thofe great improvements in voluntary induftry,
more productive labour, and the mitigation and
final abolition of flavery, when the flave fhall have
been gradually prepared to become a free fubject.
Some of the good effects that have flowed
from the national character, and peculiar circumftances of the Spanifh and Portugueze, have been
produced alfo in Dutch America, by that great
competition of capitals, and thofe complicated
difficulties, which lay the Dutch colonifts under
the neceffity of attending to the fmalleft favings.
If from this fource, combined with the facility
of importation, has arifen a cruelty unknown in
other colonies, it may be doubted whether a
compenfation for the evil is not afforded by
another effect of the fame circumftances, the
general introduction of tafk-work, which the
keen-fighted fpirit of a neceffary avarice, has
taught the planter of Dutch Guiana to view as
the moft profitable manner of working his flaves. *
Nothing, indeed, can conduce more immediately to the excitement of induftry than the introduction of tafk-work. It feems the natural and
eafy tranfition from labour to induftry ; it forms
in the mind of the flave thofe habits which are
                                        neceffary

* Malouet, Mem. fur les Col. III. 133.

neceffary for charaↄter of the free man: it
thus prepares him for enjoying, by a gradual
change, thofe rights and privileges which belong to freedom. But this manner of employing the negroes muft be coupled with mildnefs
of treatment, and with the entire abolition of
all other labour, in order to produce its good
effeↄts. Tafk-work is known in the windward
iflands of France and Britain, without bringing
any relief or improvement whatever. The toil
of grafs-picking is, indeed, the moft intolerable nuifance to which thofe unhappy men are
fubjeↄted. But that is a work impofed upon
them in addition to all their other toils, during the intervals of the field work: it is made
to interfere with their hours of reft and relaxa-
tion. In the Dutch colonies, the cruelty of the
flave fyftem prevents even the complete adoption of tafk-work from producing all its natural confequences; for the toil impofed, and
the punifhments with which the negleↄt is attended, are infinitely too fevere. The odious
plan of working out the negroes, prevails both
in the iflands and on the continent; and while a
fupply of flaves is eafily procured, the good
effeↄts produced by the fyftem of management
peculiar to Peru and Brazil, can never be ex-
peↄted to take place in the colonies of France,
Britain, and Holland—until either the manners of the nations fhall be changed, fo as to
refemble

refemble thofe of the indolent Spaniards and
Portugueze, or the views of the planters fhall
be fo enlightened, as to imprefs them with a
conviction that humane treatment is the moft
beneficial to their interefts. Such a change of
character is not to be wifhed, and fuch an enlargement of views is furely not to be expected.

We are, therefore, again led to the fame
conclufion, in which every view of this large
fubject ends—that the only means of improving the negro fyftem is the abolition of the
flave trade. This great meafure, affifted by
fubordinate arrangements, fimilar to thofe adopted in the ancient ftates, in the feudal kingdoms, and in the South American colonies,
will moft undoubtedly alter the whole face of
things in the New World. The negroes, placed in almoft the fame circumftances with the
bondfmen of ancient Europe, and the flaves of
the claffic times, will begin the fame career of
improvement. The fociety of the Weft Indies
will no longer be that anomalous, defective,
and difgufting monfter of political exiftence,
which we have fo often been forced to contemplate in the courfe of this Inquiry. The
foundation of rapid improvement will be fe-
curely laid, both for the Whites, the Negroes,
and the mixed race, out of the materials which
force and cruelty and fraud have collected.

A

A ſtrong and compact political ſtructure will S E C T.
ariſe, under the influence of a mild, civilized, II.
and enlightened ſyſtem. The vaſt continent
of Africa will keep pace with the quick improvement of the world which ſhe has peopled;
and in thoſe regions where, as yet, only the
warhoop, the laſh, and the cries of miſery,
have divided with the beaſts the ſilence of the
deſert, our children, and the children of our
ſlaves, may enjoy the delightful proſpect of that
benign and ſplendid reign, which is exerciſed
by the Arts, the Sciences, and the Virtues of
modern Europe.

That this view of the future is altogether
viſionary, I am ready to admit; but it is viſionary, only becauſe there is little chance of
that great meaſure being adopted, which every
argument of neceſſity, and every temptation of
expediency concurs to enforce. All conſider-
ations of juſtice being kept out of view, it
might be thought that the evident dangers of
the preſent ſyſtem, as exhibited to us, firſt in
Dutch, and afterwards in French America, would
awaken men to a right feeling upon their critical ſituation; that the melancholy example
of a noble province, ſacrificed to the riſks
which every other ſlave colony runs, almoſt
within the viſible horizon of the remaining ſettlements, would inſpire the European powers
with an anxiety to ſearch for that internal diſ-
order

order which is rapidly working the diffolution of the colonial fyftem, and a diftruft of thofe rafh or interefted counfellors, whofe advice has in other countries been attended with ruin.

‘ *Multa funt occulta reipublicæ vulnera, mul-*
‘ *ta nefariorum civium perniciofa confilia : nullum*
‘ *externum periculum eft, non rex, non gens ulla,*
‘ *non natio pertimefcenda eft : inclufum malum,*
‘ *inteftinum ac domefticum eft. huic pro fe quifque*
‘ *noftrûm mederi, atque hoc omnes fanare velle*
‘ *debemus.* ’ *

But it feems to be the lot of nations to derive inftruction from experience, rather than example ; and however acutely they may difcern the confequences of folly in the conduct of their neighbours, no fooner has the cafe become their own, than indolence, or timidity, or a fenfelefs confidence in good fortune, blinds them to the moft obvious applications of the leffons before their eyes ; difcourages all ideas of reformation ; and gives birth to the fame ftrange delufion, fo often fatal to individuals, that the circumftances and the conduct which have ruined others, may prove harmlefs or beneficial to themfelves.

NOTES

---

* Cicero, Orat. I. de Lege Agraria.

NOTES and ILLUSTRATIONS.

Note A a. *p. 22.*

The tenor of the two laws laſt referred to in the text, is ſufficiently ſingular to deſerve more minute attention.

The ordinance of Valentinius and Valens is conceived in the following terms :

' Univerſi fiduciam gerant, ut, ſi quis eorum ab actore
' rerum privatarum noſtrarum, ſive à procuratore vexatus
' fuerit injuriis, ſuper ejus contumeliis vel deprædationibus
' deferri quærimoniam ſinceritati tuæ, vel rectori provinciæ,
' non dubitet, et ad publicæ ſententiam vindictæ ſine ali-
' quâ trepidatione convolare : quæ res cum fuerit certis pro-
' bationibus declarata, ſancimus, et edicimus, ut ſi in pro-
' vincialem hanc audaciam quiſquam moliri auſus fuerit,
' publice vivus concremetur. ' *Cod. lib. III. tit. 26. leg.* 9.

I would here take the liberty of ſuggeſting an emendation of the laſt clauſe. Inſtead of ' *in provincialem hanc auda-*
' *ciam,* ' I would ſubmit the following reading : ' *in pro-*
' *vinciâ talem hanc audaciam.* ' The preamble is ſo general, that we cannot by any means conceive the reaſon for the re-ſtraining enactment in the end. Why ſhould the provincial ſubjects alone have the benefit of this law ? Is it probable that the Roman citizens, reſident in the provinces, would have leſs regard paid to the violation of their privileges ? But whichever reading we may adopt, the ſpirit of the en-actment is equally plain and deciſive. The edict of Con-ſtantine is as follows :

' Præſides

' Præfides provinciarum oportet, fi quis potentiorum ex-
' titerit infolentior, et ipfi vindicare non poffunt, aut exami-
' nare, aut pronuntiare nequeunt ; de ejus nomine ad nos,
' aut certe ad Prætorianæ Præfecturæ fcientiam referre :
' quo provideatur, qualiter publicæ difciplinæ, et læfis te-
' nuioribus confulatur. ' *Cod. lib. I. tit. XL. leg.* 2.

Thefe two laws prefent us with a ftriking illuftration of
the wide difference between the fkill, or the tafte, of the ancients and moderns, in the great arts of adminiftration. The
fanguinary punifhment awarded to fo high an officer as the
Emperor's reprefentative, for an offence extremely common
in all the provinces of the Roman dominion, would never have
been thought of in the prefent times, although enormities
much greater called for vengeance : and the open, direct, and
plain terms in which the edict of Conftantine prefcribes the
performance of what is always a matter of much nicety—the
reftraining of perfonal influence—clearly prove how little the
moft enlightened ftates of antiquity knew or valued the grand
fecrets of adminiftration, particularly the method of ruling
by influence, fo much and fo juftly valued in modern times.

NOTE B b. *p.* 36.

ONUPHRIUS PANVINIUS has given a very elaborate enumeration of all the Italian colonies. It is to be found in
Grævii Thefaurus, tom. I. The *Treatife of Robortellus* on
the Roman provinces deferves alfo to be confulted.

The number of the colonies planted in Italy, amounted
to one hundred and fixty-four ; while thofe planted in all
the provinces were only one hundred and ninety-nine.—
Onuph. Panv. cap. XXI. It appears from this confideration alone, that the Italian colonies were materially different,
in their conftitution and ufes, from the colonies of the provinces.

The

The firſt foreign colony which the Romans planted was
in Carthage, A. U. C. 710, when Julius Cæſar formed the
plan of reſtoring that deſerted city by means of a colonial
eſtabliſhment. The firſt colony planted in Italy was that of
Cænnia, A. U. C. 4.—*Dion. Caſſ. lib. XLIII. cap.* 50.
The practice of ſending Roman colonies to the provinces
(where they did not enjoy all the privileges of the Italian
coloniſts, *Onuph. Panvin. cap. I.*), was very common after the experiment of Julius Cæſar. He himſelf tranſplanted eighty thouſand citizens in this manner, *Sueton. in Jul.
Cæf. cap. XLII.* After the time of Auguſtus, who planted
twenty-eight colonies in Italy (*Sueton. in Octav. cap. XLVI.*)
the cuſtom of planting Italian colonies ſeems to have been
abandoned. His ſucceſſors did not plant ſo many as twenty ;
and preferred forming thoſe ſettlements beyond ſeas. Livy
does not once mention a tranſmarine or tranſalpine colony ;
although he conſtantly relates the foundation of thoſe in
Italy.

Dacia and Britain, the moſt difficult and inſecure of the
Roman conqueſts, had only, the former four, the latter five
Roman colonies. Africa (the moſt peaceable of all the Roman poſſeſſions long before the downfal of the Commonwealth) received, after the uſurpation of Julius Cæſar, no
leſs than fifty-ſeven colonies, excluſive of Egypt.

We may therefore conclude, that the Italian eſtabliſhments were founded with different views, and in a different
age of the Roman hiſtory, from the ſettlements in the provinces.

NOTE C c. *p.* 52.

THE plan of removing the ſeat of the Portugueſe government from Europe to South America, is not altogether imaginary.

ginary. It has on feveral occafions (I believe as recently as during the late war) been entertained by the regency of Lifbon ; *Dumouriez, Etat prefent de Portugal, liv. II. c. 6.* The Portuguefe character and habits are peculiarly favourable to the conception and execution of fuch a project. Placed in a corner of Europe in which their political importance is extremely trifling, they are fond of contemplating the magnitude and natural wealth of their foreign dominions. Diftinguifhed by their manners and turn of mind, as well as by their blood, from all the other European nations, they have little intercourfe with, or knowledge, of foreign countries, and feem to regard the affairs of Afia and America with more intereft than thofe of France and Germany. *Murphy's Travels in Portugal, p. 206. 4to—Murphy's State of Portugal, chap. XXIV.*

In mentioning the weaknefs of Portugal, as fhe is fituated with refpect to Spain, I have not alluded to the advantages which fhe derived from the unaccountable weaknefs of the Spanifh generals, and the bad condition of the troops during the war 1762 ; becaufe, at that period, the armies of Portugal were in a condition ftill more wretched, and as little provided for the operations of the field as in the war of the ' *Acclamaçion.* ' Soon after the invafion of 1762, the military talents of La Lippe, and the bold political genius of Pombal, reformed a multitude of abufes in all the departments of government, and greatly augmented the refources of the nation—its army, navy, and revenues. But fuch improvements, in a comparative view of two European nations, placed in the relative fituations of Portugal and Spain, may almoft always be difregarded ; for, unlefs circumftances exift in the one ftate effentially different from thofe of the other, any material augmentation in the force of the one will be attended with a proportionate increafe in that of the other. Accordingly, during the period of which we are fpeaking, Spain did not fit an idle fpectator

of

of the falutary meafures purfued in Portugal. The various N O T E S
domeftic improvements, the freedom of the colonial trade,   AND
and the increafe of the navy, are proofs of this pofition. I L L U S T,
The number of guns in the Spanifh line in 1776 was only
three thoufand nine hundred and ninety-eight; in 1788, it
had increafed to five thoufand four hundred and ten.—
Townfend's Trav. II. 397.

Where fome extraordinary event, indeed, places one nation in circumftances which another cannot emulate, we
may argue from the fuperiority which this difference will
confer ; as, for inftance, the emancipation of a colony, a
fudden revolution in the mother country, or the transference
of a feat of empire. But even thefe events tend generally
to operate fome change on neighbouring ftates, and they
are commonly attended with fuch a change, even if they do
not influence it ; becaufe, as we have feen elfewhere, (Book
III. Sect. I.) in nations forming one community, like the
European kingdoms, or the American colonies, the fame
circumftances which predifpofe to extraordinary events in
any one member of the body, tend to operate fome fimilar
effect in all the neighbouring parts.

In eftimating the relative ftrength of Spain and Portugal in South America, we ought always to recollect, that
the province of Chili has never been completely fubdued,
and that the natives would be ready to join any foreign
power againft the Spaniards ; that Portugal poffeffes the
coaft next to Europe, commands the navigation of the Am-
azons, and may eafily feize the keys alfo of the Plata ; and
that Peru is feparated from the Atlantic by a vaft ridge of
mountains, and an extenfive tract of country, level indeed,
but neither drained of its moraffes nor cleared of its forefts.

The authority which I have cited for this fact is indeed anonymous, and the work is, in this country, very little known. But, befides that a fimilar circumftance has occurred in other inftances which might be enumerated, great confidence may be repofed in the ftatements of the two travellers. Their work abounds in plain and fober narrative, delivered with a minutenefs bordering upon prolixity. The information contained in it is full, various, and explicit, even to tedioufnefs. Of its accuracy in all particulars, I am inclined to form the moft favourable opinion, from finding it completely fo in thofe parts which I have had an opportunity of verifying by perfonal obfervation. The title of the book is, *Voyage de deux François au nord de l'Europe,* 1791 & 1792. The route lay through Denmark, Sweden, Ruffia, Poland, Auftria, and part of the north of Germany.

Note E e. p. 71.

No fmall diverfity of opinion exifts among the authors who have exprefsly written upon, or only occafionally referred to the fubject of the Attican population. As the inquiry is curious, and as fome errors feem to have prevailed in the writings of thofe who are in general moft correct upon claffical fubjects, I fhall offer a few ftatements, which may perhaps fet the matter in a true light.

Mr Hume, in his admirable effay on the populoufnefs of ancient nations, (a rare fpecimen of a branch of fcience almoft wholly new—the application of philofophy to claffical antiquities),

quities), has ftated that Athenæus gives the population of A-
thens at twenty-one thoufand citizens, ten thoufand ftrangers,
and four hundred thoufand flaves, *(Effays, vol. I. p.* 416.
edit. 1793.) He then proceeds to argue againft this ftatement, as if Athenæus meant to enumerate only the population of the city. The ftrongeft of his reafons proceed upon
the idea that this was the author's fenfe ; and it muft be acknowledged that they are fufficiently conclufive. But afterwards he infers, rather inconfiftently, that Athenæus muft
have meant to give the population of all Attica. ' Be-
' fides, ' fays he, ' we are to confider that the number af-
' figned by Athenæus, whatever it is, comprehends all
' the inhabitants of Attica, as well as thofe of Athens,'
(p. 419.) His opinion, upon the whole, then, is, that Athenæus muft be underftood to fpeak of Attica ; but that, even
for Attica, the number is too great ; and Mr Hume fuppofes
the error of one cypher.

Now, in the *firft* place, let us attend to the words of
Athenæus, which Mr Hume appears not to have examined
with his ufual accuracy.

Αθηνησιν εξετασμον γενεσθαι απο Δημετριε τε φαλερε των
κατοικεντων την Αττικην· και ευρεθηναι Αθηναιες μεν δυσμυριες
προ τοις χιλιοις, μετοικες δε μυριες, οικετων δε μυριαδας τεσσα-
ρακοντα.—*Deipnofophift. lib. VI. cap.* 20. *edit. Cafaubon.
Lugdun.* 1657.

This paffage is precifely a ftatement of that which Mr
Hume infers from circumftances to be the author's meaning.
It is a ftatement of the whole *Attican* population, while Mr
Hume's arguments apply chiefly, if not entirely to the pofition, never made by Athenæus, that the *Athenian* flave
population was four hundred thoufand. The term Αθηναιες,
is evidently introduced to denote free and native citizens, in
oppofition to foreigners and flaves ; the ftatement obvioufly
applies to the word Αττικην ufed immediately before.

Such,

Such, accordingly, is the interpretation of it given not only by Cafaubon and the beft editors, but by the Abbé Barthelemy, in his *Voyage du Jeune Anacharfis, tom. II. p. 97. edit. 12mo. Deux-ponts,* 1791.

Mr Millar adopts the error of Mr Hume, *Diftinction of Ranks, Part V. Sect. IV. fecond edit.*

We may obferve, in the *fecond* place, that the emendation fuggefted by Mr Hume is not fatisfactory. How the error of a cypher fhould have crept into a Greek text, where the Arabic numerals were not ufed, it does not feem eafy to conceive. Neither is it fair to conclude, that the number of flaves fit to bear arms is alone meant to be ftated in this enumeration. The term Αθηναιης obvioufly applies to the number of citizens fit to bear arms, and it is probable that the word μετοικες means the ftrangers fit to bear arms. So far Mr Hume's arguments muft be admitted. But why, after reducing the four hundred thoufand flaves to forty thoufand, fhould he conceive that this forty thoufand means flaves capable of bearing arms? It is evident that all enumerations of ancient population had but two objects in view, the wealth and force of the community. The ftatement of free males come to the years of puberty, affords a criterion of the one: the ftatement of all the flaves (the labouring part of the people) captured or purchafed, and faleable, is neceffary to furnifh a meafure of the other.

We may conclude, that the enumeration of Demetrius, as given by Athenæus, made the free males of ripe years amount to thirty-one thoufand, and the whole flaves to forty thoufand. The total population of Attica, then, was one hundred and twenty-four thoufand free inhabitants, and four hundred thoufand flaves. This is furely neither fo great a proportion of flaves to free people, nor of inhabitants to extent of territory, as to render the plain ftatement of the ancient author incredible.

Mr

Mr Hume, it may be added, feems again to miftake Athenæus
in talking of Corinth.   He tells us, that the account of the
city of Corinth having four hundred and fixty thoufand flaves,
is entirely abfurd and impoffible, *(Effays, I.* 419.*)* Athenæus
fays that the Corinthian cities had altogether forty-fix myriads of flaves.

NOTE F f. *p.* 92.

THE recital of the many commercial privileges which
have been extorted by force, or obtained by diplomatic addrefs, or procured in exchange for temporary aids of various
forts, from the trading nations of modern times, would occupy a large fpace in the annals of mercantile policy.   The
hiftory of the Dutch trade, and that of the Hans Towns,
afford many of the moft remarkable inftances of this fpecies
of national munificence.

The readinefs of Pruffia and Ruffia to accept of fuch
boons as thofe which the new Weft Indian ftate could
eafily offer, fcarcely requires any proof.   Perhaps, however, it is not generally known how near thofe two
powers have fometimes been brought to the accomplifhment of their commercial fchemes, by the acquifition of diftant territories.   Not to mention the various voyages of
difcovery projected, and the refpectable number actually
fitted out by Ruffia, during the laft half century, we know
that the acquiring of territory in the Mediterranean has always been a favourite object with the Cabinet of St Peterf-
burgh.   Befides different fchemes more immediately connected with views of conqueft, we have obtained undoubted
information, fince the death of Katharine, that a project
had actually been conceived, of a nature entirely commercial,
and not the leaft fingular, of the various plans which diverfi-
fied the noble and dignified ambition of that renowned Princefs.

NOTES AND ILLUST.

cefs. It was in contemplation of the Emprefs, at the fuggeſtion of Prince Polemkin, to purchaſe from a private proprietor the ſmall iſlands of Lampedoſa and Linoſa, ſituated on the African coaſt, and to obtain the ſovereignty from the Court of Naples. The reader may ſee a copy of the Prince's project in the Appendix to *Eton's Survey of the Turkiſh Empire*, p. 505. The propoſed regulations are minute, and conceived with confiderable ſkill.

The Cabinet of Verſailles in 1756 endeavoured to engage Frederic II. in an alliance againſt the Elector of Hanover, by making him an offer of the iſland of Tobago. The Duke de Nivernois was entruſted with the management of this intrigue ; and it is worth while to obſerve the terms in which Frederic ſpeaks of it. He begins by calling this offer, ' *l'argument le plus fort qu'employa le Duc de Niver-* ' *nois.* ' He then mentions ſome circumſtances which oppoſed obſtacles to its being accepted. He adds, that it appeared ' *trop ſinguliere pour etre recue.* ' He then condeſcends to tell us, that he was pleaſant upon the occaſion, and that he compared the propoſed acceſſion of territory to the iſland of Barataria. But he adds a very material reaſon for all his coyneſs and pleaſantry. The treaty with London, which was the means of preſerving his exiſtence, had been ſigned ſome weeks before theſe overtures came from Verſailles ; and he lays down, with much preciſion, the reaſons which induced him to prefer the Britiſh to the French alliance ; (*Hiſt. de la Guerre de Sept-ans, chap. II. Oeuv. tom. III. p.* 69. *edit. Berlin,* 1788.) In arguing from this fact to the probable views of a Berlin cabinet, if placed in ſimilar temptations at the preſent day, we ſhould remember that the intrigue alluded to was planned by France, then in a ſtate of extreme weakneſs, againſt the intereſts of Britain, at that time the undiſputed arbitreſs of Europe, and rejected by Pruſſia, when her European exiſtence was at ſtake.

Note

THE opinion of Dr Smith upon the fubject of the French   N O T E S
and Englifh flaves, appears to have been rafhly adopted by   A N D
him, in order to fupport a theory more plaufible than con-   I L L U S T.
fiftent with the facts, that flaves under defpotic governments are neceffarily more protected by the laws than thofe
of free ftates ; becaufe the protection of a flave is an interference with private property.—*Wealth of Nations, vol. II.
p.* 395. *edit.* 1799. If this reafon is of any weight, it muft
be confined to the pure defpotifms of the Eaft, or of favage
communities where the right of property is not regarded.
It cannot furely apply to fuch governments as that of
France before the Revolution—a government as remarkable for facred regard to the property of individuals as the
Britifh conftitution itfelf. To fuppofe any fuch difference
between the effects of the French and thofe of the Britifh
forms of government, is in the higheft degree chimerical.
M. Laborie has eagerly laid hold of Dr Smith's admiffion, and given it as an indifputable teftimony in favour of his
countrymen.—*Appendix to the Coffee-Planter of St Domingo,
Art. IV.*

    Baron Wimpffen tells us, that in St Domingo the women
arepeculiarly cruel miftreffes ; a circumftance which generally
takes place where the treatment of the flaves is upon the whole
cruel, as in the Dutch fettlements both of Afia and America.—*Lett. XXXI.* The fame author ftates, that even re-
putable miftreffes hire out their negreffes to proftitution,
and fhare their gains. A fimilar accufation has never been
brought againft our countrywomen in the Weft Indies.—
Lett. XXX. It is well known that the regulations of the
Code Noire, fo humane towards the negroes, were altogether
prevented from being executed, or even thought of, by the
determined oppofition of the conftituted authorities, and ftill

                                more

more by their incongruity with the state of manners.—*Wimp-*
ffen, Lett. VII. ; Edwards's St Domingo, chap. I.

The privileges of the inferior classes, which in all the
other colonies have been gradually on the increase, were continually diminishing in the French islands previous to the
Revolution. Thus, until 1674, all Mulattoes were free at
the age of twenty-four, by the common law of the islands.
In that year an edict was made, introducing the maxim of
the Roman law, ' *Partus sequitur ventrem.* ' The edict
of 1776 abridged many of the most important privileges
which the *Code Noire* had nominally secured to the people
of colour.

The evidence contained in the Report of the Committee
1798, proves clearly that the treatment of the negroes in
the French islands was such as to render their mortality
greater than in the British settlements.—*Part V.*

NOTE H h. *p.* 101.

OUR information with respect to the progress of the importation and of the population in the French West Indies,
is by no means very full or correct. Even the history of St
Domingo, in this point of view, does not begin to be satis-
factory, until a short time before the Revolution. We are,
however, furnished with sufficient *data* upon these subjects,
to authorise a very positive conclusion, that the treatment of
slaves must have been bad ; and that, among the various
causes of the revolt, ill treatment deserves to be mentioned.

The authors of the *Encyclopedie Methodique* estimate
the negro population of St Domingo in 1775 at three
hundred thousand, after making allowance for the falsity
of the returns, which were only two hundred and forty
thousand

thoufand and ninety-five.—*Econ. Polit. et Diplom. tom. II. p.* 140.

The whole of the article of St Domingo, is to be found in *Ricard, Traite du Commerce, tom. III. p.* 692 ; fo that either he is the author mentioned in the Encyc. Method. or he has borrowed from that author, or from the Encyclopedie.

Jeffreys, in his Weft Indian Atlas, gives the negro population in 1764 at two hundred and fix thoufand.

Malouet ftates the numbers in 1775 at three hundred thoufand. *Mem. fur les Colonies, IV.* 117.; evidently making allowance for concealments.

Neckar ftates the number in 1779 at two hundred and forty-nine thoufand and ninety-eight. *Finances, tom. III. chap.* 13.

It is fair to conclude, from thefe authorities, that in 1775 the official returns of negroes in St Domingo made the number amount to two hundred and fifty thoufand. It was about four or five years after this period that the great importation began, which continued till the Revolution.

According to the official returns, the importation for the year 1787 was thirty thoufand eight hundred and thirty-nine ; and in 1788 twenty-nine thoufand five hundred and fix.—*Rapport à l'Affemblée Legiflative,* 1790; and *Edwards's St Domingo, Appendix.*

The average export from Africa in French veffels, about the fame time, was reckoned at twenty thoufand.—*Edwards' Weft Indies, Book IV. chap.* 2.; *Report of Com.* 1789, *Part IV.* But the French ftate themfelves, that of the forty thoufand exported from Africa by Britain, only thirteen thoufand three hundred are retained in the Britifh Weft Indies.—*Report of Com.* 1789, *Part VI.* If this is accurate, the greater part of the remaining twenty-fix thoufand feven hundred muft go to the French iflands.

Malouet

Malouet ſtates the annual importation of negroes into St Domingo in French veſſels at above eighteen thouſand ; and the importation by the Britiſh traders at twelve hundred and fifty. This ſtatement was written in 1775, and re-publiſhed in 1802 ; but no alteration appears to have been made on this paſſage.—*Mem. ſur les Col. IV.* 150. The average export of France from Africa, is given at thirty thouſand for 1786, 1787, and 1788, by Arnould.—*Balance de Commerce, Part II. Sect. III.* And Barré St Venant gives the importation between 1788 and 1791 (that is, in two years) at ſixty thouſand.—*Colonies Modernes, p.* 81.

If, then, we conſider the period from 1775 to 1790 as divided into two periods, one ending 1780, and the other ending 1790, we may reckon the average importation of the firſt period at fifteen thouſand, on the loweſt computation, and the average importation of the ſecond period at a-bout twenty-ſix thouſand. The numbers in 1784 had only increaſed to two hundred and ninety-ſeven thouſand and ſeventy-nine, according to the official return.—*Laborie, Coffee-planter, Appendix, Art. IV.* The returns for 1789 give this number at four hundred and thirty-four thouſand four hundred and twenty-nine. But this is fairly aſcribed by Laborie to the alterations in the mode of obtaining theſe. It is utterly impoſſible to conceive that there could have been in five years an increaſe of a hundred and forty thouſand. Yet ſome have raſhly aſſerted, that the numbers of the St Domingo negroes were increaſed by a hundred and fifty thouſand during the five years ending 1790, evi-dently comparing the looſe returns of 1784 and 1785 with the more accurate enumerations of 1789 and 1790.—*Wimp-ffen, Let. XXVII.*

Let us, however, in the firſt place, admit this in-ſpection of the returns to be always an equally fair cri-terion. The returns for 1790 give four hundred and fifty-five thouſand as the total number of the ſlaves.—*Laborie, Appen. ; Wimpffen, Let. XXVIII. ; Edwards's*

St

*St Domingo, Appen. and chap. I. ; Barré St Venant, Col. Mod.
p.* 102. ; *Malouet, &c. &c.* Morfe has indeed (*American
Geography*) ftated this number at fix hundred thoufand, and
Laborie at five hundred thoufand ; but thefe ftatements proceed upon rough calculation of the numbers probably omitted even in the moft accurate returns ; and that of Morfe
is in all probability much exaggerated. We are therefore
to confine ourfelves entirely to the official number of four
hundred and fifty-five thoufand, and to compare this with
the official number, two hundred and fifty thoufand, of the
year 1775.

We have here, then, a total increafe of two hundred and
five thoufand negroes in fixteen years. But according to the
progrefs of the importation, and the natural progrefs of the population, the natural and forced increafe combined ought to
have been much greater. Suppofe that, by the natural mode,
no increafe ought to have taken place, and that the propagation only balanced the mortality, both in the original ftock
of 1775, and in every fubfequent increafe by importation ;
the total increafe of the firft fix years, admitting that there
were two males to every female imported, and that no ac-
account of the odd males is to be kept, fhould have been
fixty thoufand ; and of the fecond period, (ten years), on
the fame fuppofitions, about a hundred and feventy-four
thoufand ; and the whole increafe fhould have been about
two hundred and thirty-four thoufand, or above twenty-nine
thoufand more than the actual increafe.

But this difference is evidently much lefs than the truth ;
for no account has been taken of five thoufand male negroes annually imported during the firft fix years, and eight
thoufand fix hundred and fixty-four during the laft ten. In
order to correct the calculation, we fhall fuppofe that one
death in twenty of the population is a fair eftimate for the
Weft Indian climate, being much more than in the worft
climates of Europe. It may eafily be computed, that at the
end

end of the fixteen years, there would remain, of the odd males imported during that period, above eighty thoufand.

Befides, no account has been taken of the fuperior accuracy with which the returns were made at the end of the period under confideration. This circumftance muft evidently increafe the difference ftill farther. For we find, that during nine years ending 1784, the total numbers had only increafed from two hundred and fifty thoufand to two hundred and ninety-feven thoufand : whereas, fuppofing the propagation only to have kept up the ftock, the importation during that period fhould have produced an augmentation of a hundred and twelve thoufand at leaft. Inftead, therefore, of a difference of a hundred and nine thoufand, in the whole period of fixteen years, we may fafely conclude, that there was a difference of nearly a hundred and forty, or that the common good treatment experienced by the lower orders of the moft unhealthy countries in the world would have produced on the population of St Domingo an increafe greater, in the proportion of feven to four, than the increafe which actually took place during the fixtecn years of great importation.

The nature of the treatment experienced by the negroes in that ifland, may from this ftatement eafily be eftimated. But feveral calculations have been prefented to us, directly confirming the fame pofition, and demonftrating, that the cruelty or hard ufage of the French colonifts was extreme. I have mentioned, in the text, the general ftatements of the Report of 1789 upon the treatment experienced by the flaves in all the French iflands. I fhall now add the particular teftimony of two able men, who drew their obfervations from perfonal knowledge. Baron Wimpffen (*Lettres, No. XXV.*) ftates, that of the negroes imported into St Domingo, twenty *per cent.* die during the firft year, while only five *per cent.* are born ; and of thefe five, one infant dies of the tetanus in the firft fortnight. M. Malouet fays that it requires from

four

four to five thoufand births, befides the annual importation of
eighteen thoufand flaves to keep up the ftock ; and that the
only total addition is the contraband with the Englifh
iflands.—*Effai fur St Domingue, p.* 148. *& feqq.* Thus, according to Wimpffen, the deaths among the imported negroes are above five times more numerous than among the
people of any other country, and the births five times lefs
numerous ; and according to Malouet, the mortality of
the whole ftock is between two and three times greater than
that of the natives of any other country on earth—a fufficient commentary upon the boafted humanity of the planters
in the French iflands, and a ufeful leffon upon the profits of
the flave fyftem.

Note I i. *p.* 194.

As a fpecimen of the inconfiftencies and mifreprefentations
which diftinguifh the cavillers upon this fubject, I fhall ad-
vert to the remarks of a very celebrated author, whofe truly
philofophical fpeculations have done much to introduce plain
and found fenfe into political inquiries, and to affift us in
forming large and extenfive views of the hiftory of nations.
After taking notice of the policy which induced Vortigern
king of the Britons to call in the affiftance of the Saxons
againft the Romans, Mr Millar obferves, that this meafure
has been univerfally blamed as weak and foolifh ; and he
adds, that Vortigern acted exactly upon the principles of
the balancing fyftem.—*Hiftorical View of the Englifh Government, p.* 25, *4to edit.* Now, it muft be evident to every
one, that this conduct of Vortigern was not juftified by the
principles of the balancing fyftem ; for, of all events, that
fyftem holds an invafion to be the leaft defirable ; and, inftead of demanding the aid of allies on your own ground, it
prefcribes

prescribes the granting of aid to allies upon their ground, in order to prevent invasion. In fact, nothing could be less politic than Vortigern's conduct, upon the plainest principles of common sense. He actually called in a conqueror, whom he armed with the power of destroying his kingdom. He imitated exactly the policy of the horse in the fable. The reader will find many good ideas upon the general subject of the European community, mingled with several obvious misconceptions and puerilities, in Voltaire's ' *Histoire* ' de la Guerre de 1740, ' *Part I. chap.* 1.

Note K k. *p.* 276.

The subject of the Austrian alliance was one of the most interesting discussions, in the politics of the eighteenth century previous to the French revolution, and perhaps not a little connected with that great and deplorable event. Those who wish to study this question of foreign policy, may consult, in the first place, the very interesting collection of state papers, published in two volumes octavo by the French government soon after the King's flight, and republished lately in three volumes, with some additions and notes by M. Segur, a gentleman well known in the diplomatic circles of the Continent, as the able negotiator who concluded the commercial treaty between France and Russia. This publication consists, chiefly, of a ' *Tableau speculatif,* ' or ' *Raisonne* ' of the foreign relations of France, drawn up by the Sieur Favier, under the direction, and with the assistance of the ministry. The object of the treatise is evidently to decry the Austrian alliance, as the cause of every calamity that befel France during the remainder of Louis XV.'s reign. The notes of M. Segur contain the chief arguments on the other side of the question. While Favier ascribes

every

every evil to the Auſtrian ſyſtem, Segur, without denying
the calamitous ſtate of affairs ſubſequent to 1756, both in
Poland and Germany, attributes all to the mal-adminiſtra-
tion of French affairs in the Seven-years war, and during
the whole interval between the peace of Hubertſburgh and
the Revolution. He argues the queſtion rather upon ſpeci-
alties ; Favier adopts the more general views of the ſubject,
which his antagoniſt condemns as unſound. As Favier perpetually recurs to the ſame text, endeavouring, like moſt
theoriſts, to reduce every thing under one head, and twiſt-
ing all facts to humour his main poſition : ſo, the new editor follows him through his whole courſe, and, under the
head of each power whoſe relations to France are diſcuſſed
by Favier in the text, we meet with a ſeparate argument in
Segur's notes, tending either to modify or overthrow the
favourite concluſions of the former politician. In general,
Favier, though a practical ſtateſman, and writing for a ſpecial purpoſe, ſeems to be an advocate for thoſe enlarged ſpeculations which I have attempted to defend in the Second
Section of the Third Book. Segur is very decidedly an advocate for the minute and detailed views of foreign policy
into which diplomatiſts ſo naturally fall. His talents in this
line are, however, unqueſtioned ; and it affords no ſmall
proof of his liberality in political matters, that he whoſe
fame in the diplomatic world reſts on the negotiation of a
commercial treaty, ſhould be the loudeſt in condemning all
ſuch conventions as abſurd and impolitic.

The hiſtorical writings of Frederic II, by far the moſt
valuable of all that lively and clever Prince's works, afford
much inſtruction upon the ſubject of this controverſy, beſides exhibiting to us a conciſe and connected view of the
relative poſitions of different powers at the moſt important
periods of his reign. He has left us, in the ' *Hiſtoire de la*
' *Guerre de Sept-ans,* ' a very valuable, and apparently a very authentic narrative of that moſt important conteſt, which

was the firſt fruit of the new alliance. This treatiſe is, indeed, a model of compoſition in the branch of hiſtory to
which it belongs—the mere detail of military tranſactions.
It is full and minute, without being tedious ; it is ſufficiently profeſſional and even deep, without any obſcurity or dry-
neſs ; it is written by one who could really ſay, ' *pars mag-*
' *na fui :* ' yet in the whole courſe of the performance, we
are never offended with the ſlighteſt violation of modeſty or
coolneſs, while we read the tale of the hero with all the intereſt natural to ſo rare an occaſion. Laſtly, as the ' *Hiſtoire* ' is compoſed by one who was a ſtateſman, as well as a
general and an author, although politics bear a very ſubordinate part in this book, the narrative is ſo drawn up, as to
throw a full and ſatisfactory light upon the whole political
tranſactions of the day, and, as it were, to fit any hiſtory
which ſhall comprehend the politics, in the ſame manner
that it embraces the military affairs of the war.

The introduction to this work contains ſome general remarks upon the ſtudy of hiſtory, and the importance of rightly
uſing collections of facts. Theſe opinions of the Royal author countenance many of the ſpeculations in which I have
indulged in the text, and are well worthy of the attention of
thoſe men of detail who laugh at all general views of policy,
as the effuſions of theoriſts, and productions of the cloſet.
For it can hardly be aſſerted that the King of Pruſſia was,
what Auſtria and Poland would indeed have wiſhed he had
been, a viſionary and ſpeculative man.

Some anecdotes and intereſting facts with reſpect to the
ſecret hiſtory of the Auſtrian alliance, may be found in
Soulavie's Memoirs of the reign of Louis XVI., and may
tend to complete the knowledge of the ſubject which the
reader has acquired from Favier, Segur, and Frederic II.
I am confident, that the reſult of the whole inquiry will lead
him to adopt the opinion which I have curſorily ſtated upon this affair in the text.

═══════

THE Methuen Treaty has been held up by all French writers, down to the Abbé Raynal (who affects to write upon
political as well as fentimental topics), as the *chef-d'œuvre* of
Britifh policy, and the pitch of Portuguefe dependence.
Moft of our Englifh ftatefmen were of the fame opinion
before the days of Smith and Hume. The former of
thefe celebrated writers has fully difcuffed the fubject, and
endeavoured to fhew that this treaty was highly difadvantageous to England, even upon the principles of the mercantile fyftem. In his general reafonings againftall fuch treaties,
it would be impoffible to find any weaknefs or difficulty ;
but he feems to have mifapprehended the ftate of things
which led to the Methuen Treaty ; and his arguments a-
gainft it, on this fpecial view, are not fatisfactory. In fact,
it muft ftrike every one who fees his ftatement, that it
proves too much ; for furely, if the ftipulations of the contract are fo leonine as he defcribes them, it is impoffible to
fuppofe that any man of common underftanding, I mean any
perfon endowed with the faculty of counting his ten fingers,
could for one moment have miftaken the nature of the
bargain.

The ftatements of Dr Smith (*Wealth of Nations,
Book IV. chap. VI.*) are the more impofing, that he pre-
faces them with a literal tranflation of the treaty, the ftipulations of which are fhort and fimple. He then proceeds to
obferve, that, by this bargain, Englifh woollens are admitted on no better terms than before the prohibition which is
thus repealed ; but that they are admitted on no better terms
than that of other nations, while the Portuguefe wines are
admitted into England with a great preference. ' So far,
' therefore, ' (fays he) ' the treaty is evidently advanta-
' geous to Portugal, and difadvantageous to Great Britain. '
—*Vol. II. p.* 327. *edit.* 1799.

This

This ſtatement, however, is fundamentally erroneous, in-aſmuch as it omits to conſider the extent and nature of the prohibition repealed in the treaty. In 1644, (the jealous ſpirit of the French cabinet having a ſhort time before pro-hibited Brazil goods), Portugal prohibited the entry of all French goods. The hands of the nation were, during the remainder of the ſeventeenth century, turned to manufac-tures, particularly thoſe of wool ; and with ſo much ſuc-ceſs, that in 1684 the government under Erricira's admi-niſtration prohibited all importation, either of the raw ma-terial or of woollen goods. This occaſioned great mur-murs, chiefly on account of the diminution ſuſtained by the revenue ; and at the ſame time Britain was endeavouring to ſupplant the French wines in her home market, by the in-troduction of the Portugueze. Both governments, there-fore, were ſoon diſpoſed to conclude a bargain, which ſhould again open the Portugueze market to Britiſh woollens, and ſhould promote in Britain the uſe of Portugueze wines. This gave riſe to the arrangements which terminated in the Methuen treaty. The paction, then, is ſhort and ſimple ; it is, that Portugal ſhall repeal the law of 1684, in favour of Britain, and that Britain, in return, ſhall admit Portugueze wines at two thirds of the duties paid by French wines. The preference is mutual. The prohibition of 1644 againſt French goods remains in full force : the prohibition of 1684 remains alſo in full force againſt French and all other woollens, except Britiſh woollens. Britiſh woollens alone are admitted ; all others excluded. Here, then, is a mo-nopoly of the Portugueze market granted to Britiſh goods, in return for a preference given to Portugueze wines over thoſe of France. Wherefore, the advantage granted to Britiſh woollens is much more general than that given to Portugueze wines. Dr Smith's objection proceeds entirely from confining his view to the terms of the treaty, which do not expreſsly ſay that the laws of 1644 and 1684 are to re-

main

main in force, unlefs in fo far as the latter is repealed by
the treaty.

I fhall only add, that the French wines having before the treaty been heavily loaded in England, and the
Portugueze wines encouraged, the Methuen treaty produced a very trifling effect in favour of Portugal ; not
much above a thirty-fecond part being for fome years added to the former importation by the diminution of duty ;
while the repeal of the law 1684, in favour of England,
gave her woollens an immediate monopoly of the Portu-
geze importation market, from which they had been totally
excluded fince that law was enacted.   Whatever truth, then,
there may be in all Dr Smith's reafonings againft commercial treaties, (and no one can for one moment doubt their
accuracy), we muft admit, that by the Methuen treaty
Britain gains more than Portugal ; that the mutual advantages are exactly of the kind propofed by the lovers of the
mercantile fyftem ; and that the bargain, upon the principles of thofe men, is mutually advantageous, but more fo to
Britain than to Portugal.   The law of 1644 might indeed
have been repealed next year (in 1704), and that of 1684
might have been repealed in favour of France, or any other
country.   But this would evidently have annulled the Methuen treaty, as much as if a preference had been granted to
French wines by Britain, in direct violation of the compact ; or as if Portugal had inftantly renewed the exclufion
of Britifh goods.

Although, therefore, the letter of the treaty is certainly
a little defective from extreme concifenefs, the fpirit and intention of it is clear, and, on the principles of the mercantile fyftem, unexceptionable.

—————

THE fubſtance of the general reaſonings and views detailed
in this Section, was publiſhed in the Second Number of a
periodical work, conducted by a ſociety of Literary Gentle-
men in Edinburgh, entitled the ' *Edinburgh Review.* '

—————

Note N n.   *p. 295.*

THE confidence with which I have termed the conduct of
France, during the American war, a blunder, is fully juſtified by the addition of ' *acknowledged,* ' which we are
entitled to make, from attending to the ſentiments uniformly
expreſſed by the ableſt ſtateſmen of France, both at the
time and ſince the American revolution. Such views are
extremely intereſting in diſcuſſing the American colonial
politics of the preſent day ; becauſe they ſhew us clearly
what would have been the advice of thoſe enlightened men
upon the great ſubjects of Weſt Indian policy. To us who
have, on many points of the ſubject, the benefit of twenty-
ſeven years experience, the errors of ſuch men are no leſs
inſtructive than their happieſt conjectures. They may teach
us what meaſure of modeſty is becoming in political diſcuſ-
ſions, and guard us againſt raſhly founding our practical
deductions upon the moſt plauſible general theories.

M. de Vergennes having, about the beginning of the
American troubles, laid before the cabinet a memorial upon the conduct ſuggeſted to France and Spain, by the ſtate
of the colonial affairs of England, M. Turgôt drew up a
long memorial upon this ſubject. The original paper of
Vergennes is loſt ; but the memorial of Turgôt was found
                                                       among

among Lewis XVI.'s papers ; and feveral long extracts from
it are inferted in the publication formerly referred to, ' *Po-*
' *litique de tous les Cabinets de l'Europe.* ' The excellence
and importance of thefe fpecimens leave the greateft room
to lament, that the whole of this interefting ftate paper was
not laid before the public.

The firft extract contains the conclufion of the whole
effay ; in which the author recapitulates, with his ufual accuracy, the inferences deduced from all the former parts ;
and probably adds new force to his previous arguments, by
again placing the refults before his reader in a varied arrangement and more luminous concentration.

The general opinion to which all M. Turgôt's reafonings
lead him, is, that the fuccefs of England in her colonial
ftruggles, would be the iffue moft advantageous both to
France and Spain. Some of the views upon which this juft
and philofophical conclufion is founded, feem not to be marked with the liberality that formed fo diftinguifhing a feature in almoft all the opinions of this enlightened ftatefman.
Thus, he fays, *(Vol. II. p.* 395. *edit.* 1793.) that if the
colonies are not reduced without a fevere effort, it is fo
much the better for France ; becaufe the ftruggle will leave
them completely exhaufted, and in no condition to affift
the wealth and power of the mother country for many
years ; and if the ftruggle is fhort, the flourifhing ftate
in which it leaves America muft be a fufficient d'verfion
to the force of England. The latter view is analogous
to thofe pofitions which I attempted to lay down in the
Second Book of this Inquiry. The former view is in
fome refpects illiberal and inaccurate. The commercial advantage of England, whether derived from her colonies, or
the other branches of her dominion, or her foreign trade, is
evidently an advantage to the commerce of France alfo ;
and this benefit reaped by France muft improve her refour-

ces,

ces, while the direct advantages of the colonial trade are promoting thofe of Britain.

M. Turgôt expreffes himfelf in a tone of confiderable confidence with refpect to the event of the American war, then only begun. ' La fuppofition de la feparation abfolue des ' colonies de la metropole, me paroìt infiniment probable. '— *p.* 395. He then ftates his opinion upon the general queftion—' Je crois fermement que toutes les metropoles feront ' forcées d'abandonner tout empire fur leur colonies. '— *p.* 396. The views which lead him to form this and other fimilar conclufions, are apparently dictated, in fome degree, by his confidence in the principles of national progreffive improvement, which he deems to be connected with the abolition of colonial relations, in the true fpirit of the œconomifts, a fect whofe tenets he appears greatly to have favoured.—See, particularly, p. 396.

In the reft of the firft extract, we meet with many forcible arguments againft the interference of either France or Spain in the affairs of North America. He alfo obferves, that a reunion of England with America, if prompt and fudden, might menace France and Spain with danger.— *p.* 397.

In another extract from the fame memorial, we meet with the following fingular opinion, introduced at the end of an invective fomewhat declamatory againft colonies in general, formerly quoted (Book I. Sect. 1.) ' Il n'eft pas ' vraifemblable que les Anglois foient les premiers à quitter ' des prejugés qu'ils ont long-tems regardés comme la fource ' de leur grandeur. En ce cas, *il n'eft pas poffible de douter* ' *que leur obftination n'entraine l'union de leurs colonies à fucre* ' *avec celles du continent feptentrional.* '—*p.* 415.

The opinion of Vergennes appears to have been in all material refpects the fame with that of Turgôt, upon the conduct which France fhould purfue with regard to American affairs. His memorial is loft ; but reference is conftant-

ly

ly made to it by Turgòt. Malouet, an author well verfed
in colonial affairs, was of the fame way of thinking ; and
drew up two memorials in fupport of this opinion, at the
defire of Sartine, then minifter of the marine and colonies.
Sartine was decidedly againft the interference, and wifhed to
lay the arguments forcibly before the King, who yielded
with great difficulty to weaker counfels.—*Mem. fur les Col.
tom. III.*

NOTE N n. *p.* 332. *

THE plan of an invafion, fuch as we have been confidering,
was actually entertained at one time by the late Emprefs of
Ruffia. At the period of the dreaded rupture with England on account of Oczacow, a plan was prefented to her
Majefty by Prince Naffau, minutely detailing all the particulars of the route by which a Ruffian force might pafs
through Bochara to Cafhmir, and thence to Bengal. The
avowed object of the expedition was to be the re-eftablifhment of the Mogul ; a trick by which the good will of the
Bocharians was expected to be gained. But as little could
be apprehended from that weak and difunited people, we
are naturally difpofed to look upon the invention as a very
ignorant one ; for it would enfure the enmity of the much
more powerful Mahometan princes in the Peninfula. Be
this as it may, the Emprefs highly approved of the plan ;
and counted on the junction of the difcontented from all
parts with her forces in the north of India. Potemkin
turned the fcheme into ridicule ; and the pacification that
immediately

---

* The letter N n is repeated in this reference by an
error of the prefs.

immediately followed prevented any farther fteps from being taken.—*Eton's Survey, p.* 501. *(Appendix.)*

The direct attack of India feems not to be the only mode of annoying the Englifh power which the Ruffian court has thought of. Plans appear to have been entertained hoftile to Japan, and even to China, for many years.—*Ibidem, p.* 504. *(Appendix.)*

Note O o. *p.* 334.

IT is ridiculous to think that the late exertions which have been made, and the new exertions which it is to be feared may foon be neceffary againft France in Egypt, are at all connected with the interefts of Turkey. To that weak power it fignifies indeed little how many of her nominal provinces fhe ceafes to call her own. That Egypt was of no manner of ufe to Turkey, for many years before the French invafion, is an undeniable fact. So long ago as when Norden travelled there, the Bafhaw ruled, or rather obtained the tribute only by intrigue.—*Norden's Travels, I.* 63. But in the fubfequent part of the century, the dependence of the Beys and their fubjects was reduced ftill lower.—*Irwine's Travels up the Red Sea, p.* 340-392. *4to edit.—Brown's Travels, chap. V.* We are informed by Bruce, that at one time there have been in Cairo alone four hundred perfons poffeffing abfolute power, and dependent only on the Beys, unlefs when one of them ufurped the chief dominion.—*Travels, vol. I. p.* 27.—a clear proof of the anarchy which fubfifted there at that time, and of the little power which the Porte could exercife over the province by any means. At a ftill later period, the very acknowledgment of fubjection was almoft withheld, the Pacha's
authority

authority openly denied, and the tribute fent or refufed at
pleafure, until it became a mock ceremony, confifting in
the annual departure of mules fuppofed to be laden with
money for the Porte, but in reality carrying rice bags, or
ftones.—*Eton's Survey, p.* 287. *8vo edit.*

NOTE P p. *p.* 336.

SOME authors have alleged that the navigation of the Red
Sea is only dangerous to the unfkilful feamen who at prefent frequent its coafts in badly conftructed veffels.—*Ricard,
Traité de Commerce, tom. III. p.* 439. M. Niebuhr, too,
in every refpect a better authority, tells us, that though
the eaft coaft is very dangerous (on account of fhoals) for
coafting, yet it is ftudded with good harbours ; and that
clear failing is as eafily performed from Djidda to Suez, as
from Djidda to the Straights of Babelmandeb ; a run which
Europeans make without a pilot.—*Defcript. de l'Arabie,
p.* 303.

If, however, we may credit the accounts of various
other perfons, particularly of Mr Bruce, *(Travels, vol. I.
paffim)*, there are in the Red Sea natural impediments to
a tolerably fafe navigation. Not to mention the violent
ftorms and the currents (particularly in the Straights)
which all authors admit, and the fhifting fands produced by
thofe currents and ftorms, it appears that this channel, perhaps more than any other, is ftudded with funken rocks ;
and, what is almoft as bad, with folitary rocks in every quarter ; in fuch a manner that, to ufe the language of Mr
Bruce, the ftem of the veffel may be ftriking, while the
ftern is in good anchorage, or in a hundred fathoms of water.
In fuch a fea it is vain to think of fafety even from the beft
charts ;

charts; at leaſt, to a perſon unacquainted with practical navigation, it muſt appear very ſtrange, if the moſt accurate
delineation of thoſe rocks could enable the moſt ſkilful ſeaman
to avoid them, when we know how wide an approximation
is given by all the operations of the compaſs and quadrant.

The force of the currents and winds appears to be conſtantly driving ſand up the Red Sea, ſo that veſſels of ſome
bulk cannot now approach ſo near Suez as formerly.—*Niebuhr's Voyage, I.* 175.

NOTE Q q. *p.* 337.

MR CAPPER, in his work on winds and monſoons, (a work
much more valuable for the number of 1 cts which it contains, than for the illuſtrations afforded by theſe to his general theory), ſeems, from the flat contradiction which one
page gives to another in ſeveral inſtances, to have fallen into
ſome material errors. In p. 45. & 68. we are informed,
that the S. W. monſoon blows on the Malabar coaſt from
April to November; and the N. E. from November to A-
pril. In page 72. Mr Capper tells us, on the authority of
M. D'Après, that the ſoutherly monſoons blow in the Red
Sea from the end of Auguſt to the middle or end of May;
and the northerly monſoons the reſt of the year. In the
very next page he ſays, that the ſoutherly monſoon blows
from the Straights to Yambo, at the ſame ſeaſon that it
blows in the Gulf of Said, (commonly called the Indian
Sea), or, he adds, from April to September; and that, from
the middle of May to Auguſt, the ſoutherly monſoon extends
from Yambo to Suez. Here are two flat contradictions;
firſt, in the duration of the Malabar monſoon; and next, in
the time of the Red Sea monſoon. Our confidence in Mr
C.'s

C.s acuracy is certainly fo newhat fhaken by fuch a circumftance ; and perhaps its effect may be fomewhat increafed
by the manifeft inftances of careleffnefs or error which one
is furprifed to meet with upon other matters.

In Mr C.'s very ftrange differtation *(p.* 217-222.*)* upon
the omniprefence of the Tartars, (if I may ufe the expreffion),
we find a comparifon between the Perfic and Saxon languages
introduced as decifive of the author's hypothefis—not that
the Perfians and Saxons were radically the fame people, but
that the Tartars and Saxons were one nation. The final and
ftrongeft inftance of fimilarity is taken from the famous word
Wittenagamote, *(Wittenagemote),* ' a compound word (fays
' Mr C.) of high political import, that has the fame found
' both in Perfic and Saxon. In the former, it is derived from
' *Wetten,* a native country, and *Gemmaiet,* an affembly.—
' According to Blackftone and Hume, it is the affembly of
' of Wife men ; but in both languages it literally means
' the National Affembly '—*p.* 221. Now, not to mention
that the fimilarity is entirely confined to the latter part of
the compound word, by the author's virtual admiffion, it is
a little fingular that he fhould have quoted the two terms,
Wetten and *Gemmaiet,* as *Perfic,* when they are in fact precifely *Arabic.* In like manner we find him, in one page,
carefully inferting vocables in the Oriental characters, and
in another fo completely mifpelling Eaftern names, of known
etymology, as to make us fufpect his accuracy, if not his
proficiency in thofe languages ; for inftance, *Irang* and *Tur-
ang,* for *Irany* and *Turany* ; *Guardafui,* for *Gardefan* ; *Babelmandel,* for *Babelmandeb.*—*pages* 218. 41. & 73. For
fuch reafons as thefe, I have been inclined to queftion Mr
Capper's general accuracy in minute particulars, and to prefer the authority of other writers upon the fubject of the
monfoons, where he happens to differ from them in his ftatements.

NOTE

ALMOST all the authors who have difcuffed the fubject of a communication with India by Egypt, have founded their reafonings rather upon the political than the phyfical obftacles to fuch an intercourfe. Thus Maillet, who difcuffes this point, contents himfelf with mentioning, that under Colbert's adminiftration the fcheme failed, from the prejudice of the natives and of the Turkifh government, which he defcribes.—*Edit. de Mafcrier, part. II. p.* 200. Niebuhr only difputes the advantages which France would derive from a commerce with India, through Egypt, by enumerating the various difficulties arifing from the political circumftances of the country, as the taxes, extortions, and delays impofed by the Arabians, the Porte, and the Beys.—*Voyage, tom. I. p.* 225. *& tom. II. p.* 10.

NOTE S s.   *p.* 353.

IN the obfervations which I have been led to make upon the connexion between the Afiatic colonies, and the improvement of Egypt, I have never expreffed any doubt upon the advantages which would refult both to the colonies and the mother countries, from the abolition of the company trade and government at prefent eftablifhed; nor have I taken at all into the confideration of this fubject the injurious confequences of fuch an event, to the perfons interefted in the actual fyftem. It may, however, be obferved, that any fudden deftruction, even of fo ruinous a plan as the Afiatic adminiftration, would be attended with confiderable inconvenience, and even with fome danger to the credit of the mother country.

' Such, '

' Such,' as Dr Smith well obferves, ' are the unfor-
' tunate effects of all the regulations of the mercantile fyf-
' tem! They not only introduce very dangerous diforders
' into the ftate of the body politic, but diforders which it is
' often difficult to remedy, without occafioning, for a time
' at leaft, ftill greater diforders.'—*Wealth of Nations, vol.*
II. p. 427. *edit.* 1799.

It is not, however, to be fuppofed, that the cultivation
of Egypt can at once ruin the prefent fyftem of colonial government in the Eaft. Ample time will be given for making
thofe arrangements which may be requifite to withftand the
fhock, and when the downfal of the companies has been
prepared, it will produce, to the whole commercial interefts
of each mother country, advantages amply fufficient to counterbalance, even in the very beginning of the new arrangement, any inconvenience refulting from the change. See
alfo Book I. Sect. III. Part II. at the end.

In a political point of view, the fame remark may be
made. The trifling affiftance received by the government
from the companies, will be nothing compared with the
vaft increafe of refources which the free trade and reformed
colonial government will place within reach of the ftate.
The naval force of the nations poffeffing Eaft Indian territory, is indeed clofely connected with the refources of their
Indian Companies. Thus, we have feen how very powerful the Dutch Eaft India Company was in former times;
and the Eaft India Company of England is, I fuppofe, one
of the firft maritime powers in Europe—probably the third;
that is to fay, it could fit out a greater and better fleet of
men of war than any power, except England and France.
But this force would certainly not be loft to the nation.
The government, if occafion required, would, after a few
years, have the ufe of almoft as many large fhips from the
open trade, as formerly from the Company. Large veffels
muft always, as we have already feen, (Book I. Sect. II.
Part

Part I.) be employed in the very diftant branches of traffic ;
and the beft way to multiply thofe, is furely to extend that
traffic which requires them.

NOTE T t. *p.* 377.

THERE is a confiderable variation in the ftatement of different authors upon the fubjeƈt of the Egyptian population.
That the reader may judge of the grounds on which I have
fuppofed it to be four millions, I fhall lay before him the
different ftatements, after premifing that the falfehoods
which have at different times been related about every thing
conneƈted with Egypt, and more particularly about the
numbers of its inhabitants, feem to have made M. Volney
wifh rather to avoid exaggeration, by running into the oppofite extreme ; and that the accuracy of M. Savary is in
general acknowledged by all writers—by none more than
by M. Volney.

Maillet, after ftating the ancient population of Egypt
at feven millions five hundred thoufand, and remarking that
the Arabian writers call it twenty millions, allows its prefent
amount to be four millions, and that of Cairo to be five hundred thoufand.—*Edit. de Maferier, Part. I. p.* 24. Ricard,
in one part of his work, fays, ' On y compte cinq ou fix
' millions d'habitans. '—*III.* 434. ; and in another part he
adds (after eftimating the population of Cairo at feven or
eight hundred thoufand), ' On ne craint pas de s'ecarter
' beaucoup de la vérité en fuppofant à l'Egypte fix ou fept
' millions d'habitans. '—*Ibid.* p. 443.

The treatife on Commerce in the *Encyclopedie Methodique,*
mentions the number of towns to have been anciently twenty
thoufand ; and adds, that at prefent there are nine thoufand
towns and twelve hundred villages.—*Tom. II. p.* 790.

Savary

NOTE T t.

NOTE T t.   555

Savary gives nine hundred thousand for the population of Cairo, and four millions for that of all Egypt. The former sum appears to be exaggerated.—*Tom. III. Let. I. & II.*

According to Volney, the population of Cairo is only two hundred and fifty thousand, and that of all Egypt two millions three hundred thousand.—*Egypt and Syria, vol. I. p.* 238. Eton follows him in his account of the latter, and confirms that of the former by a private interlineation.—*Survey, chap. VII.* And as Browne has given nearly the numbers mentioned by Volney, viz. three hundred thousand, and two millions five hundred thousand, it is probable he follows him too ; but he speaks with evident uncertainty.— *Travels in Africa, Egypt, and Syria, chap. V.*

It may be observed, that Volney founds his conclusion on a very rough estimate, from the number of towns and villages, which he says is only two thousand three hundred, and the average of inhabitants only a thousand to each, including the capital and Alexandria.

NOTE U u. *p.* 407.

THE valuable work of M. Malouet contains pretty full information upon this scheme (in the preparation of which he was employed) for introducing the free-negro system into Guiana. The reader will particularly find this matter discussed in the second section of the Memorial, (in vol. V.) entitled, ' *Nouvelles Observations.* ' He will also find in this, and in other parts of the collection, notices of the experiment actually tried (it is needless to say without any success) for cultivating Guiana by a colony of peasants from Alsace and Lorrain ; an experiment never exceeded in costly absurdity, except perhaps in the Spanish colony of the Sierra Morena.

Morena. M. Malouet (*p.* 114. *et feqq.*) argues, though
without much of his ufual acutenefs, againft the general
plan of cultivation by free negroes. His reafonings are applicable to a variety of plans, which appear at different
times to have been propofed by fpeculative men, for the abolition of the flave fyftem, by providing fubftitutes in the colonial cultivation. This branch of his argument was written
very lately ; but in other parts of his collection we meet with
fimilar topics urged againft plans of a like nature, which
appear to have found advocates among French ftatefmen
at the beginning of Lewis XVI.'s reign.—*Vol. IV.*

In this country, various crude and ill-digefted fchemes
have been propofed at different times for the cultivation of
the Weft Indian territories. The fyftem of free blacks has
been urged more lately, and with much greater ability,
in a pamphlet entitled the ' *Crifis of the Sugar Colonies,* '
publifhed about a year ago, by a gentleman who has not
chofen to give his name to the public. Widely as the opinions contained in this Inquiry differ from many of thofe
delivered in the ' *Crifis,* ' it is impoffible not to admit the
merits, and to praife the motives of this performance, which,
though very hafty, and written apparently under the warm
impreffions of the moment, difplays fufficient talents and acquaintance with the fubject, to make us regret that profef-
fional avocations have prevented the author from fully difcuffing the interefting topics of negro flavery.

NOTE V v. *p.* 462.

OTHER inftances are not wanting in Mr Edwards's writings,
more particularly in his Hiftory of St Domingo, which
prove how very rafhly he was inclined to admit, upon the
moft fufpicious teftimony, facts favourable to his opinions,

or

or rather his interefts, as a flave proprietor. The fame rafhnefs, however, appears to have directed his belief, in o- ther inflances where he had not even that excufe.

In the firft edition (1796), he publifhed, among a variety of facts obtained from ' perfonal converfation with a gentle- ' man of St Domingo, on whofe veracity and honour he ' could place the fulleft dependence,' a charge of unparalleled atrocity, againft a very worthy and refpectable French plant- er, fon of the celebrated Count de Graffe. This gentleman was ftated, in the moft pofitive terms, to have been prefent at the deftruction of the Cape, and to have warmly affifted the negro infurgents in their diabolical work of maffacre and devaftation.

During four years was the character of this unfortunate gentleman ruined in the eyes of all Mr Edwards's readers. And, in the next edition of 1800, appears a certificate from twenty refpectable perfons, that M. de Graffe had, during the whole time of the infurrection, acted with the utmoft vi- gour and fidelity, as Adjutant-General of the forces againft the rebels, and that no part of his conduct had ever furnifh- ed the flighteft grounds for a murmur of fufpicion againft him, from the time of his arrival in St Domingo to the moment of his expulfion, when, after various miferies, he fhared in the univerfal ruin of his countrymen, and was driv- en pennylefs from his home. In publifhing this *reparation* of M. de Graffe's injured character, Mr Edwards ftates, that experience has convinced him that no great dependence can be placed on the accufations raifed ' by men againft ' their fellow citizens in times of civil commotion, and a- ' midft the tumult of conflicting paffions.'—*p. 19. edit.* 1801. and he omits the recital which he had publifhed in 1796 againft M. de Graffe : yet, ftrange to tell, fo enamoured is he of every bit of private information he can fcrape together, that he republifhes every other fact in the lift of thofe which he had received from the fame quarter ; and repeats his at- teftation

teftation of the honour and veracity of the gentleman from whom thefe facts, together with the foul calumny againft M. de Graffe, were received !—p. 147.

The ' *Teftament de Mort d'Ogé*, ' is alfo inferted in both editions of this work.

This document is the foundation of a black charge a-gainft the Council of the Cape, and all the military chiefs of the colony under the ancient *regime*. They are indeed convicted, if this paper be authentic, of having been in league with the people of colour, and of having actually caufed every one of the dreadful fcenes which have, fince the revolution, overwhelmed St Domingo in countlefs horrors. Now this paper was received by the author from an emi-grant, to whom he acknowledges his obligations for the chief part of his information through the whole work. This gentleman had belonged to the revolutionary government ; had been arrefted, perfecuted, and fent over to France in chains ; but had been captured by the Englifh, and faved. At the time of publication he had returned to St Domingo to look after his property : he had again fallen into the hands of his enemies ; and the laft act of his liberty was to tranfmit the document in queftion to Mr Edwards, with o-other valuable papers—p. 13. & 14.

Now, two circumftances fhould have unqueftionably pre-vented Mr Edwards from giving credit or place to this tef-timony, even if we fhould omit the previous and general confideration of the high improbability of the charge.

In the *firft* place, the anonymous informer did not com-municate the document to Mr Edwards, when he faw him in England, and received from him many obligations, (*p.* 140.) ; but he fent it after his return to St Domingo ; Governor Blanchelande and all his affociates implicated in the charge, being then dead.

But, *fecondly*, it is evident that the anonymous informer was a perfon of moft fufpicious credibility. He was of the

party

oppofite to the men whom he accufes, ...ıce. He was one of the numerous colo- ...zans who believed, and firmly believed, that ...er-revolutionifts were as much their enemies as the , des noirs, and who hefitated not to impute, partly to their weak, and partly to their treacherous counfels, all the miferies of the rebellion. If the furious difputes of thofe difmal times could infpire the contending factions with fchemes fo mad as an appeal to the inferior races, any accufation brought by one party againft the other, fhould be received with the moft fcrupulous caution.

Although Mr Edwards did not receive the copy of Ogé's ' Teflament de Mort' until the year 1795, (p. 242.) the accufation founded upon it was brought forward againft Governor Blanchelande and the reft of the ancient adminiftration, nine months after Ogé's death, and before the fall of the perfons accufed, (p. 72.) It had therefore an evident and important purpofe to ferve. It was meant to haften the fate which foon afterwards overtook thofe unhappy men. The fpirit of the remarks made by the anonymous gentleman, in his letter to Mr Edwards fent along with the paper, and inferted in page 242. (edit. 1801), ought furely to have imprefled Mr Edwards with fome fufpicions of his partiality and rancour.

The rafhnefs of admitting this document as evidence, is greatly increafed by the anecdote which I firft related, concering the avowed error into which a fimilar credulity in another inftance led our author. It will be difficult, I apprehend, to prove that any circumftances could prevent Mr Edwards's own obfervation upon the little faith due to accounts of partizans, from applying to the teftimony of the anonymous informant.

In chapter V. we meet with a new and fignal inftance of rafhnefs in our hiflorian. He fays, after relating the mutiny of Colonel Mauduit's regiment (1791), that this unhappy man,

The rafhnefs of Mr Edwards in admitting facts, is not greater than his rafhnefs in adopting opinions. What fhall we fay of the judgement of a man well verfed in Weft Indian politics, who could account for the unnatural horrors of negro warfare by fo extravagant an hypothefis as the following, which he fays is incontrovertibly proved by the ftatements contained in his work?

'The rebellion of the negroes in St Domingo, and the
'infurrection of the mulattoes, to whom Ogé was fent as
'ambaffador, had one and the fame origin. It was not the
'ftrong and irrefiftible impulfe of human nature groaning
'under oppreffion, that excited either of thofe claffes to
'plunge their daggers into the bofoms of unoffending wo-
'men and helplefs infants. They were driven into thofe
'exceffes, reluctantly driven, by the vile machinations of
'men calling themfelves philofophers (the profelytes and
'imitators in France of the Old-Jewry affociates in Lon-
'don), whofe pretences to philanthropy were as grofs a
'mockery of human reafon, as their conduct was an out-
'rage on all the feelings of our nature, and the ties which
'hold fociety together.' p. 16. (Edit. 1801.)

It muft furely be no common meafure of prejudice which can induce any one to go farther than the nature of untamed favages, in order to find out reafons for their bloody proceedings. It is no ordinary degree of thoughtlefs violence which can fo far blind this author, as to make him forget his conftant topic of declamation againft the civilized friends of the negroes, and afcribe to their machinations, and not to the ferocious paffions of the flaves, all the horrors of the infurrection, after declaiming fo often againft their proceedings, merely becaufe they tended to awaken thofe very paffions in the negroes. In one page, the unnatural cruelties of the rebels are accounted for, by imputing them to the inftigation of their European abettors; in another, thofe abettors are accufed of blind imprudence, for letting loofe
uncivilized

uncivilized men, whofe habits rendered fuch enormities inevitable.

I have judged it neceffary to enter into thefe details,
that the reader may be mafter of the grounds upon which I
venture to call in queftion fo refpectable an authority as the
very popular writer of the Hiftory of the Weft Indies. I
truft, that the circumftances mentioned in the text, with
thofe contained in this note, will fufficiently juftify the caution which I have uniformly difplayed in receiving his ftatements, upon fubjects immediately connected with the negro
queftions. When a work has for fome time been known to
the world under the name of a hiftory, it is fometimes not
ufelefs to examine its pretenfions to this important title—
whether they are derived from right, or only admitted by
courtefy. And when the fubject of the performance is interefting to a variety of paffions and feelings; when, in
fhort, it forms one of the leading topics in the politics of
the day, it is prudent to inquire, whether this hiftory is the
mature and deliberate work of a fober-minded and impartial
writer, or the effufion of a partizan, who, if his fubject had
been lefs extenfive, and the fize of his tract confequently
fmaller, would have ranked, not among the hiftorians, but
the pamphleteers of the day.

The anecdote of Mr Edwards, with refpect to Gallifet's
flaves, which I have alluded to in the text, is not, fo far as
I know, related by any other writer in favour of the negro
fyftem, except by M. Laborie, an author in many points
guilty of confiderable unfairnefs in his ftatements. His
work, however, was not publifhed till after Mr Edwards's
firft edition (from which I quoted that anecdote) had appeared ; and, at any rate, he differs materially from that author. He imputes the rebellion of Gallifet's flaves, not to
the wife and indulgent treatment which they met with, but
to the exceffive laxity of their difcipline, and their extravagant wealth. Some of them were poffeffed of above 300l.
currency ;

currency; almoft all of them had excellent clothes, furniture, plate, &c. The plantation, according to Laborie, was a perpetual fcene of feafting and merriment. If we fhould take this as the whole account of the fact, it would be fufficient to account for the prevalence of licentioufnefs, riot, and a rebellious fpirit among Gallifet's flaves; for furely the poffeffion of fo much property, perhaps the enjoyment of fo great indulgence, is inconfiftent with the condition of bondage. When confiderable wealth is acquired by flaves, fome provifion ought always to be made for the purchafe of their freedom; otherwife they are placed in a fituation which, if it continues, muft lead to licentioufnefs and indifcipline, or, if checked, muft produce infurrection. But the material circumftance mentioned by Mr Clarkfon, and omitted by Laborie, who moft probably knows it, is the change of management which had been introduced into Gallifet's plantation for fome years previous to the revolution. This had the effect of rendering a fupply of new and unfeafoned hands neceffary, and at the fame time muft have irritated to the higheft pitch thofe who remained, and felt the effects of the new regimen. If M. Laborie's account be combined with the ftatement of Mr Clarkfon, (although it is very poffible that the latter ftatement may be complete in itfelf, and that Laborie's addition may contain an exaggerated picture), we fhall have ample grounds upon which to explain the circumftance fo unfairly ftated by Mr Edwards: for what materials could the wit of man have devifed more prone to explofion, than a mixture of new and unbroken flaves with wealthy and licentious creoles, who have been fuddenly fubjected to a vigorous fyftem of management, after a life of eafe and indulgence?

═══

NOTE Ww. *p.* 480.

ONE argument has been repeatedly urged in favour of the flave trade, certainly too abfurd to merit a ferious analyfis or refutation, had not many very refpectable perfons lent it the fanction of their names. It has been faid, that the African flave market is fupplied almoft entirely by the wars which diftract that continent, and by the execution of certain judicial fentences prefcribing flavery for fome offences, as witchcraft and adultery. It is well known, that no man, according to the cuftoms of moft African nations, can fell his home-born flave, unlefs in the cafe of famine. I fhall for the prefent admit, that the flave market on the coaft never furnifhes any temptations fufficiently powerful to induce the breach of this African law ; and I fhall fuppofe that no flaves are ever brought to the traders, who have not been either taken in war, or fold in confequence of their crimes. It is evident that the argument for the traffic gains much by thefe gratuitous conceffions ; yet, in what ftate do they leave it ? If the flaves captured in war, and the criminals condemned for witchcraft, are fold at a good price, is it not obvious that a premium is held out for the encouragement of wars, and of futile accufations ? It is faid, that if the flave market were fhut up for ever, the fame wars and accufations would continue ; with this difference, that captives would be butchered, and criminals put to death.

No doubt, the abolition of the flave trade would neither eradicate war, nor falfe accufations from the ftates of Africa. To a certain degree, both of thefe evils would continue in that barbarous quarter of the globe, becaufe both

of

of them are produced by other caufes, as well as by the flave trade ; by other paffions, as well as by avarice. It may, however, fairly be eftimated, that more of the wars and falfe accufations which keep Africa in a ftate of difcord and barbarifm, are engendered by the temptations of the flave market, than by any other caufe. Does any one deny, that the common receivers of ftolen goods encourage, beyond any other caufe, the commiffion of robberies and thefts ? Yet the expulfion of every common receiver from a country (were fuch a thing poffible), would not abolifh either of thofe crimes. But furely nothing could be more abfurd, than to difpute the propriety of taking all poffible fteps for rooting out fuch pefts of fociety, merely becaufe a complete cure of the evil would not be effected by this remedy.

As to the argument, that maffacres and executions would be the confequence of the abolition, we may be fure that, for a few campaigns of African warfare, or a few terms of the African courts, victories and convictions would end in the death of fome men, who would otherwife have been fold. This would be exactly the confequence of the previous demand for men occafioned by the trade. It always takes fome time before the fupply can accommodate itfelf to the varied demands of any market, whether the variation be that of increafe or of diminution.

No meafure, furely, could be better calculated to preferve the lives of wild beafts in any well ftocked country, than the prohibition of exportation to foreign menageries ; yet, for a few feafons, this law would certainly increafe the number of animals devoted to death ; becaufe thofe whofe habits had been formed by the old practice, would continue to hunt, and many would ftill hunt for amufement, or the gratification of cruel paffions : and as the price of wild beafts would fall in the home market, men would grow carelefs of preferving their lives : nay, more being for fome

time

time caught than the fupply of the home menageries required, many muft of neceffity be killed. But the fupply would
foon accommodate itfelf to the leffer demand ; and though
fome men continued to hunt for paftime, an infinitely fmaller number of beafts would be taken and killed than formerly. This cafe is precifely that of the African flave trade.

The abolition of this traffic will diminifh the demand
for flaves by feventy or a hundred thoufand. The flave
trade carried on by the Eaft, through Egypt, is extremely
trifling. In Cairo, which is the flave market of Egypt,
and the entrepôt of other countries, there are only fold
annually from fifteen hundred to two thoufand negroes ;
and the price never exceeds one hundred crowns, the average
being about ten pounds Sterling ; not above one fifth of
the price in the Weft Indies, and not one half of the price
on the weft coaft.—*Sonnini's Voyage in Egypt, chap. XXXVI.*
—*Report of Committee* 1789, *Part VI.*—*Edwards' Weft
Indies. B. IV. c. 2.*

Befides, it is univerfally admitted, that no comparifon
whatever can be drawn between the eaftern and the weftern
flave traffic. The treatment of the negroes in thofe Oriental
nations which employ them as flaves, is mild and gentle :
they are ufed entirely for domeftic, and even honourable
purpofes : they foon acquire their freedom with the favour
of their mafters, and partake as much of the refinement and
comforts of the fociety in which they refide, as our menial
negroes do in Europe.—*Sonnini, chap. XXXVI.*—*Bruce's
Travels, vol. I. p.* 392.

It is maintained by fome, that the flave trade both in
the eaft and weft of Africa, has abolifhed the ufe of human
flefh, and the practice of human facrifices.—*Bruce, I.* 392.
But, befides that this fact appears extremely repugnant to
the character of the negroes, which the beft and lateft travellers have given, (*Park's Travels, chap. XX. XXI. XXII.*)
admitting all the advantage juft now ftated to have been

gained

gained from the flave traffic, do we by the inftant abolition of this traffic, lofe any of the fteps already gained in improving Africa ?   For who can be fo fooiifh as to imagine that the Africans, in whatever manner they have been civilized, will ever return to their ancient habits of cannibalifm and human facrifices ?   Let us, then, by abolifhing the trade, fecure and carry forward thofe very improvements which the trade may have been the means of beginning.

The labours of the African Affociation cannot be mentioned with too much refpect.   An inftitution more purely difinterefted, more unqueftionably influenced by the higheft motives of utility, and the moft exalted views of univerfal benevolence, has never yet arifen among men.   Their fucceffes have been proportioned to their deferts ; and the public are waiting with impatience for the annunciation of new and fplendid achievements, planned by their wifdom, and effected by their affiftance.   That Africa will probably owe much to the labours of the Society, we may fafely affert ; but while the great caufe of barbarifm exifts, and while thofe who wifh well to that quarter of the globe in the Affociation, yet cling to the root of the evil, we cannot expect any fenfible effects to refult from this very praifeworthy Eftablifhment.

It is indeed a matter deeply to be regretted, that the Society fhould, except at firft, always have entrufted the important office of fecretary and editor to perfons patrimonially interefted in the negro flave trade.   The narratives which have been publifhed by Mr Edwards, for inftance, are evidently influenced by his views of the negro fyftem.   If we may credit common report, confirmed by the ftatements of Sir William Young, in his edition of his friend's laft volume, (*Policy of the Weft Indies*, vol. III. *Prefatory advertifement*, p. 8.), Mr Park's Narrative was the work of Mr Edwards. Our confidence in many of the traveller's ftatements is by

this

this circumftance greatly diminifhed ; yet enough is ftill contained in Mr Park's work to juftify ftronger inferences than
any of thofe which I have drawn with refpect to the connexion between the flave trade and the barbarifm of Africa.
As this work is in the hands of every one, I fhall only refer
my readers to the various admiffions made by the traveller
and his *redacteur*, of the extent to which plunder is carried on
in Africa, for the purpofe of felling the captives. The
whole account of the negroes, above referred to, and the
previous ftatements contained in chapter II. deferve particular attention, as coming from perfons evidently inclined to
favour the negro fyftem.

To Mr Edwards has fucceeded in the office of fecretary
and editor, Sir William Young ; and he fcruples not, in the
laft publication (*Horneman's Journal*), to augur moft favourably of the effects of the Society's labours in civilizing the
great African continent. This ftrenuous advocate of the
flave trade ferioufly imagines, that the efforts of a few
learned men to explore the interior of the country, will be
fufficient to enlighten and humanize its barbarous inhabitants, whom the conftant exertions of traders and factories
are inciting to war and plunder, by the irrefiftible temptation
of fetting a price upon their enemies taken alive. The men
who can fo eafily conceive hopes of human improvement,
muft furely wonder how the premiums of our old Saxon
king fhould have extirpated the wolf from this country,
when a few nobles and *virtuofi* would every now and then
defire to obtain a living fpecimen for fport or fhow.

INDEX.

B

*B*_{*Ahamas*} and Bermudas, expence of their civil eftablifhment, how de-
frayed, i. 5 8.
Balance of power, how reprefented by different parties, ii. 192. Example of its utility in the beginning of laft century, ii. 199. Ufurpation of Silefia to be attributed to the actual dereliction, and not
the inefficacy of the balancing fyftem, 200. Partition of Poland
does not prove its futility, 2 2. Memorable events at the clofe of the
18th century, the immediate confequence of adherence to its principles,
2c6. Has not yet attained perfection, 209. Its grand and diftinguifhing feature, 210. Said to be a difcovery of the 15th century,
211. Circumftances of the European ftates fingularly favourable to
its developement, 212.
Baltic, exports from, of what they confift, i. 225.
Barbadoes, &c. fubject to the duty of 4½ *per cent.* i. 550. Extraordinary taxes levied from, *ib.*
Batavians remarkable for their maritime fkill at a very early period, i.
291.
Bedouins, their character, ii. 377.
Berbice, origin of the colony of, i. 345.
Brazils, character of the Portugueze in, i 87. How firft colonized,
469. Privileges granted to the fettlers, 470. Its traffic confined to
a few ports, 471. Diamond mines in, when difcovered, 473. Regulations in the internal policy of, made by Pombal, 477. Loft by
the Portugueze after their fubjugation by Spain, 480. Recovered, *ib.*
Importance of to the mother country, how to be eftimated, 483.
Gives Portugal no inconfiderable weight in the continental politics,
484.
Britain, Great, unacquainted with the real calamities of war, i. 131.
Derives a confiderable clear income from her colonies, 134. Cuftom-
houfe rates there of a very old date, 185. Wealth of, arriving at a
ftate of overgrown magnificence, 215. Regulations of, for encourag-
ing colonial produce, 241. 244. How an eftimate may be formed
of the comparative advantages derived by Britain and France from
their colonial poffeffions, 502. Infurrections in the Weft India fettlements of, 510. Extent of her poffeffions in, and imports from,
&c. in 1796, 529. Average export of negroes from Africa to the
Weft Indies, 531. Amount of the population in the Britifh Weft
Indies, before the rebellion in St Domingo, 539. Value of exports
and imports, &c. *ib.* Expence of the civil government of the Britifh North American colonies previous to the Revolution, 546. Of
the eftablifhments of Canada, Nova Scotia, &c. 547. Revenue of
the Britifh Weft Indies, whence derived, 546. Expence to Britain
of the civil eftablifhments of her Weft India colonies, 559. Revenue
derived from them, *ib.*

D

E

K

Population, natural increase of, proceeded rapidly in the ancient states, i. 13. Superabundant, how disposed of, *ib*. Striking analogy between the emigrations of men and the transference of stock in modern states, 218.

Porto-Rico, consequences of the establishment of the negroes in St Domingo to, ii. 160.

Portugal, colonial policy of, i. 455. Circumstances of, in many particulars resemble those of Spain, *ib*. By its relative situation, &c. forms a subordinate branch of the European commonwealth, *ib*. In what respects she resembles Holland, 456. In what different from Spain and Holland, 457. Has never made any conspicuous figure in Europe, 459. Great extent of the Portuguese empire during the 16th century, 461. Direction of the Portuguese trade with India generally retained in the hands of the sovereign, 467. Brazil, how colonized, 469. Gold and diamond mines when discovered in, 472. Inconsistency of the colonial history of Portugal since that time, *ib*. Had attained her highest pitch of glory at the death of King Sebastian, 479. Cruelly oppressed under the reigns of the three Philips, 479. Trade of, at that time only supported by the African and East Indian settlements, 480. Has suffered an irretrievable loss in the ruin of her East Indian commerce, 482. Importance of Brazil to, how to be estimated, 483. Gives Portugal no inconsiderable weight in the continental politics, 484.

Portugal, supposition of consequences which would ensue on her transferring the seat of government to the Brazils, ii. 50. Internal state of, 280. How rendered the natural ally of Britain, *ib*. Foreign connexions of, have always varied according to the circumstances of Austria and Spain, &c. *ib*. Plan of removing the seat of, from Europe to South America, not altogether imaginary, 523. Advantages she enjoys over Spain in South America, 525.

Portuguese, their character in Europe, i. 85. In the New World, *ib*.

Possessions, distant, of a despotic government, never ruled with the same energy as the parts nearer the centre of the system, ii. 9.

Potidea, a Corinthian settlement takes the part of Athens, i. 28.

Provinces, contiguous, of a state, do not furnish supplies to, in proportion to the benefits they receive from government, i. 108. Exemplified in Britain, 109. In Holland, *ib*.

Prussia, seizes upon Silesia, i. 124. Attempts to raise the commercial importance of her dominions, 290. Desperate situation of, in 1740, 126.

——— acquisition of power by, dangerous to the Imperial House, ii. 229. Object of the assistance given by Britain to, during the Seven years war, 273.

F I N I S.